MW01079532

HANDBOOK OF RESEARCH METHODOLOGIES AND DESIGN IN NEUROENTREPRENEURSHIP

Handbook of Research Methodologies and Design in Neuroentrepreneurship

Edited by

Mellani Day

Dean, Business and Technology Division, College of Adult and Graduate Studies, Colorado Christian University, USA

Mary C. Boardman

Affiliate Faculty, Business and Technology Division, College of Adult and Graduate Studies, Colorado Christian University, USA

Norris F. Krueger

Senior Research Fellow, School of Advanced Studies, University of Phoenix, USA

Edward Elgar
PUBLISHING

Cheltenham, UK • Northampton, MA, USA

Published by
Edward Elgar Publishing Limited
The Lypiatts
15 Lansdown Road
Cheltenham
Glos GL50 2JA
UK

Edward Elgar Publishing, Inc.
William Pratt House
9 Dewey Court
Northampton
Massachusetts 01060
USA

A catalogue record for this book
is available from the British Library

Library of Congress Control Number: 2017936578

This book is available electronically in the **Elgar**online
Business subject collection
DOI 10.4337/9781785365041

Printed on 30% PCR Stock
ISBN 978 1 78536 503 4 (cased)
ISBN 978 1 78536 504 1 (eBook)
Printed and bound by Thomson-Shore, Inc.

Typeset by Servis Filmsetting Ltd, Stockport, Cheshire

Contents

PART II   NEUROSCIENCE APPLICATIONS –
ENTREPRENEURIAL JUDGMENT, DECISION
MAKING, AND COGNITION

Figures

Tables

Contributors

William Becker is Associate Professor of Management at Pamplin College of Business at Virginia Tech. He received his PhD from the University of Arizona. His work has appeared in leading journals including *Academy of Management Journal, Journal of Applied Psychology, Journal of Management*, and *Personnel Psychology*. His work has received press coverage including *The Wall Street Journal, Financial Times*, CNBC, Fox News, U.S. News & World Report, *TIME, Business News Daily*, Psych Central, *Popular Mechanics*, among others. His research interests include work emotion, turnover, organizational neuroscience, and leadership. He is currently co-editing an organizational neuroscience column in *TIP: The Industrial-Organizational Psychologist*. ORCID: 000-002-4648-4122.

Cristiano Bellavitis is Lecturer (Assistant Professor) of Innovation and Entrepreneurship at the Faculty of Management and International Business of Auckland Business School. He obtained his doctorate in management from Cass Business School, London. He serves as Chair for the track of Entrepreneurial Finance for the European Academy of Management annual conference, and is a guest editor for *Venture Capital: An International Journal of Entrepreneurial Finance*. His research interests include network theory, strategic partnering, and interfirm networking in entrepreneurial finance settings.

Mary C. Boardman, PhD, is an entrepreneurship scholar with expertise in entrepreneurial cognition, social and sustainable entrepreneurship, and philanthropy. She holds positions as a methodologist for Globalytica, LLC, affiliate faculty in the Business and Technology Division at Colorado Christian University, and is a courtesy professor in the School of Library and Information Science at the University of South Florida. She has published articles in peer-reviewed journals including *Small Business Economics, Public Administration Review*, and *World Health and Medical Policy*. She holds a PhD in Public Policy from the Schar School of Policy and Government at George Mason University. ORCID: 0000-0002-0065-8449.

Marco Colosio is Junior Researcher at the Centre for Cognition & Decision Making (Neuroeconomics group) at the National Research University

Higher School of Economics, and a PhD candidate in Psychophysiology at the Faculty of Psychology. He obtained a master's degree in experimental psychology and cognitive science at the University of Padova. His research interests span from the investigation of psychobiological basis of individual and collective human decision making at the interface of neuroscience, psychology, and economics to the applications of scientific findings in business, finance, and public policy. He is a member of the *Society for Neuroeconomics* and *Society for Neuroscience*.

Cyril Couffe, PhD, is working for the Research Chair "Talents of digital transformation" at Grenoble Ecole de Manament, France. His work is centered around the critical cognitive abilities at work that will be able to compete with the digital tools in a near future. His work is also centered around understanding the specific cognitive abilities of entrepreneurs and challenging pre-existing models. His approach to this matter relies on applying techniques that were previously exclusive to medicine and neuroscientific research. In 2016, he completed his thesis in Cognitive Psychology at the University of Lyon, France under the mentorship of Dr George A. Michael. His doctoral studies were focused on the influences that working conditions can have on different cognitive processes, especially attention-related ones. During his PhD, he worked as a scientific consultant for several companies in order to improve employee well-being. He used different concepts and cognitive models to develop a set of best practices and passed them on to hundreds of workers. Such recommendations were targeting both the physical environment and the impacts of new technologies on mental focus. In 2013, he became a neuropsychologist after several internships in the fields of gerontology and neurology.

Mellani Day is Dean of the Business and Technology Division in the College of Adult and Graduate Studies at Colorado Christian University. Over the course of her career she has worked in both higher education and in business in the USA and for over 13 years in Germany. On the business side she has been a founder of and worked primarily in entrepreneurial ventures, including over five years as Chief Financial Officer of a small high-tech entrepreneurial company in Colorado, and an import business in Germany. She earned her doctorate in business administration from Nova Southeastern University and a master's degree in systems management from the University of Southern California. Her research interests include environmental influences on entrepreneurship, entrepreneurial decision making, and most recently neuroentrepreneurship. She is a co-editor of *Neuroeconomics and the Firm* (2010). ORCID: orcid. org/0000-0001-5278-2225.

Pablo Martin De Holan is Dean (Founding) of Graduate Studies and Research at the MBSC College of Business and Entrepreneurship in KAEC, Kingdom of Saudi Arabia. Previously, he was Dean of MBAs (EMLYON France). He is Associate Editor of the *Journal of Management Inquiry*, and publishes regularly in academic journals such as *Management Science*, *Journal of Management Studies*, *Industrial and Corporate Change*, among others, and in professional journals such as *Sloan Management Review* and the *Financial Times*. His research interests revolve around two general themes: the unintended consequences of social action, and the process and outcomes of entrepreneurial agency. Over the past few years, he has been working with colleagues to introduce neuroscience techniques and methods into the field of entrepreneurship. He earned his PhD at McGill University (Canada), and his two masters' degrees at the Sorbonne University in Paris, France. He has been a full-time professor at the University of Alberta and at IE Business School, and a visiting professor at Purdue, MIT, INCAE, and other schools around the world.

Aleksei A. Gorin is a second-year PhD student at the Faculty of Psychology, National Research University Higher School of Economics. He earned his master's degree in biology from the Department of Higher Nervous Activity of Saint-Petersburg State University, Russia. Currently, he is working as Research Assistant in the Centre for Cognition and Decision Making at the Higher School of Economics. He works as scientific consultant for "mail. ru group" and "Sberbank." His main research interests include decision making, brain mapping, brain–computer interfaces, and neuroeconomics. He is a member of the *Society for Neuroeconomics*.

Sean Guillory is a data scientist (currently at TheIntelligenceCommunity. com) with cognitive neuroscience training (PhD, Dartmouth College). His previous work includes researching the neuroscience of humor and laughter (graduate work), improving brain mapping methods for neurosurgery patients (postdoctoral work), and helping lead a start-up incubator aimed at ideas that would help improve humanity (Fruition Technology Labs). His current interests include analytical methods and their application across different domains (recent work in intelligence analysis, sales enablement, and entrepreneurship).

Norris F. Krueger, PhD. Norris Krueger gets at least part of the blame for coining the term "neuroentrepreneurship" and has long been fascinated by the genesis of entrepreneurial thinking and the deep cognitive changes that entails. He has training and experience in cognitive science, especially developmental and cognitive developmental psychology as applied to human learning. His 2007 ETP "What Lies Beneath" is widely cited (http://bit.ly/ETP2007) and he is looking forward to meeting like-minded colleagues! In 2008 under the auspices of the Max Planck Institute of Economics, he and Dr Isabell Welpe issued a white paper encouraging entrepreneurship research that focused on experimental research using theory and tools from neuroscience and cognitive science. This was followed by a series of workshops and symposia at MPI and at major entrepreneurship conferences. In 2014, Krueger and Welpe published "Neuro-entrepreneurship: what can entrepreneurship learn from neuroscience?" in the *Annals of Entrepreneurship Education and Pedagogy*, with a strong emphasis on the implications of neuroscience to entrepreneurial learning (and thus education). Dr Krueger has a long history in entrepreneurship and is the most-cited author on the topic of entrepreneurial intentions. While an early pioneer using theory and tools from social and cognitive psychology, he is one of very few entrepreneurship scholars with training and experience in developmental and cognitive developmental psychology, which has afforded him useful insights into how humans – and entrepreneurs – learn. ORCID: 0000-0002-9824-928X.

Angela Passarelli, PhD is Assistant Professor of Management at the College of Charleston and Research Fellow with the Coaching Research Lab at Case Western Reserve University. Her research focuses on how developmental relationships support behavior change, particularly in the context of leader development. She draws on neuroscience and psychophysiology to explore the implicit dynamics of these relationships. Her work has been published in various journals including *Leadership Quarterly*, *Consulting Psychology Journal: Practice and Research*, and *Journal of Experiential Education*. Angela also maintains an executive coaching practice with clients from various sectors including financial services, healthcare, manufacturing, and education.

Víctor Pérez-Centeno, PhD, received his master's degree in International Political Economy and Policy Management from the University of Tsukuba, Japan and his doctorate in Economics and Business Administration from the University of Jyväskylä, Finland. He has worked as Associate Expert to the United Nations Conference on Trade and Development (UNCTAD). Currently he is a brain-driven entrepreneurship scholar at the Graduate School of Business Administration at the University of Kobe. His work applies a neuroscientific perspective to the assessment of the phenomena of entrepreneurship. Particularly, his research focuses on the interlace of emotions and learning on the entrepreneurial mindset and decision making. He is the founder of the World Network of Young Leaders and Entrepreneurs (WNYLE), an organization specialized in non-formal entrepreneurship education and applied research.

Crystal Reeck earned her bachelor's and master's degrees at Stanford University and completed her doctorate in Psychology and Neuroscience at Duke University. She worked as Postdoctoral Research Scholar in Decision Making and Negotiations at Columbia Business School before joining the Fox School of Business at Temple University as Assistant Professor of Marketing. Combining both neuroscience and behavioral approaches, her research examines how emotions influence decision making and how different strategies help people to manage that influence. She has published her research in peer-reviewed journals that span multiple fields, including *Science, Journal of Cognitive Neuroscience*, and *Journal of Experimental Social Psychology*. Her work has been featured in media outlets and funded by national granting agencies, including the National Science Foundation.

Leon Schjoedt, PhD (University of Colorado at Boulder), is Professor of Entrepreneurship and Management at Mahasarakham Business School, Mahasarakham University, Thailand. His research focuses on entrepreneurial and entrepreneurs' behavior. He has published more than 40 articles and book chapters. Leon's work has appeared in journals such as *Entrepreneurship Theory and Practice, Journal of High Technology Management Research, International HR Journal, Management Research News, Organizational Dynamics, Small Business Economics*, and *Journal of International Management Studies* and has been featured in *The Wall Street Journal*. His research has been presented at numerous academic meetings, including the annual meeting for the Academy of Management and Babson College Entrepreneurship Research Conference. Leon serves on the editorial review boards of several journals, including *Entrepreneurship Theory & Practice, Journal of Business Venturing*, and *Journal of Small Business Management*, and he serves as Associate Editor of *Small Business Economics: An Entrepreneurship Journal.* ORCID: 000-0002-0721-6344.

Kelly G. Shaver is Professor of Entrepreneurial Studies at the College of Charleston. He is a Fellow of the American Psychological Society, past Chair of the Entrepreneurship Division of the Academy of Management, and a Justin Longenecker Fellow of the United States Association for Small Business and Entrepreneurship. Kelly's previous appointments include the College of William & Mary, the Entrepreneurship and Small Business Research Institute in Stockholm, and the National Science Foundation. He has won a teaching award from the Entrepreneurship Division of the Academy of Management, a Best Paper Award from the National Federation of Independent Businesses, the 2014 Distinguished Research Award from College of Charleston School of Business, and the 2016 Distinguished Research Award from the College of Charleston (the first business professor to win this award in its 39-year history). His internationally recognized entrepreneurship research has been supported by the Ewing Marion Kauffman Foundation and the National Science Foundation. He has served as Editor of *Entrepreneurship Theory and Practice*, and is currently Associate Editor of the *Journal of Small Business Management*. He is the founder of MindCette, LLC, an entrepreneurship testing and consulting company. ORCID: 0000-0002-0699-374X.

Aparna Sud has experience as an intrapreneur, designing, developing, and launching new products, ventures, and models for companies such as Pfizer and CVS. Aparna was previously a founding member of a higher education consulting firm catering to Latin America with flagship programming focused on innovation and internationalization. She holds a dual degree from MIT in Neuroscience and Management and is pursuing a Master's in Design and Management at Pratt Institute. Aparna is passionate about entrepreneurship and believes an entrepreneurial skillset will become increasingly pivotal for companies to retain and disseminate to their workforce as the economy continues to be redefined by advances in technology and manufacturing. She hopes to spread ways to consciously practice and develop an entrepreneurial skillset on an individual basis by seeking to first uncover the entrepreneurial mindset from a neuroscientific standpoint. Aparna also conducts ideation workshops that combine yoga, lateral thinking, and strategic planning to help others step out of their set pathways and spark their inner creativity in order to develop new business ideas.

Theresa Treffers is Associate Professor in Entrepreneurship at Seeburg Castle University in Seekirchen am Wallersee, Austria, and research fellow at the chair for strategy and organization at TUM school of Management, Germany. Before that, Theresa worked as Assistant Professor in Entrepreneurship in the Innovation, Technology Entrepreneurship, & Marketing Group at Eindhoven University of Technology in the Netherlands. She received her PhD in Management from the Ludwig Maximilian University Munich, Germany. Theresa's research interests lie in the intersection of economic and psychological concepts, with a special focus on entrepreneurship, innovation, and strategy and their implications in management trainings and coaching. In particular, she examines the impact of emotions on economic, entrepreneurial, and strategic decisions, mainly using quantitative-experimental approaches. Her research is published in journals such as *Plos One*, *Journal of Economic Psychology*, *Entrepreneurship Theory & Practice*, and *Economica*. In addition, she is the author of several book chapters and practice-related articles.

M.K. Ward, PhD, is a postdoctoral research fellow in the business school at the University of Western Australia. She earned an MS and PhD in Industrial/Organizational Psychology from North Carolina State University. M.K. has published in the *Annual Review of Organizational Psychology and Organizational Behavior* and other peer-reviewed journals. She is the editor of a column titled "Organizational Neuroscience" in *The Industrial/Organizational Psychologist*. In 2014, she received the Student Research Award from the Association for Psychological Science. Her research program focuses on organizational neuroscience, entrepreneurship, performance, and measurement. In addition to researching entrepreneurship, she has been an entrepreneur and completed an accelerator program through the largest co-working organization in North Carolina. ORCID: 0000-0002-1253-1744.

Preface

As entrepreneurship researchers, if we ever hope to move beyond treating phenomena such as entrepreneurial cognition, affect, and decision making as little more than a black box in the brain, then we need the right tools. Since this has been the domain of neuroscience for some time, albeit with different foci, those tools already exist. Because of this, fortunately we do not have to reinvent any wheels. Instead our time and effort are best used learning how to take advantage of these existing tools. If entrepreneurship researchers are interested in the scientific method, to answer questions and to add to the body of knowledge in the world, then this is a path that must be followed.

You will find in this book that there are interested neuroentrepreneurship researchers around the globe who agree with us. Researchers in Russia, France, Saudi Arabia, Finland, Spain, Germany, the USA, and New Zealand, among others, are exploring this topic. You will also find neuroscientists here who are fascinated with entrepreneurs and entrepreneurship theory and interested in contributing to this conversation.

However, the primary challenge that neuroentrepreneurship research currently faces is that neuroscience is a strange new world for many of us. At this time there are few entrepreneurship researchers who are experts in both entrepreneurship and neuroscience. This book is a first attempt to truly and formally bring these two disciplines together with practical ways and means to do so. We are so fortunate to have the opportunity to feature research designs across the spectrum. Simply put, this handbook would have not been possible without the incredible support, enthusiasm, and (most importantly) chapter submissions from a broad range of scholars in these fields. Our neuroscientists detail specific designs applicable to studying entrepreneurs, and entrepreneurship scholars design research questions that ultimately require brain-based experiments.

For the vast majority of us exploring questions related to neuro-entrepreneurship, there are significant gaps in our knowledge and understanding. It is our hope that this handbook can fill in some of those gaps. Use this handbook to inform your own research designs in this field. We hope this handbook is a significant initial tool for you as you make your own valuable contributions to the field of neuroentrepreneurship. We are optimistic that this important field of research will gain the momentum it needs to truly create a useful body of knowledge and insight into the mind and brain of the entrepreneur. Regardless of your background, if you are interested in neuroentrepreneurship, this book has something for you.

Acknowledgments

Not only are we grateful for the support of this emerging community of scholarship, but also for the support of our publisher, Edward Elgar (EE). Neuroentrepreneurship is an emerging field in its infancy. We are grateful for EE's support and commitment to staying on the cutting edge of research and scholarship.

We are also grateful for the support and encouragement of those in the entrepreneurship research and neuroscience communities, as well as those in our circle of family and friends who have played their own significant parts in making this handbook a reality. To name just a few: Zoltan Acs, Randy and Kathy Pherson, and everyone at Pherson Associates/Globalytica, Jim Kajdasz, Colorado Christian University, the Entrepreneurship Division at the Academy of Management for providing the opportunity to discuss and present research on this topic, Alan Gay, Angela Stanton, Isabelle Welpe, the Max Planck Institute for Economics, Matthew Carter, Mary Harrington, and many others who have provided both insight and support over the past few years.

1. Introduction

*Mellani Day, Mary C. Boardman, and
Norris F. Krueger*

This handbook presents an exploration into the nascent field of neuroentrepreneurship. At this point, the general body of entrepreneurship research has examined global, national, local, individual, and cognitive levels of entrepreneurship. With the advancement of technology and neuroscience-inspired methodologies in other business and economics fields, it was inevitable that entrepreneurship researchers would venture even deeper into the realm of the curious entrepreneurial brain. However, where to begin?

As with the other social sciences, the study of entrepreneurship uncovers many seemingly conflicting behaviors in its subjects. We see entrepreneurs coming from various backgrounds, experiences, and environments in virtually every culture, with a complexity that stretches the limits of the deep and narrow study that is common in academic research. Even focusing on a "narrow" area such as cognition quickly becomes complex due to perceived and unperceived influences (chemical and physical) in the brain of the entrepreneur, along with his or her interpretations and reactions to those influences before any action is ever taken.

It is not difficult to conclude that entrepreneurship is a "mindset," a concept that is wide currency today. We no longer teach about entrepreneurship, we attempt to teach the entrepreneurial mindset (see for example Kriewall and Mekemson, 2010). Though we do this without ever really defining what we mean by "mindset," or how to measure it properly. The cognitive and neuroscience fields may offer us exactly what we need: the deeper structures that characterize entrepreneurial thinking and behavior. Only now do we have the technology to seriously begin to explore this and to offer definitions.

Over the past decade, researchers have revealed an increased interest in studying these perceived and unperceived influences and responses. This is partly because of the brain-based tools that are increasingly accessible through neuroscience avenues (See Krueger and Welpe, 2008; Stanton et al., 2010; Krueger and Day, 2010). Indeed, like their neuroresearch cousins in economics, marketing, and other behavioral sciences, entrepreneurship researchers have tentatively begun to step into this research space. However, faced with hurdles such as a lack of familiarity with and training in neuroscience research design and implementation, along with interpretation of reactions in the brain to stimuli in laboratory experiments, this can be daunting.

Experimental studies in entrepreneurship research in their own right, however valuable, are still relatively uncommon. Most social scientists simply do not have training or experience using functional magnetic resonance imaging (fMRI), magnetoencephalography (MEG), or positron emission tomography (PET). Neuroscientific studies are conducted in a laboratory setting and require trained specialists to set up and run the equipment and then to assist with the interpretation of the results. As much as we might want to become masters of the neuroentrepreneurship laboratory domain as well, this type of research may stretch the limits of many entrepreneurship researchers' current methodological capacities. We strongly encourage you to reach out to neuroscientists and cognitive scientists to develop and execute sound, generalizable research.

We present the chapters in this handbook as examples of approaches that some of the pioneers in this new field of neuroentrepreneurship have taken or plan to take. The authors of these chapters reflect the breadth of expertise that entrepreneurship scholars can draw upon. Within this handbook, you will find technical chapters that explain the various types and methods available to researchers. You will find examples of the types of hypotheses that can be tested with these methods, and you will find specific examples of theories in a variety of areas such as risk, decision making, and cognition that can be fruitfully tested through these methods.

Before we get started, it is important to consider some philosophical issues with which one must wrestle within the realm of brain-based research. In fact, neuroscientists do not conclusively know if and how the brain correlates to the mind. Per Mary Harrington (2011, p. 38), *The Design of Experiments in Neuroscience*, she writes: "In my opinion, figuring out how mind arises from brain is the largest and most enduring question in neuroscience."

Regarding neuroentrepreneurship, are we interested in the entrepreneurial mind, the entrepreneurial brain, or possibly both? Within this handbook, we are interested in the mind and/or brain of someone who is entrepreneurial. We do not know whether there is a type of mind or a type of brain that is entrepreneurial. In fact, we may find no evidence for this. Early entrepreneurship researchers thought that there would be measurable personality traits that could predict who would be entrepreneurs, but found no evidence for such. Skeptics believe that neuroentrepreneurship researchers are going down a similar path. Still, none of us can deny that there is something different in the mind, if not the brain of entrepreneurs.

It is entertaining to imagine something similar to the "sim-man" in medical education, to have a "simulated entrepreneur brain" created after hundreds of thousands of brain scans and other experiments with entrepreneurs that could then be studied under various environments and treatments. Could this lead to artificial intelligence – simulated entrepreneurs' brains and predicted simulated responses? Imagine a virtual test database rooted in theories around various constructs found in the entrepreneurial experience, such as failure, autonomy, altruism, loss, or success. Researchers could then test a wide variety of hypotheses using data from actual entrepreneurs when they become more easily accessible for studies.[1]

As interesting as the possibility of building a sim-entrepreneur is, it is also important to remember that such designs will always be rule-governed and controlled by instructions, without the physiological constraints that exist in actual humans (Epstein, 1984). However, that does not stop scientists from trying to create a brain-like computer. For instance, scientists in Japan are taking a new "beyond Turing" approach, presenting a "multilayered seed structure" that filters sensory input, "learns by itself," and writes its own programs to solve problems (Ghosh, et al., 2014). Perhaps within the next few decades we could have a sim-entrepreneur that might recognize opportunities and create solutions?

It may seem impossible to re-create brain-based scenarios of past entrepreneurial successes or failures. However, in the competitive world of pop music, major labels have algorithms that they run on songs that have been hits previously – in an attempt to re-create that success. Songs are not entrepreneurs, but given developments such as these, could entrepreneurship be just another field waiting to be understood deeply enough for us to make use of tools such as the sim-entrepreneur?

ENTREPRENEURIAL MIND, ENTREPRENEURIAL BRAIN?

Instead of a reductionist approach, we take a nomological stance that the mind is not the same thing as the brain, but that the mind arises from the brain. In Chapter 3, Colosio, Bellavitis, and Gorin present the field of psychophysiology that explores this relationship between mind and brain (body), between chemical and electrical signals, and physiological activity such as increased heart rate, movements, emotions, or risk-seeking behavior. Do these signals cause the activity or does the activity cause the signals? Where does the mind fit in?

A reductionist would say that behavior could be fully explained by the neural activity in the brain.[2] In Chapter 5, Ward, Reeck, and Becker discuss several variations of reductionist theory and its criticisms. Kurthen (2010) presents a thorough analysis of several philosophical positions: reductionism (materialism where "the mental reduces to the cerebral" and parallelism where there is "no interaction between the mental and cerebral"), dualism (epiphenomenalism where "mental events are caused by physical events" and not vice versa), and Kurthen's own position: non-reductive physicalism (where "the mental is asymmetrically dependent on the cerebral, without being reducible to it . . . mental events are 'realized' by cerebral events" (p. 8)).

An example: ". . .while it seems obvious that my intention to raise my arm causes my arm to raise, it is not part of our commonsensical understanding (unless we are neuroscientists) that my intention to raise my arm causes my brain to build up a certain pattern of activation in the primary motor area of the cerebral hemisphere contralateral to the arm to be raised. But this is exactly what would have to be the primary effect of my intention, if it should also manage to cause my arm to raise" (Kurthen, 2010, p. 6).

An interesting research question would then be: do chemical and/or electrical signals in one part of the brain, as might be activated in some type of experimental entrepreneurial treatment, appear to affect other parts of the brain and somehow affect a mental response occurrence? This is an example of a question that, while seemingly elementary in the world of neuroscience, could be a first step toward application in neuroentrepreneurship experiments. As a neuroentrepreneurship researcher, you might design your methodologies and perhaps interpret your results differently depending upon your philosophical assumptions about mind–brain causation. Rather than intentionally, what if Kurthen's arm raised as a result of an errant electrical impulse in the brain, or in response to a fight-or-flight activation where "intent" may exist at some instinctual level. It could be "realized" by the cerebral, but not necessarily perceived at a consciousness level. Is this important to know for neuroentrepreneurship research? Or is it enough to know that there is concurrence, whichever way?

If direction is important, this would speak to a need for a basic notion of causation. Kurthen (2010) argues that "[n]euroscience can only demonstrate concurrence, but if lawlike [nomological] concurrence is all we need for stating causation, then neuroscience can give evidence for causation" (p. 18). This type of groundwork can serve a valuable role, enhancing and informing our theory and research methodologies in neuroentrepreneurship. Harrington (2011, p. 48) explains that hypotheses related to the "proximate causation of the phenomena" would answer "how" questions, and those related to "ultimate causation" would answer "why" questions.

This brain–mind relationship represents a different presentation of causation than what we find in traditional social science research, but it is not new. For instance, Fodor (1983) references mental faculty theories, the beginnings of which go back to antiquity. These are "theor[ies] of the structure of the causal mechanisms that underlie the mind's capacities" (p. 24). Quoting Spearman (1930): "[t]he general intention (in faculty theories) [. . .] is to represent the countless transient mental experiences by a small number of relatively permanent – particularly innate – different principles" (p. 26).

Neuroscience has shown how amazingly complex is the brain and its parts, functions, and interrelationships. Yet it is the nature of theory building to reduce the complexity to somewhat manageable heuristics, another type and process of reductionism. In Chapter 5 Ward, Reeck, and Becker demonstrate how this integrates with neuroentrepreneurship theory-building and research design methodology.

Liu et al. (2014) conducted an experiment partially funded by the National Institute of Health that examined "neural and behavioral correlates of face pareidolia."[3] In their article entitled "Seeing Jesus in toast . . ." the authors found that those who were able to distinguish faces in random pixels exhibited a higher level of communication activity between different parts of the brain than those who could not see faces in the same random set of pixels. Along similar lines, perhaps instead of there being entrepreneur-specific location characteristics of the brain (that is, the BOLD patterns resulting from fMRI scanning[4]), there may be levels of electrical and chemical pattern characteristics that cause or facilitate the entrepreneur to recognize an opportunity. Or perhaps it is all of the above combined.

These types of questions will need to be answered before we get to the point where we can create a simulated entrepreneur. Direction, or causality, would also need to be addressed and controlled for. Carter and Shieh (2010) note that: "activity in the visual cortex increases not only when human subjects are exposed to visual stimuli, but also when subjects are told to *imagine* visual stimuli" (p. 24, emphasis theirs). Stokes (2013)[5] presents an in-depth discussion of the possible relationships between seeing, perceiving, and cognition, and how a person's relationship with a given perceived phenomena changes with familiarity. While seeing is not necessarily believing, what one believes may influence what one sees. Whether this is due to conditioning (learning), or some innate "cognition-to-perception" ability would also be grounds for testing.

If opportunity recognition produces the same responses as facial recognition, then random pixels might correspond to an environmental context that the entrepreneur sees but others do not. Could imagining itself (if not entrepreneurial imagining) be the representation of a type or series of chemical and electrical patterns? Would it be enough to know that such activations were concurring or does, going back to our previous discussion, direction (causality) matter? These are potentially rich areas for neuroentrepreneurship research.

In a recent concrete example (no pun intended), Robinson and Hayes (2012) tested the proposition that experience and social and institutional factors explain patterns of opportunity recognition. They shot video of a broken-down, graffiti-ridden, boarded-up store front on a corner in Harlem, New York. Then they showed the footage to entrepreneurial individuals familiar with the area and some who were not (as a control) to test if and how they perceive entrepreneurial opportunity within that location. Since the perception and recognition of an opportunity would vary across individuals and cultures, imagine the electrical and chemical variances and/or patterns that might occur. A controlled neuroentrepreneurship experiment such as this would be another fertile area to apply neuroexperimental research methods such as those represented in this handbook.

THIS HANDBOOK

As you peruse the various chapters in this handbook, it is our hope that you the reader will find guidance and inspiration in designing neuro-based experiments to enhance your own research. The rest of this book is organized as follows:

Chapter 2: for anyone reading this volume, Pérez-Centeno provides a helpful overview of the various ways in which neuroscience methods can contribute to entrepreneurship research. As neuroscientists who are also entrepreneurship scholars are rare, this chapter brings together a helpful integration of the two fields. To do this, Pérez-Centeno first provides an overview of existing brain-based entrepreneurship research. Especially helpful is how the chapter walks the reader through basic experimental design to entrepreneurial cognition and brain-based research, and then an overview of strengths and limitations.

Then, Pérez-Centeno provides an in-depth, critical review of the neuroentrepreneurship literature. Specifically, the chapter covers strengths, limitations, and opportunities for better understanding the field and specific neuroscience methods (fMRI, EEG, and so on) applicable to entrepreneurship research. The chapter then concludes with an agenda for future research, along with several possible research questions.

Chapter 3: Colosio, Bellavatis, and Gorin make two significant contributions in their chapter. First, they outline a variety of physiological and neurological processes that are potentially relevant to entrepreneurial decision making. This can help neuroentrepreneurship researchers work through and formulate research questions. For entrepreneurship scholars who are unfamiliar with physiology and/or neuroscience, this section would be helpful as a primer.

Their second main contribution is to outline the various ways in which these physical processes can be measured. Especially for entrepreneurship researchers who do not have a background in physiology or neuroscience, this section is helpful. The authors provide a useful outline of which techniques and tools are best for measuring which processes, along with a brief overview of the relevant benefits and limitations.

Chapter 4: De Holan and Couffe provide an overview of the potential for entrepreneurship research using electroencephalogram (EEG), a neuroimaging technique. For scholars who are specifically interested in this technique, or are considering this as one of several options, this chapter is useful. Specifically, the authors make the argument that research using EEG technology can be used both as a useful triangulation tool, as well as a central one. They then break down in detail specifically how EEG can be used, along with strengths, limitations, and ideas for future research.

Chapter 5: for scholars who are specifically interested in research using fMRI, a neuroimaging technique, this chapter provides first an excellent primer and then a deep dive into fMRI that is both useful and accessible for social scientists. Specifically, this chapter has several main contributions. First, the authors present the primary benefits and limitations of using neuroimaging techniques in general. For neuroentrepreneurship scholars considering neuroimaging techniques generally, and fMRI specifically, these sections are essential.

Ward, Reeck, and Becker then go on to define and describe fMRI in detail. Specifically, they discuss the types of hypotheses and designs in fMRI studies and how they can be useful for neuroentrepreneurship research as well as the benefits and limitations of each type of design. These discussions can help to set up neuroentrepreneurship scholars for success.

Particularly useful is the presentation of data analysis that is both general and specific to fMRI studies. Several of the techniques, such as regression analysis, should be familiar to entrepreneurship scholars. For the techniques that are not necessarily familiar, the authors identify these clearly.

Equally important is their section on communicating fMRI results. Even the most experienced researchers may inadvertently and unintentionally report results that do not accurately reflect the research when the methods used are unfamiliar. We strongly suggest that researchers using fMRI studies review again the communication section before drafting the results.

Chapter 6: Pérez-Centeno builds upon the presumption that a fusion between entrepreneurship and neuroscience is justified by the methodological and technological advantages facilitated by the former. He first suggests that the joint use of neuroscience tools such as laboratory experiments and brain-driven technologies are propitious to entrepreneurship research because they allow a deeper level of analysis: the entrepreneurial brain. Second, focusing on one of these tools – laboratory experiments – he unveils nine principles to take into account in good design of an experiment within the structure of a brain-driven entrepreneurship study.

Chapter 7: Day and Boardman present part of a stream of research that seeks to identify the intangible return-on-investment calculations that an individual makes in his or her decision to become an entrepreneur. This research pares down 33 cost and benefit decision variables to a handful of constructs that significantly explained the variance in their model. Then, specific to the point of this handbook, they present several hypotheses to test the model using neuroexperimental methods. These internal calculations in the mind of the pre-nascent entrepreneur may not be intentional but rather generated by the subconscious, and then "realized" by the cerebral. If however, there were such a thing as an "entrepreneurial brain" it would follow that electrical and chemical impulses came together at such a time (or maybe time and time again) to affect the mental to evaluate an opportunity that it identifies.

Chapter 8: Shaver, Schjoedt, Passarelli, and Reeck make several main contributions in applying neuroscience methods to entrepreneurial decision making and risk. Specifically, they discuss the differences between neuroimaging and electrophysiological methods, and when to use both. Importantly, the authors complement the Colosio, Bellavatis, and Gorin chapter (Chapter 3) in providing an overview of the various methods relevant to neuroentrepreneurship. They also complement the Day and Boardman chapter on entrepreneurial return on investment (ROI) (Chapter 7) by providing a deeper dive on a specific aspect of Day and Boardman's broader concept.

As experimental design is integral to neuroentrepreneurship research, the authors provide an excellent refresher on the topic. Specifically, the chapter contains overviews of method selection, methodology, and study design, along with technological and human factors. Then, the chapter walks readers through specific experimental designs relevant to neuroentrepreneurship. Particularly useful are the multiple examples of experiments that are both applicable to entrepreneurial risk and measurable using neuroscience.

Chapter 9: Sud provides an overview of experimental design, discusses brain plasticity, then advocates for an intervention-based approach to this research. The chapter concludes with specific examples of intervention-based neuroexperiments to explore entrepreneurial cognition.

Chapter 10: Treffers features a helpful discussion on neuroentrepreneurship research design, focusing on entrepreneurial cognition and affect. She first presents an argument for the use of neuroscience methods to explore these phenomena. Then, this chapter provides an in-depth review of the relevant neuroscience literature. Finally, the primary contributions of this chapter involve a presentation of five neuroentrepreneurship designs that relate to entrepreneurial cognition and/or affect.

Chapter 11: Pérez-Centeno covers seven neuroscience technologies and four criteria to guide the appropriate selection of a neuroscientific tool for a given research question.

Finally, in Chapter 12: Guillory, Boardman, and Day provide a quick overview of the topics discussed in previous chapters, and then place this in context. Specifically, we discuss the benefits and limitations of neuroentrepreneurship research, and lay out what researchers should assess when deciding to devote the time and resources to pursuing this field of study.

NOTES

1. See, for example, the ASA Experiment Manager (pdf), http://human.cbtc.utoronto.ca/tutorials/ANT-PDFs/ASA_Experiment_Manager.pdf.
2. For an analysis see Sullivan, J. (2009), "The multiplicity of experimental protocols: a challenge to reductionist and non-reductionist models of the unity of neuroscience," *Synthese*, **167**, 511–39.
3. "Face pareidolia is the illusory perception of non-existent faces" (Liu et al, 2014).
4. BOLD stands for blood-oxygen-level dependent, which is explained in more detail in Chapter 5 of this handbook.
5. See also Mathen (2005) for a discussion on seeing, doing, and knowing.

REFERENCES

Carter, M. and J. Shieh (2010), *Guide to Research Techniques in Neuroscience*, Burlington, MA: Elsevier.

Epstein, R. (1984), "Simulation research in the analysis of behavior," *Behaviorism*, **12** (2), 41–59.

Fodor, J. (1983), *The Modularity of Mind*, Cambridge, MA: The MIT Press.

Ghosh, S., K. Aswani, S. Singh, S. Sahu, D. Fujita, and A. Bandyopadhyay (2014), "Design and construction of a brain-like computer: a new class of frequency-fractal computing using wireless communication in a supramolecular organic, inorganic system," *Information*, **5** (1), 28–100; Doi:10.3390/info5010028.

Harrington, M. (2011), *The Design of Experiments in Neuroscience*, 2nd edn, Los Angeles: Sage Publishing.

Kriewall, T. and K. Mekemson (2010), "Instilling the entrepreneurial mindset into engineering undergraduates," *The Journal of Engineering Entrepreneurship*, **1** (1), 5–19.

Krueger, N. and M. Day (2010), "Looking forward, looking backward: from entrepreneurial cognition to neuroentrepreneurship," in Z. Acs and D. Audretsch (eds), *Handbook of Entrepreneurship Research: An Interdisciplinary Survey and Introduction*, 2nd edn, New York: Springer, 321–57.

Krueger, N. and I. Welpe (2008), "Experimental entrepreneurship: a research prospectus & workshop," *United States Association for Small Business and Entrepreneurship Conference Proceedings*, 1070–80.

Kurthen, M. (2010), "Pushing brains: can cognitive neuroscience provide experimental evidence for brain-mind causation?," *Psyche*, **16** (2), 5–22.

Liu, J., J. Li, L. Feng, L. Li, J. Tian, and K. Lee (2014), "Seeing Jesus in toast: neural and behavioral correlates of face pareidolia," *Cortex*, **53** (April), 60–77.

Mathen, M. (2005), *Seeing, Doing, and Knowing: A Philosophical Theory of Sense Perception*, Oxford: Oxford University Press.

Robinson, J. and R. Hayes (2012), "Opportunity recognition in inner-city markets: An exploratory study," *Journal of Developmental Entrepreneurship*, **17** (2); doi: http://dx.doi.org/10.1142/S1084946712500112.

Spearman, C. (1930) *Psychology Down the Ages*, vol. 1, New York: MacMillan.

Stanton, A., M. Day, and I. Welpe (eds) (2010), "Introduction," in *Neuroeconomics and the Firm*, Cheltenham: Edward Elgar.

Stokes, D. (2013), "Cognitive penetrability of perception," *Philosophy Compass*, **8** (7), 646–63.

Sullivan, J. (2009), "The multiplicity of experimental protocols: a challenge to reductionist and non-reductionist models of the unity of neuroscience," *Synthese*, **167**, 511–39.

PART I

NEUROSCIENCE PRINCIPLES, TECHNIQUES, AND TOOLS

2. Brain-driven entrepreneurship research: a review and research agenda
Víctor Pérez-Centeno

INTRODUCTION

Since the 1980s entrepreneurship research has been a focus of interest in society as well as in education and academic research (Landström, 2004). While there is a significant knowledge base for entrepreneurship, there are still challenging research gaps that cannot be addressed more deeply with existing approaches. In the interest of moving this research forward, technologies and methods from the field of neurosciences are beginning to resonate within the minds of several entrepreneurship scholars (Blair, 2010; de Holan, 2014; McMullen et al., 2014; Nicolaou and Shane, 2014; Smith, 2010). Although entrepreneurship researchers seem to love the mind and its workings, many of the concepts within entrepreneurship research can be explained only very poorly with the instruments used now (de Holan, 2014). Work done on entrepreneurial cognition is the major intellectual driver toward this new era. Research includes entrepreneurs' cognition[1] (R.K. Mitchell et al., 2002), knowledge (Shane, 2000), intuition (J.R. Mitchell et al., 2005), and mindsets (Haynie et al., 2010), among many other phenomena taking place within the human mind (de Holan, 2014).

Instead of focusing on what entrepreneurs think, how they think, why they think the way they do, and how they came to think that way, a majority of scholars are still assessing what entrepreneurs are or have (attributes), or what they do (behaviors) (de Holan, 2014). This omission is surprising, given that the focus of entrepreneurship research lies in how entrepreneurs think and make decisions (de Holan, 2014). In this sense, de Holan (2014) highlights the relevance of neurosciences, arguing that we have not yet begun to explore what neuroscience can do for entrepreneurship, and we only know how little we know. This research gap should be addressed and the field must come to incorporate neuroscience theory and methods (Nicolaou and Shane, 2014).

To address these concerns conceptually, the aim of this chapter is to assess the contribution of neurosciences to entrepreneurship research. This chapter strives to accomplish that through a review and research agenda for entrepreneurship research from a neurosciences angle, building upon existing research and knowledge of the entrepreneurial phenomenon through the lenses of neuroscience. The review and research agenda are developed in three steps.

First, I build on entrepreneurship research undertaken using neurosciences and highlight the conceptualization of a brain-driven approach. Second, I discuss entrepreneurship research relevant to understanding the use of neurosciences in this field. Third, to better identify avenues for future entrepreneurship research, I assess the manner and extent to which entrepreneurship research leverages the potential for a brain-based approach. Through content analysis of existing articles incorporating a neuroscience method in their studies, I depict the current state of knowledge with regard to a brain-driven research perspective. I show that for all its achievements, research has yet to leverage the full potential of applying such an approach into entrepreneurship research. I build on these observations to formalize the research agenda. I suggest a definition of brain-driven entrepreneurship research and propose a series of strategies to address and expand this approach in more in-depth ways.

CONCEPTUALIZING BRAIN-DRIVEN ENTREPRENEURSHIP RESEARCH

I start with the use of neurosciences in entrepreneurship research and discuss key conceptualizations advocated in that spectrum. Towards the end of this section the advances in entrepreneurial cognition research are also discussed: those that are likely to be essential for understanding the roots of using neurosciences in the field of entrepreneurship. The application of neurosciences to entrepreneurship research is new; thus, it is imperative to frame the scope of it within this chapter. Just as new technologies are a primary source of innovation and opportunity in entrepreneurship (Drucker, 2014; Schumpeter, 1934), the same might also be said of science (Sanders, 2007). Neuroscience did not exist even 20 years ago, but thanks to technological advances it has become one of the fastest-growing areas of the biological sciences, and a revolutionizing force across social sciences that challenges disciplines ranging from economics to sociology and psychology (McMullen et al., 2014). Taking into account that entrepreneurship draws on many of these disciplines, the field is unlikely to be immune to neuroscience's transformative impact (McMullen et al., 2014). In simple terms, neuroscience entails the study of how the nervous system develops, its structure, and what it does (Nordqvist, 2014). It is an interdisciplinary science that liaises closely with

Table 2.1   Basic concepts

Conceptualizations	Determining Characteristics
Neurosciences	Known also as neural science, it studies how the nervous system develops, its structure, and what it does.
Cognitive neurosciences	Use evidence from behavior and the brain to understand human cognition.
Brain imaging	A branch of medical imaging that concentrates on the brain. It can be useful in the study of the brain, how it works, and how different activities affect the brain.
Cognitive psychology	Understands human cognition by using behavioral evidence.
Brain-driven entrepreneurship research	Combines the use of experiments and brain-imaging technologies to explore entrepreneurial phenomena.
Entrepreneurial cognition	Aims to understand the knowledge structures that people use to make assessments, judgments, or decisions involving opportunity evaluation and new venture creation and growth.
Experimental entrepreneurship	Use of natural, economic, and hypothetical experiments in entrepreneurship research.

other disciplines, such as mathematics, linguistics, engineering, computer science, chemistry, philosophy, psychology, and medicine (Nordqvist, 2014).

In addition to the set of basic concepts (See Table 2.1), there are eight branches of neuroscience that are of special interest to the field of entrepreneurship: cognitive neuroscience, affective neuroscience, behavioral neuroscience, cultural neuroscience, computational neuroscience, neuroinformatics, systems neuroscience, and social neuroscience. Nordqvist (2014) succinctly defines these branches: cognitive neurosciences study the higher cognitive functions that exist in humans and their underlying neural bases. Affective neuroscience examines how neurons behave in relation to emotions. Behavioral neuroscience studies the biological bases of behavior, whilst cultural neuroscience looks at how beliefs, practices, and cultural values are shaped by the brain, minds, and genes over different periods. Computational neuroscience attempts to understand how brains compute, using computers to simulate and model brain function. Neuroinformatics integrates data across all areas of neuroscience to help understand the brain and treat diseases. Neuroinformatics involves acquiring data, sharing, publishing, and storing information, analysis, modeling, and simulation. Systems neuroscience follows the pathways of data flow within the central nervous system to define the kinds of processing going on there and uses that information to explain behavioral functions. Social neuroscience is an interdisciplinary field dedicated to understanding how biological systems implement social processes and behavior (Nordqvist, 2014).

There are two fundamental elements, which when applied jointly, link the contribution of the above branches of neuroscience to entrepreneurship research: the experimental research paradigm and brain-imaging technologies. On the one hand, unlike entrepreneurship, where the usage of experimental methodologies has been limited (Patel and Fiet, 2010; Schade and Burmeister, 2009; Simmons et al., 2016), neuroscience research is performed fundamentally through experimental design and the use of brain-imaging technologies. An experiment is the controlled test of a hypothesis (Huettel et al., 2009) and an experimental design can allow effective hypothesis testing through the way in which a scientist sets up the manipulations and measurements of an experiment (Huettel et al., 2009). Experiments entail pluses and minuses (Coolican, 2014); nonetheless, their use might be more beneficial than detrimental to entrepreneurship research (Krueger and Welpe, 2008; Schade and Burmeister, 2009; Shepherd et al., 2015; Simmons et al., 2016). Because much of the focus of entrepreneurship research is on the individual, experiments can be used to provide the most reliable and valid assessment of individual-level behavior and processes (Patel and Fiet, 2010).

Thus, the successful application of a neuroscientific approach to the investigation of any entrepreneurship theme presupposes the elaboration of a well-designed experiment. On the other hand, equally relevant is the technological element. The human mind has been studied for thousands of years, but the human brain has only been studied for about a century (Carter and Shieh, 2015). Only 150 years ago, the ability to study the nervous systems of humans was limited to direct observation and by examining the effects of brain damage in people and other organisms (Carter and Shieh, 2015). Technologies have developed at such a speed that modern neuroscientists now have hundreds of techniques that can be used to answer specific scientific questions (Carter and Shieh, 2015).

Technically known as whole-brain technologies, they can be either structural or functional. Structural techniques produce images of the anatomical architecture of the brain, whereas functional techniques produce images of the physiological processes that underscore neural activity (Carter and Shieh, 2015). For instance, functional magnetic resonance imaging (fMRI) and magneto-encephalography (MEG) are functional imaging techniques and, as such, are suitable to be applied to the field of entrepreneurship.

Although these technologies may enable a deeper study of the brain by facilitating higher spatial and temporal resolution (Carter and Shieh, 2015), there is discussion about their relevance to the field. Some scholars argue that these technologies may advance the state of the art in entrepreneurship research (Blair, 2010; de Holan, 2014; Krueger and Welpe, 2014), allowing a better understanding of how decision making (Smith, 2010), entrepreneurial cognition, and emotions (Krueger and Welpe, 2008; Wargo et al., 2010) are processed in the brain. Other experts are cautious about any collaboration between neuroscience and entrepreneurship (Beugré, 2010; Tracey and Schluppeck, 2014).

Brain-driven entrepreneurship research refers to the study of any suitable topic of entrepreneurship, using both an experimental design in any of its forms and any existing or forthcoming brain-imaging technologies. Defined as such, a brain-driven approach to entrepreneurship is different from neuroentrepreneurship or entrepreneurial neuroscience in that the scope of these terms remains generic. For instance, neuroentrepreneurship is tacitly referred to as being located at the intersection of neurosciences, entrepreneurship/entrepreneurial cognition, and experiments (Krueger and Welpe, 2008). Other scholars describe it as a new field that has borrowed from work in neuroscience, neuropsychology, and neuroeconomics to better understand and test how entrepreneurs think, behave, and make decisions (Blair, 2010). It is also different from experimental entrepreneurship, because such an approach implies the sole use of experiments to investigate entrepreneurial behavior from the perspectives of economics, cognitive, social, and developmental psychology, neuroscience, philosophy, and evolutionary anthropology (Krueger and Welpe, 2008).

A brain-driven approach to entrepreneurship entails the analysis of cognitive/affective/motivational/hormonal processes, which can be depicted in a single entrepreneur or team of entrepreneurs at a neural and behavioral level. The cognitive/affective/motivational/hormonal level concerns the internal mental processes reflected as neural substrates and behavioral responses. The neural level focuses on identifying the brain regions that are activated when entrepreneurs display a particular type of behavior and the behavioral level focuses on the entrepreneurs' responses to various stimuli. Figure 2.1 presents a summary of the key components of a brain-driven perspective to entrepreneurship research.

In order to understand the scope and contribution of a brain approach to entrepreneurship research, an understanding of the basic concepts

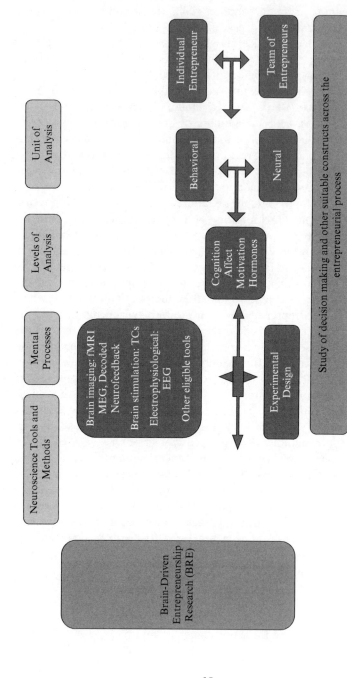

Figure 2.1   A brain-driven approach to entrepreneurship research (BRE)

highlighted in Table 2.1 is necessary. From now on, the term brain-driven entrepreneurship research is used as such or in its abbreviated form, BER.

FROM ENTREPRENEURIAL COGNITION TO BRAIN-DRIVEN ENTREPRENEURSHIP RESEARCH

The possibility to investigate deeper knowledge structures within the arena of entrepreneurial cognition marks the genesis of scholarly interest in the use of neuroscientific tools (Krueger and Day, 2010). Entrepreneurial cognition is an important perspective in entrepreneurship (R.K. Mitchell et al., 2007; R.K. Mitchell et al., 2002; R.K. Mitchell et al., 2004). To put it simply, entrepreneurial cognition deals with the question: 'how do entrepreneurs think?' (R.K. Mitchell et al., 2007). While earlier approaches to entrepreneurial cognition focused on the psychological processes that underlie behavior (Shaver and Scott, 1991), the area has broadened to focus on heuristic-based logic (Simon et al., 2000), perceptual processes (Gaglio and Katz, 2001), expertise (R.K. Mitchell et al., 2000), and effectuation (Sarasvathy, 2001).

Recent contributions on entrepreneurial cognition have shed light on the transition from static to dynamic cognitive research conceptualizations through some degree of emphasis on socially situated cognition (Randolph-Seng, Mitchell, and Mitchell, 2014). Randolph-Seng, Mitchell, and Mitchell (2014) argue that these new developments concentrate on four themes: theory, entrepreneurial affect, entrepreneurial neuroscience, and entrepreneurial thought. Carsrud and Brännback (2014) suggest a linkage-focused work connecting cognitive factors such as intentions and motivations to subsequent behaviors such as goal setting. Bird (2014) highlights the crucial role that entrepreneurial behavior plays as a concrete outcome: one of cognition's most observable outcomes. Randolph-Seng, Williams, and Hayek (2014) integrate the research literature on non-conscious cognition with research in entrepreneurial intentions and intuition.

The interface of feeling with thinking is also relevant. Foo et al. (2014) suggest that the affective/cognitive connection exists and exerts influence across both time and levels of analysis. Grégoire (2014) draws attention to different types of affective/cognitive forces in entrepreneurship, depending on their enduring versus episodic nature and their plane of influence. Other scholars propose and test a culturally situated model that relates entrepreneurial emotions/passion and cognition/self-efficacy, exploring how these factors impact venture performance (Drnovsek et al., 2014). Baucus et al. (2014) demonstrate how entrepreneurs' brains are physiologically the same as most people's, but are different in terms of their experiences and knowledge. McMullen et al. (2014), in addition to explaining the formation and successful implementation of opportunity beliefs, provide a new view that points to the theme of entrepreneurial neuroscience.

On entrepreneurial thought, Forbes (2014) proposes a new way of thinking about advances in large-scale codification processes (media and so on) and in network formation (markets and social structures), in part because such advanced symbol systems (as well as even the conceptualization of new opportunity) depend upon language as primary to idea transmission and understanding. Clarke and Cornelissen (2014) make a claim for the formative role of language in shaping the ideas of entrepreneurs and their attempts to gain a broader understanding and recognition for a new venture from stakeholders and resource providers. This account attempts to present some of the key findings on entrepreneurial cognition and unveil a concern about its methodological and technological limitations, which call for consideration of a brain-driven perspective to advance the frontiers of entrepreneurship research. Some of these limitations are pointed out by Omorede et al. (2015), who argue that: 'some cognition topics that are interesting to advance are methodologically challenging, because it is difficult for people to reflect on their own conscious processes, studies of the brain and procedures such as brain scanning are suggested as next step' (p. 766). Baucus et al. (2014) contend that neuroscience renders the entrepreneur as human.

Strengths and Limitations

There are optimistic and critical voices concerning the academic added value of a brain-driven perspective to entrepreneurship research. The optimists argue that neuroscience methods, technologies, and tools may contribute to entrepreneurship research in several ways (Nicolaou and Shane, 2014) from the new possibilities afforded by these new tools (de Holan, 2014). The use of these technologies may help to understand how entrepreneurs think, a major part of what research on entrepreneurial cognition seeks to explain (R.K. Mitchell et al., 2007). Neuroscience may complement aspects of the biological perspective on entrepreneurship (Nicolaou and Shane, 2014) and allow understanding of many facets of the practice of entrepreneurship and those who carry it out, by providing evidence that can be developed and taught in classrooms (de Holan, 2014). Schade (2005) highlights the ability of neuroscience to focus closely on individual decisions. Along the same direction, Krueger and Welpe (2014) claim that neuroscience might be useful for a better understanding of entrepreneurs and entrepreneurship.

Neuroscientific tools allow the examination of the mind itself as it is doing something, as it is being done elsewhere (de Holan, 2014). For example, its tools enable analysis of what happens in the mind of a person who is looking at something that he or she considers beautiful or ugly (Cela-Conde et al., 2004) without having to ask, and therefore avoiding the issues of confusion, desirability, or outright lies (de Holan, 2014). De Holan (2014) contends that the research potential of neuroscience is vast, broad, and not limited to the topics of behavioral decision theory, game theory, perceptions, emotions, and affect. Hoskisson et al. (2011) point out that these questions might be better approached from a neurological spectrum: what happens in the brain of an entrepreneur that allows him or her to recognize or construct an opportunity, be resourceful, or do bricolage? Is the functioning of his or her brain superior, or just pathologically biased and impervious to the rather slim odds of the success of new ventures? Is success in entrepreneurship related to the capacity to recognize an opportunity, or, as has recently been argued, the capacity to organize resources around that opportunity, or to ignore reality?[2] Is successful entrepreneurship related to a superior ability to reason, or is it more a capacity to seduce people, or both, or neither? And are these differences created? Can they be developed? Do entrepreneurs detect opportunities faster than other people? And if they do, are they more error prone?

De Holan (2014) suggests that Hoskisson's questions can be better answered with neuroscientific tools than with most of the tools used now, and the answers produced may permanently change the way the entrepreneur is seen, the entrepreneurial process, and entrepreneurial management in general. If what is needed is more research on the micro antecedents of innovation and performance, one cannot afford to keep ignoring the foundational micro antecedents of any human decision and action: the brain (de Holan, 2014). Entrepreneurship can use theories and techniques developed in the neurosciences to help better understand these phenomena, while neuroscientific research can exploit scientifically interesting phenomena in the field of entrepreneurship (Blair, 2010). Put simply, the application of neurosciences in entrepreneurship represents a unique opportunity to ask questions that could not be answered before, to test questions that could not even be thought to have been asked before, to test questions in a better way, and to get better answers (Krueger and Welpe, 2014).

On the other hand, the potential of neurosciences in entrepreneurship research is treated with some skepticism. McBride (2014) argues that studies linking questions of interest to techniques from cognitive science and neuroscience have been less than impressive, mixed, muddled, or only partially true. Tracey and Schluppeck (2014) claim that neuroimaging at the present time is incapable of shedding meaningful light on the questions that de Holan suggests it could answer. The cognitive processes are so complex and the uncertainties so great, that it is unclear, for example, as to whether opportunity recognition is rooted in particular cognitive functions that exist in a particular part of some brains, but not in others, and far less easy to disentangle these functions from the broader social and cultural contexts in which individual entrepreneurs (and their brains) are embedded (Tracey and Schluppeck, 2014). To suggest otherwise is to stretch the power of neuroimaging beyond the limits of credibility and may expose entrepreneurship research to ridicule (Tracey and Schluppeck, 2014).

Most neuroscientists do not believe that higher-level cognitive functions can be localized to a small selection of brain areas: it is very likely that such functions involve a distributed pattern of neural activity across different areas of the brain (Tracey and Schluppeck, 2014). Just because one part of the brain appears more active when a person performs a particular task does not necessarily imply that it is the part of the brain responsible for that task (Logothetis, 2008). Tracey and Schluppeck (2014) claim that there is still debate in the literature on neuroscience about the extent to which fMRI reflects excitatory or inhibitory neural responses in any particular brain region. Statistical correlation in neuroimaging data with performance in a task or behavioral traits does not imply that the identified areas play a causative role. As Wade (2006) notes, "If a scan shows that a brain area 'lights up' when someone is doodling, that does not mean the area is a doodling centre!" (p. 23).

Coupled with the above-mentioned technical and methodological limitations of neuroscience tools, another explanation why neuroentrepreneurship is not gaining credibility is that it is built on and/or around a view of entrepreneurship that is not a theory (individual/opportunity nexus), and that view itself is built on very dubious ontological grounds (McBride, 2014). As is the case with any methodology used to study a social phenomenon, both the tools that neuroscience uses and the way they are used are subject to limitations, biases, and boundary conditions (Eastman and Campbell, 2006; Vul et al., 2009). Neuroscience is not a solution to all research questions; nevertheless, not using such a powerful and available research methodology would be a mistake (de Holan, 2014).

RESULTS OF THE REVIEW

The analysis unveils the early findings of a set of entrepreneurship studies carried out at a brain level. The study covered the totality of peer-reviewed eligible empirical articles published between 1900 and 2016. A summary of the studies is presented in Table 2.2.

Findings and Contributions Using BER in Entrepreneurship Research

I illustrate what I know about the added value of a brain-driven perspective in entrepreneurship research through the empirical findings and the conceptual ideas put forward from five perspectives: theoretical, behavioral, neural, experimental, and technological.

Decision-making Efficiency Over Decision Speed

Entrepreneurs' brains are physiologically the same as other persons' brains, but in terms of experiences and knowledge they are different (Baucus et al., 2014). One of these differences has to do with how the entrepreneurial context of high uncertainty, ambiguity, time pressure, emotional intensity, and/or high risk affects decision making (Baron, 2008; Busenitz and Barney, 1997; Mullins and Forlani, 2005). These studies address the issue of decision making in a context of uncertainty from a brain-level perspective and focus on what is claimed to be substantial to entrepreneurs: finding what differentiates the decision-making ability of entrepreneurs from non-entrepreneurs (Stanton and Welpe, 2010). Applying differing conceptual perspectives and methods, these studies focus on 'entrepreneurial decision making'. Judgment and decision making are well-established topics of interest in management, psychology, sociology, and political science, to name but a few (Gilovich and Griffin, 2010; Hastie, 2001). Within entrepreneurship the topic of entrepreneurial decision making is relevant as well (Baron and Ward, 2004; Shepherd et al., 2015). A recent review categorizes seven decision-making frameworks along the primary activities associated with entrepreneurship: opportunity assessment decisions, entrepreneurial entry decisions, decisions about exploiting opportunities, entrepreneurial exit decisions, heuristics and bias in the decision-making context, characteristics of the entrepreneurial decision maker, and environment as decision context (Shepherd et al., 2015).

These studies implicitly touch upon three dimensions of entrepreneurial decision making: opportunity assessment decisions, decisions about exploiting opportunities (Laureiro-Martínez et al., 2014), and

Table 2.2   Summary of studies

Key Items	Laureiro-Martínez et al. (2014)	Ortiz-Terán et al. (2014)
Research question	What are the neural bases of individual differences in decision-making efficiency?	What are the relationships between key neurophysiological and personality characteristics in entrepreneurial decision making?
Definitions	Decision-making efficiency operationalized as total payoff divided by response time	Decision making is a common task that plays a pivotal role in translating perception into action and is affected by factors such as personality or attention. It consists of multiple operations, including multiple option evaluation, actions, and outcome monitoring
Hypothesis	While engaged in a task requiring fast and efficient decision making, individuals with experience in facing a broad range of pressing, heterogeneous decisions, compared with a group experienced in making more specialized choices, will show better performance	Decision making is different both neurophysiologically and in terms of reaction times in founder entrepreneurs when compared with non-entrepreneurs
Decision-making measure	Performance divided by response time	Reaction time
	Exploitative/explorative decision making	Decision-making speed
Task	4-armed bandit task	Stroop reaction time task
Other measures		Personality: Temperament and character inventory-revised
Data-collection tool	fMRI	Electroencephalography (EEG)
Sample	24 entrepreneurs and 26 managers	25 founder entrepreneurs and 20 non-entrepreneurs (people who never created a company)
Statistics	SMP toolbox, Matlab v7.4, GLM, ANOVA	Non-parametric Mann-Whitney test, linear regression, ANOVA F-tests, logistic regression analysis

Table 2.2 (continued)

Key Items	Laureiro-Martínez et al. (2014)	Ortiz-Terán et al. (2014)
Main results	The groups were comparable in terms of payoff Compared with managers, entrepreneurs get the same result in less time, showing higher decision-making efficiency and a stronger activation in the frontopolar cortex Neural signature of entrepreneurs found in the prefrontal cortex Exploitation and exploration are linked with the activation of different brain areas Exploitative choices recruit ventromedial prefrontal activation Explorative choices engage the fronto-parietal region, anterior cingulate cortex and locus coeruleus	Reaction times indicate that founder entrepreneurs make faster decisions than non-entrepreneurs, both behaviorally and physiologically Faster decision could be linked to better capacity to selective visual attention, response selection, and executive control Unlike non-entrepreneurs, founder entrepreneurs' brains display activity in the supplementary motor areas (inferior parietal sulcus) and the orbitofrontal cortex The novelty-seeking parameter is prominent among founder entrepreneurs

characteristics of the entrepreneurial decision maker (Ortiz-Terán et al., 2014). Opportunity is at the core of entrepreneurship, so understanding how entrepreneurs arrive at decisions relating to opportunity recognition, evaluation, and exploitation is critical to advancing our knowledge of the field as a whole (Shane, 2003; Shane and Venkataraman, 2000). At the same time, individuals are heterogeneous in their beliefs and desires, and these differences help explain why some choose to become entrepreneurs and why others choose managerial or other employment-related roles (Shepherd et al., 2015). Laureiro-Martínez et al. (2014) examine the neurobiological mechanisms behind decision-making efficiency among entrepreneurs and managers. They operationalize decision-making efficiency as total payoff divided by response time. They highlight that the ability of making decisions quickly is vital to keep up with fast environmental changes, survival, and market performance. Ortiz-Terán et al. (2014) assess the relationship between neurophysiologic and personality characteristics in entrepreneurial decision making. They mainly focus on how decision making differs between founder entrepreneurs and non-founder entrepreneurs. To put it simply, Laureiro-

Martínez et al. (2014) evaluate decision making in terms of quality and time, whereas Ortiz-Terán et al. (2014) focus mainly on the reaction time, known also as decision-making speed, and the cognitive mechanisms behind it.

Reaction time is the time taken between the onset of a stimulus/event and the production of a behavioral response (for example, a button press) (Bear et al., 2007). Laureiro-Martínez et al. (2014) conclude that entrepreneurs make more efficient decisions compared to managers. Their results suggest that expert decision-making success may be enhanced by the individual's ability to track evidence and in disengaging attention from current reassuring options, both mechanisms leading to more efficient decision making. The evidence obtained by Ortiz-Terán et al. (2014) indicates that founder entrepreneurs make faster decisions compared to non-founding entrepreneurs. In their view, founding entrepreneurs might be more oriented toward opportunity recognition and capture and eager to make more rapid decisions about which opportunities to pursue. However, they dedicate significant cognitive resources to decision closure and resolution of residual conflicts (Ortiz-Terán et al., 2014). Entrepreneurs have to invest more mental effort in this process, partly because they need to check the decisions they have just made (Baron and Ward, 2004). These studies make reference to a cognitive approach to entrepreneurial decision making. The cognitive perspective is concerned with mental processes such as perceiving, remembering, reasoning, deciding, and problem solving, and it assumes that only by studying mental processes is it possible to fully understand what organisms do (Nolan-Hoeksema et al., 2014). Entrepreneurial activity is influenced by cognitive biases, and cognitive biases strongly influence entrepreneurial decision making (Baron, 2004; Busenitz and Arthurs, 2007; Shaver and Scott, 1991). To examine decision-making efficiency, Laureiro-Martínez et al. (2014) combine a cognitive and exploration–exploitation view. Ortiz-Terán et al. (2014) instead mix a cognitive and personality-trait angle to assess decision making.

These studies use a cognitive view, and further value could have been achieved by characterizing it within the context of existing approaches to entrepreneurial decision making such as the two modes of entrepreneurial decision making: effectuation and causation (Maine et al., 2015), naturalistic decision making (Gustafsson, 2006), the stimulus-organism-response model to entrepreneurial decision making (Michl et al., 2009), and so on. The interplay between the level of certainty (high, medium, low) and elicited cognitive processes portrayed in these studies (intuitive cognition, heuristics, analysis) could have been aided, for instance, by the cognitive continuum theory (Hammond, 1988), or the factors influencing differential susceptibility to cognitive errors by entrepreneurs and others (Baron, 1998).

Baron (1998) confirms that due to the peculiar characteristics of entrepreneurs' environment (notably high levels of uncertainty, novelty, emotions, and time pressure) they are apt to demonstrate decision-making biases or heuristics. The list of these includes counterfactual thinking, affect infusion, attributional style, the planning fallacy and self-justification, and self-serving bias (Baron, 1998).

Since entrepreneurs are more liable to use decision-making biases and heuristics than are managers (Busenitz and Barney, 1997), these studies could have profited from the particular assessment of a suitable heuristic within their design. Entrepreneurial cognition-based concepts might be used to distinguish entrepreneurs from non-entrepreneurs (R. K. Mitchell, 1994), but they cannot be solely used to assess entrepreneurial decision making. Emotions and motivations also play a key role in entrepreneurial decision making (Michl et al., 2009; Reed, 2010). Evidence shows that the brain is easily fooled by emotional states, which prevent it from making fully rational decisions (Camerer et al., 2005). Lawrence et al. (2008) found that successful entrepreneurs and managers share great ability at rational analysis ('cold' cognition), but entrepreneurs display a significant edge in analyses that engaged both rational and emotional thinking ('hot' cognition). Perhaps unsurprisingly, 'hot' and 'cold' cognition tend to occur in different areas of the brain's front lobes (Krueger and Welpe, 2014).

Baron (1998, 2000, 2008) postulates that entrepreneurs will experience very intense emotions in their decisions, including the effect of positive and negative emotions. Positive emotions such as joviality and happiness might lead entrepreneurs to not fully evaluate all possible outcome alternatives, which consequently results in hasty and premature decisions (Ardichvili et al., 2003; Baron, 2004, 2008). Negative emotions such as anxiety and shame do not have an exactly opposing effect compared to positive emotions, but they are rather heterogeneous (Michl et al., 2009).

Although some researchers still see emotions and cognitions as two independent but interacting phenomena, it is common sense that emotions and cognitions cannot be studied separately from each other, and only an integrative view will lead to an understanding of their effects on entrepreneurial decision making (Michl et al., 2009). The consideration of emotions and motivations within the analysis of entrepreneurial decision making from a brain perspective remains a task pending for future studies. These studies denote an effort to assess the decision-making process through the theoretical articulation of a cognitive/exploitation–exploration view (Laureiro-Martínez et al., 2014) and cognitive/personality-traits view

(Ortiz-Terán et al., 2014), having in common a brain-level of analysis, never attempted before within the field. I consider these findings as the beginning of a deeper analysis of the phenomena of entrepreneurial decision making, while acknowledging the need for the consideration of the emotional and motivational component to entrepreneurial decision making.

Behavioral Modulation

The cognitive perspective studies mental processes by focusing on specific behaviors, but interprets them in terms of underlying processes (Nolan-Hoeksema et al., 2014). Decision making is one of these processes. Just as in neuroscience, brain-driven research in entrepreneurship requires the use of experimental tasks to modulate behavior. Research in neuroscience comprises two steps: the first aims to assess the behavioral effects of interest, and only if these work out is a neuroimaging tool then applied to investigate the neural correlates of the studied phenomena (Palva, 2014). Avoiding the behavioral component may result in lack of credibility of the result (Palva, 2014). Hence, any brain-oriented research in entrepreneurship should adhere to this requirement. These studies rightly undertake behavioral analysis first. They modulate the participant's decision making via the application of two tasks: the basic Stroop reaction time task (Ortiz-Terán et al., 2014) and the 4-armed bandit task (Laureiro-Martínez et al., 2014). The former consists of words about a variety of colors (blue, green, red) printed in colors different from that of the word itself (for example, the word 'blue' is printed in green or red) on a computer screen (Ortiz-Terán et al., 2014). The latter is a classical task of exploitative–explorative decision making (Daw et al., 2006), which involves repeated choices among four different slot machines that lead to variable gains in successive trials, all having the same structure (Laureiro-Martínez et al., 2014). Both tasks are generally accepted as reasonable proxies, since decisions within the spectrum of entrepreneurship are normally made under the constraints of limited time, knowledge, and computational capacity (Rieskamp and Hoffrage, 2008). The Stroop task is one of the best-known paradigms in cognitive psychology (MacLeod, 2005). The explanation that reading words was much more practiced than naming pictures or colors introduced the concept of 'automacity' to psychology (Cattell, 1886).

The accounts of what causes the interference produced during the Stroop task are various: degree of practice (Cattell, 1886), speed of processing (Dyer, 1973), competition between ongoing processing of the word and the color dimensions at the same time (Logan, 1980), and build-up of practice for the word pathway being greater than that for the color pathway (Cohen et al., 1990). This variety of possible causal factors suggests that interpreting the results of Stroop experiments as evidence for a particular type of processing or for a particular process is suspect (MacLeod, 2005). The reasons behind the interference should be taken as a first step in attempting to explain how entrepreneurs react when presented with an ambiguous stimulus. The scientific measurement of the speed factor in decision making nonetheless provides concrete scientific evidence that proves that founding entrepreneurs make faster decisions as compared to non-founding entrepreneurs. In doing so, it adds value to the topic of entrepreneurial decision making.

Prior studies argued that entrepreneurs rely on heuristics in their decision making more than managers (Deligonul et al., 2008); that the founders of new firms must make quicker decisions than the managers of established firms (Shepherd et al., 2015); that heuristics facilitate entrepreneurial decision making (Busenitz and Barney, 1997); and that optimism, experience, and overconfidence affect entrepreneurial decision making (Shepherd et al., 2015). However, none of them measured the moment in which decision making takes place nor attempted to explain the neural mechanisms behind it. Since every task is subject to improvement, a natural next step is to include the emotional aspect that can be assessed within the context of the Stroop task (McKenna and Sharma, 1995). On the other hand, the 4-armed bandit task used by Laureiro-Martínez et al. (2014) is appropriate to modulate entrepreneurial decision making, because entrepreneurs make decisions about where to search for new opportunities, and how to exploit known opportunities (Bryant, 2014). They also concentrate their enquiry on measuring performance, which has also been a subject of interest in cognitive neuroscience (Cohen et al., 2007; Daw et al., 2006).

Similar to Ortiz-Terán et al. (2014), the investigation of Laureiro-Martínez et al. (2014) is the first of its kind to apply the 4-armed bandit task in the context of entrepreneurial exploration and exploitation. The task used by Laureiro-Martínez (2014) is a modified version of the original bandit problem, which is a dynamic decision-making task that is simply described, well-suited to controlled laboratory study, and representative of a broad class of real-world problems (Steyvers et al., 2009).

Some of the reasons for the suitability of this task to entrepreneurship are the following: bandit problems provide an interesting and useful task for the study of human capabilities in decision making and problem solving (Steyvers et al., 2009). They provide a challenge similar to many real-world problems that is nevertheless simple to understand. They require people to search their environment in intelligent ways to make decisions, exploring uncertain alternatives and exploiting familiar ones

(Steyvers et al., 2009). The ability to search effectively, striking the right balance between exploration and exploitation, is a basic requirement for successful decision making (Gigerenzer and Todd, 1999) and bandit problems shed light on how people make decisions in general and on how information is integrated into decisions in particular (Schulz et al., 2015).

The results obtained by Laureiro-Martínez et al. (2014) are the first to assess decision-making efficiency based on data collected directly from entrepreneurs' brains and elaborate on the possible processes taking place. They also confirm that entrepreneurs are quicker than managers and as equally efficient as managers when faced with a simulated task of exploration and exploitation. The depth of analysis and results achieved by Laurie's team is germane when taking into account that a growing body of research on exploration and exploitation study the phenomena from a narrow perspective, mostly within larger, well-established firms (Jansen et al., 2012; Stettner et al., 2014), SMEs to a lesser extent (Frigotto et al., 2014), and entrepreneurial behavior from an individual-level perspective (Kuckertz et al., 2010; Voutsina et al., 2014).

In addition to the appropriateness of the task and the implied cognitive mechanisms trailing decision-making efficiency, the measures of the task could have been improved had the emotional and personality-trait aspect been considered, because performance in bandit problems also seems to have natural links to the personality traits that control risk behavior. Too much exploration in solving a bandit problem could be regarded as a form of risk-seeking behavior, while too much exploitation could be regarded as risk-averse behavior (Steyvers et al., 2009). Moreover, the analysis of individual differences in solving bandit problems, which is also said to be feasible and important (Steyvers et al., 2009), is also a relevant construct to entrepreneurship research, and hence remains a topic for future study.

Experimental Design

A common complaint among brain-imaging specialists is the misconception that you can simply place a human subject into a scanner, tell them to look at some stimulus, and then publish the results. Like any other technique, whole-brain imaging experiments must be carefully designed and interpreted, more than the non-specialist may sometimes appreciate (Carter and Shieh, 2015). A brain-driven approach to entrepreneurship requires exactly the same level of accuracy. Like any other experiment in neuroscience, experiments examine the effect of an independent variable on a dependent variable. The independent variable is the experimental variable that is intentionally manipulated by the researcher and is hypothesized to cause a change in the dependent variable (Carter and Shieh, 2015).

Experiments, in a technical sense of the word, first manipulate some aspect of the world and then measure the outcome of that manipulation (Huettel et al., 2009).

Experiments can isolate cause and effect because the independent variable is controlled (Coolican, 2014) and can control many extraneous influences so that validity is high and alternative explanations of events are eliminated or weakened (Coolican, 2014). Experiments in entrepreneurship research are not prevalent (Schade and Burmeister, 2009; Simmons et al., 2016) in spite of the fact that they may address the internal validity problem of empirical research in entrepreneurship (de Holan, 2014), are effective for theory building (Colquitt, 2008), and facilitate the effective discrimination of the factors of interest from other factors that are often rapidly changing (Krueger and Welpe, 2014).

An exploratory search performed on the SSCI database using the keyword entrepreneur* AND experimental design from 2000 to date revealed that out of 996, only 13 articles have been produced using either an experimental (eight articles) or quasi-experimental (five articles) design. This suggests that experiments in entrepreneurship research represent 3 percent of the papers produced. Though the studies differ in terms of their design and measurement tools, so a strict comparison among them is not feasible, it is possible to assess the coherence of their experimental design. A well-designed experiment shares three key characteristics: appropriateness of the independent variable, appropriateness of the dependent variable, and testability of the hypothesis (Huettel et al., 2009). In an experiment, the independent variable can be a stimulus, task, or even a difference in the subjects being tested, such as their age, gender, or disease state (Carter and Shieh, 2015). Ortiz-Terán et al. (2014) measured event-related potentials (ERPs), specifically N200,[3] P300,[4] and N450[5] generated by a Stroop task and complemented by the Temperament and Character Inventory revised.[6] They collected brain electrical activity using electroencephalogram (EEG). Laureiro-Martínez et al. (2014) measured BOLD signal intensity generated by a 4-armed bandit task. In their case, indirect brain activity data was gathered using fMRI.

The employed independent variables are suitable: Stroop task (Ortiz-Terán et al., 2014) and 4-armed bandit task (Laureiro-Martínez et al., 2014). The use of subject-generated event boundaries seems appropriate, in that it provides a better estimate of how each subject performs as compared to having other people do the task for them (Huettel et al., 2009). Because the participants do not know that they are going to respond to the tasks until after they have finished viewing them for the first time, no bias is introduced by the chosen independent variables (Huettel et al., 2009). The dependent variables: ERPs (Ortiz-Terán et al.,

2014) and BOLD signal (Laureiro-Martínez et al., 2014), are appropriate despite the inevitable pluses and minuses of EEG and fMRI. For instance, the pulse sequence used can provide good BOLD and ERP contrast and thus can provide appropriate dependent measures (Huettel et al., 2009). Finally, the hypothesis predicts a straightforward relationship between the independent and dependent variables: that changes in BOLD signals and ERPs should preferably occur at event boundaries as compared to other time points. They are also falsifiable, in that it is possible for there to be no significant BOLD or ERP differences associated with event boundaries (Huettel et al., 2009). Based on the above, these studies appear to be well-designed and capable of answering the stated experimental questions.

Neurocognitive Mechanisms of Entrepreneurial Decision-making

Social and psychological sciences can investigate the effects that changes in the environment and/or in personality traits have on behavior, and can, at most, infer the cognitive and emotional underpinnings (Polezzi et al., 2012). However, to have a proper understanding of the complexity of the interaction going on during a decision process, it is fundamental to also investigate the mutual effects that changes in the environment, behavior, and neural underpinnings have on each other (Polezzi et al., 2012). For this reason, neuroscientific methods can lead to a better understanding of decision making (Polezzi et al., 2012). Aided by comprehensive experimental designs and standard neuroimaging technologies, these studies were successful in locating the brain regions concerned with decision making and provided explanations on how the decision-making processes may take place in the brains of entrepreneurs. Ortiz-Terán et al. (2014) found that founder entrepreneurs need less time to visualize stimuli before making a decision, a task undertaken mainly in the occipital area, which they claim is due to greater attention to stimuli. Founder entrepreneurs required a longer time for post-evaluation, and the researchers proposed that this might be due to a complex interaction between systems affecting memory, active searching, attention, complex computations, establishing comparisons, decision making, and checking of answers. They also found that entrepreneurs can be differentiated by brain location with regard to two cognitive processes: an early one linked with motor response initiation, mostly localized around supplementary motor areas, and a late one linked to integrative cognitive processes, which serves to analyze and evaluate a given response, mainly in the anterior frontal regions.

Laureiro-Martínez et al. (2014) found that, compared with managers, entrepreneurs show higher decision-making efficiency and a stronger activation in regions of the frontopolar cortex (FPC). They confirm that exploitative choices recruit ventromedial prefrontal activations involved in reward anticipation (Tobler et al., 2007) and tracking the value of the current choice (Boorman et al., 2009; Kolling et al., 2012). Explorative choices engage the frontoparietal regions, alongside the dorsal sector of the anterior cingulate cortex (dACC) and locus coeruleus, associated with executive and attentional control (Boorman et al., 2009; Corbetta and Shulman, 2002). They conclude that decision-making success might be enhanced by the individual's ability to track evidence in favor of constantly evolving alternative options, and in disengaging attention from current reassuring options, both mechanisms leading to more efficient decision making. These same skills are likely to promote success in entrepreneurial endeavors that require adaptation to rapidly changing and unforgiving environmental circumstances.

Though perfect research is neither necessary nor possible (Davidsson, 2007), these findings represent the first efforts to understand the decision-making process among entrepreneurs at a brain level, and they add depth to the analysis of existing theories (Endres and Woods, 2006), processes (Gibcus and Hoesel, 2008; Schade and Burmeister, 2009; Vermeulen and Curseu, 2008), and models (Khefacha and Belkacem, 2015; Macchione et al, 2013; Miao and Liu, 2010; Olayinka et al., 2015; Pech and Cameron, 2006; Vermeulen and Curseu, 2008) in entrepreneurial decision making. The explanatory power of their results would have been strengthened by embedding their results within the three stages of the decision-making process: emergence of an idea, elaboration of an idea, and implementation of the decision (Gibcus and Hoesel, 2008), or the six steps in the decision-making process: recognition, formulation, search, evaluation, choice, and implementation. If the decision-making processes of entrepreneurs is influenced by the interplay between the attributes of the decision maker and the specifics of the situation that he or she is facing, it may have been helpful to consider the entrepreneurial decision styles that are argued to be characterized by distinct cognitive decision content (Lucas et al., 2008).

Since the design of these studies is based on a cognitive view, the analysis of the cognitive components in relation to decision making would have been enhanced with the use of tools such as cognitive maps (Gómez et al., 2000) and cognitive scripts, both viable ways of examining the cognitive structures of entrepreneurs and understanding the differences between entrepreneurs and managers (Brännback and Carsrud, 2009). These studies are the first to explore the neural correlates of entrepreneurial decision making under an ambiguous task (Ortiz-Terán et al., 2014) and an exploratory–exploitative task (Laureiro-Martínez et al., 2014) and confirm their results with prior evidence found in neuroscience research. They conclude that entrepreneurs make faster decisions, and this time issue is relevant because a basic finding in cognitive science is a relation called the speed–accuracy trade-off: a decision maker can increase accuracy at the cost of increasing decision time (Busemeyer, 2015). Decisions take time and the time taken to make a choice can change the decision (Busemeyer, 2015).

Furthermore, EEG and fMRI technologies were used for the first time in the analysis of entrepreneurial decision making and provide evidence that links decision making with speed (Ortiz-Terán et al., 2014) and with efficiency (Laureiro-Martínez et al., 2014). The causal evidence achieved at the experimental level by Ortiz-Terán et al. (2014) and Laureiro-Martínez et al. (2014) enhances theory building in a field that is dominated by retrospective, self-reporting, and correlational research methods (Simmons et al., 2016). For those who doubt the potential of a brain-level approach to entrepreneurship, these results may possibly tell little, but for those who assess this evidence as the natural perfectible steps of an emerging research stream, this evidence may represent the opportunity to get involved.

EEG and fMRI

One of the major aims of entrepreneurship is to explore how entrepreneurs think differently from non-entrepreneurs (Busenitz and Barney, 1997; R.K. Mitchell, 1994; R.K. Mitchell et al., 2002) and from other entrepreneurs (Baron, 2004, 2006; R.K. Mitchell et al., 2007). Whether decisions are made consciously or unconsciously, they rely heavily on neural processes that entail selection, inhibition, planning, and other aspects of executive control (Purves et al., 2008). To understand the cognitive processing that underlies decision making means to investigate different factors that collectively can contribute to the final decision (Polezzi et al., 2012). Several techniques allow neuroscientists the opportunity to study the neural basis of cognition, emotion, sensation, and behavior in humans (Carter and Shieh, 2015). These methods are known as functional brain-imaging techniques, and they are used to measure neural activity in the central nervous system without physically penetrating the skull (Carter and Shieh, 2015), that is, to determine which neural structures are active during certain mental operations (Carter and Shieh, 2015). These tools can show that information is represented in certain places within the brain without being consciously perceived (Carter and Shieh, 2015). Palva (2014) contends that the neural correlates might be found only if there is prior confirmatory behavioral data. These studies examine the neurocognitive decision-making mechanisms among entrepreneurs and non-entrepreneurs by making use of two brain-imaging techniques: fMRI (Laureiro-Martínez et al., 2014) and EEG (Ortiz-Terán et al., 2014). Since fMRI or EEG training is outside the scope of this chapter, those interested should consult additional resources for detailed information about fMRI design and analysis (Buxton, 2009; Huettel et al., 2009; Jezzard et al., 2001) or EEG (Picton et al., 2000).

Both tools are appropriate to these studies since their use within neuroscience is known to monitor the evidence or preference accumulation process during decision making (Busemeyer, 2015). Within entrepreneurship, it is the first time these technologies have been applied to the study of decision making. EEG is a non-invasive technique that measures the gross electrical activity of the surface of the brain (Carter and Shieh, 2015). Though it is not truly a brain-imaging technique, since no meaningful images of the brain can be produced using this technique alone, it can be used to ascertain certain particular states of conscious-ness with a temporal resolution of milliseconds (Carter and Shieh, 2015). A powerful application of EEG is in event-related potentials (ERPs), which are distinct, stereotyped waveforms in an EEG report that corresponds to a specific sensory, cognitive, or motor event. For example, if a human subject hears a sudden alarm, the perception of the sound may be represented as an ERP in the EEG waveform (Carter and Shieh, 2015). An ERP waveform is an electrical signature of all the different cognitive components that contribute to the processing of that stimulus. Systematically varying certain aspects of the stimulus may lead to system-atic variations in particular aspects of the ERP waveform. This enables inferences to be drawn about the timing and independence of cognitive processes (Bear et al., 2007).

What is of interest in ERP data is the timing and the amplitude of the task (Bear et al., 2007). Ortiz-Terán et al. (2014) employed ERPs to compute the reaction time among founding entrepreneurs and non-founding entrepreneurs. Aided by LORETA software, they also pursued identification of the brain locations generated by the Stroop task. Yet beyond the explanation of possible decision-making mechanisms, they are unable to disentangle the series of decision-making stages produced. The application of a general method for dividing reaction times into different stages, such as the additive factors method (Sternberg, 1969), could help to single out the decision-making stages in a more comprehensive fashion.

fMRI on the other hand, is a tool to study the neural basis of cognition (Aldrich and Carter, 2004). The main goal of fMRI is to detect the local variation of the BOLD signal in the brain and its potential correlation with a given task or action (Charron et al., 2008). BOLD is a marker of neuronal metabolism based on the principle that neurons that are becoming rapidly more active require nutrients from the blood to support their energy requirements. As part of this hemodynamic response, active neurons will quickly extract oxygen from the blood. This leaves more oxyhemoglobin in the region of the active neurons compared to deoxyhemoglobin, each of these displaying different magnetic properties. This variation in magnetic signal can be detected using fMRI to obtain what is referred to as a BOLD signal (Hart, 2015). One of the biggest limitations of this technique is that the signal actually represents an indirect measure of cerebral activity; however, it is a non-invasive, safe, and relatively available technique (Polezzi et al., 2012).

Laureiro-Martínez et al. (2014) applied fMRI to assess decision-making efficiency and identify the neural correlates of exploration and exploitation among entrepreneurs and managers. Their findings are important because, apart from indicating which areas in the brain light up under one condition or another, fMRI can provide access to processes that overt behavior and self-reporting measures cannot. These results can lead to the identification of causal brain mechanisms that underlie important and complex phenomena (Norris et al., 2007) such as entrepreneurial decision making. fMRI and EEG studies are also complementary, and combining information from them is a useful way to examine the spatial and temporal dynamics of brain processes (Babiloni et al., 2004; Dale et al., 2000; Liebenthal et al., 2003). Each method has its strengths and limitations: the spatial resolution is in the range of millimeters with fMRI, and the time resolution is in the range of milliseconds with EEG (Mulert et al., 2004). This means that the integration of more techniques (fMRI, ERPs and so on) and different kinds of data (behavioral and neurophysiological) can lead to more robust and reliable conclusions compared to those exclusively based on behavioral data (Polezzi et al., 2012).

The combined use of fMRI and EEG might also be beneficial to entrepreneurship research, but it is challenging to implement due to the significant amount of new knowledge required. In short, these methods hold much promise (Foo et al., 2014). Brain imaging is making real and important methodological progress, and it is no longer a field that can be characterized as being in its infancy. The practical consequence of all this is that contemporary researchers can no longer afford to be unaware of the methods and language of neuroimaging generally and fMRI in particular (Norris et al., 2007).

AGENDA FOR FUTURE DEVELOPMENT AND RESEARCH

The research agenda suggests paying increased attention to the added value of using a brain-driven approach to entrepreneurship research, particularly, but not only, to the facet of entrepreneurial decision making. It is argued that there is value in grounding entrepreneurship research in neuroscience (Baucus et al., 2014; de Holan, 2014), and neuroscience can be beneficial to entrepreneurship scholarship (Blair, 2010) both in developing understanding of the many facets of the practice of entrepreneurship and those who carry it out (de Holan, 2014).

To encourage future research in this direction I then proposed the term 'brain-driven entrepreneurship' and suggested the following definition: brain-driven entrepreneurship research refers to the study of any suitable topic of entrepreneurship using both an experimental design in any of its forms and any existing or forthcoming brain-imaging technologies. The accelerated development of brain-imaging technologies in neuroscience has attracted the attention of scholars from various fields. Although relatively new for our field, these tools have been validated in other disciplines such as economics and marketing, and have shown great potential to help clarify questions such as how entrepreneurs perceive and act upon opportunities, what areas of their brain are mobilized when they do so, and whether these differ from other, less entrepreneurial subjects (de Holan, 2014).

While neuroscientific technologies hold much promise (Foo et al., 2014), they do have limitations that need to be taken into account: they rely on reverse inference, in which the engagement of a particular cognitive process is inferred from the activation of a particular brain region (Poldrack, 2006), and these technologies produce largely correlative measures of brain activity, making it difficult to examine the causal role of specific brain activations for a chosen behavior (Glimcher et al., 2009). Also, research questions related to the interaction of environmental factors with individual characteristics, to predict how people make decisions, are difficult to operationalize with fMRI studies because only a small number of individuals, and consequently a small number of environments, are available (Foo et al., 2014). Nonetheless, the advantages afforded by these tools, such as the possibility to pinpoint what happens in the brain when people make decisions and the precise neural analysis of the links between affective and cognitive processes (Foo et al., 2014), should not be neglected by entrepreneurship scholars, especially by those interested in cognitive, affective, and motivational issues of entrepreneurial behavior.

The use of any of the technologies highlighted in this chapter is not straightforward. Their application requires the elaboration of a well-designed experiment and the existence of behavioral evidence. Any attempt to bypass this 'golden rule' of neuroscience will result in non-credible evidence (Palva, 2014). Further, the multidisciplinary nature of this research methodology demands the collaboration of experts from at least three fields: entrepreneurship, psychology, and neuroscience. Those interested in joining this camp will possibly need to upgrade their skills in experimental design, cognitive psychology, and, possibly others of the more specialized neuroscience areas.

Broadening the Scope of Research Streams

Investigation into how entrepreneurs think has become one of the major targets within entrepreneurship research, but a thorough examination of this phenomenon entails methodological (Omorede et al., 2015) constraints and technological opportunities (Foo et al., 2014; Smith, 2010; Wargo et al., 2010) that may be afforded by neuroscience. In fact, neuroscience may provide new ways to conceptualize and measure important facets of decision making (Smith, 2010). These studies reveal that entrepreneurship research at the brain level is scarce and thus far limited to the topic of entrepreneurial decision-making speed between entrepreneurs and non-entrepreneurs (Ortiz-Terán et al., 2014) and decision-making efficiency (Laureiro-Martínez et al., 2014) among entrepreneurs and managers. The techniques used and the results achieved might not be perfect, as is usual in any new and emerging approach, but the potential is there (Blair, 2010; de Holan, 2014; Nicolaou and Shane, 2014; Smith, 2010).

Neuroscientific tools facilitate a breadth of potential topics and research areas (Smith, 2010). The potential of entrepreneurship research using neuroscientific technologies and tools is broad (Nicolaou and Shane, 2014) and not limited to the topics of behavioral decision theory, game theory, perceptions, emotions, and affect (Krueger and Welpe, 2014). In addition to the need for more brain-driven research on traits, adaptation, expertise, and mindset (McMullen et al., 2014), future research is highly encouraged, particularly from four perspectives: importing concepts and theories from other branches of neurosciences, combining multiple levels of analysis, taking into consideration the mechanisms of each of the stages of the entrepreneurial process, and exploring the links between entrepreneurial mental processes and business sectors.

First, future studies may take into account the inputs of affective neuroscience, behavioral, cultural, computational, social neuroscience, neuroinformatics, and systems neuroscience, as these fields may allow a profound level of analysis of cognitive, motivational, affective, and hormonal processes and mechanisms behind entrepreneurial decision making in particular, and the entrepreneurial process in general. They may also complement research on how hormonal (Nicolaou and Shane, 2014) and genetic differences influence the wiring, structure, and function of the brain (Toga and Thompson, 2005). These topics may represent a completely new world for the majority of entrepreneurship scholars, and its progressive incorporation to the field will take some time. Questions of interest include, for example:

- How do entrepreneurs emotionally process decisions under situations of certainty and uncertainty?
- What are the motivational mechanisms that are activated before, during, and after decision making?
- How do hormones impact upon entrepreneurs' decisions?
- How do all of these factors together affect decision making among entrepreneurs?
- How does the leverage of these factors differ from non-entrepreneurs?
- Where in the brain do these phenomena take place?

Second, Low and MacMillan (1988) argue that entrepreneurship studies could and should be carried out at multiple levels of analysis, and that these analyses complement each other. Entrepreneurship research can be performed at various levels: individual, team, firm, industry/population, regional, and national (Davidsson and Wiklund, 2001). The reasons for studying entrepreneurship on multiple levels of analysis lie in the characteristics of the entrepreneurial phenomenon itself (Low and MacMillan, 1988). In addition to the need for more studies at the individual level, new investigations are required at the team level. For instance, the two major aims of entrepreneurial team research: how the interaction (Breugst et al., 2015) and composition of the team influence the team's and the venture's development (Knockaert et al., 2011) might be explored at a brain level. An exercise of this nature will need a well-thought-out experimental design and a smart combination of available brain-imaging tools, but it is certainly feasible.

Investigations at other levels: firm, industry/population, regional, and national, might prove to be more challenging to implement. Interesting questions include, for example:

- How does cognition influence decision making among entrepreneurial teams?
- How does affect impact upon decision making among entrepreneurial teams in situations of uncertainty?
- How does motivation operate among entrepreneurial teams compared to managerial teams?
- How do these factors change in terms of gender, age, level of education, and culture?
- Which of the brain regions are related to these factors?

Third, the entrepreneurial process is defined as a set of stages and events that follow one another. These stages are the idea or conception of the business, the event that triggers the operations and implementation, and growth (Bygrave, 2009). These studies do not mention the stage to which participating entrepreneurs belong, but they specify that at the time of the study the entrepreneurs had created at least one company (Ortiz-Terán et al., 2014) and they had implemented their idea and were running their firms (Laureiro-Martínez et al., 2014). That means that participating entrepreneurs may belong to the stage of either implementation or growth. Further studies should delve deeper into the mechanisms of decision making that take place along the entrepreneurial process from a brain perspective. For instance, studies that examine entrepreneurial decision making during the conception of the business or across the event that triggers the entrepreneurial action may provide new evidence on the interplay of decision making as the entrepreneurial process evolves. The questions of interest include, for example:

- How do cognitive mechanisms of decision making evolve across the stages of the entrepreneurial process?
- What is the interplay of affect and motivation during the conception of the business and the triggering of operations?
- How are these processes reflected in the brain?
- Which brain regions are involved?

Fourth, 'necessity' entrepreneurial activities are commonly observed in the traditional (and informal) sectors, whereas 'opportunity' entrepreneurial activities occur more in the modern sectors (Caliendo and Kritikos, 2010; Desai, 2011; Naudé, 2011). 'Necessity' entrepreneurs are those who are forced to go into entrepreneurship for reasons such as poverty and lack of employment opportunities. Starting a business is not their prime consideration until they have exhausted other options. On the other hand, 'opportunity' entrepreneurs are those who desire to go entrepreneurial to exploit some identifiable business opportunities such as the perception of a market opportunity, an innovative idea, or an existing network to exploit (Cheung, 2014). These studies do not provide much information about the sectors in which entrepreneurs operate, which is a relevant issue since it may provide further evidence of their necessity/opportunity orientation and may imply different decision-making mechanisms. Future research should take this into account to be able to parse out the possible cognitive, affective, motivational, and hormonal similarities or differences during decision making and their possible link to traditional or technology-oriented sectors. Questions of interest include, for instance:

- What are the cognitive and affective decision-making mechanisms of a necessity entrepreneur compared to an opportunity entrepreneur?
- How does motivation impact on decision making among necessity entrepreneurs in contrast to opportunity entrepreneurs?
- How does the brain represent these mechanisms?
- Which brain areas are linked to these processes?

Enhancing the Use of Experimental Designs

One of the primary challenges for a researcher in entrepreneurship is to engage in more systematic, theory-driven efforts (Tan et al., 2009). But, despite the number of published papers that might be considered related to the theory of entrepreneurship, no generally accepted theory of entrepreneurship has emerged (Bull and Willard, 1993). Rather than explaining and predicting a unique set of empirical phenomena, entrepreneurship has become a broad label under which a wide range of research is housed (Shane and Venkataraman, 2000). Entrepreneurship as a field of research is in need of experimental methodologies to fully study key phenomena (Shane, 2003), but the field is dominated by retrospective, self-reporting, and correlational research methods (Simmons et al., 2016). These research methods do not usually allow researchers to establish causality because the variables are all measured concurrently, therefore one cannot assume that one variable influences another as the result of a significant correlation (Simmons et al., 2016).

On the other hand, research streams within the field such as, but not limited to, entrepreneurial cognition are facing growing methodological constraints (Omorede et al., 2015) and technological opportunities, which, if adopted, may enhance causality and thus theory-building. Causality is relevant to theoretical contributions as testing causality can validate or reject relationships predicted by theory and answer the question of what triggers the dependent variable and perhaps even why (Simmons et al., 2016). An experiment enables the plausible establishment of causality and, if properly designed, can exclude alternative interpretations by direct and indirect control. Experiments thus address the internal validity problem of empirical research in entrepreneurship (Foo et al., 2014; Krueger and Welpe, 2014). Gatewood et al. (1995) also advocate the use of experimental designs in entrepreneurship research in order to randomize the allocation of respondents to research conditions.

In addition to the advantages of the experiments listed above, experiments are especially suited to investigate entrepreneurial decision making, due to its dynamic nature. Only with experimental control might the factors of interest be discriminated from 'noise' (Schade, 2005). On a review of 29 academic entrepreneurship-related journals published over the period 2000–15 (Simmons et al., 2016), 40 articles were found with single or multiple designs that employed experimental methods to explore diverse themes, including entrepreneurial decision making, emotions, intentions, opportunities, risk propensity and perception, team dynamics, education, and methodological approaches. The majority of entrepreneurship studies that use experimental design focus on opportunity identification and entrepreneurial intentions.

A lack of use of experiments in entrepreneurship research is a critical issue, not only because it reduces the theory-building possibilities for the field, but also because the methodological component that precedes the use of any neuroimaging technique (EEG, fMRI and so on) is certainly the articulation of a well-designed experimental design. Not even the most advanced brain-imaging technology can replace the faults of a poor experimental design. Further experimental research is needed not only in entrepreneurial decision making, but also other research streams such as cognitions and emotions, social and human capital, business exits and failure, corporate venture logic and methods (Simmons et al., 2016). It is the articulation of both elements – experimental designs and the use of brain-imaging technologies – that makes a brain-oriented approach to entrepreneurship promising. I anticipate a challenging learning process, especially for scholars unfamiliar with this approach, but at the same time an opportunity to test causality and enhance theory-building within the field.

Promoting the Use of Brain-assessment Technologies

We do not need to reinvent the wheel in entrepreneurship research as there are external concepts and theories in other fields that could be tested in the entrepreneurial context (Landström and Benner, 2010). Brain imaging is an important new addition to the toolbox of empirical researchers, as it provides new behavioral hypotheses and data that can evaluate current theories (Pushkarskaya et al., 2010). It may also provide useful information about the timing and location of brain activation during performance of an enormous range of cognitive tasks. Such information (when combined with behavioral evidence) has proved to be of much value in increasing our understanding of human cognition (Eysenck, 2006).

Besides EEG and fMRI mentioned in previous sections, there are at least three other technologies that deserve consideration. These are magneto-encephalography (MEG), transcranial direct current stimulation (tDCS), and decoded neurofeedback. MEG involves using a superconducting quantum interference device (SQUID) to measure the magnetic fields produced by electrical activity. It has excellent temporal resolution and its spatial resolution can be reasonably good (Eysenck, 2006). In the same way as fMRI, MEG might be used to examine the neural correlates and the cognitive/affective mechanisms of any them within the scope of entrepreneurial thinking.

Transcranial direct current stimulation (tDCS) is a safe method for non-invasively (Nitsche and Paulus, 2011) modifying the behavior of neurons and/or neural networks using weak electrical currents (usually 1-2mA) (Lewis et al., 2016) circulating between two scalp electrodes (such as an anode and a cathode) placed over the target cortical regions (Nitsche and Paulus, 2011). tDCS might be useful for entrepreneurial research and practice, because it modulates decision making (Ouellet et al., 2015) and allows studying the interplay of behavior and a specific brain region based on the excitation or inhibition of neuronal activity. Decoded neurofeedback is a technique that helps individuals learn how to self-regulate brain activity with the help of neurological feedback provided by sensory devices. Recent studies suggest that neurofeedback is capable of extinguishing fear memories, changing facial preferences, and so on, at a subconscious level (Kawato and Koizumi, 2016). The application of this method in entrepreneurship might be influential as well, for example the possibility of subconsciously mitigating fear of failure among novice entrepreneurs.

The selection of the appropriate method depends on five factors: the type of phenomena to be investigated, the availability of theoretical/conceptual skills, the suitability of the chosen techniques, the availability of statistical skills, and the budget. EEG and tDCS are the most economical technologies, whereas the use of MEG, fMRI, and decoded neurofeedback is rather expensive. Despite the advantages that tools like fMRI may afford to entrepreneurship research, there is a deeper methodology known as neuronal recording (Rolls, 2014). At this level it is possible to measure the full richness of the information being represented in a brain region by measuring the firing of its neurons. This is impossible with brain-imaging techniques, which also are susceptible to the interpretation problem that whatever causes the largest activation is interpreted as what is being encoded in a region (Rolls, 2014). Tough neuronal recording can reveal fundamental evidence crucial for our understanding of how the brain operates. It is an invasive method, which significantly limits its application (Rolls, 2014). Neuroscience may generate new ways to conceptualize and measure important facets of decision making, but it should not be forgotten that there is also a role to be played by qualitative research methodologies such as in-depth interviews, observational techniques, self-reflective action research (Smith, 2010), and so on. In addition to recommending the triangulation of neuroscience tools and field studies (Foo et al., 2014), future research should also aim to intensify the individual and combined use of electrophysiological methods such as EEG; functional brain-imaging techniques such as fMRI and MEG; brain stimulation tools such as tDCS; and novel techniques such as decoded neurofeedback, as long as their use is preceded by a well-designed experiment and backed by behavioral evidence.

Fostering the Development of Skills in Psychology, Neuroscience, and Brain-imaging Tools

Entrepreneurship researchers have already borrowed concepts and theories from mainstream disciplines such as economics, psychology, and sociology and adapted them to the study of entrepreneurship (Lohrke and Landström, 2010). This intellectual borrowing of concepts and theories from other fields has already produced several major benefits (Lohrke and Landström, 2010). Certainly, undertaking research using a brain-driven approach may become a challenging journey for an entrepreneurship scholar familiar with traditional research methods, because the execution of such an approach requires the posing of new concepts and theories outside the walls of business schools.

Importing theories from other fields of research is often a necessary first step toward developing unique theories of one's own (Zahra, 2007). For example, terms such as N200, P300, and N450, quite usual in EEG research, or concepts like dopaminergic mesocorticolimbic system, quite common in neuroscience undergraduate courses, might not be under-stood by an entrepreneurship scholar. Therefore, future investigators interested in embracing a brain-oriented research approach should focus on enhancing their knowledge of experimental design, cognitive and affective neuroscience, social neuroscience, brain-imaging technologies, data collection, and analysis tools. This is the minimum toolbox to be equipped with to start this journey.

Entrepreneurship research from a brain perspective is a multidisciplinary endeavor, which requires the accumulation of expertise from various fields. However, when borrowing theories from other disciplines, we need to contextualize the theories that we use (Zahra, 2007). Imported theories and concepts from neurosciences must be adapted because imported theories from other disciplines have been developed to under-stand fundamentally different phenomena from entrepreneurship; there-fore, a mismatch between theory and context can result in inconclusive or even incorrect findings (Lohrke and Landström, 2010). These studies reveal the high level of cooperation required among disciplines. An average of six scholars contributing from various fields such as economics, management, neurosciences, technology, psychiatry, and business took part in these studies. To increase the production of new evidence and the quality of it within this approach, future efforts should encourage the establishment and formalization of interdisciplinary teams, interfaculty teams, research groups and, ultimately, a research community. The setting and formalization of such initiatives is vital in that it will enhance the implementation of research projects, facilitate knowledge exchange among participating scholars, and ensure the academic quality of resulting evidence. Some steps in this direction have already been carried out with the organization of two consecutive neuroentrepreneurship symposia during 2014 and 2015 by the Academy of Management, and the preparation of a Massive Open Online Course (MOOC) on brain-driven entrepreneurship. Nonetheless, to date no other initiatives are known to have taken place at an international or university level.

NOTES

1. Cognition focuses on the knowledge structures that people use to make assessments, judgments, or decisions related to evaluating opportunities and creating growing ventures (R.K. Mitchell et al., 2002).
2. Each involves different parts of the brain, different neuronal paths, and different skills, some of which are acquired (de Holan, 2014).
3. N200 is associated with changing features in the stimulus environment and has been interpreted as an automatic filtering stage for selective attention toward novelty (Luck and Hillyard, 1994). Two specific cognitive processes (response selection and executive control), both related to response inhibition, have been identified in the N200 (Falkenstein et al., 1999).
4. P300 is a marker of memory in evaluation of environmental stimuli whenever an ongoing task requires identification of salient information (Donchin and Coles, 1988).
5. Cognitive tasks that require detection of processing conflicts between competing response options (for example, incongruent condition of the Stroop task) reliably elicit a N450 (Appelbaum et al., 2009). The N450 is present following both stimulus and response conflict (West et al., 2004).
6. (TCI) is an inventory for personality traits devised by Pelissolo et al. (2005). Ortiz-Terán et al. (2014) focused on the dimensions of novelty seeking, harm avoidance, reward dependence, persistence, and self-directedness (Gutiérrez-Zotes et al., 2004).

REFERENCES

Aldrich, H. and N.M. Carter (2004), "Social Networks," in W.B. Gartner, K.G. Shaver, N.M. Carter, and P.D. Reynolds (eds), *Handbook of Entrepreneurial Dynamics: The Process of Business Creation*, London: SAGE, pp. 324–35.
Appelbaum, L., K. Meyerhoff, and M. Woldorff (2009), "Priming and backward influences

in the human brain: processing interactions during the stroop interference effect," *Cerebral Cortex*, **19** (11), 2508–21.

Ardichvili, A., R. Cardozo, and A. Ray (2003), "A theory of entrepreneurial opportunity identification and development," *Journal of Business Venturing*, **18** (1), 105–23.

Babiloni, F., D. Mattia, C. Babiloni, L. Astolfi, S. Salinari, A. Basilisco, . . . and F. Cincotti (2004), "Multimodal integration of EEG, MEG and fMRI data for the solution of the neuroimage puzzle," *Magnetic Resonance Imaging*, **22** (10), 1471–6.

Baron, R. (1998), Cognitive mechanisms in entrepreneurship: why and when entrepreneurs think differently than other people. *Journal of Business Venturing*, *13*(4), 275-294.

Baron, R. (2000), "Counterfactual thinking and venture formation: the potential effects of thinking about 'what might have been'," *Journal of Business Venturing*, **15** (1), 79–91.

Baron, R. (2004), "The cognitive perspective: a valuable tool for answering entrepreneurship's basic 'why' questions," *Journal of Business Venturing*, **19** (2), 221–39.

Baron, R. (2006), "Opportunity recognition as pattern recognition: how entrepreneurs 'connect the dots' to identify new business opportunities," *The Academy of Management Perspectives*, **20**, 104–19.

Baron, R. (2008), "The role of affect in the entrepreneurial process," *Academy of Management Review*, **33**, 328–40.

Baron, R. and T. Ward (2004), "Expanding entrepreneurial cognition's toolbox: potential contributions from the field of cognitive science," *Entrepreneurship Theory and Practice*, **28** (6), 553–73.

Baucus, D.A., M.S. Baucus, and R.K. Mitchell (2014), "Lessons from the neural foundation of entrepreneurial cognition: the case of emotion and motivation," in J.R. Mitchell, R.K. Mitchell, and B. Randolph-Seng (eds), *Handbook of Entrepreneurial Cognition*, Cheltenham: Edward Elgar, pp. 254–315.

Bear, M.F., B.W. Connors, and M.A. Paradiso (2007), *Neuroscience*, vol. 2, Boston: Lippincott Williams and Wilkins.

Beugré, C.D. (2010), "Brain and human behavior in organizations: a field of neuro-organizational behavior," in A.A. Stanton, M. Day, and I.M. Welpe (eds), *Neuroeconomics and the Firm*, Cheltenham, UK: Edward Elgar, pp. 289–303.

Bird, B. (2014), "Toward a taxonomy of entrepreneurs' behaviour," in J.R. Mitchell, R.K. Mitchell, and B. Randolph-Seng (eds), *Handbook of Entrepreneurial Cognition*, Cheltenham: Edward Elgar, pp. 113–31.

Blair, E.S. (2010), "What you think is not what you think: unconsciousness and entrepreneurial behavior," in A.A. Stanton, M. Day, and I.M. Welpe (eds), *Neuroeconomics and the Firm*, Cheltenham, UK: Edward Elgar, pp. 50–65.

Boorman, E.D., T.E. Behrens, M.W. Woolrich, and M.F. Rushworth (2009), "How green is the grass on the other side? Frontopolar cortex and the evidence in favor of alternative courses of action," *Neuron*, **62** (5), 733–43.

Brännback, M. and A.L. Carsrud (2009), "Cognitive maps in entrepreneurship: researching sense making and action," in A.L. Carsrud and M. Brännback (eds), *Understanding the Entrepreneurial Mind*, Heidelberg: Springer, pp. 75–96.

Breugst, N., H. Patzelt, and P. Rathgeber (2015), "How should we divide the pie? Equity distribution and its impact on entrepreneurial teams," *Journal of Business Venturing*, **30** (1), 66–94.

Bryant, P.T. (2014), "Self-regulation and entrepreneurial ambidexterity," in U. Stettner, B.S. Aharonson, and T.L. Amburgey (eds), *Exploration and Exploitation in Early Stage Ventures and SMEs (Technology, Innovation, Entrepreneurship and Competitive Strategy*, vol. 14, Bradford: Emerald Group Publishing Limited, pp. 15–37.

Bull, I. and G.E. Willard (1993), "Towards a theory of entrepreneurship," *Journal of Business Venturing*, **8** (3), 183–95.

Busemeyer, J.R. (2015), "Cognitive science contributions to decision science," *Cognition*, **135**, 43–6.

Busenitz, L.W. and J.D. Arthurs (2007), "Cognition and capabilities in entrepreneurial ventures," in B.J. Robert, M. Frese, and R. Baron (eds), *The Psychology of Entrepreneurship*, London: Lawrence Earlbaum Associates Publishers, pp. 131–50.

Busenitz, L.W. and J.B. Barney (1997), "Differences between entrepreneurs and managers in large organizations: biases and heuristics in strategic decision-making," *Journal of Business Venturing*, **12** (1), 9–30.

Busenitz, L.W. and C.-M. Lau (1996), "A cross-cultural cognitive model of new venture creation," *Entrepreneurship Theory and Practice*, **20** (4), 25–40.

Buxton, R.B. (2009), *Introduction to Functional Magnetic Resonance Imaging: Principles and Techniques*, Cambridge: Cambridge University Press.

Bygrave, W.D. (2009), "The Entrepreneurial Process," in W.D. Bygrave and A. Zacharakis (eds), *The Portable MBA in Entrepreneurship*, 4th edn, Hoboken, NJ: John Wiley and Sons, pp. 1–26.

Caliendo, M. and A.S. Kritikos (2010), "Start-ups by the unemployed: characteristics, survival and direct employment effects," *Small Business Economics*, **35** (1), 71–92.

Camerer, C., G. Loewenstein, and D. Prelec (2005), "Neuroeconomics: how neuroscience can inform economics," *Journal of Economic Literature*, **43** (1), 9–64.

Carsrud, A.L. and M. Brännback (2014), "Linking achievement motivation to intentions, goals and entrepreneurial behaviors," in J.R. Mitchell, R.K. Mitchell, and B. Randolph-Seng (eds), *Handbook of Entrepreneurial Cognition*, Cheltenham: Edward Elgar, pp. 86–112.

Carter, M. and J.C. Shieh (2015), *Guide to Research Techniques in Neuroscience*, 2nd edn, San Diego: Academic Press.

Cattell, J.M. (1886), "The time it takes to see and name objects," *Mind*, **11** (41), 63–5.

Cela-Conde, C.J., G. Marty, F. Maestú, T. Ortiz, E. Munar, A. Fernández, . . . and F. Quesney (2004), "Activation of the prefrontal cortex in the human visual aesthetic perception," *Proceedings of the National Academy of Sciences of the United States of America*, **101** (16), 6321–5.

Charron, S., A. Fuchs, and O. Oullier (2008), "Exploring brain activity in neuroeconomics," *Revue d'Economie Politique*, **118** (1), 97–124.

Cheung, O.L. (2014), "Are we seeing 'necessity' or 'opportunity' entrepreneurs at large?," *Research in Business and Economics Journal*, **9**, 1.

Clarke, J.S. and J.P. Cornelissen (2014), "How language shapes thought: new vistas for entrepreneurship research," in J.R. Mitchell, R.K. Mitchell, and B. Randolph-Seng (eds), *Handbook of Entrepreneurial Cognition*, Cheltenham, Edward Elgar, pp. 383–97.

Cohen, J.D., K. Dunbar, and J.L. McClelland (1990), "On the control of automatic processes: a parallel distributed processing account of the Stroop effect," *Psychological Review*, **97** (3), 332.

Cohen, J.D., S.M. McClure, and J.Y. Angela (2007), "Should I stay or should I go? How the human brain manages the trade-off between exploitation and exploration," *Philosophical Transactions of the Royal Society of London B: Biological Sciences*, **362** (1481), 933–42.

Colquitt, J.A. (2008), "From the editors publishing laboratory research in AMJ: a question of when, not if," *Academy of Management Journal*, **51** (4), 616–20.

Coolican, H. (2014), *Research Methods and Statistics in Psychology*, Hove: Psychology Press.

Cooper, A.C., C.Y. Woo, and W.C. Dunkelberg (1988), "Entrepreneurs' perceived chances for success," *Journal of Business Venturing*, **3** (2), 97–108.

Corbetta, M. and G.L. Shulman (2002), "Control of goal-directed and stimulus-driven attention in the brain," *Nature Reviews Neuroscience*, **3** (3), 201–15.

Dale, A.M., A.K. Liu, B.R. Fischl, R.L. Buckner, J.W. Belliveau, J.D. Lewine, and E. Halgren (2000), "Dynamic statistical parametric mapping: combining fMRI and MEG for high-resolution imaging of cortical activity," *Neuron*, **26** (1), 55–67.

Davidsson, P. (2007), "Method challenges and opportunities in the psychological study of entrepreneurship," In B.J. Robert, M. Frese, and R. Baron (eds), *The Psychology of Entrepreneurship*, London: Lawrence Earlbaum Associates, pp. 287–323.

Davidsson, P. and J. Wiklund (2001), "Levels of analysis in entrepreneurship research: current research practice and suggestions for the future," *Entrepreneurship Theory and Practice*, **25** (4), 81–100.

Daw, N.D., J.P. O'Doherty, P. Dayan, B. Seymour, and R.J. Dolan (2006), "Cortical substrates for exploratory decisions in humans," *Nature*, **441** (7095), 876–9.

de Holan, P.M. (2014), "It's all in your head: why we need neuroentrepreneurship," *Journal of Management Inquiry*, **23**, 93–7.

Deligonul, Z.S., G.T.M. Hult, and S.T. Cavusgil (2008), "Entrepreneuring as a puzzle: an attempt to its explanation with truncation of subjective probability distribution of prospects," *Strategic Entrepreneurship Journal*, **2** (2), 155–67.

Desai, S. (2011), "Measuring entrepreneurship in developing countries," in W. Naudé (ed.), *Entrepreneurship and Economic Development*, Basingstoke: Palgrave Macmillan, pp. 94–107.

Donchin, E. and M.G. Coles (1988), "Is the P300 component a manifestation of context updating," *Behavioral and Brain Sciences*, **11** (3), 357–427.

Drnovsek, M., A. Slavec, and M.S. Cardon (2014), "Cultural context, passion and self-efficacy: do entrepreneurs operate on different 'planets'?," in J.R. Mitchell, R.K. Mitchell, and B. Randolph-Seng (eds), *Handbook of Entrepreneurial Cognition*, Cheltenham: Edward Elgar, pp. 227–53.

Drucker, P. (2014), *Innovation and Entrepreneurship*, New York: Routledge.

Dyer, F.N. (1973), "Interference and facilitation for color naming with separate bilateral presentations of the word and color," *Journal of Experimental Psychology*, **99** (3), 314.

Eastman, N. and C. Campbell (2006), "Neuroscience and legal determination of criminal responsibility," *Nature Reviews Neuroscience*, **7** (4), 311–18.

Endres, A.M. and C.R. Woods (2006), "Modern theories of entrepreneurial behavior: a comparison and appraisal," *Small Business Economics*, **26** (2), 189–202.

Eysenck, M.W. (2006), *Fundamentals of Cognition*, Hove: Psychology Press.

Falkenstein, M., J. Hoormann, and J. Hohnsbein (1999), "ERP components in Go/NoGo tasks and their relation to inhibition," *Acta Psychologica*, **101** (2), 267–91.

Foo, M.-D., C.Y. Murnieks, and E.T. Chan (2014), "Feeling and thinking: the role of affect in entrepreneurial cognition," in J.R. Mitchell, R.K. Mitchell, and B. Randolph-Seng (eds), *Handbook of Entrepreneurial Cognition*, Cheltenham: Edward Elgar, pp. 154–81.

Forbes, D.P. (1999), "Cognitive approaches to new venture creation," *International Journal of Management Reviews*, **1** (4), 415–39.

Forbes, D.P. (2014), The infrastructure of entrepreneurial learning. In J. R. Mitchell, R. K. Mitchell, and B. Randolph-Seng (eds), *Handbook of Entrepreneurial Cognition* (pp. 364-382), Cheltenham, UK: Edward Elgar Publishing, Inc.

Frigotto, M.L., G. Coller, and P. Collini (2014), "Exploration and exploitation from start-up to sale: a longitudinal analysis through strategy and MCS Practices," *Exploration and Exploitation in Early Stage Ventures and SMEs (Technology, Innovation, Entrepreneurship and Competitive Strategy*, vol. 14, Bradford: Emerald Group Publishing, pp. 149–79.

Gaglio, C.M. and J.A. Katz (2001), "The psychological basis of opportunity identification: entrepreneurial alertness," *Small Business Economics*, **16** (2), 95–111.

Gatewood, E.J., K.G. Shaver, and W.B. Gartner (1995), "A longitudinal study of cognitive factors influencing start-up behaviors and success at venture creation," *Journal of Business Venturing*, **10** (5), 371–91.

Gibcus, P. and P. v. Hoesel (2008), "Strategic decision-making processes in SMEs: an exploratory study," in P.A.M. Vermeulen and P. L. Curseu (eds), *Entrepreneurial Strategic Decision-making: A Cognitive Perspective*, Cheltenham, UK: Edward Elgar, pp. 89–104.

Gigerenzer, G. and P.M. Todd (1999), *Simple Heuristics that Make Us Smart*, New York: Oxford University Press.

Gilovich, T.D. and D.W. Griffin (2010), "Judgment and decision making," in S.T. Fiske, D.T. Gilbert, and L. Gardner (eds), *Handbook of Social Psychology*, Hoboken, NJ: John Wiley and Sons, pp. 542–88.

Glimcher, P.W., C.F. Camerer, E. Fehr, and R.A. Poldrack (2009), "Introduction: a brief history of neuroeconomics," in P.W. Glimcher, C.F. Camerer, E. Fehr, and R.A. Poldrack (eds), *Neuroeconomics: Decision Making and the Brain*, New York: Academic Press, pp. 1–12.

Gómez, A., A. Moreno, J. Pazos, and A. Sierra-Alonso (2000), "Knowledge maps: an essential technique for conceptualisation," *Data and Knowledge Engineering*, **33** (2), 169–90.

Grégoire, D.A. (2014), "Exploring the affective and cognitive dynamics of entrepreneurship across time and planes of influence," in J.R. Mitchell, R.K. Mitchell, and B. Randolph-Seng (eds), *Handbook of Entrepreneurial Cognition*, Cheltenham, UK: Edward Elgar, pp. 182–226.

Gustafsson, V. (2006), *Entrepreneurial Decision-Making: individuals, Tasks and Cognitions.* Cheltenham, UK: Edward Elgar Publishing Inc.

Gutiérrez-Zotes, J.A., C. Bayón, C. Montserrat, J. Valero, A. Labad, C. Cloninger, and F. Fernández-Aranda (2004), "Inventario del Temperamento y el Carácter-Revisado (TCI-R), Baremación y datos normativos en una muestra de población general," *Actas Españolas de Psiquiatría.*

Hammond, K.R. (1988), "Judgement and decision making in dynamic tasks," Colorado University at Boulder Center for Research on Judgment and Policy.

Hart, J. (2015), *The Neurobiology of Cognition and Behavior*, Oxford: Oxford University Press.

Hastie, R. (2001), "Problems for judgment and decision making," *Annual Review of Psychology*, **52** (1), 653–83.

Haynie, J.M., D. Shepherd, E. Mosakowski, and P.C. Earley (2010), "A situated metacognitive model of the entrepreneurial mindset," *Journal of Business Venturing*, **25** (2), 217–29.

Hoskisson, R.E., J. Covin, H.W. Volberda, and R.A. Johnson (2011), "Revitalizing entrepreneurship: the search for new research opportunities," *Journal of Management Studies*, **48** (6), 1141–68.

Huettel, S., A. Song, and G. McCarthy (2009), *Functional Magnetic Resonance Imaging*, 2nd edn, Sunderland, MA: Sinauer Associates.

Jansen, J.J., Z. Simsek, and Q. Cao (2012), "Ambidexterity and performance in multiunit contexts: cross-level moderating effects of structural and resource attributes," *Strategic Management Journal*, **33** (11), 1286–303.

Jezzard, P., P.M. Matthews, and S.M. Smith (2001), *Functional MRI: An Introduction to Methods*, Oxford: Oxford University Press.

Kawato, M. and A. Koizumi (2016), *Decoded Neurofeedback for Extinction of Fear Memory* (manuscript submitted for publication).

Khefacha, I. and L. Belkacem (2015), "Modeling entrepreneurial decision-making process using concepts from fuzzy set theory," *Journal of Global Entrepreneurship Research*, **5** (1), 1–21.

Knockaert, M., D. Ucbasaran, M. Wright, and B. Clarysse (2011), "The relationship between knowledge transfer, top management team composition, and performance: the case of science-based entrepreneurial firms," *Entrepreneurship Theory and Practice*, **35** (4), 777–803.

Kolling, N., T.E. Behrens, R.B. Mars, and M.F. Rushworth (2012), "Neural mechanisms of foraging," *Science*, **336** (6077), 95–8.

Krueger, N. and M. Day (2010), "Looking forward, looking backward: from entrepreneurial cognition to neuroentrepreneurship," in Z.J. Acs and D.B. Audretsch (eds), *Handbook of Entrepreneurship Research*, New York: Springer, pp. 321–57.

Krueger, N. and I. Welpe (2008), "Experimental entrepreneurship: a research prospectus and workshop," paper presented at the USASBE Annual Conference, San Antonio, TX, 10–13 January.

Krueger, N. and I. Welpe (2014), "Neuroentrepreneurship: what can entrepreneurship learn from neuroscience?," in M. H. Morris (ed.), *Annals of Entrepreneurship Education and Pedagogy*, Cheltenham: Edward Elgar, pp. 60–90.

Kuckertz, A., M. Kohtamäki, and C. Droege gen. Körber (2010), "The fast eat the slow – the impact of strategy and innovation timing on the success of technology-oriented ventures," *International Journal of Technology Management*, **52** (1/2), 175–88.

Landström, H. (2004), "Pioneers in entrepreneurship research," in G. Corbetta, M. Huse, and D. Ravasi (eds), *Crossroads of Entrepreneurship*, Dordretch: Kluwer Academic Publishers, pp. 13–32.

Landström, H. (2007), *Pioneers in Entrepreneurship and Small Business Research*, New York: Springer.

Landström, H., M. and Benner (2010), "Entrepreneurship research: a history of scholarly migration," in H. Landström and F. Lohrke (eds), *Historical Foundations of Entrepreneurship Research*, Cheltenham: Edward Elgar, pp. 15–45.

Laureiro-Martínez, D., S. Brusoni, N. Canessa, and M. Zollo (2014), "Understanding the exploration–exploitation dilemma: an fMRI study of attention control and decision-making performance," *Strategic Management Journal*, **36**, 319–38.

Lawrence, A., L. Clark, J.N. Labuzetta, B. Sahakian, and S. Vyakarnum (2008), "The innovative brain," *Nature*, **456**, 168–9.

Lewis, P.M., R.H. Thomson, J.V. Rosenfeld, and P.B. Fitzgerald (2016), "Brain neuromodulation techniques: a review," *The Neuroscientist*, **22** (4), 406–21.

Liebenthal, E., M.L. Ellingson, M.V. Spanaki, T.E. Prieto, K.M. Ropella, and J.R. Binder (2003), "Simultaneous ERP and fMRI of the auditory cortex in a passive oddball paradigm," *Neuroimage*, **19** (4), 1395–404.

Logan, G.D. (1980), "Attention and automaticity in Stroop and priming tasks: theory and data," *Cognitive Psychology*, **12** (4), 523–53.

Logothetis, N.K. (2008), "What we can do and what we cannot do with fMRI," *Nature*, **453** (7197), 869–78.

Lohrke, F., and H. Landström (2010), "History matters in entrepreneurship research," in H. Landström and F. Lohrke (eds), *Historical Foundations of Entrepreneurship Research*, Cheltenham: Edward Elgar, pp. 1–11.

Low, M.B., and I.C. MacMillan (1988), "Entrepreneurship: past research and future challenges," *Journal of Management*, **14**, 139–61.

Lucas, G.J., P.A. Vermeulen, and P.L. Curseu (2008), "Entrepreneurial decision styles and cognition in SMEs," in P.A.M. Vermeulen and P.L. Curseu (eds), *Entrepreneurial Strategic Decision Making: A Cognitive Perspective*, Cheltenham, UK: Edward Elgar, pp. 105–22.

Luck, S.J. and S.A. Hillyard (1994), "Spatial filtering during visual search: evidence from human electrophysiology," *Journal of Experimental Psychology: Human Perception and Performance*, **20** (5), 1000–1014.

Macchione S,M.S., M.A.C. Rocha, and P.S. Bigio (2013), "Entrepreneurial decision-making using the knightian uncertainty approach," *Revista de Administração*, **48** (4), 716–26.

MacLeod, C.M. (2005), "The Stroop task in cognitive research," in A. Wenzel and D.C. Rubin (eds), *Cognitive Methods and their Application to Clinical Research*, Washington, DC: American Psychological Association, pp. 17–40.

Maine, E., P.-H. Soh, and N. Dos Santos (2015), "The role of entrepreneurial decision-making in opportunity creation and recognition," *Technovation*, **39**, 53–72.

McBride, R. (2014), "Toward a study of neuroentrepreneurship," paper presented at the Annual Academy of Management Conference "In Search of the Entrepreneurial Mindset: Insights from Neuroscience," Philadelphia, 1–5 August.

McKenna, F.P. and D. Sharma (1995), "Intrusive cognitions: an investigation of the emotional Stroop task," *Journal of Experimental Psychology: Learning, Memory, and Cognition*, **21** (6), 1595.

McMullen, J.S., M.S. Wood, and L.E. Palich (2014), "Entrepreneurial cognition and social cognitive neuroscience," in J.R. Mitchell, R.K. Mitchell, and B. Randolph-Seng (eds), *Handbook of Entrepreneurial Cognition*, Cheltenham: Edward Elgar, pp. 316–63.

Miao, Q. and L. Liu (2010), "A psychological model of entrepreneurial decision making," *Social Behavior and Personality*, **38** (3), 357–63.

Michl, T., I.M. Welpe, M. Spörrle, and A. Picot (2009), "The role of emotions and cognitions in entrepreneurial decision-making," in L.A. Carsrud and M. Brännback (eds), *Understanding the Entrepreneurial Mind*, Heidelberg: Springer, pp. 167–90.

Mitchell, J.R., P.N. Friga, and R.K. Mitchell (2005), "Untangling the intuition mess: intuition as a construct in entrepreneurship research," *Entrepreneurship Theory and Practice*, **29** (6), 653–79.

Mitchell, R.K. (1994), "The composition, classification, and creation of new venture formation expertise," PhD thesis, University of Utah, Salt Lake City, UT.

Mitchell, R.K., L. Busenitz, B. Bird, M. Gaglio, J. McMullen, E. Morse, and B. Smith (2007), "The central question in entrepreneurial cognition research 2007," *Entrepreneurship Theory and Practice*, **31** (1), 1–27.

Mitchell, R.K., L. Busenitz, T. Lant, P. McDougall, E. Morse, and J.B. Smith (2002), "Toward a theory of entrepreneurial cognition: rethinking the people side of entrepreneurship research," *Entrepreneurship Theory and Practice*, **27** (2), 93–104.

Mitchell, R.K., L. Busenitz, T. Lant, P. McDougall, E. Morse, and J.B. Smith (2004), "The distinctive and inclusive domain of entrepreneurial cognition research," *Entrepreneurship Theory and Practice*, **28** (6), 505–18.

Mitchell, R.K., B. Smith, K. Seawright, and E. Morse (2000), "Cross-cultural cognitions and the venture creation decision," *Academy of Management Journal*, **43** (5), 974–93.

Mulert, C., L. Jäger, R. Schmitt, P. Bussfeld, O. Pogarell, J.-J. Möller, . . . and U. Hegerl (2004), "Integration of fMRI and simultaneous EEG: towards a comprehensive understanding of localization and time-course of brain activity in target detection," *Neuroimage*, **22** (1), 83–94.

Mullins, J.W., and D. Forlani (2005), "Missing the boat or sinking the boat: a study of new venture decision making," *Journal of Business Venturing*, **20** (1), 47–69.

Naudé, W. (2011), "Entrepreneurship is not a binding constraint on growth and development in the poorest countries," *World Development*, **39** (1), 33–44.

Nicolaou, N. and S. Shane (2014), "Biology, neuroscience, and entrepreneurship," *Journal of Management Inquiry*, **23** (1), 98–100.

Nitsche, M.A., and W. Paulus (2011), "Transcranial direct current stimulation – update 2011," *Restorative Neurology and Neuroscience*, **29** (6), 463–92.

Nolan-Hoeksema, S., B.L. Frederickson, G.R. Loftus, and W.A. Wagenaar (2014), *Atkinson and Hilgard's Introduction to Psychology*, Mason, OH: Cengage.

Nordqvist, C. (2014), "What is neuroscience?" *Medical News Today*, accessed 11 October 2016 at http://www.medicalnewstoday.com/.

Norris, C.J., J.A. Coan, and T. Johnstone (2007), "Functional magnetic resonance imaging and the study of emotion," in J.A. Coan and J.J.B. Allen (eds), *Handbook of Emotion Elicitation and Assessment*, Oxford: Oxford University Press, pp. 440–59.

Olayinka, I., A.K. Olusegun, G. Kellikume, and K. Kayode, K. (2015), "Entrepreneur decision making process and application of linear programming technique," *European Journal of Business, Economics and Accountancy*, **3** (5), 1–5.

Omorede, A., S. Thorgren, and J. Wincent (2015), "Entrepreneurship psychology: a review," *International Entrepreneurship and Management Journal*, **11** (4), 743–68.

Ortiz-Terán, E., A. Turrero, J.M. Santos, P.T. Bryant, T. Ortiz, E. Ortiz-Terán, . . . and T. Ortiz (2014), "Brain cortical organization in entrepreneurs during a visual Stroop decision task," *Clinical, Cosmetic and Investigational Dentistry*, **6**, 45–56.

Ouellet, J., A. McGirr, F. Van den Eynde, F. Jollant, M. Lepage, and M.T. Berlim (2015), "Enhancing decision-making and cognitive impulse control with transcranial direct current stimulation (tDCS) applied over the orbitofrontal cortex (OFC): a randomized and sham-controlled exploratory study," *Journal of Psychiatric Research*, **69**, 27–34.

Palva, S. (2014, 14 August), Personal communication.

Patel, P.C. and J.O. Fiet (2010), "Enhancing the internal validity of entrepreneurship experiments by assessing treatment effects at multiple levels across multiple trials," *Journal of Economic Behavior and Organization*, **76**, 127–40.

Pech, R.J. and A. Cameron (2006), "An entrepreneurial decision process model describing opportunity recognition," *European Journal of Innovation Management*, **9** (1), 61–78.

Pelissolo, A., L. Mallet, J.M. Baleyte, G. Michel, C. Cloninger, J.F. Allilaire, and R. Jouvent (2005), "The temperament and character inventory-revised (TCI-R): psychometric characteristics of the French version," *Acta Psychiatrica Scandinavica*, **112** (2), 126–33.

Picton, T., S. Bentin, P. Berg, E. Donchin, S. Hillyard, R. Johnson, . . . and M. Rugg (2000), "Guidelines for using human event-related potentials to study cognition: recording standards and publication criteria," *Psychophysiology*, **37** (02), 127–52.

Poldrack, R.A. (2006), "Can cognitive processes be inferred from neuroimaging data?" *Trends in Cognitive Sciences*, **10** (2), 59–63.

Polezzi, D., C. Guarneri, and C. Civai (2012), "The point of view of neuroscience on decision-making," in K.O. Moore and N.P. Gonzalez (eds), *Handbook on Psychology of Decision-Making: New Research*, New York: Nova Science Publishers, pp. 1–31.

Purves, D., E.M. Brannon, R. Cabeza, S.A. Huettel, K.S. LaBar, M.L. Platt, and M.G. Woldorff (2008), *Principles of Cognitive Neuroscience*, vol. 83, Sunderland, MA: Sinauer Associates.

Pushkarskaya, H., M. Smithson, X. Liu, and J.E. Joseph (2010), "1. Neuroeconomics of environmental uncertainty and the theory of the firm," in A.A. Stanton, M. Day, and I.M. Welpe (eds), *Neuroeconomics and the Firm*, Cheltelham: Edward Elgar, pp. 13–28.

Randolph-Seng, B., J.R. Mitchell, and R.K. Mitchell (2014), "Introduction: historical context, present trends and future directions in entrepreneurial cognition research," In J.R. Mitchell, R.K. Mitchell, and B. Randolph-Seng (eds), *Handbook of Entrepreneurial Cognition*, Cheltenham: Edward Elgar, pp. 1–60.

Randolph-Seng, B., W.A. Williams, and M. Hayek (2014), "Entrepreneurial self-regulation: consciousness and cognition," in J.R. Mitchell, R.K. Mitchell, and B. Randolph-Seng (eds), *Handbook of Entrepreneurial Cognition*, Cheltenham: Edward Elgar, pp. 132–53.

Reed, S.K. (2010), *Cognition: Theories and Application*, Belmont, CA: Wadsworth Cengage Learning.

Rieskamp, J., and U. Hoffrage (2008), "Inferences under time pressure: how opportunity costs affect strategy selection," *Acta Psychologica*, **127** (2), 258–76.

Rolls, E.T. (2014), *Emotion and Decision-Making Explained*, Oxford: Oxford University Press.

Sánchez, J.C., T. Carballo, and A. Gutiérrez (2011), "El emprendedor desde una orientacion cognitiva," *Psicothema*, **23** (3), 433–9.

Sanders, M. (2007), "Scientific paradigms, entrepreneurial opportunities and cycles in economic growth," *Small Business Economics*, **28** (4), 339–54.

Sarasvathy, S.D. (2001), "Causation and effectuation: toward a theoretical shift from economic inevitability to entrepreneurial contingency," *Academy of Management Review*, **26** (2), 243–63.

Schade, C. (2005), "Dynamics, experimental economics, and entrepreneurship," *The Journal of Technology Transfer*, **30**, 409–31.

Schade, C. and K. Burmeister (2009), "Experiments on entrepreneurial decision making: a different lens through which to look at entrepreneurship," *Foundations and Trends in Entrepreneurship*, **5** (2), 81–134.

Schulz, E., E. Konstantinidis, and M. Speekenbrink (2015), "Exploration-exploitation in a contextual multi-armed bandit task," paper presented at the International Conference on Cognitive Modeling, Groningen, 9–11 April.

Schumpeter, J.A. (1934), *The Theory of Economic Development: An Inquiry into Profits, Capital, Credit, Interest, and the Business Cycle*, Cambridge, MA: Harvard University Press.

Shane, S. (2000), "Prior knowledge and the discovery of entrepreneurial opportunities," *Organization Science*, **11** (4), 448–69.

Shane, S. (2003), *A General Theory of Entrepreneurship: The Individual-Opportunity Nexus*, Aldershot: Edward Elgar.

Shane, S. and S. Venkataraman (2000), "The promise of entrepreneurship as a field of research," *The Academy of Management Review*, **25**, 217–26.

Shaver, K.G. and L.R. Scott (1991), Person, process, choice: the psychology of new venture creation," *Entrepreneurship Theory and Practice*, **16** (2), 23–45.

Shepherd, D.A., T.A. Williams, and H. Patzelt (2015), "Thinking about entrepreneurial decision making review and research agenda," *Journal of Management*, **41** (1), 11–46.

Simmons, S., D. Hsu, A. Wieland, and M. Begelfer (2016), "Experimental methodologies: applications and agendas for entrepreneurship research," paper presented at the USASBE Annual Conference, San Diego, CA, 8–14 January.

Simon, M., S.M. Houghton, and K. Aquino (2000), "Cognitive biases, risk perception, and venture formation: how individuals decide to start companies," *Journal of Business Venturing*, **15** (2), 113–34.

Smith, R. (2010), "Mapping neurological drivers to entrepreneurial proclivity," in A.A. Stanton, M. Day, and I.M. Welpe (eds), *Neuroeconomics and the Firm*, Cheltenham: Edward Elgar, ch. 11.

Stanton, A.A. and I.M. Welpe (2010), "Risk and ambiguity: entrepreneurial research from the perspective of economics," in A.A. Stanton, M. Day, and I.M. Welpe (eds), *Neuroeconomics and the Firm*, Cheltenham: Edward Elgar, pp. 29–49.

Sternberg, S. (1969), "The discovery of processing stages: extensions of Donders' method," *Acta Psychologica*, **30**, pp. 276–315.

Stettner, U., B.S. Aharonson, and T.L. Amburgey (2014), "The interplay between exploration and exploitation in SMEs," in U. Stettner, B.S. Aharonson, and T.L. Amburgey (eds), *Exploration and Exploitation in Early Stage Ventures and SMEs (Technology, Innovation, Entrepreneurship and Competitive Strategy)*, vol. 14, Bradford: Emerald Group Publishing Limited, pp. 3–13.

Steyvers, M., M.D. Lee, and E.J. Wagenmakers (2009), "A Bayesian analysis of human decision-making on bandit problems," *Journal of Mathematical Psychology*, **53** (3), 168–79.

Tan, J., E. Fischer, R.K. Mitchell, and P. Phan (2009), "At the center of the action: innovation and technology strategy research in the small business setting," *Journal of Small Business Management*, **47** (3), 233–62.

Tobler, P.N., J.P. O'Doherty, R.J. Dolan, and W. Schultz (2007), "Reward value coding distinct from risk attitude-related uncertainty coding in human reward systems," *Journal of Neurophysiology*, **97** (2), 1621–32.

Toga, A.W. and P.M. Thompson (2005), "Genetics of brain structure and intelligence," *Annual Review of Neuroscience*, **28** (1), 1–23.

Tracey, P. and D. Schluppeck (2014), "Neuroentreprenuership: 'brain pornography' or new frontier in entrepreneurship research?" *Journal of Management Inquiry*, **23** (1), 101–3.

Vermeulen, P.A.M. and P.L. Curseu (2008), "Entrepreneurs and strategic decisions," in P.A.M. Vermeulen and P.L. Curseu (eds), *Entrepreneurial Strategic Decision-Making: A Cognitive Perspective*, Cheltenham: Edward Elgar, pp. 1–10.

Voutsina, K., G. Mourmant, and F. Niederman (2014), "The range of shocks prompting entrepreneurial employee turnover through the lenses of exploration and exploitation framework," in U. Stettner, B.S. Aharonson, and T.L. Amburgey (eds), *Exploration and Exploitation in Early Stage Ventures and SMEs (Technology, Innovation, Entrepreneurship and Competitive Strategy*, vol. 14, Bradford: Emerald Group Publishing Limited, pp. 39–66.

Vul, E., C. Harris, P. Winkielman, and H. Pashler (2009), "Puzzlingly high correlations in fMRI studies of emotion, personality, and social cognition," *Perspectives on Psychological Science*, **4** (3), 274–90.

Wade, C. (2006), "Some cautions about jumping on the brain-scan bandwagon," *Observer*, 9 September, accessed 11 October 2016 at http://www.psychologicalscience.org/

Wargo, D.T., N.A. Baglini, and K.A. Nelson (2010), "What neuroeconomics informs us about making real-world ethical decisions in organizations," in A.A. Stanton, M. Day, and I.M. Welpe (eds), *Neuroeconomics and the Firm*, Cheltenham: Edward Elgar, pp. 235–62.

West, R., R. Bowry, and C. McConville (2004), "Sensitivity of medial frontal cortex to response and nonresponse conflict," *Psychophysiology*, **41** (5), 739–48.

Zahra, S.A. (2007), "Contextualizing theory building in entrepreneurship research," *Journal of Business Venturing*, **22** (3), 443–52.

3. Human psychophysiological and genetic approaches in neuroentrepreneurship

Marco Colosio, Cristiano Bellavitis, and Aleksei A. Gorin

The field of neuroscience has considerably expanded in the last decades. Researchers have used neuroscientific techniques to study a wide range of phenomena in entrepreneurship, business, economics, and marketing. Notwithstanding the current progress of the field of neuroentrepreneurship, so far, entrepreneurship researchers did not take full advantage of the incredible research possibilities of neuroscientific methods (Krueger and Welpe, 2014). The purpose of this chapter is to provide, in a single source, an outlook on the state-of-the-art techniques in cognitive neuroscience useful to address questions within business and economics realms. Here, we particularly focus on non-invasive highly insightful psychophysiological techniques – electroencephalography (EEG), magnetoencephalography (MEG), electrocardiogram (ECG), electromyogram (EMG), electrooculography (EOG), eye tracking, and electrodermal activity. Along with electrophysiological approaches, we also provide the reader with basic principles of behavioral genetics (twins studies, family studies, adopted studies) and we introduce the reader to psychoneuroendocrinology, namely the relation between hormones and behavior. These techniques can complement more commonly used methods – for example, functional magnetic resonance imaging (fMRI).

The chapter is structured in two main sections. The first section describes the "psychophysiological correlates of behavior," while the second section describes "genetics, hormones and behavior." In particular, the first section discusses the techniques related to the central nervous system (EEG and MEG), as well as those related to the peripheral nervous system (ECG, EKG, electrooculography, and eye and electrodermal activity tracking). The second section discusses behavioral genetics and psychoneuroendocrinology. For each technique we provide a brief description, followed by a discussion of its advantages and disadvantages, and we conclude each section with examples of previous studies and potential research questions that can be answered by using the focal technique.

PSYCHOPHYSIOLOGICAL CORRELATES OF BEHAVIOR

Psychophysiology is a branch of physiology that non-invasively deals with the relationship between mind and body. This relationship is substantiated by the electrical impulses generated by the human activity. Thoughts, movements, feelings, and emotions occur in response to chemical and electrical signals triggered by the brain and then transmitted to the organs or generated in response to peripheral events (for example, pain after a wound). Psychophysiology investigates physiological activation (as in electric signals) following the manipulation of psychological variables in experimental settings. It observes the interactions between physiological changes and psychological processes. For example, it is possible to determine the relationship between particular behaviors (such as risk seeking, risk avoidance, emotional responses to particular stimuli) and somatic indexes (the heart rate, the blood pressure, or the brain activity). By combining psychophysiological approaches, scholars might answer fundamental questions such as: "how do we measure emotions, for example in relations to entrepreneurial success?" "How can we assess implicit (unconscious) responses to particular situations such as failure?" "What happens in the brain when we take entrepreneurial decisions?" "How can we predict a particular behavior such as entrepreneurial intentions?" Traditionally, psychophysiology has investigated phenomena such as emotions, stress, decision making, and cognitive processes. It has explored these phenomena within several areas of investigation, such as cognitive psychophysiology (psychophysiological changes during cognitive tasks) and social psychophysiology (investigation of psychophysiological phenomena in social processes). Since the ultimate goal of the growing field of neuroentrepreneurship is the understanding of the psychological and biological factors that determine entrepreneurial outcomes (for example, behavior, success), entrepreneurship and business scholars can obtain terrific insights by exploring psychophysiological indexes.

Human psychophysiology has been largely studied and, nowadays, a large set of tools is available to scientists to investigate the correlations between cognitive, psychological, emotional events and consequent body responses. In the first section of this chapter, we describe the traditional approaches in psychophysiology, focusing on non-invasive tools that can be useful to investigate entrepreneurs' behavior. Since psychophysiology studies the activity of both the *central nervous system* (the brain) and the *peripheral nervous system* (the organs and glands), this section is divided into the following parts: (1) common approaches for the brain's exploration (the central system), and (2) common approaches for the body's explorations (the peripheral system).

The Central Nervous System

Since the brain receives electrical and chemical signals to process information, researchers have developed tools to examine the brain's electric currents by measuring electric potentials or magnetic fields: electroencephalography (EEG) and magnetoencephalography (MEG). EEG provides information about the electrical activity of the brain, while MEG studies the magnetic activity. Both techniques allow researchers to investigate how the brain reacts to determined stimuli. In the next sections, we introduce these non-invasive approaches in detail.

Electroencephalography (EEG)

How does EEG work? Since the German psychiatrist Hans Berger succeeded in recording the brain activity of humans in a non-invasive fashion, EEG rapidly became one of the fundamental tools to explore living brains. EEG offers two main types of information. First, EEG provides information about the state of the brain at a given time. An example of the modern approach to explore brain state is the time-frequency analysis that disentangles the signal by taking into account time and frequency domain. Second, through EEG it is possible to retrieve information about changes of cortical activity induced by certain events within a specific time window. The latter are known as event-related potentials (ERPs) that provide useful information regarding the brain response to specific stimuli or events, compared to other experimental conditions (such as how our brain reacts to a worse-than-expected feedback/outcome or a mistake; see Figure 3.1).

Nowadays, due to its high temporal resolution – the ability to accurately discriminate and record two points in time is within a window of 2 milliseconds (hereafter, ms). EEG is largely used in both clinical and cognitive neuroscience settings. The signal that is recorded through EEG is the result of the electrical activity of a large population of neurons (Figure 3.2). The excitation of the neuron's membrane changes the permeability of the membrane, and different ions flow inside and outside the neuron. The following changes in electrical potentials of neuronal membrane generate local electric currents. Subsequently, the local current activity propagates along the axon of the neuron until it reaches the synapses (the region of neurons where the signal is transmitted). It is in the synapses that the information is transmitted to neighboring neurons. When many

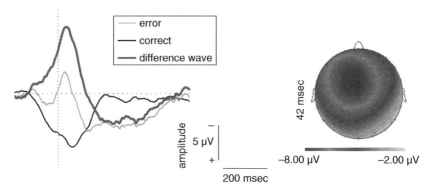

Note: When an individual makes or detects a mistake as well as an erroneous response during a cognitive task, an ERP component is observable in the processed EEG signal. The ERP component observed in this figure is known as error-related negativity (ERN) and it appears as a negative deflection that occurs within 100 milliseconds after an error or mistake. The ERN has been suggested to be a fundamental component of behavioral adaptation and learning. The ERN is shown on the left side of the picture. The thin-gray line ("error") indicates the ERP obtained by averaging the neural activity following erroneous responses in 15 participants during a cognitive task. Researchers compared erroneous responses and correct answers (black line). *Difference wave* indicates the difference in the brain activity during error and correct condition. Please note that the ERP negative deflections are traditionally oriented upward. As it is clearly observable, after errors a negative peak was generated after approximately 42 milliseconds. ERP are observable only after signal analysis and are not observable in raw EEG. On the right, the authors showed topography distribution of ERN. Traditionally, the ERN is thought to be generated in a brain region called anterior cingulate cortex, a structure below the prefrontal cortex. ERN is observable as a frontocentral negativity (the central striped area).

Source: Images adjusted from Bellebaum and Colosio (2014).

Figure 3.1   An example of event-related potential

neighboring neurons are excited within short time windows, EEG is able to detect the electrical current generated.

A standard EEG device is composed by compact digital multichannel amplifiers connected to a PC as data collector. The usual research setting involves participants performing a task while they wear electrodes placed on their scalp. These electrodes (Figure 3.3: A) are connected to an amplifier (Figure 3.3: B). Yet, it is important to note that, on the market, a broad amount of EEG devices is available, and each device can offer different configurations. For example, it is very common that electrodes are embedded into an elastic cap (Figure 3.3: C) that participants must wear. The use of the cap reduces preparation time and guarantees a more stable electrodes' positioning throughout the whole experiment. The number of electrodes (often called *channels*) ranges from 8 to modern

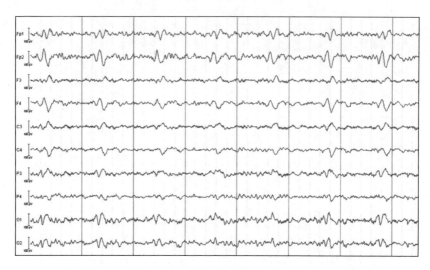

Note: Each EEG signal line corresponds to a EEG channel, named on the left column.

Source: Yeji Han (2014).

Figure 3.2   An example of a raw EEG signal

high-density devices that have 128/256 electrodes. However, the majority of studies involved 32 or 64 electrodes.

Advantages of EEG   The main advantages of EEG are represented by the fact that this technique is non-invasive, safe, and a well-studied tool to address a large range of research questions. Further, as mentioned above, a strong advantage of EEG lies in its superior time resolution that makes it a powerful tool to investigate brain dynamics and detect rapid changes of the brain's activity. High temporal resolution is a fundamental feature to detect the changing nature of cognitive functions such as attention and perception (that is, changes occurring within a few milliseconds). It is also germane to create models of relatively slower brain responses related to cognitive functions such as memory, learning, motivation, and decision making, among others (that is, electrical activity arising over hundreds of milliseconds).

Modern technological development led to the generation of small and portable devices and electrodes that are largely used in marketing studies and can be potentially very proficient in exploring the entrepreneurship mind in a real environment. Finally, modern devices are cheap to purchase and run compared to other machines such as MRI scanners. The cost of

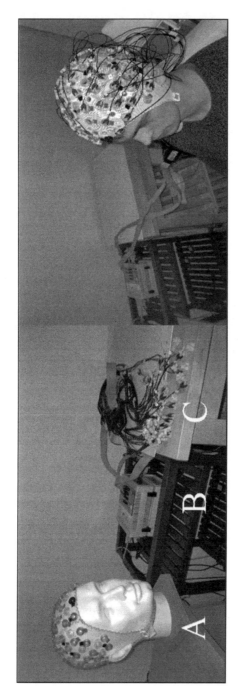

Note: On the left: (A) 128-channel elastic cap; (B) EEG amplifier (top) and its battery (below); (C) electrodes – on the right, one of the authors wears a 64-channel montage.

Figure 3.3   An example of an EEG setting

purchasing EEG equipment ranges from a couple of hundred dollars for basic models to approximately US $10000. This compares with more expansive MRI scanners whose prices range from $150000–$500000 or more. EEG also has low maintenance and running costs (such as electrode replacement, gel).

Disadvantages of EEG   EEG is not a perfect tool and has its limitations. First, EEG may offer misleading results. Indeed, EEG can detect a certain amount of *noise* generated by different sources than the brain (such as muscular activity/tension, eye blinking and 50–60 Hz ambient electrical noise). Thus, it is important that researchers pay particular attention to reduce these sources of noise. Noise reduction and filtering can be achieved by employing specific software and a free toolbox. Once signals have been filtered, they can be processed and analyzed.

Second, although EEG offers very accurate temporal resolution, it lacks spatial resolution – the capacity to discriminate two points in space (for more detail about temporal and spatial resolution see Burle et al., 2015). Recent innovations involve the use of high-density electrode arrays that are more accurate in making inferences on spatial distribution of the electrical activity. In order to obtain a more reliable signal, it is also very common to reduce the impedance of the skin by applying conductive/ abrasive gel between the electrodes and the surface of the scalp. It has been noted that hair does not significantly interfere with the EEG signal. This solution is not necessary using modern devices. These machines are usually equipped with "dry-electrodes" that do not require (or require a very small amount) of conductive gel.

The poor spatial resolution is not a trivial problem that requires careful handling by professional staff. This problem is associated with a fundamental issue called the "*inverse problem*". As suggested by the name, the inverse problem refers to the difficulty of reconstructing the source of the EEG signal. Indeed, this problem arises because the signal detected on the scalp may be generated by either cortical layers or deeper structures of the brain and then propagated to the scalp. Thus, starting from the signal (effect), scientists need to localize its source (cause). Understanding *where* the signal is generated (*source localization*) and addressing the inverse problem is challenging and is crucial to obtain reliable neural models as well as to generate strong causal predictions. However, modern approaches (such as combining EEG and fMRI), reliable neural models, and advanced statistical analysis allow better information about the source of observed EEG signals (for a more exhaustive description we recommend a review by Grech and colleagues, 2008).

Which research questions can be answered using EEG? Despite its merits, to the best of our knowledge EEG has never been adopted to answer entrepreneurship research questions. However, this technique has been used in related fields that can inspire entrepreneurship-related research. For example, Studer et al. (2013), through a modern EEG (and fMRI) approach, explored the correlation between brain activity at rest (no task), psychological traits (such as sensitivity to punishment and reward), and risk-taking behavior. Their results showed that specific baseline activity of the prefrontal cortex (a brain area important for high-level cognitive processes, behavioral control, and decision making) and psychological traits can predict risk-taking behavior. A similar research design could be implemented to explore risk-taking behavior such as entrepreneurship activities. Through a design similar to the one of Studer et al. (2013) it is possible to understand whether psychological traits and brain activity are good predictors of the choice to become an entrepreneur or get involved in entrepreneurial activities.

In another recent study published in the *Journal of Behavioral Finance,* Vieito and colleagues (2015) explored a symmetrical question. The authors investigated whether certain market outcomes influenced brain activity and response. In particular, they used an EEG to explore whether different market conditions (such as growing versus high-volatility market) influence the brain activity of 20 investors (volunteers) during different financial activities (such as selling, buying, and holding). Participants were divided into two groups of ten participants. Each participant underwent 100 investment decisions (50 decisions in each market). Experimenters manipulated the order of market sequence in such a way that the investors of the first group played in a growing market and then in a high-volatile market, whereas the individuals of the second group performed the opposite sequence, playing first in a high-volatile marked and then in a growing market. The researchers used a particular EEG analysis (principal component analysis) to look at the brain activity of the investors. The authors found that the brain responded differently between the two groups of investors. Albeit both groups performed well during the experiments, the research showed that trading in a different market sequence (from a growing market to a high-volatility market and vice versa) not only affected financial decision-making processes but also activated different neural circuits in the brain. The authors posited that different market predictability (and subsequent emotional activation) activates different brain networks to successfully predict market trends and optimizes the decisions. A similar design could be adopted to investigate how entrepreneurs react to negative business outcomes or setbacks.

These studies show that very detailed and interesting research questions can be answered with EEG. It is surprising that the entrepreneurship field did not take full advantage of this technique. As previously mentioned, future studies might use EEG to understand how different entrepreneurs respond to certain market or business situations. This research could explain what leads entrepreneurs to start a company, or to shut it down. Also, it would shed light on how market events shape an entrepreneur's motivation or particular decision making. Borrowing from the study of Vieito et al. (2015), entrepreneurship researchers could investigate important dynamics of the venture financing industry, including equity crowdfunding. Possible research questions could be: are venture capitalists investments' decisions affected by particular market situations? How do venture capitalists react when their investee company underperforms or when they have a disagreement with the management? What type of information mostly affects the brain activity of the investors, that in turn affects their decision to invest (or not to)?

Magnetoencephalography (MEG)

How does MEG work? Magnetoencephalography studies the brain's magnetic activity by detecting the magnetic fields generated by the neurons' activity. As previously mentioned, researchers can detect electrical activities with an EEG. However, it is well known that the movement of local electrically charged particles through a conductor generates a magnetic field. On the basis of this physical principle, it is possible to make inferences about the brain activity, understanding its magnetic activity through an MEG.

MEG was invented by David Cohen in 1968. This method is based on the principle that electrical activity generated by populations of neurons is always accompanied by the generation of magnetic fields. Similarly to the electric signals observed through an EEG, magnetic fields' fluctuation has similar temporal features and can be observed either as a sequence of oscillatory waves or as changes in response to particular events (like time-lock ERPs). Moreover, magnetic fields are not significantly affected by the density of the skull. However, the activity generated by neurons is extremely weak (approximately 10^{-15} Tesla).

In order to detect such weak fields, MEG systems use special sensors called superconducting quantum interference devices (or SQUIDs) placed in liquid helium contained in a special vacuum thermos, called *dewar flasks*. By cooling SQUIDs to very low temperatures, these sensors turn into superconductors able to detect very small magnetic fields' changes. These sensors can be of two types: (1) *magnetometers* that measure magnetic fields directly; (2) *gradiometers* that measure gradients of fields at some particular direction (planar or radial).

In a standard experimental setting, the study subject sits on a chair where his or her head is placed in a helmet called a "dewar". The dewar contains hundreds of SQUIDs sensors that detect magnetic fields at an extraordinary temporal resolution and permits solid inferences on both temporal and spatial properties of the neurons that generate the magnetic fields.

Advantages of MEG   MEG offers several advantages, especially compared to EEG. First, MEG is a non-invasive tool that can address a wide number of research questions without incurring ethical concerns. Second, MEG provides highly precise data in terms of temporal as well as spatial resolution. This is due: (1) because the magnetic fields detected by MEG are not distorted by the skull and the skin; and (2) because MEG is equipped by the large number of sensors (SQUIDs). These peculiarities allow MEG to clearly retrieve the topography of the signal. In other words, it can locate where the brain signal is generated on the cortex with an extraordinary temporal and spatial accuracy. As a consequence, through MEG, researchers can make direct inferences about the location and the duration of the brain's cortical activity. Third, MEG is relatively easy to set up. The amount of time required to prepare an MEG system is significantly shorter than an average EEG study. In fact, MEG does not require a large number of electrodes (to reduce muscular artifacts few electrodes are needed) and conducive gel is not necessary. This also leads to a more comfortable experimental setting and more reliable data. Finally, MEG can be easily combined with other techniques such as structural MRI. Coupling MEG with structural MRI allows imaging to overlap the brain structure and the brain activity on an individual basis.

Disadvantages of MEG   Despite the above-mentioned advantages, a few major disadvantages limited the wide adoption of this technique. First and foremost, the cost of setting up an MEG scanner and the necessary shielded laboratory are very high. Indeed, the environment is affected by numerous electromagnetic sources such as electronic devices and motors; SQUIDs are so sensitive that even the magnetic fields generated by the earth can impact MEG readings. In order to avoid any signal interference, it is fundamental to install the MEG equipment in a chamber that is shielded from any kind of external magnetic fields. Along with a magnetic-shielded chamber, MEG needs liquid helium to work properly. MEG centers have two ways to source liquid helium. The first option is to purchase it from a provider when it is needed. The second option is to build a helium recovery system. Unfortunately, both options are very expensive. Thus, MEG requires an investment of usually more than US $2 million. Maintenance and running costs (such as highly specialized staff) are also substantial. Albeit MEG centers are not numerous, we recommend the reader to consult the list of known MEG centers worldwide, available on the website megcommunity.org.[1] Second, although spatial resolution is more accurate compared to an EEG, it is less accurate if compared to an MRI.

Third, due to physical limitations, MEG does not collect satisfactory data from deep structures of the brain. Thus, MEG is appropriate to study the most widely investigated brain regions such as cortical areas, but has a low sensitivity to subcortical areas.

In conclusion, the MEG is a powerful tool to access neural mechanisms underpinning entrepreneurship processes, since it gives high-quality data that is more exhaustive than other similar techniques such as EEG. However, due to its peculiarities, the MEG is often discharged in favor of EEG studies and fMRI approaches to investigate the human brain.

What research questions can be answered using MEG?   MEG has been rarely used to investigate research questions specifically targeted to entrepreneurship scholars. The limited adoption of this technique is mainly due to the costs involved. However, despite these cost limitations, MEG has been used in related fields. Previous research used MEG to study emotions, higher cognitive processes, and perception. For example, Ioannides et al. (2000) employed MEG to investigate how the brain responds to cognitive and affective stimuli. Results found that the brain responds differently to cognitive and affective stimuli. In particular, cognitive stimuli activate – more than affective stimuli – the brain areas related with high-order cognitive processes and executive control.

MEG has been used to study how monetary concepts are represented in the brain. A study by Tallon-Baudry et al. (2011) published on *PloS One*, investigated how the human brain is activated when either money and neutral stimuli are presented. Money, as any other physiological incentive, activates the reward system in the brain. However, contrary to physiological incentives, money is a cultural artifact and its value is arbitrary. Thus, the authors explored how the properties of monetary stimuli are identified by the brain. Moreover, the authors tested whether similar brain response occurs when a neutral stimulus (such as a metal disk), whose value is experimentally assigned, is presented. Using the MEG, the authors found that a brain region called the ventral visual pathway is able to recognize and distinguish valid and invalid coins in less than 175 ms, regardless of familiarity with the coins (euros and Australian dollars). This data supports the hypothesis that money representation is non-specific and is independent from daily experience. Moreover, it supports the idea that the ventral visual pathway is involved in representing cultural-defined symbols.

Table 3.1   Differences between EEG and MEG

Method	EEG	MEG
Basic principle	Electric field detection	Magnetic field detection
Unit of measurement	Microvolt (μV)	Femtatesla (fT)
Detector	Electrode	SQUID
Temporal resolution	1 ms	1 ms
Space resolution	Bad, >10 mm	Good, 2–8 mm
Signal purity	Tissues attenuation	Little effect of tissues attenuation
Size	Compact (a suitcase)	Huge
Mobility	Mobile	Immovable
Consumable material	Conductive gel	Liquid helium
Cost	Approximately $6 000	Approximately $2.5 million
Areas of interest	Clinical research, cognitive neuroscience	Clinical research, cognitive neuroscience
Applications	Sleep disorders, pre-surgical mapping of the brain, epilepsy, psychiatric and neurodegenerative disorders, several cognitive mechanisms, human factors, brain–computer interface	Epilepsy, neurodegenerative disorders, perceptual, attentional and emotional mechanisms, decision making, memory, language

Altogether, these studies provide a glimpse into the possible applications of MEG to unravel entrepreneurial questions. For instance, it would be of interest to study the neural response (such as the activation of emotion-related areas) of investors and businesspeople to start-ups and innovative projects. Understanding these reactions could clarify what components and brain area are relevant in certain kinds of decision making. Similarly, researchers could investigate what type of ideas, presentations, or events trigger certain emotions or rational responses in investors. Table 3.1 compares EEG and MEG.

Peripheral Nervous System

As previously mentioned, the nervous system is composed of the *central nervous system* (brain) described in the previous section, and by the *peripheral nervous system* (organs and glands). The latter nervous system transmits information from the brain to the rest of the body and vice versa. Motor nervous cells transmit brain inputs through the spinal

Table 3.2   Modulation of physiological indexes by sympathetic and parasympathetic nervous system

Physiological function / Nervous System	Sympathetic Nervous System	Parasympathetic Nervous System
Heart rate	Increment	Decrement
Respiration rate	Increment	Decrement
Pupil	Dilatation	Constriction
Digestion	Inhibition	Stimulation
Salivation	Inhibition	Stimulation
Sexual arousal	Orgasm	Erection/vaginal lubrication
Fight-or-flight	Activates fight-or-flight response (stress)	Reset homeostasis (relaxation)
Sweating	Sweating	—

cord and nerves to muscles, organs, and glands. At the same time, information originated by organs, sensations, and external stimuli are carried to the brain by sensory nervous cells. A portion of the peripheral nervous system in particular has attracted the attention of researchers: the autonomic nervous system (ANS). The ANS regulates numerous body functions such as heart rate, pupil dilatation, respiration rate, sweating, and more complex responses such as fear (embedded into a mechanism called *fight-or-flight response*). Two branches of the ANS are responsible for the modulation of the body functions: (1) the sympathetic nervous system and (2) the parasympathetic nervous system. These two work in opposition to each other and are responsible for the general activation and relaxation of the body. Arousing events activate the sympathetic branch of the ANS, whereas relaxing situations trigger physiological relaxation, and the subsequent homeostasis. The latter is a gradual activation of the parasympathetic nervous system. Table 3.2 summarizes the effects of the activation of each system on several physiological processes.

Since peripheral psychophysiological indexes are continuous and fast-changing, psychophysiologists used peripheral physiological markers directly linked to the activity of the ANS to explore human behavior. In this section, we provide an outlook on the main peripheral psychophysiological methods and their possible applications.

Electrocardiogram (ECG or EKG), heart rate, and blood pressure
The heart is an involuntary muscle that represents the central element of the cardiovascular system and is one of the most important organs

of the human body. Its activity ensures the constant flow of blood all over the body tissues. Blood is pumped through a distribution system (called *vasculature*) by alternating contractions and relaxation of atrial and ventricular fibers. The cardiac cycle consists in a sequence of events that occur from one beat to another and it is composed by two main moments. First, during the *diastole* the heart is at rest and the blood flows into the heart. Second, during the *systole*, the electrical activity generated by specific groups of cells (a natural pacemaker) leads muscle fibers to contract and pump the blood out of the heart. Along with the intrinsic activity of the heart, the cardiovascular system is under the control of both sympathetic and parasympathetic branches of ANS.

As Krueger and Welpe (2014) stated, there are substantial "emotional underpinnings to entrepreneurial action." Considering how the heart is related to our emotional perception, investigating how the heart rate (or blood pressure) changes under certain stimuli or situations can provide important insight into entrepreneurial decision making. In particular, using cardiovascular techniques, researchers can better understand how, when, and why entrepreneurs show a "hot cognition" advantage over other economic actors (Lawrence et al. 2008).

How do cardiovascular techniques work?   As we introduced in the previous section, the sympathetic and parasympathetic activity of ANS is strongly connected with cognitive, emotional, and perceptive processes. Thus, heart-related indexes have been largely studied to investigate psychological and cognitive processes. Here, we focus our attention on three of the most common-studied parameters, which are (1) electrical activity of the heartbeat; (2) the heart rate; and (3) blood pressure.

The *electrical activity of the heart* can be detected via an ECG or EKG. These tests use a number of positive and negative electrodes (from two to ten electrodes depending on the level of accuracy needed) placed on the subject's body. The electrodes record the electrical potential originated by the heart's muscle contraction over a period of a heartbeat, generating an electrical waveform called *PQRST complex* (see Figure 3.4). The latter reflects each stage of a heartbeat, where *P–S* indicates the systole, *T–P* the diastole, and *R* the point of maximum ventricular excitation. In a healthy adult human at rest, the normal duration of a cardiac cycle (intended as *P–P* interval) is approximately 0.86 seconds. However, the duration of a heartbeat is influenced by various factors such as physical demand, chemical factors (caffeine and nicotine increases the number of heartbeats), circadian rhythm (during the day the *P–P* interval is shorter compared to night heartbeat frequency), and emotional factors and stress levels (stress increases the amount of cardiac cycles per minute).[2] The

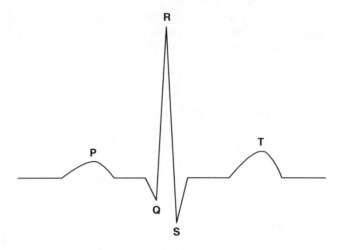

Note: The P wave represents excitation of the atria followed by the QRT activity that reflects ventricular excitation; T precedes relaxation of the heart.

Figure 3.4   An example of the PQRST complex

latest instruments are relatively small, portable, and wireless and can be used for experimental purposes in real settings, adopted to explore cardiac responses in entrepreneurial situations. Finally, we want to outline that ECG is a method for recording the duration of the electrical impulses generated during heartbeats and should not be confused with a measure of the heart rate (explained below), although the latter can also be directly measured via ECG.

The *heart rate* (HR) is a biological index obtained by converting the *heart period:* defined as the amount of R spikes (in the PQRST complex) that arise within a time window of one minute (whereas the variation between two adjacent R–R peaks is the heart rate variability – see below). Because of the conversion, the HR index is expressed in beats/minute or simply as bpm.

The HR is impacted by both personal characteristics as well as environmental conditions. At rest, an adult human being HR ranges from 60 to 100 bpm, with an average of 75 bpm. This variability is given by (1) permanent subject's characteristics, (2) temporary subject's characteristics, (3) environmental factors. HR is affected by permanent characteristics such as age (heart rate is slower for older subjects), level of fitness, lifestyle habits, and diet, among others. In addition, temporary characteristics such as the level of hydration (dehydration leads to faster HR to compensate constriction of arteries), stress, and emotional states such as love or anger.

Finally, environmental factors such as temperature (for example, very cold environments reduce the HR) affect heart rates. Therefore, it is important to control for such parameters in experimental settings.

Blood pressure is another index that is largely used to detect cardiovascular activity. Blood vessels' pressure is generated when the heart contracts and the blood flows throughout the body. Since blood pressure is strictly related with the cardiac cycle, two distinguished phases can be observed with blood pressure measurement: (1) a phase of higher pressure generated by systolic activity of the blood, called *systolic pressure,* and (2) a subsequent pressure decrease caused by diastole, called *diastolic pressure.* Thus, blood pressure is reported as a ratio between systolic and diastolic pressure. Normally, average blood pressure in an adult human is 120/80 mmHg (120 over 80 mm of mercury displacement) and can range within 95–140 mmHg for the systolic pressure and 60–90 mmHg for the diastolic pressure.

Blood pressure can be detected in both invasive and non-invasive fashion. Among the non-invasive methods, the most common is the *auscultatory measurement.* The first measurement can be done with a sphygmomanometer (pressure cuff) and a stethoscope (manual), or a microphone embedded in an arm or wrist cuff (automatic). This kind of measurement detects systolic pressure by detecting the *K-sound* (where K stands for Korotkoff) that is emitted after the cuff has been sufficiently inflated to interrupt arterial blood flow (no systolic sound is perceived). In the same way, diastolic pressure corresponds to the pressure of the cuff when the K sound disappears.

Although blood pressure appears simple to measure, it is important to follow specific rules, as recommended by the American Heart Association (Pickering et al., 2005). First, it is recommended to measure the blood pressure at the same body location, as the blood pressure slightly changes from one location to another (ideally, it should be recorded as close as possible to the aorta). Importantly, differences between left and right arm are common. Second, the size of the cuff needs to be correctly adjusted in order to fit correctly one's arm or wrist. Third, in order to avoid pressure miscalculation, it is recommended to conduct multiple measurements and take the average pressure. This approach significantly reduces the effect of high blood pressure variability within the same experimental session. Fourth, considering that blood pressure is affected – as for other cardiovascular indexes – by endogenous and exogenous factors, researchers should try to control for these factors as much as possible.

Advantages of cardiovascular measurements ECG, HR, and blood pressure are relatively easy to measure, are generally non-invasive, versatile, and are low-cost techniques (from $400). The latest portable instruments allow scientists to measure cardiovascular indexes in different experimental settings and with a more powerful external validity. Moreover, because most people are familiar with these tools, participants are more likely to feel more comfortable during the experiment as compared with other less-known devices (such as MEG). Furthermore, modern devices are able to simultaneously detect different parameters, providing a holistic picture of the physiological response of the subject under study. These markers can be fruitfully complemented with other methodologies such as EEG, fMRI, or self-reported measurements (for example, questionnaires).

Disadvantages of cardiovascular measurements   The above-mentioned techniques are generally reliable. The main drawback of these measurements is associated with the high variability of parameters within the same person and between different individuals. This variability endangers accuracy of the measurements and the correct interpretation of the results. As previously mentioned, these concerns can be eased by implementing a strict experimental design and controlling for external factors that can impact readings.

What research questions can be answered using cardiovascular measurements?   Understanding perception, evaluation, and exploitation remains central to advancing entrepreneurship research (Krueger, 2008), and cardiovascular studies can be very valuable in this respect. Cardiovascular measurements have been used in entrepreneurship research with differing degrees. The ECG is largely used in clinical studies and sport applications and less so in cognitive sciences. Nevertheless, ECG has been employed by psychologists as a marker of different personality traits. For instance, it could be used to explore whether successful entrepreneurs show ECG amplitude patterns correlated with personality and psychological traits such as warmth, agreeableness, and extraversion (Koelsch et al., 2012).

Similarly, monitoring the HR and the blood pressure can shed light on entrepreneurial intentions. Both HR and blood pressure have been associated with the modulation of emotions and personality traits. For instance, a study by Shapiro and colleagues (2001) investigated the relationship between mood states and both blood pressure and HR. The authors recorded the blood pressure and HR (every 20 minutes) in more than 200 women, over a period of four days. After every measurement, participants rated their mood on a five-point scale. The results indicated that higher levels of blood pressure and HR correlated with a reduction of self-reported positive mood and energy levels, whereas little physiological changes were followed by better mood.

In a well-designed experiment published in *Nature*, Lawrence et al. (2008) investigated the phenomenon of 'functional impulsivity' among entrepreneurs and managers. Functional impulsivity allows people to catch opportunities in fast-changing environments. The researchers recorded several parameters such as neurocognitive assessment (to test decision-making skills) and associated these parameters with behavioral tasks' performance. The main goal was to test whether entrepreneurs and managers differed in impulsivity and risk taking. The results showed that entrepreneurs and managers equally performed in behavioral tasks that requires 'cold' cognition (rational analysis), but entrepreneurs out-performed managers in 'hot' cognition. These results could explain why entrepreneurs are more likely to express risk-taking behavior in tasks that require both rational and emotional thinking. Moreover, entrepreneurs showed a higher personality impulsiveness and cognitive flexibility performance.

Understanding entrepreneurs' emotions can shed light on many processes that are otherwise difficult to disentangle. The study by Lawrence et al. (2008) demonstrates that neuroentrepreneurship can be a powerful tool to answer this type of research question. In particular, the exploration of psychophysiological indexes might contribute to a better understanding of the nature of entrepreneurial behavior. Future studies could build upon this literature and compare cardiovascular parameters between male and female entrepreneurs or investors (Bellavitis, Filatotchev and Souitaris, 2016; Bellavitis, Filatotchev, Kamuriwo and Vanacker, 2017). The study could investigate how the two groups react in different situations such as risk taking, failure, success, or uncertainty. Other studies could try to understand whether different entrepreneurial ventures trigger different emotional states that, in turn, lead an entrepreneur to choose (or discard) a particular venture based on emotions rather than economic profit maximization.

Taken together, cardiovascular markers have been extensively used to explore psychophysiological aspects of cognitive processes, especially associated with emotions, psychological traits, and cognitive workload.

Electromyography (EMG)

How does EMG work? The skeletomuscular system is represented by the combination of bones, tendons, cartilages, nerves, ligaments, and muscles. Among the several components of skeletomuscular system, muscular activity plays a central role in psychophysiological studies and it is considered a reliable index of many behavioral and cognitive processes. In this section we describe the electromyogram (EMG), a non-invasive procedure to record electrophysiological muscles' signals (for the basic principles of motor control see Freund, 1983; Pearson, 1993).

Muscle contraction is the result of a long series of biochemical events that are originated by an electrical impulse coming from special neurons placed in the spinal cord (*motoneurons*). Motoneurons innervate from one to many muscular fibers. If stimulated, fibers can reduce their length (contraction) by consuming energy. Once the stimulation is either over, or the chemical elements surrounding muscle fibers (calcium and adenosine triphosphate, ATP) are no longer available, the fibers return to their original length. During the electromagnetic changes occurring throughout muscular activity, a little part of the electrical signal reaches the skin via the extracellular fluid.

Surface (non-invasive) EMG has the capacity to detect this electrical potential generated by muscle fibers' contraction. Importantly, EMG is able to detect only the activation of a group of muscle fibers activated simultaneously. Thus, surface EMG indirectly reflects muscular activity, but it should not be considered a direct measure of muscular activity or movement (these parameters can be inferred obtrusively).

The electromyogram is a relatively small device composed by transducers that detect and convert electrical signal into digital. Normally, the signal transducers detect sequences of brief signal (whose duration goes from 1 to 5 ms). In non-invasive EMG, the signal is transmitted to the transducers via electrodes placed on the muscle of interest. The amplitude of the signal ranges from 1 to 1,000 microvolts (μV). However, these parameters change in accordance with the target muscle and may be disturbed by noise. This noise can be removed or significantly reduced with proper filters and analysis (Clancy, Morin, and Merletti, 2002).

Advantages of EMG   The EMG is a non-invasive and continuous technique that allows the detection of muscular contraction and is largely used in clinical settings to diagnose neurological disorders. The EMG, and in particular facial EMG, has been used in psychophysiological studies. It can be combined with other behavioral observation procedures and represents a promising and powerful tool for exploring entrepreneurship behavior and psychology, such as to detect stress or emotional mimicry. Since it has been posited that emotional stimuli involuntarily activate facial mimicry, the EMG approach bypasses voluntary control of emotion and detects involuntary activity.

Disadvantages of EMG   The main risks with EMG arise when placing the electrodes. Non-experienced researchers should pay particular attention to the correct placement of the electrodes. Also, as previously mentioned, noise could confound the results, and it should be properly reduced. In addition, a limitation is in the difficulty of disentangling the source of muscular activity. This limitation can be partially bypassed by strong experimental design. As for facial EMG, a strong limitation is in the limited amount of muscle activity that is possible to detect at a time, along with a possible discomforting feeling generated by electrodes placed on facial skin.

What research questions can be answered using EMG? Choosing the right business partners, creating a positive and trustworthy collaboration among team members, and developing strong resilience to failure (such as negative feedbacks and emotions such as frustration) are among the key factors to establish a successful business. Surface and facial EMG can help researchers to understand the relationship between emotions, social cooperation, and decision making in entrepreneurs. Surprisingly, hitherto, there is a dearth of experimental studies that use EMG to explore entrepreneurial activities.

However, EMG has been extensively employed by psychophysiologists to investigate psychological and emotional processes in both healthy and pathological populations. For instance, employing facial EMG, along with EEG and other behavioral measurements, Balconi and Pagani (2015) explored social hierarchies and emotions. The authors disentangled the individual reactions in a competitive cognitive task on the basis of individual hierarchical social status. Experimental results showed that negative emotions (for example, involuntary corrugator activity) and weaker cognitive performance followed a downgrade in social status. The opposite pattern emerged when the social status increased. Finally, the authors claimed that high social status positively influences cognitive processes and performances.

Entrepreneurship scholars largely debated the importance of counterfactual thinking (the cognitive process of imagining alternative scenarios to real events) on entrepreneurial efficiency. Counterfactual thinking also attracted the attention of psychologists and neuroscientists. In a series of experimental studies, researchers at the University of Cambridge and their partners explored the interrelationship between gambling and counterfactual thinking. Wu and colleagues (2015) investigated the effect of near wins/near losses on self-perceived luck, betting behavior, and facial muscular activity. By exploring zygomaticus and corrugator activity, researchers found that wins and losses activated different facial muscles. Interestingly, they also observed that near-wins situations, where participants were close to an actual win, activated the same muscles as in wins, albeit these events were perceived as unlucky. This evidence supports the hypothesis that near-wins events generate appetitive mechanisms despite the adverse outcome. Although this experiment did not directly address entrepreneurial behavior, it is a good example of experimental design that can be implemented to test differences between entrepreneurs and non-entrepreneurs. As the authors suggested, their study 'supports the utility of facial EMG and a marker of emotional reactivity in gambling and decision-making research' (pp. 365). Future studies, for example, could investigate whether an almost successful venture capital investment, or start-up, incentivizes the venture capitalists (VCs) to fund a similar start-up, and the entrepreneurs to start a similar venture.

EMG has also been used to study different stages of sleep, or to provide biofeedback for stress reduction and for patients' rehabilitation. Within psychological studies, many works addressed facial EMG to explore emotional reaction to different emotional stimuli (such as surprise), mood, and social contexts. To test the relation of involuntary facial EMG and emotion, Künecke and colleagues (2014) investigated face and emotion perception in 269 subjects during multiple tasks. Results showed that facial corrugator activity correlates with individual emotion perception activity.

In conclusion, facial EMG represents a powerful tool to investigate conscious and unconscious psychological processes and behavioral response that could arise in many entrepreneurship-related contexts.

Electrooculography and eye tracking

Vision is the most developed sense in human beings. Visual-related areas compose 30 percent of the brain cortex, whereas areas related to other senses are below 10 percent each. Thus, it is important for entrepreneurship scholars to focus on eye-related processes as the initial stage of sensual perception and cognitive processing. To detect visual activity, two methodologies exist: (1) electrooculography (EOG) and (2) eye tracking. Since EOG merely detects ocular muscles' activity (such as blinking), researchers are increasingly preferring eye tracking over EOG. Eye tracking is also easier to implement and more accurate to answer entrepreneurship-related research questions. Attention and vision are closely related. Exploring visual patterns can be crucial to explore what shapes entrepreneurial decisions. Hence, in this section we will focus more on eye tracking.

A complex chain of biochemical reactions allows our brain to elaborate visual stimuli. Visual processing of stimuli begins when the light enters the eyes and hits special cells in the retina (photoreceptors). The pupil controls the amount of light entering the eye by constantly changing its size (known as pupillary reflex). Several factors influence pupillary reflex, such as environmental lightening (for example, high level of light makes the pupil constrict), age (aging reduces pupil diameter and velocity), and cognitive load (for example, complex mental tasks increase pupil size). Photoreceptors convert the light into electrical signals that are processed by different areas of the brain and by the visual cortex. The signal is elaborated in hierarchical fashion (from basic information about shape, color, and orientation to higher-order cognitive functions associated with the object). During the visuocognitive process, eyes are constantly moving, even when the subject is intentionally fixating a point. This involuntary eye movement is referred to as *saccadic eye movement* or *saccade*. Saccades allow the fovea – the central as well as the most sensitive area of the retina – to explore several spatial points of the observed object. Each saccade, which lasts 25 ms on average, is followed by a fixation period (on average 250 ms). This mechanism is fundamental for optimal vision, as the fovea guarantees to process visual details of objects (known as *acuity*). Both eye tracking and EOG can record the saccade – fixation patterns.

Since the very beginning of the field of electrophysiology, scientists investigated visual activity studying the muscles responsible for eye movements. EOG records eye movements through 2–4 electrodes placed respectively in the *outer canti* (external corners of the eyes) and above/below one eye. These electrodes detect both saccades and blinks. EOG is largely used together with EEG to remove the electrical activity generated in correspondence of eye movement, to obtain more reliable EEG results. EOG is also used for clinical purposes, such as dyslexic diagnosis (the oculomotor program of dyslexic readers is different from non-dyslexic). However, EOG is less informative to explore attentional and visual processes of entrepreneurs, due to its high sensibility to artifacts (such as facial muscles' activity).

How does eye tracking work?   Eye tracking is a more sophisticated approach, compared to EOG, to detect visual activity. It provides a large set of indexes of the eyes' activity such as fixation point (point in space where the fovea is oriented; this parameter is returned in milliseconds), saccades and pupils' dilatation. Nowadays, eye-tracking devices are available for lab experiment setting (stable or relatively portable, but not wearable) or for field experiments (wearable and wireless). Most of the eye trackers use *corneal reflection* (often called *video-based pupil eye trackers*) to detect either monocular or binocular activity. Corneal reflection is obtained when infrared or near-infrared light illumines the eye (for example, the center of the pupil). Digital video cameras detect, with temporal and spatial precision, the corneal reflection and extract information about the eye movement, eye gaze characteristic, and pupil change, among others.

Advantages of eye tracking   As previously mentioned, modern eye-tracking devices permit collection of both quantitative and qualitative data on visual and attentional processes (for example, eye movement, fixation points and duration, saccades, and changes in pupil size) that are otherwise difficult to gauge. Eye tracking has the potential to provide an outlook on perceptual, attentional, and visual aspects of the cognitive system. Consequently, this technique provides a unique tool to explore human behavior in real environments due to a portable and non-invasive technology. Through eye tracking, as we will explain in more detail below, researchers grasped insights on what type of information investors focus their attention onto in situations of uncertainty and time constraint (Hüsser and Wirth, 2014). An eye tracker can be integrated with other techniques (such as fMRI and EEG) to provide a holistic picture of the subject behavior and responses to cognitive, visual, or entrepreneurial stimuli. When combined with other techniques (such as fMRI), it is possible to obtain more detailed information on ongoing brain (fMRI) and behavioral (eye tracker) processes.

Disadvantages of eye tracking   However, eye tracking has some limitations. The main pitfall is that not all eyes can be successfully detected. Often, contact lenses and glasses dramatically reduce the camera's efficiency. However, technological and software development are overcoming this restriction. Additionally, it has been reported (Blignaut and Wium, 2013) that ethnicity may have an impact on data quality (for example, data quality is worse in Asians than Caucasians and Africans). Furthermore, eye trackers do not provide information about the level of comprehension of a stimulus (as in a text), but rather only reveal information about eye movements. Thus, it is a common procedure to implement eye-tracking experiments with other data, such as self-reported measurement or questionnaires. Additionally, potential disadvantages come with using portable devices. For instance, camera calibration and data analysis can be more laborious than when using stable devices.

What research questions can be answered using eye tracking?   Eye tracking provides information about perceptual, attentional, linguistic, and cognitive processes. These peculiar characteristics lead eye tracking to be extensively used in a variety of fields, including entrepreneurship. Eye tracking shows visual patterns related to determined stimuli (for example, saccades and ocular movements to explore a stimulus such as an advertisement on a screen), heat maps (how much and how long stimuli are observed), and areas of interest (analysis of parameters such as eye fixation on a particular point). For example, Hüsser and Wirth (2014) used eye tracking to investigate the effect of limited attentional resources on the investing behavior of investors. Participants had only three minutes to read a fund performance disclosure before engaging in a financial game. Eye-tracking data suggested that investors, due to limited time to investigate the fund disclosure (that is, limited attention), focused their attention on past fund performance. In addition, the authors found a correlation between the attention toward past performance and investors' purchase intentions. An extension of this study would be to explore what sections of a business plan investors pay attention to. These studies could use eye tracking to explore which information sources (for instance a financial chart) are visually inspected to understand where the attention is mostly allocated and for how long (fixation time). Similarly, researchers could investigate what portions of a crowdfunding web page are most relevant to backers.

Another stream of studies looked at pupillary dilatation as an index that reflects arousal and attentional processes to stimuli. A study from Bradley et al. (2008) explored the pupillary response of 27 participants while observing 96 pictures (pleasant, neutral, and unpleasant pictures). Along with pupil reaction, researchers also recorded skin conductance and HR. Results showed that when participants were exposed to either pleasant or unpleasant pictures, the pupil dilated significantly more than during neutral stimuli. Additionally, the authors found that pupil size covaried with skin conductance activity. These results emphasize the role of pupil response and related increased sympathetic activity associated with emotional arousal. Since business success is strongly built on proper decision making, it would be interesting to explore whether entrepreneurs process information in a different way compared to non-entrepreneurs. Detailed information could be gathered by looking at eye tracking to understand information processing as well as emotional arousal.

Electrodermal activity: skin conductance (SC) and skin conductance response (SCR)

How do they work? The body skin shields our body from external agents, maintains water balance, and prevents overheating or overcooling. These functions are mainly controlled by vasoconstriction and vasodilation as well as by the activity of sweat glands. Since the skin plays a fundamental role for the equilibrium of some of the most important parameters of our body (such as temperature and water balance), it is not surprising that the brain is continuously connected with the skin. Since the dynamic and multifunctional activity of the skin is largely understood, psychophysiologists traditionally looked at electrodermal activity as a privileged source of information to infer nervous and cognitive activity. Sweat glands (skin sensors) are of two kinds: (1) *apocrine* and (2) *eccrine.* Yet, the latter have received considerably more attention due to their prominent role in thermoregulation. However, since palmar and plantar surfaces have a high density of eccrine glands, it is posited that these glands are also responsive to psychological stimuli and emotional sweating.

Electrodermal activity reflects the activity of eccrine glands. Due to its simplicity, the SC is the most studied form of electrodermal activity. It indicates the degree of conductance of a small flow of current through the skin. The SC reflects the activity of eccrine sweating, exclusively controlled by the sympathetic nervous system. Eccrine glands' activity (sweating) increases the number of electrolytes on the skin. The more sweated is the skin, the less resistance is met when a small electrical current flows between two surface electrodes. Skin conductance unit is the microsimens, whereas the resistance is expressed in kilohm (KΩ).

The SC measurement can be observed as an oscillation between tonic and phasic activity. Tonic SC indicates changes in conductance level of the skin that are not causally related to an experimental stimulus. These changes usually have a duration that ranges from ten seconds to one minute. Contrarily, phasic SC indicates conductance changes induced by stimulus presentation and it is elicited within five seconds from the stimulus. Phasic increase of skin conductance shortly after stimulus presentation is labeled as skin conductance response (SCR). Normally, the SCR is defined as an increase of 0.05 microsimens of the individual baseline at rest. The SCR must be observed within five seconds after stimulus onset. Traditionally, the SCR has been considered as a marker of emotional evaluation of stimuli. This marker has been particularly used in decision-making studies in both experimental and clinical domains.

The SCR has also been suggested to reflect the general state of arousal and alertness. When arousing stimuli activate the cognitive system, the body responds by stimulating the eccrine glands. This mechanism has been explained as a preparation to grasp. Indeed, an increment of the eccrine glands' activity leads to better sensitivity of the receptors placed on the palms' surface.

Advantages of electrodermal activity tracking   Electrodermal activity tracking has been broadly used in psychophysiological studies. The main advantage of this technique is that electrodermal activity offers unique indicators of emotional processes and arousal level. Similar to other psychophysiological methods, electrodermal activity trackers provide continuous data of electrical activity of the skin. Further, electrodermal activity is easily detectable and, therefore, offers reliable and consistent results. Finally, the available instruments are unobtrusive and non-distracting for the study subjects. Indeed, modern and very compact devices are easy to wear and are available on the market for an average cost of about $450.

Disadvantages of electrodermal activity tracking Electrodermal activity is not a constraint-free method. In fact, compared to other electrophysiological approaches, electrodermal activity (in particular the galvanic skin response, GSR) is slower than other techniques. Despite the important advantages of this technique, it is important to note that the interpretation of SC is still debated. An electrodermal signal does not reflect the valence of an emotion. In other words, based on an increase of electrodermal activity, it is not possible to conclude whether a subject is experiencing positive or negative emotions, but rather only that the subject is feeling *an* emotion. Other factors can negatively impact the quality of data, such as cognitive (for example, attention) or body fatigue, environmental temperature (people sweat more in warm environments), and predictability of experimental design (repetitive tasks suppress galvanic responses). Thus, to avoid data misunderstandings, it is highly recommended to associate this approach with other complementary techniques.

What research questions can be answered using electrodermal activity? SCR has been largely used within the very influential theoretical framework of the "somatic marker hypothesis" (for an application in economic decisions see Bechara and Damasio, 2005). The somatic marker hypothesis posited that several somatic markers (psychophysiological indexes) are associated with the normal functioning of a brain area called the ventromedial prefrontal cortex (VMPFC). This area takes strategic decisions and, if impaired, economic and strategic thinking is weakened. In fact, when this region is lesioned, the functioning of SCR is compromised as compared to healthy individuals. For example, van't Wout et al. (2006) studied physiological responses to unfair offers in an economic game (Ultimatum Game). The authors observed a significantly larger increase of the SCR for unfair offers. In addition, the SCR was also associated with the rejection of unfair offers. The authors posited that the SCR to unfairness is the consequence of emotional arousal (negative emotion). Interestingly, increase of the SCR only followed unfair offers from human players, but not when offers were made by the computer. Thus, the SCR supports the hypothesis that emotional arousal (such as feelings of inequality or unfairness) plays an important role in economic and strategic decision making. This research could be extended to study the relationship between investors and entrepreneurs (Bellavitis, Filatotchev and Kamuriwo, 2014). This type of study could extend the paper of Busenitz et al. (2004). Their findings showed that when entrepreneurs were treated in a procedurally fair manner, the chances for venture success improved.

The role of emotions in decision making is also supported by other articles (Bechara et al., 1999; Bechara et al., 2005). These studies showed that patients with impaired VMPFC failed in several economic games and did not show any SCR modulation in response to fair conditions or losses. This shows that the SCR (somatic marker) can be an optimal index to infer information about emotional arousal, decision making, and behavior. Moreover, it might contribute to exploring inefficient entrepreneurial decision-making strategies.

Along with the main theoretical framework of somatic marker hypothesis, few studies also used skin conductance and other psychophysiological indexes to test real-time, fast-changing somatic responses to financial events. Lo and Repin (2002) investigated the role of emotions in financial decision making, taking into account skin conductance and blood parameters. Ten professional traders participated in the experiment. The authors found significant differences in skin conductance during transient markets events as well as a higher cardiovascular response with high market volatility. Interestingly, they observed a significantly different psychophysiological response between highly experienced and low-experienced traders. Similar studies could be conducted to explore differences between first-time entrepreneurs and serial entrepreneurs.

These studies highlight the potentiality of electrodermal techniques. The SCR might be a fruitful index to explore entrepreneurial behavior. It provides a window on fast-changing emotional processes and it might help to disentangle factors that make successful entrepreneurs. For example, electrodermal activity might be useful to explore how partners build successful collaboration (trustworthiness), or how investors (for example, venture capitalists) react to certain investment proposals, comparing emotional and experience-related responses to investment opportunities. Table 3.3 compares the various psychophysiological indexes.

GENETICS, HORMONES, AND BEHAVIOR

In this section we introduce a second group of methodologies that offer an outlook on biological, genetic, and chemical backgrounds of cognitive

Table 3.3 Differences between psychophysiological indexes

Method	ECG	HR	BP	EMG	EOG	Eye Tracking	SCR
Organ	Heart	Heart	Heart	Muscles	Ocular muscles	Eye	Skin
Basic principle	Electrical impulses	Electrical impulses	Blood pressure	Muscular contraction	Ocular movements	Corneal reflection	Eccrine glands
Unit of measurement	Millivolt (mV)	bmp	MmHG	Microvolt (µV)	Millivolt (mV)	HZ	Microsimens (µS)
Detector	Electrodes	Electrodes	Arm cuff	Electrodes	Electrodes	Eye tracker	Electrodes
Temporal resolution	0.04 sec	NA	NA	1–5 ms	40 Hz	From 0.5 ms (2 000 Hz)	Up to 5 sec
Spatial resolution	NA	NA	NA	Variable	1 degree or less	From 0.15° visual arc	NA
Size	Compact	Compact	Small	Compact	Compact	Compact	Compact
Mobility	Portable	Portable	Portable	Portable	Portable	Portable/wearable/ Fixed	Portable
Areas of interest	Clinical application, Psychophysiology and biofeedback	Clinical application, Psychophysiology and biofeedback	Clinical application, Psychophysiology and biofeedback	Clinical application, Psychophysiology and biofeedback	Clinical application, Psychophysiology and biofeedback	Clinical application, Psychophysiology, Marketing	Clinical application, Psychophysiology and biofeedback
Applications	Clinical disorders, emotions, stress, attention	Clinical disorders, emotions, stress, attention	Clinical disorders, emotion, stress, attention	Clinical disorders, emotions, stress, attention	Reading disorders, attention, saccades, eye movements	Decision making, attention, spatial exploration	Emotional arousal, stress
Cost (approx)	From $400	From $150	From $50	From $300	From $300	From $500	From $250

functions and behaviors. Genetics can be crucial to develop the field of entrepreneurship, offering an innovative and powerful set of tools to investigate behavioral and cognitive patterns of entrepreneurs. As we previously introduced, scholars can indirectly investigate the neural and physiological correlates of human behavior. However, nowadays, a range of available techniques allows researchers to investigate precursors of behaviors, including entrepreneurial behavior. These tools can shed light over important questions related to natural (genetics-based) or nurtured (education-based) origins of entrepreneurial attitude, as well as on individual differences between successful and non-successful entrepreneurs. Here, two common approaches are presented: (1) behavioral genetics and (2) neuro-psychoendocrinology approach.

Behavioral Genetics

Behavioral genetics is a modern, interdisciplinary field that aims to weight the contribution of genetic components (*nature*) versus environmental ones (*nurture*: for example, education, family, personal experiences) on human behavior. Understanding the impact of nature as opposed to experiences is germane to contextualize human behavior. Genetic studies allow researchers to comprehend to what extent each factor determines personality and cognitive traits; how genetics and the environment shape a person's choices (such as to be an entrepreneur), behavior, and skills (such as leadership or decision-making skills). Moreover, behavioral genetics offers the chance to investigate whether there are common psychobiological patterns among people who share determined traits such as high resilience, tolerance to stress, and leadership skills. Importantly, considering the complexity of genetic studies, multiple levels of inquiry need to be taken into consideration.

There are two main non-mutually exclusive approaches to explore behavior. On one hand, researchers can address the genetic underpinnings of behavior by directly exploring the DNA structure and its genes localization. This approach largely uses animal models and advanced methodologies (such as the localization of a specific gene on a chromosome). Considering the complexity of these methodologies, they will not be covered in this section.

On the other hand, behavioral genetic studies quantify the contribution of both genetic traits and environmental influence. This approach aims to disentangle the nature–nurture issue exploring behavioral differences among individuals of specific populations (such as a family). Therefore, behavioral genetics addresses questions such as "are behavioral and personality traits inherited?". "If so, what genes explain family resemblances and differences among individuals?" "Are entrepreneurs born or made?" Since answers to these questions are fundamental for entrepreneurship researchers, it is not surprising that numerous researchers (Nicolaou et al., 2008; Nicolaou and Shane, 2010; van der Loos et al., 2011; Zhang et al., 2009) have used this approach to shed light on the genetic components of entrepreneurship. For example, Nicolaou et al. (2008) compared the activity of twins to suggest that genetics exert a strong impact on entrepreneurship, while environment and upbringing have little impact. We will elaborate more on the existing research in the following sections.

Thus, in this section we focus on the classical methodologies used in behavioral genetics: (1) family studies, (2) twin studies, and (3) adoption studies. Family studies are common to investigate the genetic effects on cognitive, behavioral, and psychological development. These studies are also very useful to disentangle the *nature* versus *nurture* question. The most common design involves the analysis of DNA from participants' blood. Researchers can observe the correlation between the presence (or absence) of specific genes and the observed behavior, and consequently infer causality between genes and behaviors.

However, family studies' results are at risk of being confounded with environmental factors. Family members often share a similar environment that, potentially, can have a strong influence on behavior. Hence, it is difficult to discern the effect of family genes (common to family members) and environment on behavioral outcomes. For instance, within a family where both the parents and the children are entrepreneurs, it cannot be implied that certain genes inherited by the children are the main cause to choose an entrepreneurial career. The environment might have played an even stronger role. For example, a local school in which entrepreneurship-related courses are taught, or the education received from the parents (which is different from the genetic inheritance), might be the cause of the children's career choices.

Twin studies offer an alternative tool to disentangle the effect of *nature* and *nurturing*. Twins can be monozygotic (*identical twins*) or dizygotic (*fraternal* twins). Identical twins share the identical genotype (the collection of genes in the DNA sequence) and have a very similar phenotype (observable characteristics, genes expression). Fraternal twins, share 50 percent of their genes, and have a different phenotype. Considering that identical twins share 100 percent of their genetic make-up, they are (1) more likely to show very similar behavioral and personality phenotypes (Plomin et al., 1977), and (2) they resemble each other more than fraternal twins.

Identical and fraternal twins differ only in the amount of DNA shared. At the same time both kind of twins share the same age and environment, and receive similar parental care. These peculiarities offer unique research opportunities to investigate the role of genetics and environment on behavioral phenotype. For example, when an observed trait is shown in identical twins but not in fraternal twins, this posits in favor of a strong genetic contribution in the expression of the trait; on the other hand, if similarities are observed in both identical and fraternal twins, it might be reasonable to assume that external factors are contributing in the generation of similar traits.

Albeit this approach is largely used to investigate entrepreneurship, scientists must take into account that this is not a constraint-free approach. The main drawbacks are related to data collection. It is indeed very difficult to retrieve enough pairs of twins willing to participate in the study.[3] Another important limit is the simplistic assumption that twins share environments to the same extent.

Adoption studies are the ideal setting to disentangle the environmental effects from the genetic effects on behavior and psychological traits. Both family and twin studies investigate subjects that share, at least to some extent, both genetics and the environment. On the other hand, since adopted individuals do not share genetic traits with their parents and the other children in the family, this setting uniquely separates genetics from environmental effects. This approach offers two levels of comparisons: in an ideal setting, it would be possible to compare the behavior of an adopted person with the behavior shown by both biological and adoptive parents. If systematic similarities are observed between the subject and his/her adoptive parents, a researcher can conclude that environmental factors shape a certain behavior. The opposite behavioral pattern may indicate a stronger genetic contribution. However, data limitations make this type of study generally unfeasible.

Although adoption studies are appealing and fascinating, it is quite complicated to find study participants. Also, in most cases, for privacy reasons, it is difficult to connect the adopted children with their natural parents (and their DNA). Therefore, the limited availability of adopted individuals, as well as ethical and legal concerns (such as confidentiality) represent two serious limits of this approach. Moreover, adopting parents are on average older, wealthier, and healthier as compared to biological parents. Thus, these factors must be considered when conducting this kind of investigation.

Taken together, in this section we presented the three most common methodologies in behavioral genetics. Each of these methods has advantages and disadvantages that permit investigation of the relationship between *nature* and *nurture* from different perspectives. Importantly, this nature/nurture contribution should *not* be considered as a dualistic relation but as a continuum. The two concurrently contribute to the behavioral phenotype. Multidisciplinary approaches are nowadays available and behavioral genetics is gaining popularity among the scientific community.

What research questions can be answered using behavioral genetics?
A large amount of research questions can be addressed using this technique. Even in entrepreneurship research a number of studies emerged in recent years. For example, numerous papers explored the heritability of certain behavioral phenotypes, such as creativity or the ability to identify business opportunities (Nicolaou et al., 2009; Shane and Nicolaou, 2015), self-employment (Nicolaou and Shane, 2010), personality traits (Shane et al., 2010), and entrepreneurial ability (Barnea et al., 2010; Nicolaou et al., 2008). Comparing large samples of monozygotic with dizygotic twins, these studies found an important heritability component impact in emerging entrepreneurial behavioral patterns, whereas the environment seemed to be less crucial to generating entrepreneurial behavior. Additionally, these results are consistent both in male and female twins.

However, other studies found that the environment also influences behavior in financial situations. An interesting study from Barnea and colleagues (2010) found a significant relationship between the family environment and the behavior of young investors. Yet, family influence is short term and rapidly replaced by experience.

Future researches might explore the longitudinal and spatial contribution of genetic and environmental factors. For example, do genetics and experience impact behavior differently in different life stages? Do they reinforce each other? Certain cultures such as the Japanese generally tend to be risk (and potentially entrepreneurship) averse. Is it possible to overcome these cultural hurdles toward entrepreneurship due to certain genetic influences? Other studies might also study the contribution of these factors toward various outcomes such as entrepreneurial success, failure, opportunism, or persistence.

Other researchers compared entrepreneurial tendencies in adopted children (for example, Lindquist et al., 2015). The authors showed that, contrary to previous evidence, the influence of adoptive parents (entrepreneurs) is twice as important as the genetic contribution (biological parents). However, when adopted children are compared with natural offspring of entrepreneurs, the environmental influence is stronger in the latter group. This evidence suggests that the genes and the environment might both play a role in shaping entrepreneurial intentions and behavior.

Other researchers used the behavioral genetic approaches to investigate differences in male and female entrepreneurs. Zhang and colleagues

(2009) explored the impact of gender differences and genetic contribution on the tendency to engage in entrepreneurial behaviors by assessing two psychological traits: (1) extraversion and (2) neuroticism. The authors accounted for both identical and fraternal twins. The results showed that the female tendency to become an entrepreneur was strongly genetic-based and largely determined by both extroversion and neuroticism. In contrast, males reported the opposite pattern, showing a fundamental contribution of shared environment and extraversion.

This section has demonstrated the huge potential of genetic studies. This research method has gained popularity in recent years. Yet despite the proliferation of studies engaging in genetic research in the realm of entrepreneurship, a large number of research questions remain unanswered.

Psychoneuroendocrinology

The human brain works through the mediation of two complementary systems: (1) the nervous system based on neurotransmitters (such as dopamine or serotonin) and (2) the endocrine system mediated by hormones. Psychoneuroendocrinology investigates endocrine functions and dysfunctions. In particular, the field applies an interdisciplinary approach from several disciplines, including psychiatry, psychology, neurology, neurobiology, neurosciences, and endocrinology (Campeau et al., 1998).

Table 3.4 summarizes the main features of both nervous and endocrine systems. Both systems are fundamental for the body and regulate several functions, such as the circadian cycle, sexual desire, body temperature,

Table 3.4   Differences between nervous and endocrine systems in humans

Feature / Nervous system	Nervous System	Endocrine System
Signals	Electrical impulses (action potentials)	Chemical impulses (hormones)
Pathways	Transmission by neurons	Transported by blood
Speed of information	Fast	Slow
Duration of the effect	Short-lived	Short- or long-lived
Type of action and response	Voluntary or involuntary	Involuntary
Target	Localized (cells connected to neurons)	Often distant (many cells can be affected)

learning, appetite, metabolism, growth, and body weight. Furthermore, nervous and endocrine systems are fundamental for maintaining the natural equilibrium of the brain and the body (*homeostasis*). Broadly speaking, what we are and what we do are regulated by the state of the neuroendocrine system at a given point in time.

Neurotransmitters are chemicals that transmit inhibitory or excitatory information in the brain and all over the body. The transmission propagates along nerve bundles. The most common neurotransmitters are dopamine, GABA, serotonin, and norepinephrine. Although neurotransmitters are commonly associated with a singular function, for example dopamine is known to be related with pleasure and behavioral reinforcement, the role of neurotransmitters is complex and quantity-dependent. Moreover, many neurotransmitters can simultaneously play both excitatory and inhibitory effects.

Hormones are chemicals that are secreted directly into the blood from glands and organs such as thyroid, pancreas, gonads, and the pineal gland. Their impact is considerably slower than the one exerted by neurotransmitters, but their effect lasts longer. Insulin, testosterone, leptin, melatonin, estrogen, and cortisol are some of the most well-known hormones.[4]

Considering the concentration of neurotransmitters and hormones (and of their precursors or receptors) in the human body, and their fundamental role played, a huge amount of scientific production investigated the relation between the neuroendocrine system and behavior. For simplicity, we focus on the relationship between three of the most known chemicals and entrepreneurial phenomena: (1) dopamine, (2) cortisol, and (3) testosterone.

Dopamine is a neurotransmitter whose presence is linked with several functions such as movement, memory, attention, sleep, and mood regulation. Importantly dopamine plays a central role in reinforcing behavior by "pleasing" and "rewarding" the brain, leading to the consolidation of the neural representation of an action and the association of this action with a sensation of pleasure (Berridge and Kringelbach, 2008).

Cortisol is a key hormone that helps to maintain homeostasis. Cortisol is involved in the regulation of many body functions such as the blood glucose level, the metabolic function, the immune response, and various anti-inflammatory actions. Despite this widespread body intervention, the main function of cortisol is stress control and reaction. When people are under stress, cortisol plays a central role in generating a cascade of chemical events that drive the organisms to homeostasis. However, prolonged exposure to stressors, and the consequent presence of above-average levels of cortisol in the blood, negatively affects the capacity of the system to find its own homeostasis. This is the case of chronic stress or post-traumatic stress disorders. Moreover, researches (Simeon et al., 2007) showed a correlation between cortisol and psychological resilience (the capacity to cope with stressors and adaptation). On the other side, even a lack of cortisol negatively affects the capacity of the organism to restore homeostasis.

The most known chemical is testosterone. This hormone regulates sexual and reproductive male development. Women produce testosterone in a considerably lower amount than men. Testosterone is associated with several sexual-related functions such as development of sex organs or traits during puberty (for example, voice deepening, body-hair growth and so forth). It also drives sexual behavior and determines fat distribution. It is interesting to note that sexual development in males, and levels of testosterone, are closely related to a large set of social behaviors such as the need for dominance and competition. Indeed, in many mammals, testosterone promotes muscle growth and strength. Evidence posits in favor of higher levels of testosterone (and cortisol) in alpha males among non-humane-primates such as chimpanzees. In humans, testosterone is associated with leadership and aggression (see the review by Yildirim and Derksen, 2012). Since testosterone seems to be central to generating social and antisocial behaviors – mostly in men – it has been largely addressed as an important factor to explain individual differences between aggressive and non-aggressive personalities. In addition, it has been considered as an important factor to explain different economical decision-making behaviors (such as gamblers). However, modern research methods aim to investigate not only the role of single hormones, but the interaction of two or more. An example is the interaction between testosterone and cortisol in decision making and aggressive behavior.

What research questions can be answered using psychoneuroendocrinology?
The analysis of different hormones can offer interesting insights into entrepreneurial behavior. Considering the association between dopamine and a sensation of pleasure, this hormone is the principal candidate to explain why we love to eat our favorite dish, for example, or why individuals develop drug addiction. Similarly, a different level of dopamine precursor or receptor explains risk-seeking behavior and can be indicated as a predictor of entrepreneurial instincts. For instance, an interesting twin study from Nicolaou et al. (2011) suggested a possible connection between the presence of a gene (DRD3) that encodes a type of dopamine receptors (special protein molecules that are selectively activated by dopamine) and entrepreneurship. The authors suggested that individuals with a specific genetic makeup (that is, individuals carrying a specific variation of the

gene DRD3) are more likely to engage in entrepreneurial behaviors or other sensation-seeking activities. This might be due to higher levels of dopamine that these individuals require to "activate" rewarding circuits in their brain. However, it has to be highlighted that this work failed to be replicated in larger samples (see, for example, van der Loos et al., 2011). Thus, the dopaminergic contribution to entrepreneurial behavior is still debated and requires further attention.

Cortisol is associated with stress. Since entrepreneurs often act under stressful conditions and high uncertainty, researchers investigated cortisol as an important element that can explain individual differences between entrepreneurial and non-entrepreneurial traits (Bergen, 2011; Townsend et al., 2011). For example, Takahashi (2004) associated cortisol to time-discounting. Time-discounting refers to the degree a person prefers a small immediate reward to a bigger future reward. The author found that a lower level of cortisol predicts more impulsive behavior in intertemporal decisions. Therefore, this study might seem to suggest that the level of cortisol in the body of an individual might influence career choices (for example, self-employment as opposed to employment).

Finally, previous studies associated testosterone with competitive, aggressive, dominant, and antisocial behavior (Edwards, 1969; Mattsson et al., 1980; Scerbo and Kolko, 1994). Testosterone is traditionally considered the main candidate to investigate traits such as leadership, risk seeking, financial style of investment, and entrepreneurship. Nevertheless, its role is still debated and needs further investigation. For instance, a recent study from van der Loos et al. (2013) did not find any association between testosterone and entrepreneurial behavior, whereas Mehta and Prasad (2015) found an interaction between testosterone and cortisol in risk-taking behaviors.

In this section, we have introduced the basic concepts of psychoneuroendocrinology that can assist entrepreneurship researchers. We also indicated some of the most known chemicals that can predict, determine, or lead to entrepreneurial behavior. These chemicals can explain the neural and biological underpinnings that make an entrepreneur successful. Thus, a psychoneuroendocrinological approach represents an interesting perspective to enlarge our knowledge of entrepreneurship.

Nevertheless, we want to highlight that genetic and endocrinology components should be considered as two sides of the same coin, rather than two distinguished approaches. In fact, the endocrine system and the genes influence each other. For instance, the testosterone concentration in men is determined by specific genes and it is highly heritable. On the other side, the amount of testosterone influences the expression of determined genes (for instance appropriate levels of testosterone allow correct growth and sexual development). Thus, genetics, chemicals, and behavior are strictly interconnected and interdependent. Researchers should, therefore, design their studies accordingly.

CONCLUDING REMARKS

In this chapter we have presented several approaches and methodologies that can provide valuable insights on the neural basis of entrepreneurship. Each technique sheds light on different aspects of entrepreneurship and its biological underpinnings. The methods introduced here demonstrate how scholars and researchers can explore entrepreneurship mechanisms from different perspectives, ranging from biological aspects to more high-cognitive processes. Different techniques can be combined to provide accurate and informative insights on entrepreneurship phenomena.

As Krueger and Welpe (2014) brilliantly posited, "the entrepreneurial mindset is decidedly not a set of facts to be learned or even a set of skills to be taught, it is a way of thinking and feeling. If we need to truly understand the entrepreneurial mindset, we need to look deeper." In this chapter, we presented various tools to look deeper. We provided evidence and guidance to look at entrepreneurs' minds, hearts, eyes, and skin. Arguably, these techniques are the deepest available to today's researcher who is truly interested in understanding the primordial instincts that guide and drive entrepreneurial intentions and behaviors.

NOTES

1. http://megcommunity.org/groups-jobs/groups.
2. We recommend consulting the guidelines of the Society for Cardiological Science and Technology.
3. Some research institutes created twin registries – mainly for medical purposes – for facilitating data collection and data sharing. For example, the Swedish Twin Registry: http://ki.se/en/research/the-swedish-twin-registry; and the Australian Twin Registry: https://www.twins.org.au/.
4. Our body also produces a class of chemicals that are hormones but that act as neurotransmitters.

REFERENCES

Balconi, M. and S. Pagani (2015), "Social hierarchies and emotions: cortical prefrontal activity, facial feedback (EMG), and cognitive performance in a dynamic interaction," *Social Neuroscience*, **10** (2), 166–78.

Barnea, A., H. Cronqvist, and S. Siegel (2010), "Nature or nurture: what determines investor behavior?" *Journal of Financial Economics*, **98** (3), 583–604.

Bechara, A. and A.R. Damasio (2005), "The somatic marker hypothesis: a neural theory of economic decision," *Games and Economic Behavior*, **52** (2), 336–72.

Bechara, A., H. Damasio, A.R. Damasio, and G.P. Lee (1999), "Different contributions of the human amygdala and ventromedial prefrontal cortex to decision-making," *The Journal of Neuroscience: The Official Journal of the Society for Neuroscience*, **19** (13), 5473–81.

Bechara, A., H. Damasio, D. Tranel, and A.R. Damasio (2005), "The Iowa Gambling Task and the somatic marker hypothesis: some questions and answers," *Trends in Cognitive Sciences*, **9** (4), 159–62.

Bellavitis, C., I. Filatotchev, and D.S. Kamuriwo (2014), "The effects of intra–industry and extra-industry networks on performance: A case of venture capital portfolio firms. *Managerial and Decision Economics*, **35** (2), 129–44.

Bellavitis, C., I. Filatotchev, and V. Souitaris (2016), "The impact of investment networks on venture capital firm performance: A contingency framework." *British Journal of Management*, **28**: 102–19.

Bellavitis, C., I. Filatotchev, D.S. Kamuriwo, and T. Vanacker (2017), "Entrepreneurial finance: New frontiers of research and practice. *Venture Capital*, **19** (1-2): 1–16.

Bellebaum, C. and M. Colosio (2014), "From feedback- to response-based performance monitoring in active and observational learning," *Journal of Cognitive Neuroscience*, **26** (9), 2111–27.

Bergen, C.W. Von (2011), "Too much positive thinking hinders entrepreneur success," *Journal of Business and Entrepreneurship*, **23** (1), 30–53.

Berridge, K.C. and M.L. Kringelbach (2008), "Affective neuroscience of pleasure: reward in humans and animals," *Psychopharmacology*, **199** (3), 457–80.

Blignaut, P. and D. Wium (2013), "Eye-tracking data quality as affected by ethnicity and experimental design," *Behavior Research Methods*, **46** (1), 67–80.

Bradley, M.M., L. Miccoli, M.A. Escrig, and P.J. Lang (2008), "The pupil as a measure of emotional arousal and autonomic activation," *Psychophysiology*, **45** (4), 602–7.

Burle, B., L. Spieser, C. Roger, L. Casini, T. Hasbroucq, and F. Vidal (2015), "Spatial and temporal resolutions of EEG: is it really black and white? A scalp current density view," *International Journal of Psychophysiology: Official Journal of the International Organization of Psychophysiology*, **97** (3), 210–20.

Busenitz, L.W., J.O. Fiet, and D.D. Moesel (2004), "Reconsidering the venture capitalists' 'value added' proposition: an interorganizational learning perspective," *Journal of Business Venturing*, **19** (6), 787–807.

Campeau, S., H.E.W. Day, D.L. Helmreich, S. Kollack-Walker, and S.J. Watson (1998), "Principles of psychoneuroendocrinology," *Psychiatric Clinics of North America*, **21** (2), 259–76.

Clancy, E., E. Morin, and R. Merletti (2002), "Sampling, noise-reduction and amplitude estimation issues in surface electromyography," *Journal of Electromyography and Kinesiology*, **12** (1), 1–16.

Edwards, D.A. (1969), "Early androgen stimulation and aggressive behavior in male and female mice," *Physiology & Behavior*, **4** (3), 333–8.

Freund, H.J. (1983), "Motor unit and muscle activity in voluntary motor control," *Physiological Reviews*, **63** (2), 387–436.

Grech, R., T. Cassar, J. Muscat, K.P. Camilleri, S.G. Fabri, M. Zervakis, and B. Vanrumste (2008), "Review on solving the inverse problem in EEG source analysis," *Journal of Neuroengineering and Rehabilitation*, **5**, 25.

Hüsser, A., and W. Wirth (2014), "Do investors show an attentional bias toward past performance? An eye-tracking experiment on visual attention to mutual fund disclosures in simplified fund prospectuses," *Journal of Financial Services Marketing*, **19** (3), 169–85.

Ioannides, A.A., L. Liu, D. Theofilou, J. Dammers, T. Burne, T. Ambler, and S. Rose (2000), "Real time processing of affective and cognitive stimuli in the human brain extracted from MEG signals," *Brain Topography*, **13** (1), 11–16.

Koelsch, S., J. Enge, and S. Jentschke (2012), "Cardiac signatures of personality," *PloS One*, **7** (2), e31441.

Krueger, N. (2008), "The influence of cognitive appraisal & anticipated outcome emotions on the perception, evaluation & exploitation of social entrepreneurial opportunities (summary)," *Frontiers of Entrepreneurship Research*, 28 (6), article 10, accessed 17 April 2017 at http://digitalknowledge.babson.edu/fer/vol28/iss6/10.

Krueger, N. and I. Welpe (2014), "Neuroentrepreneurship: what can entrepreneurship learn from neuroscience?," in Michael H. Morris (ed), *Annals of Entrepreneurship: Education and Pedagogy*, United States Association for Small Business and Entrepreneurship.

Künecke, J., A. Hildebrandt, G. Recio, W. Sommer, and O. Wilhelm (2014), "Facial EMG responses to emotional expressions are related to emotion perception ability," *PloS One*, **9** (1), e84053.

Lawrence, A., L. Clark, J.N. Labuzetta, B. Sahakian, and S. Vyakarnum (2008), "The innovative brain," *Nature*, **456** (7219), 168–9.

Lindquist, M.J., J. Sol, and M. Van Praag (2015), "Why do entrepreneurial parents have entrepreneurial children?" *Journal of Labor Economics*, 33 (2), 269–96.

Lo, A.W. and D. Repin Dmitry (2002), "The psychophysiology of real-time financial risk processing," *Journal of Cognitive Neuroscience*, **8508**, 323–39.

Mattsson, Å., D. Schalling, D. Olweus, H. Löw, and J. Svensson (1980), "Plasma testosterone, aggressive behavior, and personality dimensions in young male delinquents," *Journal of the American Academy of Child Psychiatry*, **19** (3), 476–90.

Mehta, P.H. and S. Prasad (2015), "The dual-hormone hypothesis: a brief review and future research agend," *Current Opinion in Behavioral Sciences*, **3**, 163–8.

Nicolaou, N. and S. Shane (2010), "Entrepreneurship and occupational choice: genetic and environmental influences," *Journal of Economic Behavior & Organization*, **76** (1), 3–14.

Nicolaou, N., S. Shane, G. Adi, M. Mangino, and J. Harris (2011), "A polymorphism associated with entrepreneurship: evidence from dopamine receptor candidate genes," *Small Business Economics*, **36** (2), 151–5.

Nicolaou, N., S. Shane, L. Cherkas, J. Hunkin, and T.O. Spector (2008), "Is the tendency to engage in entrepreneurship genetic?" *Management Science*, **54** (1), 167–79.

Nicolaou, N., S. Shane, L. Cherkas, and T.D. Spector (2009), "Opportunity recognition and the tendency to be an entrepreneur: a bivariate genetics perspective," *Organizational Behavior and Human Decision Processes*, **110** (2), 108–17.

Pearson, K.G. (1993), "Common principles of motor control in vertebrates and invertebrates," *Annual Review of Neuroscience*, **16**, 265–97.

Pickering, T.G., J.E. Hall, L.J. Appel, B.E. Falkner, J. Graves, M.N. Hill, . . . and E.J. Roccella (2005), "Recommendations for blood pressure measurement in humans and experimental animals: blood pressure measurement in humans: a statement for professionals from the subcommittee of professional and public education of the American Heart Association cou," *Hypertension*, **45** (1), 142–61.

Plomin, R., J.C. DeFries, and J.C. Loehlin (1977), "Genotype-environment interaction and correlation in the analysis of human behavior," *Psychological Bulletin*, **84** (2), 309–22.

Scerbo, A.S. and D.J. Kolko (1994), "Salivary testosterone and cortisol in disruptive children: relationship to aggressive, hyperactive, and internalizing behaviors," *Journal of the American Academy of Child and Adolescent Psychiatry*, **33** (8), 1174–84.

Shane, S. and N. Nicolaou (2015), "Creative personality, opportunity recognition and the tendency to start businesses: a study of their genetic predispositions," *Journal of Business Venturing*, **30** (3), 407–19.

Shane, S., N. Nicolaou, L. Cherkas, and T.D. Spector (2010), "Genetics, the Big Five, and the tendency to be self-employed," *Journal of Applied Psychology*, **95** (6), 1154–62.

Shapiro, D., L.D. Jamner, I.B. Goldstein, and R.J. Delfino (2001), "Striking a chord: moods, blood pressure, and heart rate in everyday life," *Psychophysiology*, **38** (2), 197–204.

Simeon, D., R. Yehuda, R. Cunill, M. Knutelska, F.W. Putnam, and L.M. Smith (2007), "Factors associated with resilience in healthy adults," *Psychoneuroendocrinology*, **32** (8–10), 1149–52.

Studer, B., A. Pedroni, and J. Rieskamp (2013), "Predicting risk-taking behavior from prefrontal resting-state activity and personality," *PloS One*, **8** (10), e76861.

Takahashi, T. (2004), "Cortisol levels and time-discounting of monetary gain in humans," *Neuroreport*, **15** (13), 2145–7.

Tallon-Baudry, C., F. Meyniel, and S. Bourgeois-Gironde (2011), "Fast and automatic activation of an abstract representation of money in the human ventral visual pathway," *PloS One*, **6** (11), e28229.

Townsend, S.S.M., B. Major, C.E. Gangi, and W.B. Mendes (2011), "From 'in the air' to 'under the skin': cortisol responses to social identity threat," *Personality & Social Psychology Bulletin*, **37** (2), 151–64.

van't Wout, M., R.S. Kahn, A.G. Sanfey, and A. Aleman (2006), "Affective state and decision-making in the ultimatum game," *Experimental Brain Research*, **169** (4), 564–8.

van der Loos, M.J.H.M., R. Haring, C.A. Rietveld, S.E. Baumeister, P.J.F. Groenen, A. Hofman, and A.R. Thurik (2013), "Serum testosterone levels in males are not associated with entrepreneurial behavior in two independent observational studies," *Physiology & Behavior*, **119**, 110–14.

van der Loos, M.J.H.M., P.D. Koellinger, P.J.F. Groenen, C.A. Rietveld, F. Rivadeneira, F.J.A. van Rooij, and A.R. Thurik (2011), "Candidate gene studies and the quest for the entrepreneurial gene," *Small Business Economics*, **37** (3), 269–75.

Vieito, J.P., A.F. da Rocha, and F.T. Rocha (2015), "Brain activity of the investor's stock market financial decision," *Journal of Behavioral Finance*, **16** (3), 220–30.

Wu, Y., E. van Dijk, and L. Clark (2015), "Near-wins and near-losses in gambling: a behavioral and facial EMG study," *Psychophysiology*, **52** (3), 359–66.

Yildirim, B.O. and J.J.L. Derksen (2012), "A review on the relationship between testosterone and life-course persistent antisocial behavior," *Psychiatry Research*, **200** (2–3), 984–1010.

Zhang, Z., M.J. Zyphur, J. Narayanan, R.D. Arvey, S. Chaturvedi, B.J. Avolio, . . . and G. Larsson (2009), "The genetic basis of entrepreneurship: effects of gender and personality," *Organizational Behavior and Human Decision Processes*, **110** (2), 93–107.

4. Unpacking neuroentrepreneurship: conducting entrepreneurship research with EEG technologies
Pablo Martin De Holan and Cyril Couffe

We need to shake vigorously the forest of our dormant neurons; we need to shake them with the emotion of the new, and infuse in them noble and elevated quests . . . Neurons are cells of a delicate and elegant form, the mysterious butterflies of the soul whose wing movement perhaps will shed light, one day, over the secrets of our mind.

Santiago Ramón y Cajal (1888)
1906 Nobel Prize in Medicine and Physiology for pioneering work in neuroscience

INTRODUCTION

Entrepreneurship is a human endeavor that consists in detecting, transforming, and profiting from problems whose solution creates economic and/or social value, through the adequate management of a highly uncertain, non-linear, and risky process consisting of a series of sequential activities that go from a vague idea and a vague desire to a fully functioning organization. Thus defined, entrepreneurship is a human activity that shapes, to a large extent, the way one deals with forces that are beyond one's control and with life itself: it is the mechanism through which we comprehend, plan for, and deal with life, and its intractable uncertainty.

Entrepreneurship is emerging as a discipline and it is still finding its own voice. Yet, it is commonly accepted that many if not most of the activities carried out by entrepreneurs are impossible without high-level, sophisticated cognitive functions that are in turn made possible by the functioning of our brain, strongly suggesting that some of its features and limitations have relevant consequences for that process. While entrepreneurship scholars are just beginning to use the tools of neuroscience for their discipline (Laureiro-Martínez et al., 2014; Martin de Holan et al., 2013; Ortiz-Terán et al., 2013), their love of the mind and its workings has a long research tradition mainly interested in how activities that are, at their core, mental processes, impact or influence entrepreneurial antecedents (Goodale et al., 2011), narratives (Garud and Giuliani, 2013), drive (Armstrong and Hird, 2009), agency (Townsend, 2012), imagination (Cornelissen, 2013), cognition (R.K. Mitchell et al., 2002), knowledge (Shane, 2000), intuition (J.R. Mitchell et al., 2005), and even mindsets (J.M. Haynie et al., 2010) to try to understand the connection between the activities of the mind and action or lack thereof in a context of entrepreneurial activity.

Yet, for want of a tool that would allow us to observe and comprehend these operating processes, researchers generally have focused on secondary proxy measures, some of very good quality but rarely as good as the original. Consequently, it is common to study what entrepreneurs are or have (attributes) or what they do (behaviors), instead of what they think, how they think, and of course why they think the way they do and how they came to think that way because, as Ramón y Cajal noted over 100 years ago, "every man can be, if he wants, a sculptor of his own brain" and it can be safely assumed that this property extends to other genders as well.

In this chapter, we argue that this methodological limitation is being lifted by new technologies and by the new use of old ones, and propose concrete ways to incorporate one of the tools of neuroscience, the electroencephalogram (EEG), into the study of phenomena of interest for entrepreneurship scholars as a complementary, triangulating tool for our current research methodologies, and probably also as a central one. We argue here that advances in neurosciences and technological platforms upon which they are built are creating connection between researchers' theoretical ambitions and their implicit methodological and practical consequences. Indeed, the techniques and tools of neuroscience have provided a better understanding of the topology and functionality of the brain, and are providing an early understanding of how it works during the processes of interest to entrepreneurship (for example, ideation, effectuation, opportunity detection and so on).

As has been the case with medicine, early progress began with studies of brain pathology, accidental or disease-generated (Damasio et al., 1994; Ratiu et al., 2004, and well before that, Bigelow, 1850; Broca, 1861), all of which based their conclusions in the psychological and somatic changes that patients had experienced after some traumatic event, and the comparison with their abilities prior to those given a discrete damage to the brain. Yet, since these accidents or diseases were exceedingly rare, involved expansive damage to parts of the brain and the body simultaneously, and often were accompanied by additional and undesirable physical symptoms that clouded their understanding, extrapolating from them had obvious limitations. Consequently, scientists had to make inferences about human behavior and even nature from either animal studies (in some cases not even mammals), or extreme, "noisy" human cases to construct general theories, but the obvious route of trying to understand how the brain is activated remained off limits for lack of an adequate tool of inquiry, forcing scientists to infer normal processes from pathological situations.

Even today, many of the dominant theories in the social sciences are built from the explicit manifestations of some hypothesized but unrevealed thought process, natural state of the mind, or deep force that guides them both. The most obvious example is self-interest, a core assumption of several economic theories taking base on the assertions of Adam Smith, when he claimed that "it is not from the benevolence of the butcher, the brewer, or the baker, that we can expect our dinner, but from their regard to their own interest" (Smith, [1776] 2000), which presumes that most of the time the well-being of self is weighted more strongly than the welfare of others and that calculation is made constantly and as accurately as possible, and repeated before any meaningful decision. Assuming this is true, it should be possible, at least theoretically, to see how the brain understands the situations, how it assesses its interest, how it compares one's interest to someone else's, and whether this is a decision based on pure reason, emotions, or a combination of both, and, if so, in what sequence.

In comparison with other disciplines such as psychology, marketing, or economics, entrepreneurship has been slow to adopt and adapt neuroscience's tools, for three reasons at least. The first is the byzantine complexity of the technologies, adding a biological layer to any research question that entrepreneurship scholars may want to design, for which most researchers are not prepared. Then, to combine neuroscience and entrepreneurship or any social science, there is an incontrovertible need to build and manage research teams that are truly multidisciplinary (including scientists used to dealing with the specificities of these data and technicians who know how to operate these machines, and of course statisticians to deal with that data and be able to convert it into variables), with all the complexities inherent to it. Then, the complexity of the brain itself, which obliges researchers to ride steep learning curves to translate research questions into meaningful studies. Finally, the cost: using EEG is laborious and can become quite resource-intensive, and using functional magnetic resonance imaging (fMRI) prohibitively so, even if the machine itself has already been bought.

The aim of this chapter is to review and unpack EEG technology and its advantages and pitfalls, with an emphasis on its use by researchers interested in entrepreneurship. We focus on our experience using EEG in general and as an effective, affordable mechanism to study and analyze entrepreneurship processes through neuroscience, and, based on what we know about EEG in other social-science disciplines, we suggest a path that could help other researchers to use such methodologies in their study. This chapter is structured as follows. After briefly presenting the physical and technological dimensions of EEG, we discuss its potential for entrepreneurship research in general and cognition in particular, and highlight some of its limitations. We then present our experience designing and carrying out such studies, and conclude with potential lines of inquiry where this technology could be of benefit for other research streams. In so doing, we hope to contribute to increase the use of this proven and promised technology in organization studies, helping define those circumstances that are particularly adequate for its use.

EEG: HISTORY AND PHYSICS

An early device that detected and rudimentarily measured brainwaves was invented in 1924 by Hans Berger, a German psychiatrist (Sur and Sinha, 2009). At the time, the reaction of the scientific community was overwhelmingly negative, as it was very skeptical of the very notion of the possibility of recording mental states with a physical apparatus (Ellingson, 1990). However, once its results proved to be accurate for the diagnostic of a series of brain states, pathological or not, its scientific acceptance grew and rapidly it became a standard way to test brain activity. This was achieved thanks to advances in three different areas: the discovery and understanding of several specific brainwaves, the refinement of extracting methods, and towards the end of the twentieth century, the significant reduction in the cost of computing power and the increased sophistication of the machines and the software used to extract and later analyze its data.

For many decades since its discovery, EEG remained the only non-invasive method to observe features of the brain at work, and even today it continues to be one of the most widely used methods in cognitive neuroscience. Neuroscience technologies (EEG, fMRI and derivatives), due to their great explanatory power and their incontrovertible useful-ness for medicine and psychology, gradually diffused to other disciplines interested in deciphering the way our brain reacts to stimuli, basic or complex: strategy (Powell, 2011), leadership (Waldman et al., 2011), organizational behavior (Becker et al, 2011), marketing (McClure et al., 2004), ergonomics (Shen et al., 2008), and human–computer interaction (Sourina et al., 2012), among many others. More recently, Laureiro-Martínez and associates used ingenious fMRI techniques to contrast the areas of the brain and the processes associated with the activities known as exploitation and exploration, showing that each activity differs markedly from the other and mobilizes different brain resources. In addition, results also suggest that a stronger activation of the brain areas that control attention allows subjects to make better decisions (Laureiro-Martínez et al., 2014).

What the brain does matters, and EEG measures it by taking advantage of the properties of the electromagnetic force to detect brain electrical activity caused by columns of neurons being activated. Specifically, EEG detects and quantifies the changes in the electrical potential energy (voltage) between two points, caused in this case by ionic currents inside the neurons (brain cells). Indeed, brain activity is characterized by three main, distinct, and interacting physical phenomena: the electrical activation of the brain cells; the exchange of neurotransmitters at the synaptic level between neurons, leading to the exchange of specific chemicals that bind to their receptors and shape our consciousness of the world; and the physical antecedents and consequences of these processes, such as increased blood flows and varying levels of oxygen at the brain caused by our constant interaction with the world. All cognitive processes, the ones that require deep introspection and the ones that do not, are the result of a sequence of complex activities of the brain in close interaction with the rest of the nervous system, the body at large, and the person's environment, and obviously higher thought processes require a much more complex and onerous series of activities, at different moments, in different sequences, and having very likely had a different genesis depending on individual and social circumstances.

Thanks to the capacity of electrical currents to generate electromagnetic signals that move beyond thick solid objects such as the skull, EEG allows for monitoring the electrical activity occurring inside the brain non-invasively at the surface of the scalp. This is achieved through electrodes (current sensors) that are either stuck one by one to the patient's head with conductive putty or are incorporated into a neoprene helmet worn by the patients, whose cables in either case are connected to the EEG machine (see Figure 4.1)

EEG is the most used non-invasive brain-imaging device, for several technical and practical reasons: it has a quite good temporal resolution (that is, the delay between signal and detection is low and approaching real time); it is relatively easy to use, especially compared with similar technologies; and it is less expensive than the alternatives and also portable – all of which sharply contrast with the much greater complexity and cost of other technologies. We explore these below.

Figure 4.1   Standard helmets with electrodes for adults and children

BRAIN ELECTRICAL ACTIVITY: BRIEF CHARACTERISTICS

The idea that human condition is significantly determined by activities of the brain and its functioning (Raichle, 2010) has become the standard yardstick to define what life is in most of the developed world: a body may survive its brain, but when our brain dies our "universe disappears" and our organs can be harvested legally and the body laid to rest (Lock, 2002).[1] As long as there is meaningful electrical activity in the brain, a person is deemed to be alive.

Two categories can be distinguished when looking at the electrical activities of the brain: those that are induced by some external or internal force (an activity, a stimulus), and the ones that are spontaneous and uncontrollable. The brain is constantly active, but the nature and magnitude of that activity varies according to the type of task that is being carried away by the subject (voluntary/involuntary, pleasant/unpleasant, automatic/requiring cognitive processing, and so on), the state of consciousness of the person (asleep/awake, distracted/concentrated, alert/tired, and so on), the person's emotional state (happy/sad, angry/tranquil, for example), and also the environmental conditions surrounding the subject. All of these can be studied in baseline situations, or under other conditions. For example, while conducting an EEG on a subject without any stimuli other than the ones a normal person would receive when comfortably seated in a quiet room without distraction, the subject's brain electrical activity would be observed as waveforms varying in duration (milliseconds), frequency (in hertz or oscillations per second), amplitude (in microvolts Mv), polarity (negative or positive), and shape, all of which would then be translated into machine-readable data. Other relevant variables can be measured and attached to the existing data: the moment when the event or stimulus happens, its latency (time elapsed between the event and the peak of the electrical signal in the brain), the sequence of events that led to it, and the part or parts of the brain that are activated prior, after, and during that moment.

For example, one of the most documented waves issued from visual studies is the P100, a brainwave present within the posterior part of the brain after the appearance of any visual stimulus. The first letter P means that the polarity is positive, and 100 means that the mean latency is around 100 ms. Figure 4.2 depicts an example of what brainwave patterns could look like during a visual ERP procedure. After introducing the event, several components happening sequentially can be found. Early components, happening before 150 ms such as the P100 and the N100,

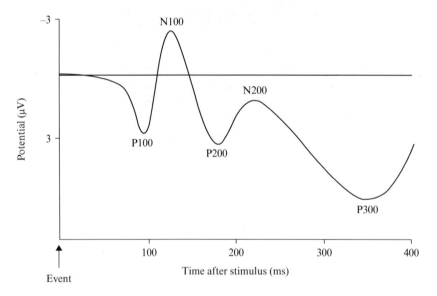

Figure 4.2   An example of a brainwave pattern during a visual ERP

represent the early processing of visual stimuli. Later components, like the N200 and the P300, are related to cognitive processing and are sometimes used to demonstrate variations between different classes of participants (Takeda et al., 1993).

EVENT-RELATED POTENTIALS

Voluntary reaction to stimuli is the preferred alternative when carrying out research with EEG. Observing how and under what circumstances a person reacts to an induced stimulus allows researchers to observe, analyze, and theorize about the different parts of the brain involved in that task, and how it is performed. Such induced brain activity is achieved typically through an approach called event-related potential (ERP), a research design that seeks to measure the mental processes related to the stimulus of interest, observing our reactions to what is called an "event." Because of the physical limitations of the brain, its specialization by areas, and the time and energy it needs to carry out these activities, reactions to stimuli appear sequentially in a process that can be described with great detail, and associated with the specialization of each area being activated.

While theoretically any mode of stimulation could be used to produce events, for practical reasons most researchers manipulate visual or auditory stimuli to produce voluntary or involuntary reactions depending on the objective of the study. The overall goal of the technique is to record, and later interpret, the specific brain activity provoked by this event in order to (1) infer the temporal aspects of its processing and the sequence of processing; (2) compare how different categories, some of them social such as education, wealth, or gender, react to the same events to show what separates them, and, (3) understand the sources and consequences of these differences. Response components are classified according to the variables mentioned above, to create a corpus of data that can be later aggregated with that of other subjects, and analyzed according to research design and need.

While recording an ERP, the electrical activity associated with the event is confounded with the spontaneous brain activity during each single trial, reducing its noise/signal ratio. To correct for this, each task is repeated multiple times by the same subject, correcting the unsystematic bias with a regression to the mean that helps highlight the central effects and eliminate noise. This method reduces the importance of the spontaneous activity while emphasizing the electrical waves of the early and late components associated with the sensory and cognitive processes mobilized by the subject as a reaction to the event. For example, it is generally believed that early waves (between 50 and 150 ms after the event) are usually indicators of involuntary, exogenous processes influenced by the physical properties of the stimuli used and not a conscious reaction or part of a voluntary thought process of the subject. Because cognition – and especially the kind of high-level cognition needed to achieve many of these tasks – requires more processing time than involuntary reactions, later waves (after 300 ms) are taken as signs of voluntary, endogenous, and cognitive-based processes that involve processing the different stimuli that the subject is receiving, and constructing an appropriate response. Both types are useful for entrepreneurship research.

EEG: POTENTIAL AND LIMITATIONS

There are five general features that make EEG of interest for entrepreneurship researchers: (1) its cost; (2) the results are less biased by consciousness; (3) an access to processes inaccessible to other traditional methods; (4) the experimental paradigms easily produced; and (5) the experiment parameters are already validated in social sciences studies.

One of the advantages of using EEG is the lower cost and practicality compared to other techniques. A portable EEG machine designed with research in mind has become quite affordable for institutions, and the cost of consumables and maintenance are trivial (although set-up of the experiment is not, please see below). The cost of designing the research protocol is similar to traditional research methods, and recording data can be done with standard computer equipment, as can the analyses. The statistical software designed to analyze such data is inexpensive as well. In contrast with other imaging techniques, the situational requirements for EEG are austere: a small, comfortable, quiet room will suffice.

Aside from these secular features, the core advantage of brain-imaging techniques in general is the fact that they can access how subjects shape their perception of the world, and how they create responses that are not mediated by conscious thought. Not only does this reduce the likelihood of biased responses because of social desirability or mere ignorance, it also opens the door to other research questions that were immensely difficult to operationalize. Before these and other imagery techniques were introduced, and in the case of entrepreneurship even today, it was common to use scales or experimental designs that required the conscious contributions of their participants, with its intrinsic, irreducible bias. In contrast, the activity measured by EEGs gives information practically before the participant is aware of what he or she is perceiving or deciding, and without the need to ask the subject to explain or even understand their rationale. While this is clearly not a panacea for research, it is easy to imagine entrepreneurship studies where this could be a desirable feature.

Given the robust literature around ERPs and EEG, it seems sensible to hypothesize that the systematic bias that neuroimaging techniques introduce in the data is not correlated with the other biases, providing a very useful tool to triangulate data gathered through more conventional means. More importantly, these families of imaging techniques allow researchers to observe and explain phenomena that are irretrievable through introspection, such as explaining whether a decision was made after evaluating a series of alternatives and selecting the best one, or whether a choice was made first and then cognition had been mobilized to justify the choice already made. Anecdotal evidence, but also scientific research, show that decisions which involve judgments are made at speeds that are incompatible with any complex cognitive elaboration, and that after the decision was made, cognitive efforts are deployed to justify it at any cost. Recently, a team of researchers have shown detectable brain activities up to ten seconds *before* a decision entered the part of the brain that handles awareness. Through the analyses of observed brain electrical patterns, they were able to predict with high accuracy what the decision might be between two different options, *before* participants had access to what they were about to choose (Soon et al., 2008). In that vein, we hypothesize that a variation of that study could be used to test how entrepreneurs make up their minds during the evaluation of opportunity, and how they reach their decisions.

One of the additional advantages of event potentials is that they do not require us to use a task. Indeed, it is possible, and in many cases desirable, to measure the automatic cognitive response to a certain stimulus in order to infer differences between groups. In medicine, this is done traditionally by comparing the mental states of healthy and pathological brains such as in attention deficit disorders (Stroux et al., 2016), schizophrenia (Wynn et al., 2015), or depression (Bridwell et al., 2015), and these approaches could be easily extended to any type of comparison between classes of subjects, which could include any type of category that may be needed, such as bilingual versus non-bilingual (Chen et al., 2015), mediation experts versus non-experts (Lomas et al., 2015), or even musicians versus non-musicians (Rigoulot et al., 2015).

As another example, Martin de Holan et al. (2013) report that entrepreneurs and non-entrepreneurs mobilize different mental resources to solve a problem: while entrepreneurs reacted rapidly to the stimulus and made a decision without too much thinking, non-entrepreneurs needed cognitive elaboration of the problem before the decision was made. The mobilization of different areas of the brain helps explain the difference in time (entrepreneurs are faster) needed by the two groups to complete the task (see Martin de Holan et al. 2013), but also supports the hypothesis that "certain cognitive factors may differentiate entrepreneurs from non-entrepreneurs" (Hoskisson et al., 2011). Finally, the experiment parameters (dependent variables, number of repetition, interval interstimuli, and so on) are easy to choose, and it is relatively easy to find parameters that have been validated outside the social sciences. This is very beneficial for researchers from across different disciplines and who might be reluctant at first to use a complicated technique, and it significantly increases the robustness of the findings by eliminating possible accusations of artifacts.

As is the case with any empirical method, EEG and imaging techniques in general have limitations. There are five families of limitations of EEG: (1) reverse inference; (2) susceptibility to artifacts; (3) crude spatial resolution and difficulty measuring the activity of deep structures; (4) limited complexity of tasks that can be proposed; and (5) the need for a multidisciplinary-based approach.

The major limitation of EEG is the reverse inference problem: when presenting a stimuli or a task, EEG establishes a correlation between a particular mental state and a specific brain region. However, that correlation cannot be reversed, so it is impossible to infer the presence of any mental state just by observing that a specific region of the brain is being activated (Theodoridis and Nelson, 2012). If a researcher were to detect a spike in the electrical activity of the frontal lobes without knowing the task at hand that produced that spike, it would be impossible to deduce the cognitive processes that led to it, since the same region could, and indeed is, recruited during numerous processes (working-memory refreshment processes, language production, evaluating the mental states of others, and so on).

Then, EEG is very susceptible to motion artifacts (blinking or movements, even breathing and heartbeats) that can be created by the most trivial of events in the environment, and also involuntarily by the subject with seemingly inconsequential actions such as scratching one's hand. In some cases, the artifacts elicit even stronger responses than the events manipulated, which makes data preparation and later analysis particularly delicate but essential for the integrity of the data. In order to compensate for these artifacts, ERP experiments require numerous task repetitions, as well as many subjects (around 20 participants) so as to reduce the signal/noise ratio, but this comes at the expense of the resources that the study consumes. As a consequence, tests last longer than other experimental designs, and probably require that participants have unusual levels of motivation and a great deal of self-control. The experimenter should therefore be careful with fatigue signs and also with strategies that their participants could use to make the task easier. Kober et al. (2013) indeed showed that different strategies used by participants during EEG procedures (visual, auditory, concentration, or relaxation) can have an impact on the data gathered.

As discussed elsewhere (Song et al., 2015), two dimensions are of interest for this type of research: what is happening in the brain, and when that is happening. Even though the spatial resolution of EEG is still crude, the temporal resolution is one of the best obtained to this day. EEG is very limited in terms of spatial resolution (around 10 cm), making it almost impossible to infer the origin of the activation observed with the current state of technologies. At best, researchers can use crude localization cues such as the anterior, posterior, right, left, or central part (vertex) of the brain areas and subareas that the participants mobilize to satisfy the requirements of the experiment. In addition, it is still very difficult to measure the electrical activity of the deep structures of the inner brain such as the amygdala, the nucleus accumbens, or the hypothalamus, all very relevant for information processing and decision making. Unfortunately, many inner structures are involved in critical aspects of cognition such as memory or emotion, making our observations partial.

In order to specifically study the inner brain, other techniques such as fMRI, coupled with magnetoencephalocraphy (MEG) can be used as a complement to EEG (Balderston et al., 2013), increasing the complexity of the research design and the cost (for an introductory explanation see Camerer et al., 2004). In spite of these shortcomings, spatial resolution is increasing rapidly with advances in the sciences of materials, in particular those that seek to augment the number of sensors in the helmet to triangulate position more reliably and those that seek to increase the sensitivity threshold of the captors, which would include more signals to process, including very weak ones. Theoretically at least, EEG could be as precise as any other imaging technique, but no imaging technique depending on BOLD (blood oxygen-level dependent) such as fMRI, which measures the transportation and consumption of oxygen as fuel to the brain, could be as rapid as EEG because of the interval that is needed for oxygen to arrive where it is used.

Also, as is often the case, ERP research designs are limited by the nature of the technology. The information processing that is being monitored is always less active than what it would be if it were a real-life equivalent, and the tasks the participants perform need to be simplified and translated into proxies. This is a common feature of any experimental design, but is particularly sensitive for EEG as the context of a mental process is important for its content and consequences. To the best of our knowledge, it has not been possible yet to design an experiment requiring the active physical participation of the subjects, or to process long and very complex and sequential tasks. In other words, results and conclusions drawn from EEG studies often seem abstract, ultra-focused on the mental processes alone, and a long way from everyday experience, but they provide valuable insights about what participants think, and how they think and engage different mental operations to interact with the world. EEG, as with all empirical techniques, is neither perfect nor fundamentally flawed.

Finally, as is prudent with any other technology, neuroscience-based studies need to be grounded on strong theoretical bases and proven research methods. An approach mixing several disciplines seems required for the neuroentrepreneurship perspective to truly take off (Martin de Holan et al., 2013; Nicolaou and Shane, 2014), as numerous research skills are required: experimental sciences (how to design a protocol, choose the appropriate independent and dependent variables, control for the influence of undesirable variables), a deep understanding of the neurosciences and brain anatomy and physiology, and statistical analyses.

WHAT WOULD NEUROENTREPRENEURSHIP LOOK LIKE?

Research that Can Be Conducted Right Away

Several researchers have already stated the importance of cognition for entrepreneurship theories and research (N.F. Krueger, 2003), and others have predicted the emergence of neuroentrepreneurship (Martin de Holan et al., 2013) driven by the advance in technologies, offering better quality at a lower cost (McMullen et al., 2014). Nevertheless, very few entrepreneurship studies have been conducted so far on using neuroscience approaches. Aside from intrinsic merits of the technology described above, the obvious advantage of using EEG for entrepreneurship research is the existence of nearly a century of accumulated experience in medicine and psychology, which has led to well-established paradigms, research designs, methods, and tools for analysis and data interpretation that have been validated and documented extensively in the cognitive sciences literature. Given the theoretical inclinations of many entrepreneurship researchers, the oversight of such vast potential seems particularly wasteful, so we are suggesting a series of research ideas that could be conducted very rapidly by researchers interested in the possibilities of neuroentrepreneurship.

Probably the most intriguing one, at least early on, is a comparative analysis of entrepreneurs and non-entrepreneurs' cognition, well beyond what has been done so far. Simply by comparing well-matched groups of entrepreneurs with non-entrepreneurs, researchers could strengthen the current theories and models by showing what cognitive processes might be more efficient, and confirm or falsify theories that require the brain to work in certain ways, such as effectuation. Shane and Venkataraman (2000, 2007) proposed that entrepreneurship researches involve studying three steps: what are the sources of opportunities; how entrepreneurs discover them; and how do they decide to exploit them. ERP-based researches allow for studying the last two steps, right away: opportunity identification and evaluation (McMullen et al., 2007) and decision making (Sánchez et al., 2011).

Opportunity Identification and Evaluation

Opportunity identification is a central concept for entrepreneurship studies, and the subject of a considerable debate, even though there is agreement that the evaluation process is essentially a cognitive phenomenon about which we do not know much (Keh et al., 2002). For example, Shane and Venkataraman (2007) claim that in order to discover opportunities, entrepreneurs must identify new means–ends relationships that are generated mostly by changes in the environment. They also state that these abilities differ from one person to another, and that entrepreneurs, particularly successful ones, should have more – and more sophisticated – skills than non-entrepreneurs, and probably different ones as well. This is eminently testable with EEG, and related technologies: if cognitive processes involved are indeed different in these two groups, a representation of the brain working would reveal exactly that. In the same vein, Gaglio and Katz (2001) proposed an elegant model of opportunity identification based on the hypothesis that entrepreneurs have a unique set of perceptual and information-processing skills that allows them to detect and act upon opportunities. Based on the alertness or readiness to react, they propose that entrepreneurs are very good at recognizing events of disequilibrium in the market, another proposition that can easily be translated into a research program for neuroentrepreneurship.

In terms of cognitive processes, Baron (2007) states that entrepreneurs could be better at detecting cues of anomalies and inconsistencies with higher pattern-recognition abilities. He postulates that entrepreneurs might be better at (1) recognizing links between trends, changes that appear at first unconnected, and (2) identifying a recurrent pattern. Such claims could be easily supported by EEG-based research using simple methods such as the Flanker task, a visual exercise where participants have to detect a target in two different experimental conditions: in the first one the target is accompanied by a congruent spatial cue, for example an arrow is pointing toward the target, and in the other condition the cue is non-congruent, in that the same arrow would be pointing toward the opposite direction. The Flanker task has already been used coupled with ERP measures to compare different clinical populations in medicine (Johnstone and Galletta, 2013), and this procedure can be easily modified to incorporate opportunity-related stimuli that could be used as congruent or non-congruent distractors. Then, by comparing entrepreneurs to non-entrepreneurs' performance and brainwave, one might easily verify if there is indeed an alertness or readiness advantage for the first group, both with behavioral and electrophysiological measures.

The literature on entrepreneurship is currently unclear about the effects of prior knowledge on inconsistencies detection, which seem to be relevant for opportunity detection and/or construction. Indeed, some authors argue that having prior knowledge and expertise allow for a more holistic view and help detect abnormalities (Johnson et al., 1991), while others state that prior knowledge might in fact increase entrepreneurs' susceptibility to a number of cognitive biases, especially the effects of prior errors on judgment (Baron, 1998). In terms of cognitive psychology, different experimental tasks can assess what is called proactive interference, the difficulty in treating or learning new information because of already existing information in the cognitive system. Some of them have recently been coupled with ERP measures, revealing interesting components such as a late frontal negativity (approximately 500 ms) involved in the resolution of the interference (Yi and Friedman, 2011). If the same paradigm was used on groups of entrepreneurs and non-entrepreneurs, it might give us more information on how they process new information in the context of pre-existing knowledge.

Entrepreneurs and Decision Making

Acting upon an opportunity is often regarded as depending on a form of rule-based decision making. Indeed, it has been observed that entrepreneurs are particularly different from non-entrepreneurs when it comes to decision making, and it has been suggested that they tend to take rapid actions with low(er) rational thinking than others, and reflect on their decisions afterwards, correcting what needs correction before initiating the process again. In fact, entrepreneurs might base their decisions to act upon an opportunity on mental images or theories of the mind about the potential reward for a particular action minus the cost of that action (Day, 2014). For example, Wood and Williams (2014) proposed that the criteria used by entrepreneurs to judge a situation are the opportunity, novelty, resource efficiency, and worst-case scenario. For an entrepreneur to choose whether to act upon an idea or not, he or she must strongly believe in the successful outcomes, ignoring sometimes the discordant elements even if some are quite apparent, suppressing at least some information that is readily available. This type of reasoning is considered the opposite of the usual prudent approach, as it does not follow the normative/rational model of thinking (R.K. Mitchell et al., 2007). Indeed, recent research has demonstrated that decision making in a context of high uncertainty recruits a complex neural network that includes the dorsolateral prefrontal cortex, located at the front part of the brain (Ernst and Steinhauser, 2015). This rather small chunk of brain matter has already been the target of ERP researches in other domains (Upton et al., 2010). Specifically, to study decision making in entrepreneurs in order to confirm or falsify current views, researchers could use experimental tasks designed to tap into decision-making processes combined with EEG measures.

The most commonly used tasks in clinical research in cognitive psychology are the go/no-go task, the Stroop task, the Hayling test, the Brixton task, the trail-making test, the Wisconsin card-sorting test, and the Tower of London task. Most of them have already been successfully coupled with ERP measures and showed reproducible brainwave components, paving the way for comparison between entrepreneurs versus non-entrepreneurs and concluding some theoretical debates.

During a go/no-go task, stimuli are presented in a continuous stream and participants have to decide for each stimulus between two predefined actions: either making a motor response (go) or withholding their response (no-go). As an example, they could be presented with either circles or triangles with the instruction to press a button as quickly and accurately as possible but only when a circle appeared. When this procedure is coupled with EEG-measures, a N200 is usually detected and interpreted as a front-central component related to inhibition of response in the no-go condition (Johnstone et al., 2005). An obvious research question to test would be the comparative behaviors of entrepreneurs versus a control group. Indeed, current models posit that entrepreneurs make quicker decisions because they use specific heuristics (as in simplified strategies they use to manage information and reduce uncertainty: see Sánchez et al., 2011) and, if it is indeed the case, the N200 component should be present earlier among entrepreneurs, indicating that they can process information more efficiently when it comes to making decisions to act given precise situation parameters.

Researchers could also look at other components in that task, such as the lateralized readiness potential (LRP). This component appears when a participant has to answer with one hand – an activation can be spotted over the motor cortex contralateral to the hand of response. It is thought to represent the moment at which the brain begins preparing the motor response and can influence the N200 (Kopp et al., 1996). Are entrepreneurs always prepared to respond, hence are more prone to take the advantage of a situation where being among the first is key?[2]

Another important field of study is the response after errors, even after careful or prudent decision processes. Is expertise in entrepreneurship related to the speed with which one recognizes an opportunity? Do entrepreneurs process their mistakes the same way that non-entrepreneurs do? Current models suggest that they do not, since successful entrepreneurs at least should be able to take more lessons from their errors in order to give a better performance at the next iteration. If this is the case, this attitude should be associated with reinforcement learning and ERP studies could show how entrepreneurs treat such information compared to non-entrepreneurs. The component of choice in this case could be the error-related negativity (ERN), generally observed after an error has been committed, even when the participant is not aware of that (Suchan et al., 2003). Virtually any paradigm requiring a motor response can be used to measure the ERN as long as it generates enough errors to analyze the participants' data. The go/no-go procedure is also widely used in that case. As a consequence, elaborating a simple paradigm to compare entrepreneurs and non-entrepreneurs can give us valuable information. Here, we make the hypothesis, based on several entrepreneurship models, that entrepreneurs would show differential ERN responses, either shorter latencies, or higher peaks. This procedure could be coupled with tasks involving gain and loss in a second time. Indeed, such tasks would be more closely related to real-life settings. The Iowa gambling task (Mapelli et al., 2014) and the game-of-dice task, (Pabst et al., 2013) have already shown promising results in demonstrating differences between different clinical groups using feedback ERN (fERN). Once again, the experimental procedure would not be very difficult to complete but the conclusions are likely to impact the field of entrepreneurship for a long time.

Marketing science and practice has embraced neurosciences earlier than most disciplines, and has used EEG and other techniques as tools to measure consumers' response to products, in the hope they could find ways to influence either the memory or the decision to buy goods. This neuroscientific-based methodology is used to complement the pre-existing methodologies such as opinion and behaviors measures. Over the last decade, neuromarketing has had some promising results: for instance, it provided data on how familiar brand logos might engage the memory and emotional systems (Esch et al., 2012), or, in an older study, researchers used EEG while participants were viewing different ads for the same products in order to determine which one had the highest chances of being remembered (Rossiter et al., 2001).

To conclude with the immediate potential of neuroentrepreneurship, we will briefly present one of the first neuroentrepreneurship published studies. Martin de Holan et al. (2013), in their recent work, compared the performance of founder entrepreneurs and non-founders/non-entrepreneurs during a Stroop decision task while recording ERP measures. Most interestingly, their preliminary results strongly suggested a cognitive and heuristic gap between these two groups, favoring the entrepreneurs during a decision task. The electrical measures showed that they were capable of making faster decisions during uncertain trials, followed by a larger post-evaluation cognitive process. These thrilling results might indicate that entrepreneurs indeed react faster than others in uncertain situations, just as several models predicted, but also that they would reflect more on their past decisions (see also Ortiz-Terán et al., 2013). More studies are obviously needed, but the data is very encouraging, especially because the task used was not directly linked to entrepreneurial routine but still showed differences.

RECOMMENDATIONS OF STUDIES FOR THE NEXT DECADE

Potential notwithstanding, some questions will still remain unanswered for the foreseeable future. Probably the most central problem facing entrepreneurship is the diversity of paradigms that populate the field, several of them containing incompatible assumptions about the functioning of the brain of the entrepreneur, and some even suggesting that an entrepreneur's brain is capable of doing things that are considered physically impossible by the field of neuroscience.

Four major paradigms were identified by McMullen et al. (2014) when seeking to explain how entrepreneurs form their opportunity identification systems and their mental theories (see Figure 4.3). Two dimensions are relevant: the locus of origin of the opportunity as external or internal (as in "whether the formation and successful implementation of opportunity beliefs is triggered primarily by a stimulus that is internal or external to the individual"), and whether the differences observed are permanent or temporary phenomena. Four paradigms emerge then: (1) the *trait* explanations, favoring permanent internal attitude such as personality traits and even genetics (Nicolaou and Shane, 2014); (2) the *adaptation* explanations, regrouping the cognitive-based approaches and the idea that one is not born an entrepreneur but rather adopts

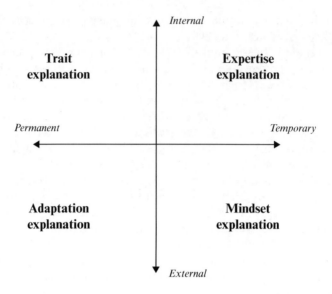

Source: McMullen et al. (2014).

Figure 4.3   Opportunity identification and theories of the mind

entrepreneurial behaviors thanks to favorable cognitive predispositions; (3) the *expertise* explanations, valuing the role of knowledge, day-to-day learning, and experience over any predisposition; and (4) the *mindset* explanations, explaining that entrepreneurs have a unique mindset (see Figure 4.3).

Neuroentrepreneurship should allow for the study and comparison of models coming from these categories, test their predictions, strengthen their interpretations, and refine the way we perceive, teach, and nurture entrepreneurship around the world. For example, studies could confirm or revise the model of opportunity perception of Dutton and Jackson (1987), the link between resilience to adversity and optimism (Baron and Markman, 2000), or the role of perceived desirability, feasibility on opportunity detection (Krueger, 2000). Many authors are pressing for the development of a unique entrepreneurship model that can incorporate, explain, and predict all the above-mentioned elements (Sánchez et al., 2011; Shane and Venkataraman, 2007). We strongly believe that ERP-grounded studies could help build the foundations of such a model, starting with the cognitive unique abilities of entrepreneurs.

Also, once the field matures, it will become important to settle the debate of whether entrepreneurs are favored by some cognitive advantages or, on the contrary, their abilities come from their acquired experience and knowledge – or a combination of both and, if so, in what sequence and with what magnitude. Longitudinal studies could follow cohorts of children of entrepreneurs, since we know they are more likely to become entrepreneurs themselves (Aldrich and Cliff, 2003), or a group of MBA students before and after an entrepreneurship-intensive program, gathering ERP, behavioral, and scale measures to contrast differences over time. That way, we could study how the cognitive abilities dedicated to opportunity seeking and decision making develop in time, as well as how environmental influences and personal abilities weight on developing an entrepreneurial attitude.

Unfortunately, there are very few examples of real distinct entrepreneurial tasks so far, mostly because we do not have a very precise definition of the phenomenon but rather different collections of partial definitions across the literature. Nonetheless, a few researchers built experimental paradigms that assess directly some aspects of entre-preneurial cognition and should be used more often. For instance, J.M. Haynie et al. (2012) created an entrepreneurial task to investigate the ability to effectively and appropriately change decision policies (that is, to learn) given feedback (inputs) from the environmental context in which cognitive processing is embedded (M. Haynie and Shepherd, 2009). Participants must evaluate the potential of different opportunities on a Likert-type scale ranging from 1 (not at all attractive) to 11 (very attractive). Each opportunity was presented with a set of decision attributes (such as the value, limits on competition, rarity, or imitability), each of which being either high or low. The procedure takes place in two steps: first, participants have to complete several decisions with a feedback after each of them to implicitly learn which configurations of decision attributes are the most attractive. Then, after a short break, they are administered a second set of decision trials with feedbacks, but this time the most rewarding configurations are completely different. In other words, they have to effectively adapt their decision policies to respond to these changes, which is what entrepreneurs have to do on a daily basis. This ingenious paradigm can tell us how fast a person can learn a set of rules, take decisions, and relearn a new set while managing the proactive interference. But how could we adapt this paradigm to ERP-recording? What would be the electrical activities tracked? It could be the reaction to feedback during the second step. Overall, it would certainly be most interesting to verify if entrepreneurs have more intense post-evaluation cognitive processes, taken as a sign of cognitive and heuristic differences as compared to non-entrepreneurs. Additionally, researchers could look at the response after an error was produced by using the ERN or other

ERP components. The take-home message is that even though using already validated procedures would be more rewarding at first, future neuroentrepreneurship studies will, sooner or later, most likely require using innovative and more targeted approaches such as this experimental task. By doing so, researchers will have more flexibility to test their hypotheses and elaborate new models.

Since EEG recording benefits from the best temporal resolution of all imaging techniques, it rends possible measurements of changes occurring during mental operations on the millisecond scale and, in a sense, EEG measures are continuous reflections of participants' cognitive states. Most domains of entrepreneurship, at the cost of paradigm adaptations, are ideal targets for future ERP-based studies: creativity (Tomasino, 2007; Ward, 2004), cognitive adaptability (as in take account of the ongoing changes, J.M. Haynie et al., 2012), social cognition (England Bayrón, 2013), metacognitive processes (M. Haynie and Shepherd, 2009), cognitive bias (Baron, 1998), international entrepreneurship (Zahra et al., 2005), personality (Brandstätter, 2011), entrepreneurship teaching (Rahmati et al., 2014), and so on.

CONCLUSION

Neuroentrepreneurship opens the way for thrilling future researches combining cognitive sciences, neurosciences, and entrepreneurship, and we believe that virtually any topic concerning the cognitive or metacognitive aspects of entrepreneurship can and should be studied using neurophysiological measures. With this chapter, we strongly suggest that its future applications are numerous and potentially fruitful, especially if the imaging techniques are combined with other existing ones (scales, behavioral, hormonal, genetic, and so on) that we use already, or if we use them to study different theoretical problems we know well.

For all its putative potential, neuroscience is not a panacea and will not resolve all the empirical questions we would like to ask. Yet, as we have shown, it constitutes a formidable additional tool with benefits and limits like any other, that should complement the researcher's pre-existing toolkit with due care because complex psychological and social processes must be studied carefully, with the right procedures and a prudent and multidisciplinary approach (Tracey and Schluppeck, 2014). We strongly believe that entrepreneurship research needs to embrace neuroentrepreneurship.

NOTES

1. See part of the debate about the moment of death in Wijdicks (2002), Rady et al. (2013), and "Legislative Fact Sheet – Determination of Death Act", Uniform Law Commission, accessed 16 July 2012 at http://uniformlaws.org/LegislativeFactSheet.as px?title=Determination%20of%20Death%20Act.
2. *The Oxford Handbook of Event-Related Potentials* (Kappenman and Luck, 2012) is an interesting platform to begin thinking about the connections between ERPs and neuroentrepreneurship, as it has studies in clinical and cognitive psychology in mind, which are compatible with the aims of entrepreneurship.

REFERENCES

Aldrich, H.E. and J.E. Cliff (2003), "The pervasive effects of family on entrepreneurship: toward a family embeddedness perspective," *Journal of Business Venturing*, **18** (5), 573–96; http://doi.org/10.1016/S0883-9026(03)00011-9.

Armstrong, S.J. and A. Hird (2009), "Cognitive style and entrepreneurial drive of new and mature business owner-managers," *Journal of Business and Psychology*, **24** (4), 419–30; http://doi.org/10.1007/s10869-009-9114-4.

Balderston, N.L., D.H. Schultz, S. Baillet, and F.J. Helmstetter (2013), "How to detect amygdala activity with magnetoencephalography using source imaging," *Journal of Visualized Experiments*, (76); http://doi.org/10.3791/50212.

Baron, R.A. (1998), "Cognitive mechanisms in entrepreneurship: why and when entrepreneurs think differently than other people," *Journal of Business Venturing*, **13** (4), 275–94; http://doi.org/10.1016/S0883-9026(97)00031-1.

Baron, R.A. (2007), "Behavioral and cognitive factors in entrepreneurship: entrepreneurs as the active element in new venture creation," *Strategic Entrepreneurship Journal*, **1** (1–2), 167–82; http://doi.org/10.1002/sej.12.

Baron, R.A. and G.D. Markman (2000), "Beyond social capital: how social skills can enhance entrepreneurs' success," *The Academy of Management Executive (1993–2005)*, **14** (1), 106–16.

Becker, W., R. Cropanzano, and A.G. Sanfey (2011), "Organizational neuroscience: taking organizational theory inside the neural black box," SSRN Scholarly Paper No. ID 1742384, Rochester, NY: Social Science Research Network; http://papers.ssrn.com/abstract=1742384.

Bigelow, H. (1850), "Dr. Harlow's case of recovery from the passage of an iron bar through the head," *The American Journal of the Medical Sciences*, **4** (14), 13–22.

Brandstätter, H. (2011), "Personality aspects of entrepreneurship: a look at five meta-analyses," *Personality and Individual Differences*, **51** (3), 222–30; http://doi.org/10.1016/j.paid.2010.07.007.

Bridwell, D.A., V.R. Steele, J.M. Maurer, K.A. Kiehl, and V.D. Calhoun (2015), "The relationship between somatic and cognitive-affective depression symptoms and error-related ERPs," *Journal of Affective Disorders*, **172**, 89–95; http://doi.org/10.1016/j.jad.2014.09.054.

Broca, P. (1861), "Sur le principe des localisations cérébrales," *Bulletins de La Société d'Anthropologie, tome II*, 190–204.

Camerer, C., G. Loewenstein, and D. Prelec (2004), "Neuroeconomics: how neuroscience can inform economics," SSRN Scholarly Paper No. ID 590965, Rochester, NY: Social Science Research Network; http://papers.ssrn.com/abstract=590965.

Chen, P., J. Lin, B. Chen, C. Lu, and T. Guo (2015), "Processing emotional words in two languages with one brain: ERP and fMRI evidence from Chinese–English bilinguals," *Cortex*, **71**, 34–48; http://doi.org/10.1016/j.cortex.2015.06.002.

Cornelissen, J.P. (2013), "Portrait of an entrepreneur: Vincent van Gogh, Steve Jobs, and the entrepreneurial imagination," *Academy of Management Review*, **38** (4), 700–709; http://doi.org/10.5465/amr.2013.0068.

Damasio, H., T. Grabowski, R. Frank, A.M. Galaburda, and A.R. Damasio (1994), "The return of Phineas Gage: clues about the brain from the skull of a famous patient," *Science (New York, N.Y.)*, **264** (5162), 1102–5.

Day, M. (2014), "Word problems: intangible returns on investment in the mind of the entrepreneur," paper presented at the Academy of Management Conference, Philadelphia, PA.

Dutton, J.E. and S.E. Jackson (1987), "Categorizing strategic issues: links to organizational action," *Academy of Management Review*, **12** (1), 76–90; http://doi.org/10.5465/AMR.1987.4306483.

Ellingson, R.J. (1990), "Introduction: the first Hans Berger lecture," *Electroencephalography and Clinical Neurophysiology*, **76** (4), 294–5; http://doi.org/10.1016/0013-4694(90)90030-N.

England Bayrón, C. (2013), "Social cognitive theory, entrepreneurial self-efficacy and entrepreneurial intentions: tools to maximize the effectiveness of formal entrepreneurship education and address the decline in entrepreneurial activity," *Griot*, **6** (1), 66–77.

Ernst, B. and M. Steinhauser (2015), "Effects of invalid feedback on learning and feedback-related brain activity in decision-making," *Brain and Cognition*, **99**, 78–86; http://doi.org/10.1016/j.bandc.2015.07.006.

Esch, F.-R., T. Möll, B. Schmitt, C.E. Elger, C. Neuhaus, and B. Weber (2012), "Brands on the brain: do consumers use declarative information or experienced emotions to evaluate brands?," *Journal of Consumer Psychology*, **22** (1), 75–85; http://doi.org/10.1016/j.jcps.2010.08.004.

Gaglio, C.M. and J.A. Katz (2001), "The psychological basis of opportunity identification: entrepreneurial alertness," *Small Business Economics*, **16** (2), 95–111; http://doi.org/10.1023/A:1011132102464.

Garud, R. and A.P. Giuliani (2013), "A narrative perspective on entrepreneurial opportunities," *Academy of Management Review*, **38** (1), 157–60; http://doi.org/10.5465/amr.2012.0055.

Goodale, J.C., D.F. Kuratko, J.S. Hornsby, and J.G. Covin (2011), "Operations management and corporate entrepreneurship: the moderating effect of operations control on the antecedents of corporate entrepreneurial activity in relation to innovation performance," *Journal of Operations Management*, **29** (1–2), 116–27; http://doi.org/10.1016/j.jom.2010.07.005.

Haynie, M. and D.A. Shepherd (2009), "A measure of adaptive cognition for entrepreneurship research," *Entrepreneurship Theory and Practice*, **33** (3), 695–714; http://doi.org/10.1111/j.1540-6520.2009.00322.x.

Haynie, J.M., D. Shepherd, E. Mosakowski, and P.C. Earley (2010), "A situated metacognitive model of the entrepreneurial mindset," *Journal of Business Venturing*, **25** (2), 217–29; http://doi.org/10.1016/j.jbusvent.2008.10.001.

Haynie, J.M., D.A. Shepherd, and H. Patzelt (2012), "Cognitive adaptability and an entrepreneurial task: the role of metacognitive ability and feedback," *Entrepreneurship Theory and Practice*, **36** (2), 237–65; http://doi.org/10.1111/j.1540-6520.2010.00410.x.

Hoskisson, R.E., J. Covin, H.W. Volberda, and R.A. Johnson (2011), "Revitalizing entrepreneurship: the search for new research opportunities," *Journal of Management Studies*, **48** (6), 1141–68; http://doi.org/10.1111/j.1467-6486.2010.00997.x

Johnson, P. E., K. Jamal, and R.G. Berryman (1991), "Effects of framing on auditor decisions," *Organizational Behavior and Human Decision Processes*, **50** (1), 75–105; http://doi.org/10.1016/0749-5978(91)90035-R.

Johnstone, S.J. and D. Galletta (2013), "Event-rate effects in the flanker task: ERPs and task performance in children with and without AD/HD," *International Journal of Psychophysiology*, **87** (3), 340–48; http://doi.org/10.1016/j.ijpsycho.2012.07.170.

Johnstone, S.J., C.B. Pleffer, R.J. Barry, A.R. Clarke, and J.L. Smith (2005), "Development of inhibitory processing during the go/no-go task: a behavioral and event-related potential study of children and adults," *Journal of Psychophysiology*, **19** (1), 11–23; http://doi.org/10.1027/0269-8803.19.1.11.

Kappenman, E.S. and S.J. Luck (2012) *The Oxford Handbook of Event-Related Potentials*, New York: Oxford University Press.

Keh, H.T., M.D. Foo, and B.C. Lim (2002), "Opportunity evaluation under risky conditions: the cognitive processes of entrepreneurs," *Entrepreneurship Theory and Practice*, **27** (2), 125–48; http://doi.org/10.1111/1540-8520.00003.

Kober, S.E., M. Witte, M. Ninaus, C. Neuper, and G. Wood, G. (2013), "Learning to modulate one's own brain activity: the effect of spontaneous mental strategies," *Frontiers in Human Neuroscience*, **7**, 695; http://doi.org/10.3389/fnhum.2013.00695.

Kopp, B., U. Mattler, R. Goertz, and F. Rist (1996), "N2, P3 and the lateralized readiness potential in a no-go task involving selective response priming," *Electroencephalography and Clinical Neurophysiology*, **99** (1), 19–27.

Krueger, J. (2000), "The cognitive infrastructure of opportunity emergence," *Entrepreneurship: Theory and Practice*, **25** (3), 5–23.

Krueger, N.F. (2003), "The cognitive psychology of entrepreneurship," in Z.J. Acs and D.B. Audretsch (eds), *Handbook of Entrepreneurship Research*, New York: Springer, pp. 105–40.

Laureiro-Martínez, D., N. Canessa, S. Brusoni, M. Zollo, T. Hare, F. Alemanno, and S.F. Cappa (2014), "Frontopolar cortex and decision-making efficiency: comparing brain activity of experts with different professional background during an exploration-exploitation task," *Frontiers in Human Neuroscience*, **7**, 927; http://doi.org/10.3389/fnhum.2013.00927.

Lock, M. (2002), *Twice Dead: Organ Transplants and the Reinvention of Death*, California Series in Public Anthropology, California: University of California Press.

Lomas, T., I. Ivtzan, and C.H.Y. Fu (2015), "A systematic review of the neurophysiology of mindfulness on EEG oscillations," *Neuroscience & Biobehavioral Reviews*, **57**, 401–10; http://doi.org/10.1016/j.neubiorev.2015.09.018.

Mapelli, D., E. Di Rosa, M. Cavalletti, S. Schiff, and S. Tamburin (2014), "Decision and dopaminergic system: an ERPs study of Iowa gambling task in Parkinson's disease," *Frontiers in Psychology*, **5**; http://doi.org/10.3389/fpsyg.2014.00684.

Martin de Holan, P., E. Ortiz-Terán, A. Turrero, and T. Alonso (2013), "Towards neuroentrepreneurship? Early evidence from a neuroscience study," *Frontiers of Entrepreneurship Research*, **33** (5); http://digitalknowledge.babson.edu/fer/vol33/iss5/12.

McClure, S.M., J. Li, D. Tomlin, K.S. Cypert, L.M. Montague, and P.R. Montague (2004), "Neural correlates of behavioral preference for culturally familiar drinks," *Neuron*, **44** (2), 379–87; http://doi.org/10.1016/j.neuron.2004.09.019.

McMullen, J.S., L.A. Plummer, and Z.J. Acs (2007), "What is an entrepreneurial opportunity?," *Small Business Economics*, **28** (4), 273–83; http://doi.org/10.1007/s11187-006-9040-z.

McMullen, J.S., M.S. Wood, and L.E. Palich (2014), "Entrepreneurial cognition and social cognitive neuroscience," in J.R. Mitchell, R. Mitchell, and B. Randolph-Seng (eds), *Handbook of Entrepreneurial Cognition*, vol. 29, Cheltenham, UK/Northampton, MA: Edward Elgar, pp. 723–40.

Mitchell, J.R., P.N. Friga, and R.K. Mitchell (2005), "Untangling the intuition mess: intuition as a construct in entrepreneurship research," *Entrepreneurship Theory and Practice*, **29** (6), 653–79; http://doi.org/10.1111/j.1540-6520.2005.00102.x.

Mitchell, R.K., L. Busenitz, T. Lant, P.P. McDougall, E.A. Morse, and J.B. Smith (2002), "Toward a theory of entrepreneurial cognition: rethinking the people side of entrepreneurship research," *Entrepreneurship Theory and Practice*, **27** (2), 93–104.

Mitchell, R.K., L.W. Busenitz, B. Bird, C. Marie Gaglio, J.S. McMullen, E.A. Morse, and J.B. Smith (2007), "The central question in entrepreneurial cognition research 2007," *Entrepreneurship Theory and Practice*, **31** (1), 1–27; http://doi.org/10.1111/j.1540-6520.2007.00161.x.

Nicolaou, N. and S. Shane (2014), "Biology, neuroscience, and entrepreneurship," *Journal of Management Inquiry*, **23** (1), 98–100; http://doi.org/10.1177/1056492613485914.

Ortiz-Terán, E., A. Turrero, J.M. Santos, P.T. Bryant, and T. Ortiz (2013), "Brain cortical organization in entrepreneurs during a visual Stroop decision task," *Neuroscience and Neuroeconomics*, **2013** (2), 33–49; http://doi.org/10.2147/NAN.S48243.

Pabst, S., M. Brand, and O.T. Wolf (2013), "Stress effects on framed decisions: there are differences for gains and losses," *Frontiers in Behavioral Neuroscience*, **7** (142); http://doi.org/10.3389/fnbeh.2013.00142.

Powell, T.C. (2011), "Neurostrategy," *Strategic Management Journal*, **32** (13), 1484–99; http://doi.org/10.1002/smj.969.

Rady, M.Y., J.L. McGregor, and J.L. Verheijde (2013) "Transparency and accountability in mass media campaigns about organ donation: a response to Morgan and Feeley," *Medicine, Health Care and Philosophy*, **16** (4), 869–76.

Rahmati, N., R. Rostami, M.R. Zali, S. Nowicki, and J. Zarei (2014), "The effectiveness of neurofeedback on enhancing cognitive process involved in entrepreneurship abilities among primary school students in District No.3 Tehran," *Basic and Clinical Neuroscience*, **5** (4), 277–84.

Raichle, M.E. (2010), "Two views of brain function," *Trends in Cognitive Sciences*, **14** (4), 180–90; http://doi.org/10.1016/j.tics.2010.01.008.

Ratiu, P., I.-F. Talos, S. Haker, D. Lieberman, and P. Everett (2004), "The tale of Phineas Gage, digitally remastered," *Journal of Neurotrauma*, **21** (5), 637–43; http://doi.org/10.1089/089771504774129964.

Rigoulot, S., M.D. Pell, and J.L. Armony (2015), "Time course of the influence of musical expertise on the processing of vocal and musical sounds," *Neuroscience*, **290**, 175–84; http://doi.org/10.1016/j.neuroscience.2015.01.033.

Rossiter, J.R., R.B. Silberstein, P.G. Harris, and G. Nield (2001), "Brain-imaging detection of visual scene encoding in long-term memory for TV commercials," *Journal of Advertising Research*, **41** (2), 13–21; http://doi.org/10.2501/JAR-41-2-13-21.

Sánchez, J.C., T. Carballo, and A. Gutiérrez, A. (2011), "The entrepreneur from a cognitive approach," *Psicothema*, **23** (3), 433–8.

Shane, S. (2000), "Prior knowledge and the discovery of entrepreneurial opportunities," *Organization Science*, **11** (4), 448–69; http://doi.org/10.1287/orsc.11.4.448.14602.

Shane, S. and S. Venkataraman (2000), "The promise of entrepreneurship as a field of research," *The Academy of Management Review*, **25** (1), 217–26; http://doi.org/10.2307/259271.

Shane, S. and S. Venkataraman (2007), "The promise of entrepreneurship as a field of research," in P.Á. Cuervo, P.D. Ribeiro, and P.S. Roig (eds), *Entrepreneurship*, Berlin Heidelberg: Springer, pp. 171–84.

Shen, K.-Q., X.-P. Li, C.-J. Ong, S.-Y. Shao, and E.P.V. Wilder-Smith (2008), "EEG-based mental fatigue measurement using multi-class support vector machines with confidence estimate," *Clinical Neurophysiology: Official Journal of the International Federation of Clinical Neurophysiology*, **119** (7), 1524–33; http://doi.org/10.1016/j.clinph.2008.03.012.

Smith, A. ([1776] 2000) *The Wealth of Nations*, ed. Edwin Cannan, introduction by Robert Reich, New York: Modern Library.

Song, J., C. Davey, C. Poulsen, P. Luu, S. Turovets, E. Anderson, . . . and D. Tucker (2015), "EEG source localization: sensor density and head surface coverage," *Journal of Neuroscience Methods*, **256**, 9–21; http://doi.org/10.1016/j.jneumeth.2015.08.015.

Soon, C.S., M. Brass, H.-J. Heinze, and J.-D. Haynes (2008), "Unconscious determinants of free decisions in the human brain," *Nature Neuroscience*, **11** (5), 543–5; http://doi.org/10.1038/nn.2112.

Sourina, O., Q. Wang, Y. Liu, and M.K. Nguyen (2012), "EEG-enabled human–computer interaction and applications," in B.Z. Allison, S. Dunne, R. Leeb, J.D.R. Millán and A. Nijholt (eds), *Towards Practical Brain-Computer Interfaces*, Springer Berlin Heidelberg, pp. 251–68.

Stroux, D., A. Shushakova, A.J. Geburek-Höfer, P. Ohrmann, F. Rist, and A. Pedersen (2016), "Deficient interference control during working memory updating in adults with ADHD: an event-related potential study," *Clinical Neurophysiology*, **127** (1), 452–63; http://doi.org/10.1016/j.clinph.2015.05.021.

Suchan, B., D. Zoppelt, and I. Daum (2003), "Frontocentral negativity in electroencephalogram reflects motor response evaluation in humans on correct trials," *Neuroscience Letters*, **350** (2), 101–4.

Sur, S. and V.K. Sinha (2009), "Event-related potential: an overview," *Industrial Psychiatry Journal*, **18** (1), 70–73; http://doi.org/10.4103/0972-6748.57865.

Takeda, M., H. Tachibana, B. Okuda, K. Kawabata, and M. Sugita (1993), "Event-related potential and visual evoked potential in patients with Parkinson's disease," *Nihon Ronen Igakkai Zasshi. Japanese Journal of Geriatrics*, **30** (5), 363–8.

Theodoridis, A.G. and A.J. Nelson (2012), "Of BOLD claims and excessive fears: a call for caution and patience regarding political neuroscience," *Political Psychology*, **33** (1), 27–43; http://doi.org/10.1111/j.1467-9221.2011.00860.x.

Tomasino, D. (2007), "The psychophysiological basis of creativity and intuition: accessing 'the zone' of entrepreneurship," *International Journal of Entrepreneurship and Small Business*, **4** (5), 528–42; http://doi.org/10.1504/IJESB.2007.014388.

Townsend, D.M. (2012), "Captains of their own destiny? Toward a theory of entrepreneurial agency in firm survival," in A.C. Corbett and J.A. Katz (eds), *Entrepreneurial Action*, vol. 14, Emerald Group Publishing Limited, pp. 125–60.

Tracey, P. and D. Schluppeck (2014), "Neuroentreprenuership: "brain pornography" or new frontier in entrepreneurship research?," *Journal of Management Inquiry*, **23** (1), 101–3; http://doi.org/10.1177/1056492613485915.

Upton, D.J., N.R. Cooper, R. Laycock, R.J. Croft, and P.B. Fitzgerald (2010), "A combined rTMS and ERP investigation of dorsolateral prefrontal cortex involvement in response inhibition," *Clinical EEG and Neuroscience*, **41** (3), 127–31.

Waldman, D.A., P.A. Balthazard, and S.J. Peterson (2011), "Leadership and neuroscience: can we revolutionize the way that inspirational leaders are identified and developed?" *The Academy of Management Perspectives*, **25** (1), 60–74.

Ward, T.B. (2004), "Cognition, creativity, and entrepreneurship," *Journal of Business Venturing*, **19** (2), 173–88; http://doi.org/10.1016/S0883-9026(03)00005-3.

Wijdicks, E.F. (2002) "Brain death worldwide: accepted fact but no global consensus in diagnostic criteria," *Neurology*, **58** (1), 20–25.

Wood, M.S. and D.W. Williams (2014), "Opportunity evaluation as rule-based decision making," *Journal of Management Studies*, **51** (4), 573–602; http://doi.org/10.1111/joms.12018.

Wynn, J.K., A.M. Jimenez, B.J. Roach, A. Korb, J. Lee, W.P. Horan, . . . and M.F. Green (2015), "Impaired target detection in schizophrenia and the ventral attentional network: findings from a joint event-related potential–functional MRI analysis," *NeuroImage: Clinical*, **9**, 95–102; http://doi.org/10.1016/j.nicl.2015.07.004.

Yi, Y. and D. Friedman (2011), "Event-related potential (ERP) measures reveal the timing of memory selection processes and proactive interference resolution in working memory," *Brain Research*, **1411**, 41–56; http://doi.org/10.1016/j.brainres.2011.07.004.

Zahra, S.A., J.S. Korri, and J. Yu (2005), "Cognition and international entrepreneurship: implications for research on international opportunity recognition and exploitation," *International Business Review*, **14** (2), 129–46; http://doi.org/10.1016/j.ibusrev.2004.04.005.

5. A brief primer on using functional magnetic resonance imaging (fMRI) in entrepreneurship research
M.K. Ward, Crystal Reeck, and William Becker

Brain imaging is increasingly used in areas outside of the neurosciences to search for answers to applied research questions, including those that relate to business. Entrepreneurship scholars have begun to consider the ways in which they can incorporate neuroscience into their work. Using tools like neuroimaging can enrich research methods and strengthen the conclusions that we can draw. Just as neuroeconomics (Glimcher and Fehr, 2013) and social neuroscience (Cacioppo, 2002) have fruitfully integrated neuroscience to form new paradigms, entrepreneurship scholars can conduct cutting-edge research using neuroscience and today's technology to make similar advances. In doing so, entrepreneurship scholars would adopt the approach of organizational neuroscience (ON), a field of scholarly inquiry that connects neuroscience to business-related research (Becker et al., 2011; Senior et al., 2011; Ward et al., 2015). For example, neuroscientific measurement techniques can measure fine distinctions to support or refute proposed relationships among constructs, including differences between various types of leaders (Balthazard et al., 2012). Drawing from and modeling the development of ON, entrepreneurship scholars use a paradigm sometimes referred to as neuroentrepreneurship. In the interest of consistency, we use the term neuroentrepreneurship in the remainder of this chapter

A promising means to integrate neuroscience with entrepreneurship will be for entrepreneurship scholars to add neuroscientific methods of data collection to their toolbox. From there, scholars can adapt their research designs to accommodate the neuroscientific tools they adopt—which is easier said than done. Although the challenge is formidable, to exclude the neural level of analysis in our research would be to ignore an opportunity to bolster both the rigor of our research and radically advance our collective understanding of entrepreneurship.

The purpose of this chapter is to support entrepreneurship scholars in their efforts to integrate neuroimaging with more traditional empirical work in entrepreneurship. To this end, we first describe potential benefits of using neuroimaging in entrepreneurship research. Second, we discuss general issues and considerations regarding neuroimaging research. Third, we present functional magnetic resonance imaging (fMRI) as a neuroimaging method to add the neural level of analysis to entrepreneurship research. Fourth, we discuss opportunity identification and evaluation, and entrepreneurial decision making as examples of topic areas ripe for using fMRI. We subsequently describe research questions, designs, and best practices in fMRI research. Finally, we close with a discussion regarding interpretation and communication of results.

This chapter is intended for those without formal training in fMRI research, yet are open to the use of neuroimaging for entrepreneurship research. Thus, we overview a selection of the topics and issues involved in neuroimaging research. At the end of this chapter, we include a list of recommended readings that provide more extensive discussions of the topics that we describe. Our aim is to support compelling and rigorous research that integrates neuroscience with existing streams of entrepreneurship research.

POTENTIAL BENEFITS OF NEUROIMAGING IN ENTREPRENEURSHIP

Put simply, neuroimaging refers to multiple ways of peering into the brain to then create an image of brain function. There are four potential benefits of using neuroimaging in entrepreneurship. First, neuroimaging provides entrepreneurship researchers with a wider range of tools for data collection (see Volk and Köhler, 2012). Furthermore, those techniques measure brain activity, which provides additional levels of measurement. For example, neuroimaging can assess cognitive processes that individual entrepreneurs draw on but are unable to consciously report (see Becker and Menges, 2013).

A second potential benefit is that neuroimaging offers alternatives to self-report measures. These additional measurement methods can complement traditional ways of collecting data. By using neuroimaging in addition to more common data collection methods, researchers can avoid mono-method bias and other familiar problems that arise from a reliance on self-report and rating-based measures (Schwarz, 2000; Volk and Köhler, 2012).

Third, neuroimaging can enhance our abilities to develop and validate entrepreneurship theories and constructs. Neuroimaging can contribute evidence of both construct validity and separability of constructs (Powell, 2011). For example, Bagozzi et al. (2013) used neuroimaging to reveal non-conscious explanatory mechanisms that clarified mixed findings regarding the relationships between theory of mind, Machiavellianism, and organizational citizenship behavior. Neuroimaging can provide new ways to refine theories that address important questions in the field of entrepreneurship. For example, neuroimaging can resolve inconsistent evidence regarding relationships between constructs (Bagozzi et al., 2013).

Fourth, neuroimaging provides the ability to link unobserved variables and investigate the emergence of within-person phenomena, such as how different types of leadership emerge (Boyatzis, 2014). A similar study could investigate how different entrepreneurial motives lead to different types of entrepreneurs. Just as quantitative electroencephalography can be used to investigate leader self-complexity and its relationship to adaptive decision making (Hannah et al., 2013), neuroimaging can reveal the complexity of entrepreneurs' self-perceptions and related outcomes. Additionally, neuroscience can adjudicate debates regarding theory (Powell, 2011). In short, from these four benefits, ON can make needed contributions to the field of organizational science if researchers, scholars, and practitioners expand their perspectives and toolboxes to include everything that ON has to offer.

In addition to these benefits of incorporating neuroimaging into entrepreneurship research, to ignore neuroimaging methods and their potential utility in entrepreneurship scholarship would be a missed opportunity. If entrepreneurship scholars and practitioners ignore the information and tools of neuroscience, then we risk becoming obsolete compared to increasingly influential subject areas such as social neuroscience (Cacioppo, 2002). Thus, to maintain the momentum that entrepreneurship scholarship has earned over the past few decades, we must strengthen our research methods by thoughtfully incorporating the information and tools of neuroscience (Ward et al., 2015). The incorporation of neuroimaging is one way to answer the call for continued exploration and refinement in entrepreneurship research and research methods (Shepherd, 2015).

ISSUES AND CONSIDERATIONS BEFORE USING NEUROIMAGING

Entrepreneurship researchers can learn from disciplines that have already integrated neuroscience into their domains, such as social neuroscience, neuroeconomics, and organizational neuroscience (Cacioppo, 2002; Camerer, 2008; Ward et al., 2015). Scholars at the forefront of each of those domains have had to define themselves, and address issues in adding the brain-level of analysis to their research. Similarly, prudent neuroentrepreneurship scholars would do well to develop a deep understanding of the nature of brain-level data in order to design studies that avoid logical fallacies. In this section we discuss three considerations related to those logical fallacies, namely: the reductionism criticism, the reverse inference issue, and the epiphenomenal nature of neuroimaging data.

The Reductionism Criticism

The utility of using neuroimaging in entrepreneurship depends on an understanding that entrepreneurial phenomena cannot be reduced down to activation of particular neural networks. This is the essence of the reductionism criticism. The fundamental assumption of reductionism is that more basic mechanisms give rise to higher-order, behavioral phenomena. Those behavioral phenomena occur in various work functions for the entrepreneur (for example, leading, strategic decision making, fundraising).

Lindebaum and Zundel (2013) describe theory reduction as a specific type of reductionism. Theory reduction is the idea that higher-order theories pertaining to complex behavioral phenomena can be reduced to theories that are focused solely on brain functioning. They contend that theory reduction is impossible because such reduction requires a fit between neural and organizational phenomena. For example, proponents of the reductionism criticism would hold that it is nonsensical to link electrochemical brain activity with a complex construct like entrepreneurship.

There are two other types of reductionism in addition to theory reduction: (1) mechanistic, and 2) hierarchical reductionism (Healey and Hodgkinson, 2015). The goal of mechanistic reduction is to identify parts of the mechanisms underlying cognitive and/or behavioral phenomena. In pursuit of that goal, mechanistic reductionism puts greater emphasis on the *organization* of those mechanisms and the ways in which those mechanisms are orchestrated to realize their effects (Healey and Hodgkinson, 2015). Mechanistic reductionism fragments phenomena (for example, opportunity identification) into underlying cognitive processes (for example, pattern recognition). Consequently, when research is conducted from this viewpoint, the knowledge gained is likewise fragmented. A complete understanding of opportunity identification requires more than knowing the brain activation association with it. Critics of neuroscience methods suggest that the goal of mechanistic reductionism is to identify the "entrepreneurial" area of the brain. This is not the case. Instead, the goal of incorporating neuroscience is to discover how neural networks function during entrepreneurial activities, in order to deepen our understanding of entrepreneurship and of the unique characteristics of entrepreneurs. In short, the emphasis is on how multiple systems coordinate to give rise to phenomena. For neuroimaging data from fMRI scans, the emphasis would be on neural networks rather than molecular biology.

In hierarchical reductionism the preference shifts from higher levels of analysis to lower levels of analysis when explaining phenomena. The continual preference for lower levels of analysis implies that the cause(s) of a given entrepreneurial phenomenon occurs in activity at lower levels. Applied to entrepreneurship, hierarchical reductionism would suggest that opportunity exploitation can be fully explained by neural activity in the brain of an entrepreneur. The perspective of hierarchical reductionism has misinterpreted the goals of other fields that aim to connect the neural level of analysis to psychological and behavioral phenomena. For example, in the field of organizational neuroscience, Becker et al.'s (2011) advocacy for organizational neuroscience has been misinterpreted as hierarchical reductionism, rather than as a way to collect data at an additional level of analysis through neuroimaging. Extending entrepreneurship research to the neural level, for example could explore how emotional reactions to setbacks are different in serial entrepreneurs versus entrepreneurs growing their first start-up.

It is imperative that researchers who use neuroimaging data in entrepreneurship research understand that neuroimaging data provides an additional level of analysis, rather than the preferred level of analysis. The goal is not to replace other types of data, but rather to enhance the richness of the data we collect. Thus, by appropriately incorporating neuroimaging data into entrepreneurship research, we can respond to calls for entrepreneurship research that takes into account multiple levels of analysis (see Shepherd, 2011).

Statements that encourage the use of neuroimaging data have been widely misinterpreted as claims of revealing *fundamental* and *sole* causes of psychological and behavioral phenomena (see Lindebaum and Zundel, 2013). For example, the potential of mirror neurons to enhance explanations of ways in which people resist change does *not* mean that the *only* contributing factor is mirror-neuron activity (Becker et al., 2011). Rather, mirror neurons are *one* potentially informative factor in phenomena such as resistance to change. Furthermore, looking at resistance to change in this way could provide promising alternatives for positive interventions. For further discussion of the reductionism criticism, see Healey and Hodgkinson (2015) and a recent response by ON proponents (Ashkanasy et al., 2014).

In sum, neural activity alone does not provide a complete understanding of constructs like entrepreneurship. While it is not sufficient, data about neural activity is necessary to fully understand entrepreneurs' sensations, perceptions, and behaviors that range from opportunity identification to exit decisions (Purves et al., 2008). We recognize that the dynamic, complex, and influential context of entrepreneurs influences entrepreneurial behaviors (Healey and Hodgkinson, 2015). Thus, we deem it necessary to collect data about neural activity in order to build an understanding of entrepreneurial phenomena, while we recognize that neuroimaging data provides only a portion of the picture.

The Reverse Inference Issue

A second key consideration for neuroentrepreneurship researchers is the issue of reverse inference. Reverse inference occurs when one starts with an outcome or a dependent variable, and then infers the condition or existence of independent or intervening variables (Huettel et al., 2008; Poldrack, 2006). For example, the outcome of fear frequently coincides with activity in the amygdala. Yet, amygdala activation is not always needed in order to elicit the experience of fear, or it may be elicited by other emotions such as anger. This illustrates the crux of the logical fallacy. When applied to neuroentrepreneurship, reverse inference would occur when reasoning from brain activation (outcome) to mental processes (independent variable).

Reverse inference may be sound if the brain activation (outcome) occurs because of a specific manipulation and *not* due to other manipulations. When one can rule out alternative manipulations, the research design has high selectivity. Thus, neuroentrepreneurship scholars who want to strengthen their ability to make causal claims should maximize selectivity in the design of their research studies.

There are specific elements of research design that neuroentrepreneurship scholars can manipulate to increase selectivity (Huettel et al., 2008). First, one type of design used in fMRI research to increase selectivity is the subtractive design. In this type of experiment, two manipulations differ in one way that allows for direct comparison and conclusions about the effect of the independent variable. Second, researchers can vary a feature of the manipulation continuously. Third, rather than looking within one brain region, it is important to look at patterns of activation across brain regions. Then it is important to analyze changes in those patterns of activation over time (Huettel et al., 2008). Taken together, the issue of reverse inference should be addressed in neuroentrepreneurship research, and there are several methods that can strengthen the validity of the reverse inference.

The Epiphenomenal Nature of Neuroimaging Data

The correlational nature of fMRI data is the third critical issue to address in any entrepreneurship study that uses such neuroimaging data. Epiphenomenalism is a secondary consequence of a causal chain of processes that plays no causal role in the process of interest. The issue for neuroentrepreneurship is that fMRI data has extremely limited utility to test experimental hypotheses. The limiting factor is the nature of the signal that fMRI uses to measure neural activity, which we describe later in this chapter. Information processing is commonly assumed to directly result from changes in neuronal activity. The assumption of this relationship may not be tenable.

For example, increased neuronal activation in the prefrontal cortex may be associated with better performance on a working memory task. However, it can also be the case that *decreased* neuronal activation in the prefrontal cortex also may be associated with better performance. How can this be? People who practice the task tend to show better performance and lower activation in the brain regions required to perform the task. The good news for entrepreneurship researchers is that the entrepreneurial environment and tasks are often novel to the entrepreneur, reducing the likelihood of encountering practice effects.

Strictly speaking, the epiphenomenal nature of fMRI data means that fMRI data could not test neuronal or psychological hypotheses. Neuronal hypotheses focus on predicting neuronal activity from specific stimuli, and psychological hypotheses focus on connecting neuronal activity with cognition. Later in this chapter, we describe the different types of hypotheses used in fMRI research. Epiphenomenalism would be a critical problem for neuroentrepreneurship – because typical research questions in entrepreneurship involve hypotheses at the psychological level. However, this overly strict definition of hypothesis testing need not be used in entrepreneurship research that uses fMRI data, given that there is an implicit causal sequence in most experimental studies in entrepreneurship. For example, in some studies we assume that entrepreneurial intention will cause new venture formation (see Bird, 1988). In sum, the correlational nature of fMRI data requires researchers to be cognizant of the assumption of an implicit causal sequence when designing studies that use neuroimaging.

fMRI DEFINED

There are a number of methods for measuring the neural activity in the brain. In general, these methods vary in terms of *temporal resolution,* the precision of time measurement, and *spatial resolution*, the precision of physical location within the brain. Currently, functional magnetic resonance imaging (fMRI) is prevalent in social cognitive neuroscience research. One reason for the popularity of fMRI is that it has excellent spatial resolution and adequate temporal resolution for investigating most psychological hypotheses currently under investigation (we discuss different types of hypotheses in more detail later in this chapter). Additionally, fMRI is non-invasive and involves no inherent health risk even for multiple or repeated sessions. This method is not used in all studies due to disadvantages of fMRI. Primary disadvantages include high costs, limitations of the types of tasks that can be investigated, and complexity of experimental design and analyses. In this section, we describe the basic elements of fMRI signal, equipment, and experimental design.

In the context of neuroentrepreneurship, neuroimaging provides a way to measure brain function related to the processes of entrepreneurship. Images constructed through fMRI indicate changes in blood flow or *hemodynamic response*, and those changes indicate changes in neural activity. For example, if a person thinks through a cost-benefit analysis regarding an opportunity, then blood flows to the brain regions that the person uses to think through the task. In this example, fMRI data may show increased activity in the ventromedial prefrontal cortex, based on the hemodynamic response that occurs shortly after the person begins thinking through the task. The way in which fMRI measures the hemodynamic response relies on atomic physics and magnetic fields.

The *functional* part of fMRI refers to a class of neuroimaging research techniques that focuses on how parts of the brain function (rather than only locating activation) and often this means looking at changes over time. The basic principle of fMRI analysis involves comparing the average signal level in a particular section of the brain during one type of task, such as a risky decision, with signal levels in that same area while resting or while performing a different task, a decision with no risk. In this way, we can infer which areas of the brain are implicated in different functions. These analyses are quite complex and require corrections for movement and timing. They are also subject to multiple comparisons issues.

Scanners are used to produce magnetic fields in order to generate the signal used to create images of neural activity. The scanners used in fMRI experiments are identical to the equipment found in hospitals or clinics. Most research, however, is conducted in scanners that are dedicated to experiments and calibrated for research. MRI scanners produce extremely strong magnetic fields that are able to produce high-resolution images of the soft tissues of the body by varying the magnetic fields. Most research is currently conducted in 3.0 Tesla (3T) scanners, and to put that number in perspective the Earth's magnetic field is 0.00005T.

The process of measuring activity levels in the brain relies on the unique magnetic characteristics of blood, which vary depending on the amount of oxygen in the blood. When neurons become active in a particular area of the brain, the oxygen level in the blood in that area changes and this can be measured and recorded by the MRI scanner. This is referred to as the blood-oxygenation-level-dependent (BOLD) signal.

A drawback of the BOLD signal is that it does not directly measure neural activity, and hemodynamics respond more slowly than neurons actually fire. The timing of the BOLD signal underlying neural activity lags behind said neural activity by a few seconds. This delay limits the temporal resolution of fMRI. The unit of spatial resolution in fMRI is called a voxel, and an image of neural activity is therefore made up of numerous voxels. Voxels in fMRI data are similar to pixels in digital photographs in that smaller voxels indicate better spatial resolution. While the spatial resolution of fMRI is on the order of a few cubic millimeters, even this small volume contains hundreds of thousands of neurons.

In addition to somewhat limited spatial resolution, the physical constraints of the scanner limit the types of tasks that can be used. Instructions and stimuli are typically presented visually using special goggles or a mirror that reflects a computer monitor just outside of the scanner. The process of recording brain images is very loud but participants typically wear headphones that can provide limited audio stimuli to be presented. Recording participant behavior is also challenging in fMRI research. Participants cannot speak during the scans so feedback is limited to selections they make by using push-button clickers (used with one or both hands).

The design of fMRI experiments have evolved to minimize the aforementioned limitations. During an fMRI session, participants lie flat, horizontally, and motionless inside the scanner during brain imaging. First, a high-resolution structural image of the participant's brain is recorded, which takes several minutes to complete. While the participant completes the experimental and resting tasks, the brain is scanned every few seconds. In order to overcome resolution and timing issues, each task of interest must be repeated many times. For example, in a study of entrepreneurs and risky choices, two sessions can be recorded with 40 decisions in each session. Each fMRI scanning session would last between 45 and 60 minutes to produce hundreds of functional images.

There are two broad categories of fMRI experimental designs. The first is a blocked design where the participant is presented with multiple similar stimuli or tasks over a period of time. The second is event-related design where stimuli or tasks are presented in a random or unscripted order. Blocked designs are simpler to analyze and require fewer trials, but they are frequently inappropriate for behavioral research that would be common in entrepreneurial research where a more natural flow of stimuli is important to ecological validity.

The cost of fMRI often limits the number of participants that are included in a single study (Mumford, 2012). Neuroimaging investigations typically include approximately 20–30 participants. While these sample sizes are relatively small compared to some other experimental approaches, the increased number of observations collected from each participant offsets the smaller sample size to preserve adequate statistical power. It is typically good practice to establish the power of one's design to identify a reasonable sample size based on the data that will be collected. Advances in technology and our understanding of the brain have led to a movement toward region of interest (ROI) analysis versus whole brain analysis. In ROI analysis, signal levels are averaged and compared across volumes that make up specific subregions of the brain rather than comparing conditions exhaustively across all areas of the brain.

While researchers should be wary of overinterpreting the results of a single fMRI study, fMRI research continues to evolve and mature. Of the currently available tools in neuroscience, fMRI offers one of the most promising windows into the minds of entrepreneurs. After understanding the technical features of fMRI, scholars can innovate research to add neural data to entrepreneurship research.

INTEGRATING ENTREPRENEURSHIP WITH NEUROSCIENCE AND fMRI RESEARCH

A first step to integrating fMRI into entrepreneurship is to identify gaps in our collective understanding of entrepreneurship. The gaps in our collective understanding of opportunity identification and evaluation are areas that could benefit from the integration of neuroimaging and entrepreneurship. In this section, we discuss two areas that show gaps in our current understanding of entrepreneurship and that are likely to benefit from attention to neural functioning: (1) opportunity identification, evaluation, and the default-mode network; and (2) entrepreneurial decision making and dual-process theories of cognition.

Opportunity Identification, Evaluation, and the Default-mode Network

Two fundamental parts of entrepreneurship are the identification and evaluation of opportunities by people we call entrepreneurs (Shane and

Venkataraman, 2000). Baron and Henry (2011) define opportunities as "perceived means of generating economic value (i.e., profit) that have not previously been exploited and are not currently being exploited by others" (p. 251). Thus, an initial step in entrepreneurship is perceiving an opportunity in the environment. Importantly, successful entrepreneurs must be able to evaluate the opportunities they identify, and to choose and pursue the opportunities that are most likely to succeed. The general research question is: how do entrepreneurs identify and evaluate opportunities?

What features of the entrepreneur's cognitive processes enable the entrepreneur to see opportunities in the environment? How does this differ across entrepreneurs who are different in terms of their experience, network, gender, socioeconomic status, and other individual differences? What thought patterns does the entrepreneur use to rule out opportunities as non-viable? How does this differ across entrepreneurs who are different in terms of their experience, network, gender, socioeconomic status, and other individual differences? After connecting particular cognitive processes with entrepreneurial performance outcomes (beyond forming a new venture), the subsequent research question becomes: can we train unsuccessful entrepreneurs to engage the cognitive processes required to identify and pursue a viable opportunity?

The aforementioned questions indicate potentially promising areas for using fMRI in entrepreneurship research. We know that opportunity identification occurs before evaluation during the general processes of entrepreneurship. Depending on the outcome of opportunity evaluation, the opportunity may be exploited with the hope that later the new venture can be sold after the entrepreneur makes an exit decision. Cognitive neuroscience can enrich our understanding of how entrepreneurs move through each step of the process. More specifically, the default-mode network may be particularly relevant to incorporate into studies of opportunity identification.

The default-mode network refers to the set of brain regions whose activation tends to *decrease* while performing active, engaging tasks, and *increase* during conditions of resting and reflection. While these relative differences are reliably seen in neuroscience, specifically in studies using fMRI, entrepreneurship researchers have given no attention to what happens when entrepreneurs are not in the act of identifying and evaluating an opportunity. Understandably, entrepreneurship research has concentrated on events when entrepreneurs are actively and consciously focusing attention on identifying and evaluating opportunities.

Predicting those events is critical to understanding entrepreneurship, yet we have much to learn about what happens before opportunities are identified. Neuroscience findings regarding the default-mode network suggest that it may benefit our understanding of entrepreneurship to investigate what happens in the minds of entrepreneurs when they are *not* actively and consciously performing entrepreneurial activities. Admittedly counterintuitive, this shift in focus seems to be a potentially rich area of untapped knowledge.

The default-mode network seems to be notably important to opportunity identification in entrepreneurship. Neuroscientists posit that the default-mode network may be important in reflecting on the past and thinking about the future (Andrews-Hanna et al., 2010; Raichle and Snyder, 2007). Particular regions of the default-mode network may be important to particular facets of opportunity identification and evaluation. The ventromedial prefrontal cortex is important to emotional decision making, particularly assessments of probable rewards for future behaviors. Looking at fMRI data in entrepreneurs with a focus on the ventromedial prefrontal cortex activation at rest may reveal cognitive differences in how entrepreneurs versus non-entrepreneurs think and feel about opportunities. A well-designed fMRI study may be able to reveal reasons why entrepreneurs decide to pursue opportunities despite the likelihood of failure. Alternatively, another study may begin to more precisely answer the cognitive steps that entrepreneurs take to manage risk and uncertainty.

In sum, the default-mode network can be described as introspective, stimulus-independent, self-directed thinking. These functions may well show different activation patterns in entrepreneurs versus non-entrepreneurs, or successful entrepreneurs versus entrepreneurs whose ventures failed. The neural patterns may show differences across entrepreneurs with different entrepreneurial experience, ethnicities, gender, and socioeconomic statuses. Those differences may indicate better ways of supporting entrepreneurs by recognizing their diversity. Furthermore, similarities in neural activation may reveal universal neural mechanisms common to all entrepreneurs.

Entrepreneurial Decision-making and Dual-process Theories of Cognition

In addition to opportunity identification and evaluation, entrepreneurial decision making is a potentially fruitful topic for integration, for two reasons. First, it is an important topic to both the practice and the theory of entrepreneurship. Second, there is a substantial amount of research in the neuroscience of business and financial decision making (neuroeconomics). There have been multiple calls for research in entrepreneurial decision making (Baron and Henry, 2011; Shepherd et al., 2015). One area with great potential to make a contribution would be to add neuroimaging data to research questions regarding the ways in which affect influences entrepreneurial decisions to enter a market, establish their new venture, and exit, (see Antonakis and Autio, 2007; Dew et al., 2009; Riaz et al., 2014; Shepherd et al., 2015). The general research question being, how does affect influence entrepreneurs' decisions and actions when exploiting an opportunity?

Baron and Henry (2011), in their three-phase model of entrepreneurship, explain that new ventures go through pre-launch, launch, and post-launch phases. In the post-launch phase, entrepreneurs make decisions in an effort to: build their customer base, hire key employees, improve product design or service offerings, conduct negotiations, and influence and motivate others (Antonakis and Autio, 2007; Vecchio, 2003). Those decisions can be influenced by affect in several ways (see Kahneman and Tversky, 1979; Västfjäll and Slovic, 2013). Affect is the feeling state that delineates the generally positive or negative quality of a stimulus (Västfjäll and Slovic, 2013). Affect directs, and to some extent controls, attention during decision making, which in turn influences information processing during decision making (Västfjäll and Slovic, 2013).

Affect influences decision making, especially when situations are characterized by uncertainty (Lerner and Keltner, 2001), which can be extremely high for entrepreneurs as they establish their new ventures (Shepherd et al., 2015). The particular emotional state of the decision maker can interact with context and influence decision making (Raghunathan and Pham, 1999). Negative emotions of sadness, fear, and uncertainty tend to facilitate systematic, detail-oriented and deliberate information processing (Visser et al., 2013).

Affect has a substantial role in dual-process theories of cognition, which hold that people interpret reality using either System 1 or System 2 thinking. When System 2 thinking is active, there is more deliberate, slow, verbal, and analytical information processing. Experiential, non-verbal, intuitive, and automatic information processing characterizes System 1 thinking. Do serial entrepreneurs engage System 1 and System 2 thinking differently from new entrepreneurs or non-entrepreneurs? Collecting fMRI data with a well-designed study could reveal the neural networks associated with each category of entrepreneurs, and a mixed design could reveal the sequence of transient neural activity associated with entrepreneurial decision making.

Previous research has demonstrated that specific affective states influence decisions differently, including monetary decisions, even when experienced affect is unrelated to the decision at hand (see Shiv et al., 2005; Stanton et al., 2014). Fear often increases estimates of risk, and anger tends to decrease risk estimates (Västfjäll and Slovic, 2013). Sadness tends to evoke a focus on reward acquisition, as well as avoidance tendencies (Västfjäll and Slovic, 2013). Neuroimaging data using fMRI could reveal the sequence of cognitive processes that entrepreneurs go through when a new venture fails, and when entrepreneurs make exit decisions. The neural activation data could reveal more precisely how entrepreneurs decide to exit.

Positive affect can also influence decision making. Optimism is an extensively researched topic in entrepreneurship that seems to be closely associated with emotional states that have a positive valence. The effects of optimism on entrepreneurial performance show mixed effects (Hmieleski and Baron, 2009). Using fMRI data may reveal multiple neural pathways or patterns of activation that correlate with the experience of optimism. Such findings could provide insight into why we see differential effects of optimism on entrepreneurial performance.

TYPES OF HYPOTHESES IN fMRI STUDIES

There are three types of hypotheses that can be made in fMRI and other brain-imaging studies: hemodynamic, neuronal, and psychological hypotheses. The *hemodynamic hypothesis* is the most specific of the three types of hypotheses, with predictions focused on the BOLD effect without inferring causes or effects of BOLD changes. *Neuronal hypotheses* do make inferences about causes of neuronal activity but restrict those inferences to a specific type of stimuli. It is important to remember that fMRI infers neuronal activity based on blood flow (the BOLD signal); fMRI does not measure neuronal activity directly. *Psychological hypotheses* are the most applicable to entrepreneurship research. These types of hypotheses focus on the relationships between cognition (for example, decision-making heuristics) and fMRI results. Carefully constructing these psychological hypotheses and building a strong study design to test such hypotheses is absolutely critical to connecting the neural level of analysis with entrepreneurial phenomena such as entrepreneurial decision making.

An example of a psychological hypothesis that could be tested in entrepreneurship falls under one of the aforementioned research questions. The first research question asks: how do entrepreneurs identify and evaluate opportunities? One could hypothesize that decisions to exploit an opportunity partially rely on increased activity in the ventromedial prefrontal cortex. This is an example of a psychological hypothesis that could be tested with an fMRI study. The sequence of neural activity that fMRI data can reveal would provide new insights into the processes by which entrepreneurs identify and evaluate opportunities.

TYPES OF DESIGNS IN fMRI STUDIES

Best practices in designing fMRI studies are similar to general rules to follow in entrepreneurship research and organizational research more broadly. As is good practice in typical social science research, studies that use fMRI data should let the research question guide decisions about design. Thus, the key is to determine the design that will enable experimental manipulation to evoke measureable differences in BOLD activation.

There are some general steps to take to ensure sound design when using fMRI data. Once a topic is in mind for an entrepreneurship study that uses fMRI, it is important to assess the appropriateness of the independent and dependent variables. Consider, for example, a hypothetical experiment in which the researchers want to examine how entrepreneurs make decisions about options involving risk. On each trial, participants view potential gambles, in which there are different probabilities of favorable and unfavorable outcomes (for example, 40 percent chance of winning $50, 40 percent chance of losing $25, 20 percent chance of winning $0). When selecting a dependent variable, the research should consider which measure is the best fit for their question. For example, do they want to collect a measure of subjective liking for the gamble, ask participants how much they want to play the gamble, or ask them to simply decide whether or not to play the gamble? The next step is to ensure the hypotheses are testable given the design; if the answers are all "yes," then proceed with the study. In short, these are important thought questions to ask oneself when designing entrepreneurship studies that incorporate fMRI data.

There are additional best practices in study design that are specific to fMRI research. The goal in designing an experiment is to ensure a study has interesting and interpretable results, and that has sufficient power. The following guidelines are not exhaustive, but do provide a helpful starting point for entrepreneurship scholars to begin conducting high-quality research using fMRI.

First, it is important to evoke the specific cognitive processes of interest. Although seemingly obvious, it is surprisingly easy for novice researchers to conduct an fMRI study with a design that seems strong but does not actually elicit the cognitive processes of interest. Consider the hypothetical experiment mentioned earlier that seeks to examine how entrepreneurs make decisions involving risk. If all of the options presented to participants included large potential losses as outcomes, both risk aversion and loss aversion might shape participants' responses. Thus, the researchers would want to carefully control the stimuli in order to avoid potentially confounding these two cognitive processes. Considering the specific cognitive processes evoked by tasks has not been a common requirement in typical entrepreneurship research. That changes when one begins to use fMRI data. When using neuroimaging, researchers need to precisely define the mental steps that participants need to take to complete experimental tasks. In other words, what specific cognitive processes will be elicited by each stimulus in the experiment?

Second, it is important to maximize the changes in cognitive processes of interest, over time. This requires the researcher to carefully choose stimulus conditions and timing of stimulus presentation. One way to maximize the effect sizes of differences is to group together experimental stimuli, then build in other periods of time when participants do not engage in cognitive processes of interest.

Third, researchers should minimize correlations among elicited cognitive processes of interest by adjusting the order of the timing of experimental stimuli. Such correlations cause issues in analysis, which is problematic when determining support for hypotheses. For instance, in the hypothetical experiment examining entrepreneurs' responses to risk, imagine that after viewing each gamble and making a decision, the participant subsequently immediately saw the outcome of the gamble. If the timing structure was the same on every trial (for example, there was always a one-second delay between making a decision and viewing the outcome), it would be impossible to disentangle neural activation related to making the decision from neural activation related to learning the subsequent outcome. One way to resolve this issue is to vary the length of the delay between making a decision and viewing the outcome.

Fourth, it is important to try to measure participants' behavior that could be connected to fMRI activation results. Similar to best practices in entrepreneurship research, it is important to collect as much data as possible from each participant and collect data from as many participants as possible (Huettel et al., 2008). When you have a research question that compares different types of individuals, you will need to integrate fMRI data across participants. In this case, an important goal is to maximize the number of participants from whom you collect data. Like more typical entrepreneurship studies, the idea is to increase sample size wherever possible to increase power and strengthen the validity of conclusions. In sum, the probability of obtaining interpretable results from a well-designed study always increases by collecting more data either within or across subjects.

Similar to typical entrepreneurship research, it is important to collect as much data as possible during the experiment. Efficiency of research design comes to the forefront in fMRI research. The high cost of fMRI data makes it important for researchers to ensure that results will answer the research question using the least amount of data. For studies collecting data via fMRI, this means determining the optimal number of trials or repetitions of the experimental task. It is important to design the experiment so that while participants are in the scanner, they are spending time on the essential experimental tasks of interest. This means it is similarly important to minimize the time that participants spend on tasks that are fillers or not relevant to evaluating the effects of the experimental stimuli. Therefore, one of the best ways to ensure efficiency is by carefully designing a neuroentrepreneurship study. Three major types of experimental designs in fMRI research are blocked, event-related, and mixed designs. We describe each in more detail below.

Blocked Designs

The simplest way to investigate the effect of an independent variable on a dependent variable is through the use of blocked designs. In a blocked design, experimental stimuli are grouped together in time to form blocks. Typically there are two types of blocks: experimental and control. The control blocks can include a control condition in which there is a task or stimulus that evokes different cognitive processes than the experimental condition. Another type of control condition is the null-task block in which there is simply a rest period without any task requirement of the participant.

In addition to the importance of carefully choosing stimuli, it is similarly important to carefully set the order as well as the timing of stimuli. Typically the blocks are ordered such that experimental and control blocks are interleaved. This is because a major purpose of the control blocks is to build in time for the hemodynamic response to return to baseline. In terms of timing of the task blocks, one goal is to allow enough time for the hemodynamic response to stimuli and tasks. The second goal is to set a block length that evokes the same cognitive processes throughout. One helpful question to answer when determining block length is whether time constraints preclude extremely short or extremely long blocks. The task (for example, gambling task) may be too difficult or too easy, depending on whether the block is too short or too long. Try to avoid fatigue effects when using long blocks or cognitively intensive tasks. It is also important to consider the potential influence of practice effects.

An experimental condition presents stimuli to the participant for a period of time that is generally between 10 and 60 seconds. It is generally recommended that block length be constant for all of the conditions in order to optimize statistical power for experiments with two conditions. However, unequal block lengths may benefit experiments with more than two conditions (for a more extensive discussion of block designs and statistical analysis see Huettel et al., 2008).

Advantages and disadvantages of a blocked design
There are advantages and disadvantages to think about when considering the blocked design. When a major aim of the study is to demonstrate differences in neural activation the blocked design can be very powerful. The simplicity and power of blocked designs to detect neural activation are two main advantages. Detection is the determination of whether or not the experimental manipulation induced a change in neural activation within a given voxel. Estimation refers to the measurement of the pattern of change over time within a voxel that shows activity changes in response to the experimental manipulation. There is a trade-off in fMRI experiments wherein a study design that is good at estimation may be poor at detection or vice versa. For instance, in the hypothetical experiment studying entrepreneurs' responses to risk, on each trial they view a gamble with different probabilities of favorable and unfavorable outcomes. The researchers may *detect* that activation during this task increases in both the lateral prefrontal cortex and the amygdala. However, they may be interested in *estimating* differences in the timing of neural responses, if for instance, they think the amygdala reaction might occur faster and automatically and feed into processing that occurs in the prefrontal cortex.

Two factors determine the detection power of blocked designs. First the difference in BOLD signal between conditions should be as large as possible. Second, the signal to noise ratio should be maximized at the task frequency. These two factors indicate that the noise at the task frequency will be greatest with relatively long block lengths and smallest with relatively short block lengths. For experiments that test cognitive processes such as attention, longer blocks are often needed because those types of cognitive processes may begin after a time lag from the start of an experimental task.

Blocked designs with long blocks of stimuli are somewhat insensitive to changes in the timing of the hemodynamic response; they would only identify effects associated with the onset of the first stimulus in the block. Superposition is a principle of linear systems that states that the total response to a set of inputs is the sum of the independent responses to the inputs. When a series of the same or similar stimuli are presented, the hemodynamic responses to the individual stimuli combine. The combining of individual hemodynamic responses impedes the researcher from determining the shapes of the individual responses. Continuing with the example of the hypothetical experiment regarding entrepreneurs and risk, a blocked design would show a series of several potential gambles in each trial. The potential gambles are similar stimuli, and when shown in succession, participants' hemodynamic responses would combine due to superposition. Consequently, it would be impossible to determine if the hemodynamic response to a scenario with 40 percent chance of winning $50, differs from the response to a scenario in which there is a 20 percent chance of winning $10. A main disadvantage of the block design is this insensitivity to the shape and timing of the hemodynamic response.

In sum, blocked designs are simple and can be a powerful way to identify significant neural activation. Extending the time of the experimental condition can evoke very heterogeneous neuronal activity, making some tasks inappropriate for blocked designs. The aim is to identify specific cognitive processes by using tasks thought to evoke said processes. Heterogeneous activity weakens the ability to identify said cognitive processes. Furthermore, blocked designs are not useful for estimating the time course of activation in voxels.

Event-related Design

An alternative to the block design is the event-related design, which assumes that following a stimulus the neural activity of interest will occur for brief, discrete periods of time. Due to the focus on the sequence of activation in event-related designs, it is more important to optimize temporal resolution relative to blocked designs. In other words, event-related designs reflect fMRI research focused on measuring transient changes in neural activation that is associated with particular events.

An *event* is a single instance of a stimulus that causes the aforementioned neural activity. Events and stimuli are related but distinct concepts. The same stimulus can be an event for a brain region, and not an event for another region that does not show activation in response to the presentation of the stimulus. For example, if an experiment presented two types of stimuli as word and non-word letter strings, a given brain region may respond to the words and not to the non-words. The presentation of non-words for that brain region would be stimuli, but not events. The presentation of words for that brain would be stimuli *and* events because that brain region would exhibit a BOLD signal following perception of the words.

Early developments in electroencephalogram research were foundational to the development of event-related designs. Specifically, the practice of time-locking or synchronizing the EEG signal to the onset of a stimulus and signal averaging across many trials made it possible for researchers to extract small electrical changes called event-related potentials. Applying these techniques to fMRI resulted in the use of the event-related design, which is very commonly used in fMRI research today.

The event is considered an impulse that individually evokes the hemodynamic response. Thus, several events or impulses can be sequenced in relatively short durations (such as two seconds). After data collection, statistical procedures can then separate out the hemodynamic responses to each individual impulse. The timing and order of events (or impulses) may be randomly ordered. Similar to blocked designs, the time between events is important to design as well. The interstimulus interval refers to the amount of time that separates successive stimuli. This means that the interstimulus interval is the time between the end of one stimulus and the onset of the next stimulus. The term "stimulus-onset asynchrony" is the time between successive onsets of stimuli.

The time between events can occur at regular intervals, making it a periodic event-related design. Alternatively, many researchers use a technique called "jittering" to randomize intervals between successive events. Best practices recommend that when using an event-related design one should use variable interstimulus intervals within which one type of successive events occur every four to six seconds on average.

Advantages of an event-related design
The advantages of event-related designs are the ability to detect the timing, shape, and sequence of the hemodynamic response to events. The detection power can be strong in event-related designs. Relative to blocked designs, there is more flexibility in the event-related design to individuate particular functions because functions can be separated in time. One reason for this flexibility is that an event can be analyzed in multiple different ways in order to test different hypotheses. For example, participants might see two types of images (objects and faces) and two types of presentations (sideways or right-side up) in a randomized sequence of one image at a time. If the hypothesis focuses on differences in cognition when viewing people versus things, then the data could be analyzed as two types of events (objects versus faces). Alternatively, the data could be analyzed as one type of event (visual stimuli), or four types of events. Researchers can also choose stimuli based on experimental data by using trial sorting. This flexibility of event-related designs improves the efficiency of the study in that it enables the researcher to test multiple, different hypotheses from one sample in a study.

The concept of efficiency in an event-related design
Efficiency is a critical facet of design for any fMRI experiment, and is relatively unfamiliar to entrepreneurship researchers. Efficiency depends on the specific experimental hypothesis and efficiency is measured by the amount of data that would be required to test that hypothesis. A key

question to ask when designing an entrepreneurship study that uses fMRI data is: how should I present experimental stimuli to maximize the size of my effects given the specific type of hypothesis that I am testing?

There are several things that determine the efficiency of an experiment. Remember that the principal goal of fMRI study design is to evoke the *intended* mental process. An efficient design makes that possible with a relatively small set of data. The ability of an experiment to differentiate among conditions is reduced when there are high correlations among the processes of interest. These correlations can be due to frequently occurring processes or because subsequent processes are too close to other processes in their timing following an event. This creates inefficiency in the study.

Another cause of inefficiency is due to a poor match between design and research question. For example, investigating the timing and shape of the hemodynamic response is poorly matched to a purely blocked design, which by design does not allow for such analyses. Finally, a third cause of inefficiency is if the design is bad at evoking the processes of interest and does not, therefore, maximize the BOLD signal. This is especially relevant to entrepreneurship researchers, who would be looking at more complex cognitive processes such as decision making. The challenge for the researcher is to ensure that participants are taking the task seriously and not thinking about other things that are unrelated to the experiment. Otherwise, those unrelated cognitive processes can render a study's design useless.

Using an event-related design with very short, but highly variable, intervals between successive stimuli is often the most efficient experimental design currently in use. There are a few reasons for this. The randomization presents events that can occur in rapid succession, thereby evoking the maximal BOLD signal. The events can also occur with short time intervals between them, or even long time intervals, which allow the BOLD signal to return to baseline. This variability in the BOLD signal translates to good detection power because voxels that are activated will undergo changes of a large magnitude over time.

Other reasons why this design is particularly efficient is that time points are relatively uncorrelated, and the randomness of events minimizes the ability of participants to predict events. Uncorrelated time points with variable intervals between events maintains good detection efficiency and maximizes estimation efficiency. The inability of participants to predict subsequent events is important for efficiency because it reduces the occurrence of extraneous cognitive processes that occur when participants are anticipating or expecting an event.

There are a few ways to improve the efficiency of a study. First, researchers can use simple randomization of an event occurring or not.

Second, researchers can jitter the time between successive stimuli by randomly drawing amounts of time for the interstimulus interval from a distribution of possible intervals within a set range. For example, a researcher can randomly select intervals from a uniform distribution of time intervals between one and seven seconds. Third, researchers can use a semi-random design to change the statistical properties of the design over time – for example, if a study trial was 90 seconds and was segmented into three 30-second blocks. The chance of an event occurring in the first and last blocks of time could be 20 percent and the chance of the middle even occurring could be set to 80 percent. Finally, there are algorithms that have been developed to calculate and maximize the efficiency of study designs in fMRI experiments (see Huettel et al., 2008 for more information about these algorithms).

Disadvantages of an event-related design
While event-related designs clearly have their advantages, there are some challenges to overcome in these types of fMRI experiments. Event-related designs are more complicated to set up and often exhibit less power to detect neural activation than blocked designs. It is also possible to miss significant differences in BOLD signals by incorrectly modeling the shape of the hemodynamic response curve. However, event-related designs are superior to blocked design in estimating the shape and timing of the hemodynamic response.

In sum, event-related designs are helpful when investigating hypotheses regarding transient cognitive processes evoked by specific types of stimuli. When the research question and hypothesis calls for an event-related design, conducting such a study can be both efficient and informative. This is one reason for the popularity of this type of research design in fMRI studies.

Mixed Design

A third major type of research design for fMRI experiments are mixed designs that combine elements of blocked and event-related design. This can be an extremely powerful design for studies that investigate research questions regarding both short-term, transient cognitive processes and long-term, sustained cognitive processes during trials. These types of cognitive processing are referred to as state-related processes and item-related processes. State-related processes are neural changes that are assumed to reflect distinct modes of functioning. Thus, blocked designs are an appropriate design to measure state-related processes. Alternatively, item-related processes reflect changes in the brain that are assumed to be caused by individual stimuli, and can be more easily measured using event-related designs.

Mixed designs present stimuli in discrete blocks, and within those blocks are multiple events often using multiple types of stimuli. Conceptually, there is a difference between mixed designs and semi-random designs that are sometimes used in event-related experiments. Unlike mixed designs that assume the grouping of events into a task block that will cause the participant to maintain a cognitive state, stimuli in a semi-random design are assumed to repeatedly evoke a specific cognitive process. Repeated, discrete neural processes in semi-random designs assume that participants do not sustain an underlying cognitive state in relation to the task. For this reason, mixed designs are best when the research question and hypothesis requires an investigation into sustained neural activation (for example, sustained for 20 seconds or longer).

Advantage of a mixed design

Mixed designs can be powerful in separating brain systems that underlie state- and item-related aspects of experimental tasks. An example of this comes from a study by Donaldson et al. (2001), who used long task blocks of 105 seconds. In each task block, there were 42 randomly ordered events of three different types (words that participants had not studied, words that participants had studied, and fixation events without words). Results showed sustained activation increases in the prefrontal and insular cortices for the duration of the task block. Meanwhile, a more diverse set of brain regions showed event-related activation. Therefore, the mixed design enabled Donalson et al. (2001) to distinguish between multiple different activations related to state- versus item-related cognitive processes.

Another example shows how a mixed design can enable conclusions about regions that constitute a system for establishing and maintaining task sets. Dosenbach et al. (2006) used ten different fMRI tasks and 183 participants to find brain regions that showed activation throughout the task block unrelated to the particular type of task performed. Without a mixed design these conclusions would be unfounded.

Overall Recommendations for fMRI Research Designs

Of the three design options discussed, the optimal design depends on its appropriateness for testing the hypothesis. The importance of experimental design is undeniable and, for a much more complete discussion of design, we refer the reader to publications by Henson (2007), Huettel et al. (2008), Liu (2004), Liu et al. (2001), Poldrack et al. (2008), and Wager and Nicholls (2003) listed in the suggested readings at the end of this chapter.

ANALYSES

Following data collection via a properly designed fMRI experiment, one must statistically analyze the data. Entrepreneurship researchers who are looking to integrate fMRI into their studies will find several points of overlap in the underlying logic, concepts, and goals of statistical analysis of fMRI data. The ultimate objective is to use statistical analyses to derive meaning from data; what differs with fMRI data is that the dataset represents neural activation. In fMRI experiments, statistical significance is one factor used to evaluate the extent to which an experimental manipulation induced meaningful changes in neural activation.

Hypothesis testing is foundational to most fMRI analyses. Like entrepreneurship studies, the basic investigation tests an experimental hypothesis and null hypothesis.

If the probability that the data (as in neural activation) could have occurred under the null hypothesis is below the alpha level, then you can reject the null hypothesis. There are Type I and Type II errors to address in fMRI experiments, just as in entrepreneurship and other areas of organizational science research. Published articles that use fMRI data commonly present significant activation in voxels by color-coding statistical maps with colors varying according to the level of significance.

Many of the statistical tests used to analyze fMRI data match the types of statistics used in entrepreneurship research. T-tests can be used to determine if mean differences in neural activity are statistically significant across people or samples. Contrasts are used to create and evaluate differences in neural activation. Such contrasts involve a statistical comparison of neural activation induced by two (or more) experimental conditions.

The t-test and other univariate statistical tests are not appropriate for multivariate experiments and are difficult to use in event-related designs that are complex. The t-test makes a relative comparison of neural activation across conditions of the experiment. Therefore, this statistic is inappropriate when you want to draw conclusions about a pattern of activation. Another challenge for t-tests is determining the time points that should be assigned to particular experimental conditions. There is a time lag between the time when the stimulus is presented, and the hemodynamic response that stimulus evoked. To capture the hemodynamic response, researchers can delay the onset of all blocks by five seconds and exclude transition time that occurs during block changes.

Correlation analyses are used to determine the relationship between the observed data (showing the actual hemodynamic response) and the predicted hemodynamic response. Correlation analysis enables a basic modeling approach to predict expected neural activation. The strengths of correlation analysis complement t-tests and can be combined in regression analyses of fMRI data.

Regression and several statistical tests used to analyze neuroimaging data are based on the general linear model. This means that the data is treated as a linear summation of independent regressors that are the effects of different experimental conditions (for example, levels of the independent variable). In fMRI research, the basic parts of the general linear model involve data matrices. The data matrix is a matrix of data points with voxels along one dimension and time points along the other dimension. The design matrix for fMRI research is the specification of how model factors change over time. In the design matrix, there are M regressors and each regressor has a length of n time points. The parameter matrix shows the relative contributions of each model to the observed data for each voxel. Voxels are the rows in the parameter matrix and M parameter weights are the columns. The error matrix represents the fMRI data that the design matrix fails to explain after the parameter matrix is fitted to the observed data. By including nuisance regressors one can improve the model by modeling factors that are not related to the experimental hypothesis, but are associated with known sources of variability. Adding nuisance regressors can increase the validity of the model by reducing the residual variation in the error matrix. In sum, the general linear model is frequently used to analyze fMRI data. It assumes that the sum of individual factors can be used to model observed data (such as neural activation).

There are some challenges to data analysis that are unique to fMRI experiments compared with entrepreneurship studies. There are lots of data points in fMRI data analysis, which necessitates numerous comparisons. Thus, it is important to control inflation of the familywise error rate or the risk of making a Type I error by falsely rejecting the null hypothesis. ROI analysis restricts the focus of the analyses to a particular region of the brain based on *a priori* anatomical distinctions. In doing so, ROI analysis offers researchers an approach that reduces statistical comparisons and ameliorates the need for correction. The interested reader can learn about other approaches to reduce the need to correct for multiple comparisons in fMRI data. False positives are problematic in fMRI data analysis and significant attention should be given to controlling for Type I error. In sum, there is both overlap and differences in statistical analyses of fMRI data compared with analyses used in entrepreneurship research. In general, the goal of analyses matches that of other empirical work in organizational science: to evaluate differences across experimental conditions and develop good models of observed data.

Communication of Results

The use of fMRI data in experiments can bring challenges in communicating research results. It will be important for entrepreneurship researchers using fMRI data to avoid things like overblown, illogical, or unfounded conclusions (Ashkanasy et al., 2014). In articles, the persuasive power of visual depictions of neuroimaging reflects an inaccurate or incomplete understanding of neuroscientific methods and of what things like brain imaging can actually tell us. Most people have little if any training in neuroscience. Therefore, the common occurrence of misinterpretation is when brain imaging results is understandable and must be addressed in neuroentrepreneurship research.

Often findings and implications become overstated when neuroscientific research is reported. Popular press reports that publish statements about brain functioning and brain images have powerful influences on public audiences. The outlandish claims that have been popularized about brain imaging spread misunderstandings regarding the meaning and consequences of neurological measurement, and can create an irrational fear of things like mind reading (Huettel et al., 2008).

While reporting neuroimaging findings as part of entrepreneurship studies certainly presents a challenge, it can be overcome, allowing accurate communication of neuroentrepreneurship research results to any audience. A major challenge lies in explaining concepts in enough detail and with appropriate diction to educate readers about the results. Equally important is an awareness of the researcher, and an ability of the researcher to explicate the logic behind the conclusions drawn from an experiment. Individual researchers and research teams should play a key part in improving research reports by taking care not to overstate their findings. Researchers should also precisely state the conclusions that can be drawn. Finally, researchers should explicitly describe the limitations of their studies, with perhaps additional explanation given the nature of this type of research and the newness of its application in neuroentrepreneurship settings (Huettel et al., 2008). A general mindset to help researchers clearly communicate their neuroimaging results can come from asking: who is my audience and what is the neuroimaging knowledge of a typical member of said audience?

One additional feature of communicating neuroimaging results is worth noting. The media and journalists tend to be interested in reporting research that uses neuroimaging. Thus, empirical results may flow from the neuroentrepreneurship researcher to members of the media and journalists, who then report to public readers. It is therefore imperative that media members and journalists retain *all* important information, while making the message digestible to those without training in neuroscience. Given that the media and journalists have a stronger incentive toward increasing readership, neuroentrepreneurship researchers would do well to advocate for accuracy in reports of their research results. In sum, conveying all important information without sensationalizing conclusions is a key challenge for researchers, which must be met for neuroentrepreneurship to have a reputation of legitimacy.

DISCUSSION AND CONCLUSIONS

From research question to hypothesis development to publishing results, neuroentrepreneurship studies that use fMRI will challenge even the most creative scholar to conduct entrepreneurship research in novel ways. Following good design in fMRI research there are the additional tasks of analyzing and interpreting data collected, as well as effectively communicating the results. Publishing research connecting entrepreneurship and neuroscience will require entrepreneurship scholars to address misinterpretations, avoid overstating conclusions from neuroimaging data, and explicate the deep as well as superficial limitations of the study.

In terms of limitations, an effective researcher in neuroentrepreneurship can employ multiple measurement methods, including neuroimaging. The challenge will be in maintaining ecological validity of entrepreneurial tasks, while making experimental tasks suitable for fMRI data collection. The prudent researcher will have numerous considerations to make and challenges to tackle in exploring this emerging area of neuroentrepreneurship research. Yet in the middle of difficulty lies opportunity, and employing neuroimaging like fMRI in entrepreneurship research can produce cutting-edge research with important implications.

REFERENCES

Andrews-Hanna, J.R., J.S. Reidler, J. Sepulcre, R. Poulin, and R.L. Buckner (2010), "Functional-anatomic fractionation of the brain's default network," *Neuron*, **65** (4), 550–62; http://doi.org/10.1016/j.neuron.2010.02.005.

Antonakis, J., and E. Autio (2007), "Entrepreneurship and leadership," in J. Baum, M. Frese, and R.A. Baron (eds), *The Psychology of Entrepreneurship*, Mahwah, NJ: Erlbaum, pp. 189–208.

Ashkanasy, N.M., W.J. Becker, and D.A. Waldman (2014), "Neuroscience and organizational behavior: avoiding both neuro-euphoria and neuro-phobia," *Journal of Organizational Behavior*, **35** (7), 909–19; http://doi.org/10.1002/job.1952.

Bagozzi, R.P., W.J.M.I. Verbeke, R.C. Dietvorst, F.D. Belschak, W.E. van den Berg, and W.J.R. Rietdijk (2013), "Theory of mind and empathic explanations of Machiavellianism:

a neuroscience perspective," *Journal of Management*, **39** (7), 1760–98; http://doi.org/10.1177/0149206312471393.

Balthazard, P.A., D.A. Waldman, R.W. Thatcher, and S.T. Hannah (2012), "Differentiating transformational and non-transformational leaders on the basis of neurological imaging," *The Leadership Quarterly*, **23** (2), 244–58.

Baron, R.A., and R.A. Henry (2011), "Entrepreneurship: the genesis of organizations," in Sheldon Zedeck (ed), *APA Handbook of Industrial and Organizational Psychology, Vol 1: Building and Developing the Organization*, Washington, DC: American Psychological Association, pp. 241–73.

Becker, W.J., R. Cropanzano, and A.G. Sanfey (2011), "Organizational neuroscience: taking organizational theory inside the neural black box," *Journal of Management*, **37** (4), 933–61; http://doi.org/10.1177/0149206311398955.

Becker, W.J., and J.I. Menges (2013), "Biological implicit measures in HRM and OB: a question of how not if," *Human Resource Management Review*, **23** (3), 219–28; http://doi.org/10.1016/j.hrmr.2012.12.003.

Bird, B. (1988), "Implementing entrepreneurial ideas: the case for intention," *Academy of Management Review*, **13** (3), 442–53.

Boyatzis, R.E. (2014), "Possible contributions to leadership and management development from neuroscience," *Academy of Management Learning & Education*, **13** (2), 300–303; http://doi.org/10.5465/amle.2014.0084.

Cacioppo, J.T. (2002), *Foundations in Social Neuroscience*, Cambridge, MA: MIT Press.

Camerer, C.F. (2008), "The potential of neuroeconomics," *Economics and Philosophy*, **24** (03), 369–79.

Dew, N., S. Read, S.D. Sarasvathy, and R. Wiltbank (2009), "Effectual versus predictive logics in entrepreneurial decision-making: differences between experts and novices," *Journal of Business Venturing*, **24** (4), 287–309; http://doi.org/10.1016/j.jbusvent.2008.02.002.

Donaldson, D.I., S.E. Petersen, J.M. Ollinger, and R.L. Buckner (2001), "Dissociating state and item components of recognition memory using fMRI," *Neuroimage*, **13** (1), 129–42.

Dosenbach, N.U., K.M. Visscher, E.D. Palmer, F.M. Miezin, K.K. Wenger, H.C. Kang, . . . and S.E. Petersen (2006), "A core system for the implementation of task sets," *Neuron*, **50** (5), 799–812.

Glimcher, P.W., and E. Fehr (2013), *Neuroeconomics: Decision Making and the Brain*, New York: Academic Press.

Hannah, S.T., P.A. Balthazard, D.A. Waldman, P.L. Jennings, and R.W. Thatcher (2013), "The psychological and neurological bases of leader self-complexity and effects on adaptive decision-making," *Journal of Applied Psychology*, **98** (3), 393.

Healey, M.P. and Gerard P. Hodgkinson (2015), "Toward a theoretical framework for organizational neuroscience," in David A. Waldman and Pierre A. Balthazard (eds), *Organizational Neuroscience*, vol. 7, Bingley: Emerald Group Publishing Limited, pp. 51–81.

Henson, R. (2007), "Efficient experimental design for fMRI," in William D. Penny, Karl J. Friston, John T. Ashburner, Stefan J. Kiebel, and Thomas E. Nichols (eds), *Statistical Parametric Mapping: The Analysis of Functional Brain Images*, London: Elsevier, pp. 193–210.

Hmieleski, K.M., and R.A. Baron (2009), "Entrepreneurs' optimism and new venture performance: a social cognitive perspective," *Academy of Management Journal*, **52** (3), 473–88; http://doi.org/10.5465/AMJ.2009.41330755.

Huettel, S.A., A.W. Song, and G. McCarthy (2008), *Functional Magnetic Resonance Imaging*, 2nd edn, Sunderland, MA: Sinauer Associates.

Kahneman, D., and A. Tversky (1979), "Prospect theory: an analysis of decision under risk," *Econometrica*, **47** (2), 263–91; http://doi.org/10.2307/1914185.

Lerner, J.S., and D. Keltner (2001), "Fear, anger, and risk," *Journal of Personality and Social Psychology*, **81** (1), 146.

Lindebaum, D., and M. Zundel (2013), "Not quite a revolution: scrutinizing organizational neuroscience in leadership studies," *Human Relations*, **66** (6), 857–77; http://doi.org/10.1177/0018726713482151.

Liu, T.T. (2004), "Efficiency, power, and entropy in event-related fMRI with multiple trial types: part II: design of experiments," *Neuroimage*, **21** (1), 401–13.

Liu, T.T., L.R. Frank, E.C. Wong, and R.B. Buxton (2001), "Detection power, estimation efficiency, and predictability in event-related fMRI," *Neuroimage*, **13** (4), 759–73.

Mumford, J.A. (2012), "A power calculation guide for fMRI studies," *Social Cognitive and Affective Neuroscience*, **7** (6), 738–42; http://doi.org/10.1093/scan/nss059.

Poldrack, R.A. (2006), "Can cognitive processes be inferred from neuroimaging data?" *Trends in Cognitive Sciences*, **10** (2), 59–63.

Poldrack, R.A., P.C. Fletcher, R.N. Henson, K.J. Worsley, M. Brett, and T.E. Nichols (2008), "Guidelines for reporting an fMRI study," *Neuroimage*, **40** (2), 409–14.

Powell, T.C. (2011), "Neurostrategy," *Strategic Management Journal*, **32** (13), 1484–99; http://doi.org/10.1002/smj.969.

Purves, D., E.M. Brannon, R. Cabeza, S.A. Huettel, K.S. LaBar, M.L. Platt, and M.G. Woldorff (2008), *Principles of Cognitive Neuroscience*, vol. 83, Sunderland, MA: Sinauer Associates.

Raghunathan, R., and M.T. Pham (1999), "All negative moods are not equal: motivational influences of anxiety and sadness on decision making," *Organizational Behavior and Human Decision Processes*, **79** (1), 56–77.

Raichle, M.E., and A.Z. Snyder (2007), "A default mode of brain function: a brief history of an evolving idea," *NeuroImage*, **37** (4), 1083–90; http://doi.org/10.1016/j.neuroimage.2007.02.041.

Riaz, M.N., M.A. Riaz, and N. Batool (2014), "Managerial decision making styles as predictors of personal and organizational outcomes of in-service employees," *Journal of Behavioural Sciences*, **24** (2), 100–116.

Schwarz, N. (2000), "Emotion, cognition, and decision making," *Cognition & Emotion*, **14** (4), 433–40.

Senior, C., N. Lee, and M. Butler (2011), "Organizational cognitive neuroscience," *Organization Science*, **22**, 804–15.

Shane, S., and S. Venkataraman (2000), "The promise of entrepreneurship as a field of research," *Academy of Management Review*, **25** (1), 217–26.

Shepherd, D.A. (2011), "Multilevel entrepreneurship research: opportunities for studying entrepreneurial decision making," *Journal of Management*, **37** (2), 412–20; http://doi.org/10.1177/0149206310369940.

Shepherd, D.A. (2015), "Party on! A call for entrepreneurship research that is more interactive, activity based, cognitively hot, compassionate, and prosocial," *Journal of Business Venturing*, **30** (4), 489–507; http://doi.org/10.1016/j.jbusvent.2015.02.001.

Shepherd, D.A., T.A. Williams, and H. Patzelt (2015), "Thinking about entrepreneurial decision making review and research agenda," *Journal of Management*, **41** (1), 11–46.

Shiv, B., G. Loewenstein, A. Bechara, H. Damasio, and A.R. Damasio (2005), "Investment behavior and the negative side of emotion," *Psychological Science*, **16** (6), 435–9; http://doi.org/10.1111/j.0956-7976.2005.01553.x.

Stanton, S.J., C. Reeck, S.A. Huettel, and K.S. LaBar (2014), "Effects of induced moods on economic choices," *Judgment and Decision Making*, **9** (2), 167–75.

Västfjäll, D., and P. Slovic (2013), "Cognition and emotion in judgment and decision making," in M.D. Robinson, E.R. Watkins, and E. Harmon-Jones (eds), *Handbook of Cognition and Emotion*, New York: Guilford Press, pp. 252–71.

Vecchio, R.P. (2003), "Entrepreneurship and leadership: common trends and common threads," *Human Resource Management Review*, **13**, 303–27.

Visser, V.A., D. van Knippenberg, G.A. van Kleef, and B. Wisse (2013), "How leader displays of happiness and sadness influence follower performance: emotional contagion and creative versus analytical performance," *The Leadership Quarterly*, **24** (1), 172–88; http://doi.org/10.1016/j.leaqua.2012.09.003.

Volk, S., and T. Köhler (2012), "Brains and games applying neuroeconomics to organizational research," *Organizational Research Methods*, **15** (4), 522–52; http://doi.org/10.1177/1094428112449656.

Wager, T.D., and T.E. Nichols (2003), "Optimization of experimental design in fMRI: a general framework using a genetic algorithm," *Neuroimage*, **18** (2), 293–309.
Ward, M.K., S. Volk, and W.J. Becker (2015), "An overview of organizational neuroscience," in *Organizational Neuroscience: Monographs in Leadership and Management*, vol. 7, Emerald Group Publishing Limited, pp. 17–50.

LIST OF RECOMMENDED READING

Henson, R. (2007), "Efficient experimental design for fMRI," in William D. Penny, Karl J. Friston, John T. Ashburner, Stefan J. Kiebel, and Thomas E. Nichols (eds), *Statistical Parametric Mapping: The Analysis of Functional Brain Images*, London: Elsevier, pp. 193–210.
Liu, T.T. (2004), "Efficiency, power, and entropy in event-related fMRI with multiple trial types: part II: design of experiments," *Neuroimage*, **21** (1), 401–13.
Mumford, J.A. (2012), "A power calculation guide for fMRI studies," *Social Cognitive and Affective Neuroscience*, **7** (6), 738–42; http://doi.org/10.1093/scan/nss059.
Poldrack, R.A., P.C. Fletcher, R.N. Henson, K.J. Worsley, M. Brett, and T.E. Nichols (2008), "Guidelines for reporting an fMRI study," *Neuroimage*, **40** (2), 409–14.
Raichle, M.E. and A.Z. Snyder (2007), "A default mode of brain function: a brief history of an evolving idea," *NeuroImage*, **37** (4), 1083–90; http://doi.org/10.1016/j.neuroimage.2007.02.041.
Stanton, S.J., C. Reeck, S.A. Huettel, and K.S. LaBar (2014), "Effects of induced moods on economic choices," *Judgment and Decision Making*, **9** (2), 167–75.
Wager, T.D. and T.E. Nichols (2003), "Optimization of experimental design in fMRI: a general framework using a genetic algorithm," *Neuroimage*, **18** (2), 293–309.
Ward, M.K. and W.J. Becker (2015), "Work at the intersection of theoretical neuroscience, entrepreneurship, and technology: a TIP interview with Dr. Vivienne Ming, part 1," *The Industrial-Organizational Psychologist*, **53** (2), 67–71.
Ward, M.K. and W.J. Becker (2016), "Enhancing cognitive ability and revolutionizing I-O psychology: a TIP interview with Dr. Vivienne Ming, part 2," *The Industrial-Organizational Psychologist*, **53** (3), 39–43.
Ward, M.K., S. Volk, and W.J. Becker (2015), "An overview of organizational neuroscience," in D.A. Waldman and P.A. Balthazard (eds), *Organizational Neuroscience: Monographs in Leadership and Management*, vol. 7, London: Emerald Group Publishing Limited, pp. 17–50.

6. Experimental methodological principles for entrepreneurship research using neuroscience techniques
Víctor Pérez-Centeno

INTRODUCTION

The successful application of neuroscientific techniques and methods to address a specific entrepreneurship research question is essentially a well-designed experiment. This approach is termed neuroentrepreneurship (N. Krueger and Welpe, 2014), entrepreneurial neuroscience (Randolph-Seng et al., 2014), and, more recently, brain-driven entrepreneurship research (Perez, 2017).[1]

Because of its newness and the level of technical and methodological competencies that this approach demands, at the time of writing only five entrepreneurship studies have been carried out using a brain-driven approach: one using neurofeedback (Rahmati et.al., 2014); three deploying electroencephalography (EEG) (Ortiz-Terán et al., 2013; Martin de Holan et al., 2013; Zaro et al., 2016), and one applying functional magnetic resonance imaging (fMRI) (Laureiro-Martínez et al., 2014). This chapter focuses on experimental design as well as nine methodological principles to account for in the design of a laboratory experiment within the context of a brain-driven entrepreneurship study.

These principles, as useful as they are, do not replace the neuroscience knowledge needed to execute an experiment. That being said, this chapter alone is not sufficient to equip entrepreneurship researchers to immediately apply a brain-driven approach in a laboratory. Rather, this chapter will prepare researchers unfamiliar with the details of laboratory experiments to understand the basic concepts of how to conduct brain-driven entrepreneurship research in a laboratory setting.

EXPERIMENTS

The appropriate design of a laboratory experiment constitutes the first pillar in applying neuroscience methods to entrepreneurship research: evaluation, discovery, and exploitation (Shane and Venkataraman, 2000).

The nature of such a design is to quantitatively measure the effects, if any, of cognitive and/or behavioral variables of interest (Charron et al., 2008).

Much as the first generation studies of empirical entrepreneurship suggested no room for laboratory research, arguing that the innate characteristics of people cannot be manipulated, many changes have occurred. These changes create an environment more welcoming to contributions from laboratory research such as experiments (Davidsson, 2007). On one hand, entrepreneurship is decreasingly seen as a dichotomous individual disposition and rather as a result of the interplay between the person, task, and environment (Shane, 2003). These are phenomena that experiments manipulate with great mastery (Davidsson, 2007). On the other hand, the approach of powerful neuroscience advancements permits researchers to directly observe the brain's responses during experiments.

Methodologists consider experiments as the "most rigorous of all research designs" and the "gold standard against which all other designs are judged" (Trochim, 2001, p. 191).[2] In entrepreneurship research, experiments are relevant for three reasons: first, they can establish causality in a relatively unambiguous manner (Davidsson, 2007), thus allowing for rigorous tests of theory that specify cause–effect relationships (Colquitt, 2008). In doing so, experiments address the internal validity problem the field faces (Martin de Holan, 2014; N. Krueger and Welpe, 2014). Second, laboratory studies are a valuable complement and sometimes an acceptable alternative when resource limitations prevent a longitudinal study in real settings (Davidsson, 2007). Finally, experiments appear to be helpful in assessing how expert entrepreneurs differ from novices (Davidsson, 2007). Nonetheless, despite the experimental method's capacity for developing and testing theory, researchers have barely touched the surface of potential in entrepreneurship research (N. Krueger and Welpe, 2008; Schade and Burmeister, 2009; Simmons et al., 2016).

Aguinis and Lawal (2012), for example, suggest that experimental methods are the most infrequently used methodology in published articles in the *Journal of Business Venturing* (JBV). While there has been a persistent increase in experimental entrepreneurship research since its introduction in 1990 (Kraus et al., 2016), experimental research remains in limited use when contrasted to other methodologies.

The lack of experiments in entrepreneurship research suggests that researchers are not utilizing experimental strategies because of a blend of three motives: the majority of entrepreneurship scholars are not aware of experiments' advantages; they do not know how to design and run an experiment; and/or their experimental studies are simply not standing up to the review process to publication. I argue that the main obstacle lies in the challenge that implies the design and implementation of a good experiment; it is not an easy task.

There are various design considerations when crafting an experiment (Simmons et al., 2016). In the case of a brain-driven entrepreneurship approach, an "experiment" refers specifically to a laboratory experiment conducted in a well-controlled environment monitored by a neuroscience technology. Other types of experiments such as quasi-experiments, field experiments, and natural experiments are not considered in this framework because they do not fulfil the requirements of internal validity and/or random assignment.

Laboratory experimentation consists of four stages: setting the stage of the experiment; constructing the independent variable; measuring the dependent variable; and planning the post-experimental follow-up (Wilson et al., 2010). The nine principles that follow depict some of the central issues to shoulder as a top priority when designing a laboratory experiment. Principles 1, 2, and 8 cover stage one; principles 3, 4, and 5 invoke stage two; principles 6 and 7 allude to stage three; and principle 9 refers to stage four. Issues related to statistical analysis are not covered, as this procedure is not part of the experimental design.

Becoming familiar with these principles is germane, yet should not be taken as the holy grail. Instead, the reader is herewith encouraged to learn the foundation of experimental design (Burns and Dobson, 1981). The section concludes with an example of an fMRI experiment that contains the essential steps to account for in order to address an entrepreneurship enquiry.

Principle 1: It is Primarily an 'Internal Validity' Game

Entrepreneurship workers should know that implementing a brain-driven approach fundamentally suggests keeping up "high internal validity" through laboratory experimentation. Internal validity fosters theory building, particularly required by the field of entrepreneurship.

Laboratory experiments are high in internal validity because they examine causality (Shaver, 2014) in a controlled environment. They have a unique advantage, taking into account that the internal validity of correlational studies dominant in the field of entrepreneurship are challenged by self-reporting and retrospective biases (Simmons et al., 2016). For instance, observational studies, self-reports, and correlational analyses do not usually establish causality because the variables are all measured concurrently. Therefore, one cannot assume that one variable influences another as a result of a significant correlation (Simmons et al., 2016).

The reasoning goes like this: laboratory experiments test causality, which if done correctly engender a high internal validity. This may nurture new theoretical insights needed to strengthen the basis of entrepreneurship research (Simmons et al., 2016). Simmons et al. (2016) remind us that causality is relevant to theoretical contributions, since testing causality can validate or reject relationships predicted by theory. In other words, causality can be established with a controlled experiment first (Simmons et al., 2016). If the experiment fails to show a significant treatment effect, researchers may revise the design and test other conditions or alternative factors and refine the lead hypothesis (Aronson et al., 1990).

Despite the fact that lab experimentation is an ideal instrument to test causality in brain-based research, once a theory is supported and a causal relationship is established by a controlled experiment, the results could be generalized to the real world using other empirical methods (Mook, 1983). These can include field studies attempting to replicate experimental findings (Simmons et al., 2016). As opposed to laboratory/controlled experiments, field and natural experiments do not fully fit within this approach, mainly because these type of experiments have lower internal validity. Their strength rather lies in their higher ecological validity, that is, the extent to which a study can be generalized to real life (Crano et al., 2014). Hence field and natural experiments are about generalizing a theory (for example, whether a relationship predicted by a theory would actually take place in various contexts) and answering the questions of who, where, and when (Simmons et al., 2016).

In addition to the lack of internal validity in field and natural experiments, the use of the neuroscience techniques suggested later in this chapter would be complicated in the former and unlikely in the latter, because the majority of these technologies are not mobile. The only tool that could potentially be used in field experiments would be EEG, due to the advantage of its portability.

Principle 2: There is No Substitute for Good Data

Though the use of neuroscience techniques provides many advantages for entrepreneurship workers, the outcome of a poorly designed experiment can neither be amended by any of these techniques nor by signal-processing methods. A well-designed experiment is as valuable with regards to the data collected, as failing to do so is damaging to the quality of results and credibility of an experiment. Kass et al. (2014) reinforce the point that statistical methods can not fix flaws in experimental design or data collection, and in the rare cases that it might, much work and adamant assumptions will be needed.

It is, therefore, necessary to allocate considerable time and effort making sure to record the cleanest possible data (Luck, 2014). To get experimental effects that are replicable and statistically significant, low levels of noise must be attained. Noise might be reduced by increasing the number of trials (Kappenman and Luck, 2010; Luck, 2014) but it is not generally recommended because, to reduce noise by 50 percent, trials must be increased by four times (Luck, 2014). This would substantially increase the budget and length of the experiment to the point of making it unviable.

Another solution could be to reduce the noise before it is picked up by whatever device is being used. For instance, in EEG/event-related potential (ERP) research much of the noise comes from non-biological signals such as skin potentials and electrical noise sources in the environment, accidentally picked up during EEG recording. In principle, it is feasible to minimize these sources of noise directly. In fact, the improvement of reducing these sources of noise could be equivalent to doubling the number of trials for each subject or the number of subjects in each experiment (Luck, 2014).

The occurrence of skin potentials might, for instance, be reduced by keeping the recording environment consistently cool and dry, to reduce abrasion of the skin under the electrode (Kappenman and Luck, 2010). This could also be reduced by puncturing the skin with a needle at the recording site (Picton and Hillyard, 1972).

From my own experience in EEG/ERP research, I can advise that focusing on decreasing every one source of noise before running an experiment pays off. It spares one-third of the time typically required per participant and, most importantly, it helps to significantly minimize the impedance between the recording electrodes and the live skin tissue from 5 kΩ to an average of 2 kΩ, which largely improves data quality.

Luck (2014) notes that in addition to tracking down noise sources and disposing of them directly, it is additionally conceivable to lessen noise by using data-processing techniques, such as filtering. However, it is important not to depend too much on post-processing techniques as these techniques are effective only under limited conditions, and because they almost always distort the data. Therefore, to enhance data quality and the probability of obtaining a statistically significant experimental effect (Kappenman and Luck, 2010), entrepreneurship scholars should take every measure to get the cleanest possible data; it will save money and time.

Principle 3: Consider a Within-subject Design for Judgment Studies

A critical decision that an entrepreneurship researcher will make is whether to manipulate the independent variable on a between-subjects or within-subjects basis (Wilson et al., 2010). Researchers should determine if participants will be exposed to multiple manipulations/treatment (within-subject design) where participants serve as their own statistical control (Grégoire and Lambert, 2015), or if participants will be exposed to only one experimental treatment (between-subject design) where the group not exposed to the treatment serves as the control (Simmons et al., 2016). Put simply, in a within-subjects design participants are allocated to several treatments or control conditions whereas in a between-subjects design participants are randomly assigned to a treatment condition or control group (Simmons et al., 2016).

Within-subject designs expose participants to various treatments and compare their results between the treatment conditions (Mark and Reichardt, 2004). This design choice makes it conceivable to inspect and control for the order in which participants see every condition (Simmons et al., 2016). The random order of treatment conditions in this design is known as counterbalancing (Simmons et al., 2016). The main advantage of within-subjects designs is that the internal validity does not depend on random assignment (Simmons et al., 2016). Because the same individual is responding to all treatments and serves as his/her own control, the sample size for within-subject designs is a fraction of that required for between-subject designs (Simmons et al., 2016). Often within-subject designs are preferred because fewer participants are required to achieve sufficient statistical power (Wilson et al., 2010).

The major weakness of this design is that participants are exposed to multiple treatments, which may provoke contrast (participants responding differently to the conditions) or assimilation effects (participants responding similarly to the conditions) (Simmons et al., 2016). These effects are known as "carryover effects," in which earlier treatments may influence responses to later treatments (Aronson et al., 1990). Within-subject designs are appropriate for so-called judgment studies when the treatments do not significantly alter participants' self-concepts. In judgment experiments, participants are more like passive observers: they are asked to recognize, recall, classify, or evaluate stimulus material presented by the experimenter (Wilson et al., 2010). The intention is to have minimal direct impact on participants except when the stimulus material captures people's attention and elicits meaningful judgmental processes (Wilson et al., 2010). Judgment experiments are easy to do because they require a less elaborate staging of the situation within which to involve participants (Wilson et al., 2010).

Wilson et al. (2010) underline that some hypotheses are judgmental in nature. For instance, emotion independent research questions on entrepreneurial decision making (hot cognitions) and opportunity discovery fit the judgmental type, because the treatments can be under-taken through recognition, classification, and evaluation tasks, without actively involving participants in a series of events that may change their self-views. For example, in the Forlani and Mullins (2000) experiment, each participant was introduced with the profiles of four ventures and asked to make a decision. The two independent variables, variability and hazard, were manipulated at various levels in each venture profile. Aware that participants need to respond to four ventures, and that their first decision may influence the next one (carry-over effect), Forlani and Mullins (2000) randomly presented the four venture profiles to participants in order to counterbalance a carry-over effect. A within-subjects design is generally recommended in a judgment study as long as the treatment applied can be counterbalanced.

Principle 4: Consider a Between-subjects Design for Impact Studies

Unlike within-subjects design, in a between-subjects design, experimenters create research procedures that expose different groups of participants to varying levels of one or more target variables (Grégoire and Lambert, 2015). Participants are relegated to either a treatment condition or the control group, and the consequences of these groups are contrasted to each other (Mark and Reichardt, 2004). Between-subject designs have the advantage of not anchoring participant responses after having been exposed to one treatment, therefore are not subject to carry-over effects (Simmons et al., 2016). This feature makes between-subject designs more appropriate for impact experiments.

In impact experiments, people are active participants in an unfolding series of events and have to react to those events as they take place (Wilson et al., 2010). Often, these events have a significant impact in people's self-views, and they thus become deeply involved in the experiment (Wilson et al., 2010). This might be a good choice for research questions that look into attitudes, behaviors (Simmons et al., 2016), and emotions-dependent decision-making processes because there is no risk of biasing the study results due to carry-over effects manipulating the attitude of the same participant via repeated treatments (Simmons et al., 2016).

For instance, entrepreneurship scholars interested in the effects of passion in entrepreneurial action should consider a between-subjects design and impact study formula. As Wilson et al. (2010) imply, it would be absurd to undertake an experiment on the influence of passion on entrepreneurial drive to action without doing something aimed at truly inducing passion among participants. Rationalizing backwards, an attempt to actively boost participant's passion in an experiment could neither be afforded by a within-subjects design, because of the carry-over effects it would generate, nor by a judgment study, because it is not suited to actively engaged participants.

Three guidelines for entrepreneurship researchers emerge from this: first, researchers should always tailor their method to their hypothesis (Wilson et al., 2010). Second, whether an experiment is an impact or judgment type depends on the phenomenon under study (Wilson et al., 2010). Third, if the research interests lie in what happens when a person's self-concept is engaged by a series of events that happen to that person, there is no substitute for an impact experiment (Wilson et al., 2010).

Principle 5: Pay Attention to the Homogeneity of the Sample

There is agreement that entrepreneurs are diverse (Hayton et al., 2002) in age, gender (Arenius and Minniti, 2005), and education[3] (Blanchflower, 2004). At a deep-seated level, neuroscience also provides evidence that variables such as age (Cabeza, 2002; Carter and Shieh, 2015), gender (Schulte-Rüther, et.al., 2008), education (Garibotto et al., 2008), and even language (Abutalebi et al., 2001) have impact on psychological processes and neural activations (Laureiro-Martínez, et al., 2015).

As a result, an experimental design that expects to examine any entrepreneurship subject from a brain-driven basis might consider these distinctions to expand the validity of the outcomes. Brain-driven entrepreneurship experimenters should afford attention to the homogeneity of their participants, because in doing so confounding variables such as age, gender, and education, among others, can be aptly decreased or controlled.

Aiming for homogeneity, however, influences the type and size of the sample required to run a laboratory experiment. For instance, finding homogeneous participants (entrepreneurs) implicitly encompasses the calculated selection of participants in terms of age, schooling level, and so on, and at the same time the identification of participants that fulfil the requirements set by the study's hypothesis: both demands are served with purposive sampling.[4] The same holds for case-study research – participant characteristics have to be specified so as to exclude trivial alternative explanations and ensure comparability of results (Eisenhardt and Graebner, 2007).

Usually a purposive sample is small, but in a brain-driven laboratory experiment at least three reasons justify a small-size sample. First, the premeditated selection of reasonably uniform participants naturally reduces the number of eligible subjects needed in a study; second, the statistical analysis, which technically claims that the optimal number of participants is sixteen (Friston, 2012). Friston (2012) argues that "if you cannot demonstrate a significant effect with sixteen subjects, it is probably not worth demonstrating." Moreover, Desmond and Glover (2002) underline that for a liberal threshold of 0.05, about 12 subjects are required to achieve 80 percent power at the single voxel level for typical activations. Third, and less important, logistical reasons such as costs per participant (Laureiro-Martínez et al., 2015) drive small sample sizes. Herein lies a core characteristic of laboratory experiments: their primary focus on internal validity in place of generalizability.

In practical terms, the sample size varies depending on the type of study. For instance, fMRI studies that focus on examining the location and magnitude of a neural activation of an action or decision (Laureiro-Martínez et al., 2015) involve small samples ranging from 15 to 20 participants (Carter and Shieh, 2015; Yarkoni and Braver, 2010). Experiments that seek to understand individual differences use samples of around 30 participants (Venkatraman et al., 2011). Studies that examine the differences between two groups of individuals apply samples of about 50 participants. For example; Ortiz-Terán et al. (2013) used a sample of 25 founder entrepreneurs and 25 non-founder entrepreneurs (50 participants) to gauge the relationship between neurophysiologic and personality characteristics in entrepreneurial decision making. One additional note has to do with the sample size needed in a within-subject study and a between-subjects study. Between-subject designs require twice the number of participants than a within-subject study (Carter and Shieh, 2015) because fewer participants are necessary to detect a mean difference between two conditions in a within-subject design than in a between-subjects design (Maxwell and Delaney, 2004).

Principle 6: Select an Appropriate Manipulation

Whether using a between- or within-subject approach, the means for manipulating target-predictor variables to probe any of the above topics in an experiment are diverse. In entrepreneurship research, there are three classes of manipulations: information manipulations, treatment manipulations, and priming manipulations (Grégoire and Lambert, 2015). It is important to understand that none of these may be connected with regards to a brain-driven research design.

Grégoire and Lambert (2015) note that information manipulations consist in systematically varying the information embedded in stories, scenarios, cases, profiles, descriptions, or audio or video recordings. Then, the extent to which the manipulations explain participants' different reactions is examined (Grégoire and Lambert, 2015). Simmons et al.

(2016) name this manipulation 'passive role playing' because the level of involvement is low, and participants are asked to make judgments on hypothetical scenarios. These manipulations are also known as vignette or conjoint experiments (Simmons et al., 2016). This is recommended in the case of judgment studies because it requires participants to read a text or observe a phenomenon and then make judgments or evaluations. To be considered within the bounds of a brain-driven entrepreneurship approach, these manipulations must be executed in a laboratory setting and be measured by an appropriate neuroscience technology.

Treatment manipulations investigate the effects of particular treatments or interventions on a subject's behavior and/or responses. In entrepreneurship research, treatment manipulations often concern the effects of various forms of pedagogical methods or content/skill training (Grégoire and Lambert, 2015). Subject to the degree of realism of the events, a manipulation might be categorized as 'active participation' (high involvement in a real-world context) or 'passive participation' (low involvement in a close-to-real-world setting). For instance, Souitaris et al. (2007) asked students to participate in an entrepreneurship training program and then assessed the effect of the program on the participants' entrepreneurial intentions. Because the participants actively took part in the experiment and responded to the manipulation (that is, the entrepreneurship program), the experiment was impactful to the participants (Simmons et al., 2016).

The application of this manipulation within a brain-based approach is extremely troublesome for different reasons. First; the internal validity of the study would be weakened because experimenting in a real- or close-to-real-world context does not match the stringent control that can be achieved in a laboratory setting. For instance, there might be extraneous variables linked with a particular treatment level, and randomization would be difficult to administer.

Second, with the possible exemption of EEG and functional near infrared spectroscopy (FNIRS), none of the existing neuroscience techniques are equipped to deal with the mobility requirements of treatment manipulations. Even if using EEG, it would be quite challenging to take simultaneous recordings of several participants at the same time in a close-to-real-world setting. On the other hand, priming manipulations use instructions, research material, and/or other aspects of an experiment's context to subconsciously prime or induce a particular state of mind (Grégoire and Lambert, 2015). Depending on the level of a participant's involvement, priming manipulations can be 'active role playing' (high involvement in a simulated scenario) or 'passive role playing' (low involvement in a hypothetical setting) (Simmons et al., 2016).

For instance, Grichnik et al. (2010) used a variety of movie excerpts to prime the positive and negative emotions embedded in a bogus visual acuity test to prime participants' positive or negative emotions before assessing their individual levels of entrepreneurial orientation. Because priming manipulations may influence a participant's self-views (Bengtsson et al., 2010), in addition to judgment studies they could also be used in impact studies. Priming manipulations are likely to be more useful because they appealingly exploit the advantages of both laboratory experimentation and neuroscience technologies. All things considered, brain-driven entrepreneurship scholars may consider the use of any manipulation with the proviso that it fulfils three conditions: adequacy to address the research question, high internal validity, and use of an appropriate neuroscience technique.

Principle 7: Find or Create a Simple and Clear Experimental Task

One of the most important parts of an experimental design is to devise a procedure that captures the independent variable perfectly without influencing any other factors (Wilson et al., 2010). So, choosing between information, treatment, or priming manipulation to control a particular independent variable is necessary but not sufficient. An entrepreneurship experimenter must also carefully engineer the way the chosen manipulation is to be executed. Such an aim is achieved through simple, clear, and repeatable procedures that resemble a simulated scenario in which a decision is taken several times (Laureiro-Martínez et al., 2015); such procedures are known as experimental tasks.

Often, the degree of elaboration of a task relates to the type of the selected manipulation. For instance, tasks in information manipulations tend to be simpler than tasks in priming manipulations, because the former primarily involve the plain display of text and images in various formats. In this case, a set of precise instructions should fulfil the task requirements.

Priming manipulations or the like require a higher level of elaboration because these manipulations require the examination of specific cognitive representations and processes without the awareness of participants (Bargh and Chartrand, 2000), such as the adoption or alteration of existing and ideally validated tasks, and sometimes the building of entirely new customized tasks.

An accurately designed experimental task is essential in order to reliably isolate activations related to the process of interest (Laureiro-Martínez et al., 2015). Tasks also should capture the attention of participants so that they remain alert and responsive (Wilson et al., 2010). In other words, experimenters must understand the world of participants well enough to build tasks that they understand in the same way as the experimenter does, even though the experimenter thinks in abstract terms and the participants think in concrete actual realities (Webster and Sell, 2014).

A way to identify appropriate tasks is to understand how neuroscientists approach these problems (Laureiro-Martínez et al., 2015). For instance, there is an accord that there is a strong positive correlation between the measure of selective attention and performance in the Stroop task (Lamers et al., 2010). Therefore, scholars interested in weighing the role of selective attention in entrepreneurial opportunity recognition could consider the Stroop task without the use of conventional selective attention measurements.

In sum, tasks for entrepreneurship studies should be uncomplicated, reproducible, and capable enough to detach specific brain processes under study from multiple neural systems that could be activated. There are many tasks used in psychology and neurosciences that could be adapted by entrepreneurship scholars to examine the distinct phases of the entrepreneurial process. If the problem framed concerns entrepreneurial discovery or exploitation, a multi-armed-bandit task could be considered. For instance, a 4-armed bandit task is a widely validated task of exploitative/explorative decision making (Daw et al, 2006) that has already been applied to assess entrepreneurial decision making (Laureiro-Martínez et al., 2015).

The task designed by Kolling et al. (2014) might also be adapted to gauge entrepreneurial discovery and exploration. This task simulates a situation of a foraging animal pursuing an imperative longer-term reward target, by asking subjects to try to repeatedly collect a target number of points. Subjects chose between safer high-probability options and riskier, but high-magnitude, options. Aside from stand-alone tasks, it is also possible to apply a combination of tasks to isolate specific processes and mechanisms (Venkatraman et al., 2009).

Principle 8: Verify the Ethical Requirements of Your Home Institution

Entrepreneurship scholars should be prepared to deal efficiently with the ethical issues arising from the use of neuroscience techniques in their experiments. Experimenting usually entails the collection of self-reporting behavioral and/or physiological data from human participants and that ought to be conducted in accord with the ethical principles of respect for persons, beneficence, and justice (Weijer et al., 2015). Most universities have established committees to review and approve research using human subjects to ensure that subjects are treated ethically, and that fair and humane procedures are followed (Levitin, 2002). The fulfilment of ethical requirements varies across universities (Levitin, 2002). For instance, ethical approval for EEG or transcranial direct current stimulation (TDCS) studies is granted automatically in some institutions while fMRI studies always require ethical approval. Levitin (2002) recommends to confirm the requirements of one's home institution before taking part in any human subject research.

Among the conventional ethical considerations,[5] there is one that merits special attention to entrepreneurship scholars applying a brain-driven research perspective: incidental findings. These refer to the discovery of physical abnormalities in brain scans after data collection (Laureiro-Martínez et al., 2015). Despite reports of unexpected findings in brain-imaging research (Katzman et al., 1999), many fMRI studies are performed by non-physicians, which leaves room for unanticipated results that may go unrecognized and thereby leave subjects without appropriate referral (Illes et al., 2002). Incidental findings can also be unveiled in magnetoencephalography (MEG) and EEG recordings; FNIRS also may detect abnormalities (Nelson, 2008). Therefore; the detection, significance, and management of incidental findings are crucial to the welfare of the research subject as well as to the integrity of the studies (Illes et al., 2002).

No guidance is available for addressing this issue within the arena of entrepreneurship research, but Illes et al. (2006) offer an ethical approach to incidental findings that could be adopted by future brain-driven entrepreneurship scholars. It consists of four recommendations: determine the potential for incidental findings at the outset of planning for the study and not after it has started; if the potential for a significant incidental finding exists, establish a process to handle discovery and reporting of such findings; determine the threshold for reporting incidental findings; and if monitoring and reporting incidental findings are not feasible or are unduly burdensome, the local ethical committee should be approached for further advice. These suggestions could be regarded as the starting point, because it is foreseeable that the discussion and establishment of protocols to specifically deal with incidental findings within entrepreneurship research will soon become a necessity.

Principle 9: Take Care of the Experimental Follow-up

It is important to emphasize that most of the success of an experiment lies in the quality of its design and the collection of the cleanest data, but a researcher's responsibility does not end when the data has been collected through a brain-imaging apparatus. Entrepreneurship scholars should recognize the importance of follow-up with the research subjects themselves and perform it accordingly. This is particularly the case if any deception has been employed within the experimental design (Wilson et al., 2010). As Wilson et al. (2010) advise, a cautious experimenter should take care that each of the four goals have been fully accomplished: make sure that participants are healthy; participants have understood the experimental procedure, the hypothesis and their own performance; take advantage of the participant's unique skills as a valuable consultant for the study; and probe for any wariness on the side of the participants, such as whether they believed the cover story.

The fact that a brain-driven approach to entrepreneurship makes use of different neuroscience techniques that are mostly unknown and, to some extent, 'scary' to participants, serves another forceful reason for entrepreneurship scholars to pay due attention to the post-experimental follow-up. Finally, in order to safeguard the validity of the experiment, the experimenter must persuade participants not to discuss the experiment with other people until it is completed (Wilson et al., 2010). Overlooking this issue may cause a few uninformed participants to undermine the entire study.

AN EXAMPLE fMRI EXPERIMENT

This example reveals some of the key steps required to address an entrepreneurship research question using fMRI. Notice that in addition to the nature of the hypothesis, the design of an experiment is also influenced by the type of the technique used – and in that sense, the structure of an experiment should be customized to the technical capabilities of the applied tool. In the case of an fMRI experiment, the following ten steps would apply:

Step 1: Formulate a Research Question

The research question should be specific enough. For example, let's say we are interested in exploring the neural basis of business opportunities among expert entrepreneurs. We conceptualize business opportunities as those who fulfil at least three conditions: generate positive net cash flow, solve a customer's problem, and its implementation involves a manageable risk (Baron and Ensley, 2006). One way to frame this question is: which brain regions are active when an expert entrepreneur recognizes a business opportunity?

Step 2: Identify the Independent and Dependent Variable(s)

The independent variable is the variable that varies from trial to trial (Carter and Shieh, 2015). In this example, the independent variable is an "opportunity." Because in this example we assume that an opportunity might be reflected regarding profit, customer's problem, and risk to the subjects (expert entrepreneurs), it can be said that the independent variable is made of three factors. On the other hand, the dependent variable is the change in the BOLD signal intensity in the brain. Note that the BOLD signal is the primary dependent variable, but some studies use other measures (Huettel et al., 2009).

Step 3: Generate the Hypothesis

Carter and Shieh (2015) assert that in an fMRI experiment the hypothesis can be framed in four ways: activity in brain region X is correlated with stimulus Y; activity in brain region X is higher under condition Y than Z; activity in brain region X changes across time as subjects learn a task, for a given stimulus; activity in brain region X precedes activity in brain region Y.

For this example, the following is our general hypothesis: *"Expert entrepreneurs will display a higher neural activity when recognizing a business opportunity than when recognizing a non-business one."* But since a hypothesis must be operationalized (Burns and Dobson, 1981) we elaborate our operational hypothesis as follows: *"Among expert entrepreneurs as defined by Sarasvathy (2008), the recognition of any of the three dimensions of a business opportunity as determined by Baron and Ensley (2006) will have significantly higher neural activity than a non-business opportunity as measured by the blood-oxygen-level-dependent (BOLD) signal."*

Sarasvathy (2008) conceptualizes an expert entrepreneur as a person who, either individually or as part of a team, had founded one or more companies, remained a full-time founder/entrepreneur for ten years or more, and has participated in taking at least one company public. Baron and Ensley (2006) suggest a total of ten dimensions, but in this example, we decide to focus only on examining the aspects of a customer's problem, net cash flow, and risk because they are the ones most relevant to the authors' model. In an experiment, we must aim for a balance between meaningfulness and simplicity.

Because fMRI can scan the entire brain and identify all regions that significantly differ between the two conditions (Carter and Shieh, 2015) it remains optional to focus the analysis on a particular brain region. In this example, we opt to scan the whole brain. The above hypothesis would be a hemodynamic hypothesis because it reflects questions about the BOLD signal itself, without making inferences about its causes (Huettel et al., 2009). Hypotheses in fMRI studies might also be psychological and neuronal (Huettel et al., 2009).

Step 4: Define an Appropriate Manipulation

Manipulations are the process by which an experimenter creates the independent variables operationally within the experimental setting (Walker, 2014). In other words, a manipulation is a mechanism by which the experimenter controls the independent variable. In this example, because we aim to use scenarios where imaginary business opportunities concerning net cash flow, customer's problems, and risk could be recognized by participants (expert entrepreneurs) we decide to apply an information manipulation. We chose this type of manipulation because it is well suited for almost any question about the judgments and decision-making processes of individuals in general, and of professionals in particular (Taylor, 2006), plus scenarios have already been used in the investigation of entrepreneurial decision making (Burmeister and Schade, 2007). Take note, we always attempt to justify our experimental choices.

Step 5: Determine the Design

In view that this experiment assesses entrepreneur's passive evaluation on many imaginary business opportunities presented to them, we decide that a within-subject design fits our experiment because it is the ideal setting for judgment studies. For the same reason, a within-subject design also fits well with an information manipulation. Because we aim to manipulate three variables (net cash flow, customer's problem, and risk) with two levels each (positive net cash flow/negative cash flow, solves/does not solve customer's problem, manageable risk/unmanageable risk) it is a 2^3 factorial experiment with eight possible scenarios or conditions. It means that in our experiment the factors are crossed (Collins et al., 2009), that is, all combinations of the levels of the three factors are formed, to create a design with eight experimental conditions. Note that in a within-subjects design, random assignment is not necessary (Simmons et al., 2016). Generally, experimental designs should be within-subjects whenever possible. (Huettel et al., 2009).

Step 6: Develop an Experimental Task

While a manipulation sets up a proper context to control the independent variable (eight scenarios) the task portrays "how" the manipulation will be executed. A task provides a reasonable context to test the hypotheses: it should be intuitive; easy-to-interpret; and should involve goals, measures of success, and the appropriate motivational mechanisms for the subjects to perform the task as expected. The level of detail of a task within the context of any manipulation using a neuroscientific technology, fMRI included, depends on the study. However, the idea is to make it clear enough that no participant can misunderstand it, but to be brief at the same time.

In this example, a summarized version of our experimental task would be as follows: *"We test eight hypothetical scenarios of a business opportunity concerning cash flow, customer's problem, and risk. Each condition has the same introduction, but different information is presented as per the manipulated condition. The scenarios are elaborated in text format and presented randomly to subjects on a computer screen. For each trial, the subject's task is to read and evaluate one scenario at a time and from the information presented judge it as either a business or non-business opportunity. Using a mouse, participants give their responses, clicking the right side of the mouse if they evaluate the presented scenario as business opportunity or the left side of the mouse if they assess the displayed case as a non-business opportunity. Subjects have a 60-second time limit to read a scenario and make their evaluation. The task entails 160 trials (20 per each condition). Before entering the scanner, subjects will be familiarized with the task using a separate set of stimuli."*

We chose 20 trials per condition because this is the suggested number of trials for fMRI decision-making experiments to acquire a stable average (Sanfey and Stallen, 2016). Keep in mind that other authors consider a range of 30–50 repetitions as the minimum number of trials for a meaningful signal extraction (Perez-Edgar and Bar-Haim, 2010). The task timing of 60 seconds is reasonable for a judgment study, considering that Huettel et al. (2009) recommend the timing limits of a task: from several seconds to two minutes, to allow for maximal signal intensity in active brain regions (Carter and Shieh, 2015). For a revision of another task to assess efficient decision making among entrepreneurs using fMRI, readers may consult Laureiro-Martínez et al. (2014), and the experiment by Krueger et al. (2014) illustrates the level of detail required in a task applied to the use of scenarios in fMRI research.

Step 7: Identify Participants

For this experiment, we consider the participation of 40 expert male healthy entrepreneurs with similar age and background (place of origin and schooling level) in order to minimize the influence of factors such as age, grades, and gender, among others, on subject's performance. This measure also reduces participant variables and avoids order effects. Regarding the quantity of participants, more often than not 10–20 subjects are needed for an fMRI experiment, but at least 20–40 should be recruited because some of the data will need to be discarded as some subjects may fail to show up, some may fall asleep in the scanner, or some may turn out to have medical conditions that may preclude them from participation in the study (Carter and Shieh, 2015).

Step 8: Get Approval from Your Local Ethical Review Committee

Once we have completed each of the above steps, but before proceeding to implement the study, it is necessary to obtain formal ethics approval for the experiment. This is a mandatory procedure for any fMRI study. Every experimenter applying fMRI must request and obtain written approval from his/her local ethical review committee. As a rule, experiments on human subjects using any neuroscience technology must be conducted following the principles of the Declaration of Helsinki set by the World Medical Association.[6]

Step 9: Run a Debriefing Interview after Data Collection

In an fMRI experiment, we use a debriefing interview to make sure participants have understood the instructions of the experiment, and each of the conditions applied. To ensure that each condition has been adequately comprehended Carter and Shieh (2015) recommend giving a brief survey in which participants indicate the level of familiarity with each condition on a scale of 1–10. We also implement a debriefing interview to provide participants with accurate information about the nature of the experiment. During the debriefing procedure, we impart to the subjects information identified with the targets of the research, along with the hypothesis for the experiment, and we take the opportunity to correct any misconception arising during this process. The final figure of this experiment is the difference in signal intensity between the eight conditions among subjects (expert entrepreneurs) set in step 5. Because the fMRI template contains coordinates for discrete brain regions, it is possible to interpret the specific regions activated in response to each tested scenario (Carter and Shieh, 2015). Remember that in this experiment we collected physiological (fMRI recording), behavioral (decision-making task), and self-report data (debriefing interview).

Step 10: Keep Improving Your Design

These can be considered some of the major steps to consider in an fMRI experiment to address an entrepreneurship research inquiry, nonetheless other steps such as pre-testing and pilot testing are said to be similarly important in an experimental design. The first because it involves examining the specific elements of the experiment in isolation and the second because it allows conducting full experimental sessions with an eye to what is and is not working as expected (Walker, 2014). As Walker (2014, p. 143) points out, "careful design must not cease when the design is in place or even after the elements have been pretested, good experiments are an exercise in vigilance."

FINAL REMARKS

In this chapter, I have provided an introduction of one of the two central components of a brain-driven perspective to entrepreneurship research: experimental design. The fact that, as of late 2016, only five articles have been published applying this approach calls for a broader dissemination of the bedrocks of this emerging line of research, and I believe this chapter helps to fill this gap. I have outlined the supremacy of laboratory experiments as an ideal research method to address a major challenge in entrepreneurship research, that is, the internal validity problem; I seek to encourage future entrepreneurship scholars to incorporate and apply these tools. Finally, I have pointed out nine methodological principles to take into account during the design of an experiment.

Laboratory experimentation traditionally entails four stages: setting the stage of the experiment, constructing the independent variable, measuring the dependent variable, and planning the post-experimental follow-up (Wilson et al., 2010). Aspects such as: careful operationalization, standardization of procedures, random assignment, and factorial designs are also seen as acute for entrepreneurship research (Shaver, 2014). It is fair to say that the minutiae of experimentation go beyond the confines of this chapter. Therefore, entrepreneurship scholars should devote supplementary time to learn the "how" of each of the methodological principles shared in this contribution. A further conclusion of this chapter is that researchers should also be able to experimentally test hypotheses in both the laboratory and field, as it is highly recommended that experiments are conducted in a variety of settings (Wilson et al., 2010). Laboratory experimenting is a necessity for entrepreneurship research and a must to those interested in exploring the entrepreneurial phenomena from a brain-based view.

NOTES

1. This approach refers to the combined use of both experiments and neuroscientific technologies to enable a deeper understanding of the phenomenon of entrepreneurship as well as its enhancement. This definition includes but does not restrict itself to brain-imaging and brain-enhancing technologies.
2. An experiment is a research method that allows the controlled analysis of a causal relationship between two variables, one called dependent (DV) and the other independent (IV). The dependent variable is the variable in the experiment whose changes depend on the manipulation of the independent variable (Coolican, 2014).
3. Particularly in richer countries.
4. According to Patton (1990, p. 169), the "logic and power of purposeful sampling lies in selecting information-rich cases for study in depth. Information-rich are those from which one can learn a great deal about issues of central importance to the purpose of the research thus the term purposeful sampling."
5. Informed consent by which experiment subjects are given an accurate description of their task, the risks involved, and the option to decline, or to discontinue their participation at any time without penalty.
6. The equivalent in the USA would be through the guidelines set by the U.S. Department of Health and Human Services (National Institutes of Health and National Institute of Mental Health).

REFERENCES

Abutalebi, J., S. Cappa, and D. Perani (2001), "The bilingual brain as revealed by functional neuroimaging," *Bilingualism: Language and cognition*, **4** (02), 179–90.

Aguinis, H., S. and Lawal (2012), "Conducting field experiments using eLancing's natural environment," *Journal of Business Venturing*, **27** (4), 493–505.

Arenius, P., and M. Minniti (2005), "Perceptual variables and nascent entrepreneurship," *Small Business Economics*, **24** (3), 233–47.

Aronson, E., J. Carlsmith, and P. Ellsworth (1990), *Methods of Research in Social Psychology*, 2nd edn, New York, NY: McGraw-Hill.

Bargh, J., and T. Chartrand (2000), "The mind in the middle: a practical guide to priming and automaticity research," in H.T. Reis and C.M. Judd (eds), *Handbook of Research Methods in Social and Personality Psychology*, New York, NY: Cambridge University Press, pp. 253–85.

Baron, R., and M. Ensley (2006), "Opportunity recognition as the detection of meaningful patterns: evidence from comparisons of novice and experienced entrepreneurs," *Management Science*, **52** (9), 1331–44.

Bengtsson, S., R. Dolan, and R. Passingham (2010), "Priming for self-esteem influences the monitoring of one's own performance," *Social Cognitive and Affective Neuroscience*, **6** (4), 417–25.

Blanchflower, D. (2004), "Self-employment: more may not be better," *Swedish Economic Policy Review*, **11** (2), 15–74.

Burmeister, K., and C. Schade (2007), "Are entrepreneurs' decisions more biased? An experimental investigation of the susceptibility to status quo bias," *Journal of Business Venturing*, **22** (3), 340–62.

Burns, R., and C. Dobson (1981), *Experimental Psychology: Research Methods and Statistics*, Lancaster: MTP Press.

Cabeza, R. (2002), "Hemispheric asymmetry reduction in older adults: the HAROLD model," *Psychology and Aging*, **17** (1), 85–100.

Carter, M., and J. Shieh (2015), *Guide to Research Techniques in Neuroscience*, 2nd edn, Burlington, MA: Academic Press.

Charron, S., A. Fuchs, and O. Oullier (2008), "Exploring brain activity in neuroeconomics," *Revue d'Economie Politique*, **118** (1), 97–124.

Collins, L., J. Dziak, and R. Li (2009), "Design of experiments with multiple independent variables: a resource management perspective on complete and reduced factorial designs," *Psychological Methods*, **14** (3), 202–24.

Colquitt, J. (2008), "From the editors publishing laboratory research in AMJ: a question of when, not if," *Academy of Management Journal*, **51** (4), 616–20.

Coolican, H. (2014), *Research Methods and Statistics in Psychology*, London: Psychology Press.

Crano, W., M. Brewer, and A. Lac (2014), *Principles and Methods of Social Research*, Mahwah, NJ: Lawrence Elrbaum Associates.

Davidsson, P. (2007), "Method challenges and opportunities in the psychological study of entrepreneurship," in B.J. Robert, M. Frese, and R. Baron (eds), *The Psychology of Entrepreneurship*, Mahwah, NJ: Lawrence Erlbaum Associates, pp. 287–323.

Daw, N., J. O'Doherty, P. Dayan, B. Seymour, and R. Dolan (2006), "Cortical substrates for exploratory decisions in humans," *Nature*, **441** (7095), 876–9.

Desmond, J. and G. Glover (2002), "Estimating sample size in functional MRI (fMRI) neuroimaging studies: statistical power analyses," *Journal of Neuroscience Methods*, **118** (2), 115–28.

Eisenhardt, K. and M. Graebner (2007), "Theory building from cases: opportunities and challenges," *Academy of Management Journal*, **50** (1), 25–32.

Forlani, D. and J. Mullins (2000), "Perceived risks and choices in entrepreneurs' new venture decisions," *Journal of Business Venturing*, **15** (4), 305–22.

Friston, K. (2012), "Ten ironic rules for non-statistical reviewers," *Neuroimage*, **61** (4), 1300–1310.

Garibotto, V., B. Borroni, E. Kalbe, K. Herholz, E. Salmon, V. Holtoff, and F. Fazio (2008), "Education and occupation as proxies for reserve in aMCI converters and AD: FDG-PET evidence," *Neurology*, **71** (17), 1342–9.

Grégoire, D. and L. Lambert (2015), "Getting inside entrepreneurs' heart and mind: methods for advancing research on affect and cognition," in T. Baker and F. Welter (eds), *The Routledge Companion to Entrepreneurship*, Abingdon: Routledge, pp. 450–66.

Grichnik, D., A. Smeja, and I. Welpe (2010), "The importance of being emotional: how do emotions affect entrepreneurial opportunity evaluation and exploitation?," *Journal of Economic Behavior & Organization*, **76** (1), 15–29.

Hayton, J., G. George, and S. Zahra (2002), "National culture and entrepreneurship: a review of behavioral research," *Entrepreneurship Theory and Practice*, **26** (4), 33–52.

Huettel, S., A. Song, and G. McCarthy (2009), *Functional Magnetic Resonance Imaging*, 2nd edn, Sunderland, MA: Sinauer Associates.

Illes, J., J. Desmond, L. Huang, T. Raffin, and S. Atlas (2002), "Ethical and practical considerations in managing incidental findings in functional magnetic resonance imaging," *Brain and Cognition*, **50** (3), 358–65.

Illes, J., M. Kirschen, E. Edwards, L. Stanford, P. Bandettini, M. Cho, and R. Macklin (2006), "Incidental findings in brain imaging research: what should happen when a researcher sees a potential health problem in a brain scan from a research subject?," *Science*, **311** (5762), 783–4.

Kappenman, E., and S. Luck (2010), "The effects of electrode impedance on data quality and statistical significance in ERP recordings," *Psychophysiology*, **47** (5), 888–904.

Kass, R., U. Eden, and E. Brown (2014), *Analysis of Neural Data*, New York, NY: Springer.

Katzman, G., A. Dagher, and N. Patronas (1999), "Incidental findings on brain magnetic resonance imaging from 1000 asymptomatic volunteers," *JAMA*, **282** (1), 36–9.

Kolling, N., M. Wittmann, and M. Rushworth (2014), "Multiple neural mechanisms of decision making and their competition under changing risk pressure," *Neuron*, **81** (5), 1190–1202.

Kraus, S., F. Meier, and T. Niemand (2016), "Experimental methods in entrepreneurship research: the status quo," *International Journal of Entrepreneurial Behavior & Research*, **22** (6), 958–83.

Krueger, F., M. Hoffman, H. Walter, and J. Grafman (2014), "An fMRI investigation of the effects of belief in free will on third-party punishment," *Social Cognitive and Affective Neuroscience*, **9** (8), 1143–9.

Krueger, N., and I. Welpe (2008), "Experimental entrepreneurship: a research prospectus and workshop," paper presented at the USASBE Annual Conference, San Antonio, TX, 10–13 January.

Krueger, N., and I. Welpe (2014), "Neuroentrepreneurship: what can entrepreneurship learn from neuroscience?," in M.H. Morris (ed.), *Annals of Entrepreneurship Education and Pedagogy*, Cheltenham, Edward Elgar, pp. 60–90.

Lamers, M., A. Roelofs, and I. Rabeling-Keus (2010), "Selective attention and response set in the Stroop task," *Memory & Cognition*, **38** (7), 893–904.

Laureiro-Martínez, D., N. Canessa, S. Brusoni, M. Zollo, T. Hare, F. Alemanno, and S. Cappa (2014), "Frontopolar cortex and decision-making efficiency: comparing brain activity of experts with different professional background during an exploration-exploitation task," *Frontiers in Human Neuroscience*, **7** (927), 1–10.

Laureiro-Martínez, D., V. Venkatraman, S. Cappa, M. Zollo, and S. Brusoni (2015) "Cognitive neurosciences and strategic management: challenges and opportunities in tying the knot," *Advances in Strategic Management: Vol. 32. Cognition and Strategy*, Bingley: Emerald Group Publishing Limited, pp. 351–70.

Levitin, D. (2002), *Foundations of Cognitive Psychology: Core Readings*, Cambridge, MA: MIT Press.

Luck, S. (2014), *An Introduction to the Event-Related Potential Technique*, 2nd edn, Cambridge, MA: MIT Press.

Mark, M., and C. Reichardt (2004), "Quasi-experimental and correlational designs: methods for the real world when random assignment isn't feasible," in C. Sansone, C.C. Morf, and A.T. Panter (eds), *The Sage Handbook of Methods in Social Psychology*, Thousand Oaks, CA: Sage Publications, Inc, pp. 265–86.

Martin de Holan, P. (2014), "It's all in your head: why we need neuroentrepreneurship," *Journal of Management Inquiry*, **23** (1), 93–7.

Martin de Holan, P, E. Ortiz-Terán, A. Turrero, and T. Alonso (2013), "Towards neuroentrepreurship? Early evidence from a neuroscience study," *Frontiers of Entrepreneurship Research*, **33** (5), Article 12; http://digitalknowledge.babson.edu/fer/vol33/iss5/12.

Maxwell, S., and H. Delaney (2004), *Designing Experiments and Analyzing Data: A Model Comparison Perspective*, vol. 1, Mahwah, NJ: Lawrence Erlbaum Associates.

Mook, D. (1983), "In defense of external invalidity," *American Psychologist*, **38** (4), 379–87.

Nelson, C. (2008), "Incidental findings in magnetic resonance imaging (MRI) brain research," *The Journal of Law, Medicine & Ethics*, **36** (2), 315–19.

Ortiz-Terán, E., A. Turrero, J. Santos, P. Bryant, T. Ortiz, and E. Ortiz-Terán (2013), "Brain cortical organization in entrepreneurs during a visual Stroop decision task," *Neuroscience and Neuroeconomics*, **2**, 33–49.

Patton, M.Q. (1990), *Qualitative Evaluation and Research Methods*, Newbury Park, CA: Sage.

Perez, V. (2017), "Brain-driven entrepreneurship research: a review and research agenda," in M. Day, M. Boardman, and K. Norris (eds), *Handbook of Research Methodologies and Design in Neuro-entrepreneurship*, Cheltenham: Edward Elgar.

Perez-Edgar, K., and Y. Bar-Haim (2010), "Application of cognitive neuroscience techniques to the study of anxiety-related processing biases in children," in Julie A. Hadwin and Andy P. Field (eds), *Information Processing Biases in Child and Adolescent Anxiety*, Chichester: John Wiley & Sons, pp. 183–206.

Picton, T., and S. Hillyard (1972), "Cephalic skin potentials in electroencephalography," *Electroencephalography and Clinical Neurophysiology*, **33** (4), 419–24.

Rahmati, N., R. Rostami, M. Zali, S. Nowicki, and J. Zarei (2014), "The effectiveness of neurofeedback on enhancing cognitive process involved in entrepreneurship abilities among primary school students in district No. 3 Tehran," *Basic and Clinical Neuroscience*, **5** (4), 277–84.

Randolph-Seng, B., J. Mitchell, and R. Mitchell (2014), "Introduction: historical context, present trends and future directions in entrepreneurial cognition research," in J.R. Mitchell, R.K. Mitchell, and B. Randolph-Seng (eds), *Handbook of Entrepreneurial Cognition*, Cheltenham: Edward Elgar, pp. 1–60.

Sanfey, A., and M. Stallen (2016), "Neurosciences contribution to judgment and decision making: opportunities and limitations," in G. Keren and G. Wu (eds), *The Wiley Blackwell Handbook of Judgment and Decision Making*, vol. 1, West Sussex: John Wiley & Sons, pp. 268–94.

Sarasvathy, S. (2008), *Effectuation: Elements of Entrepreneurial Orientation*, Cheltenham: Edward Elgar.

Schade, C., and K. Burmeister (2009), "Experiments on entrepreneurial decision making: a different lens through which to look at entrepreneurship," *Foundations and Trends in Entrepreneurship*, **5** (2), 81–134.

Schulte-Rüther, M., H. Markowitsch, N. Shah, G. Fink, and M. Piefke (2008), "Gender differences in brain networks supporting empathy," *Neuroimage*, **42** (1), 393–403.

Shane, S. (2003), *A General Theory of Entrepreneurship: The Individual-Opportunity Nexus*, Aldershot: Edward Elgar.

Shane, S., and S. Venkataraman (2000), "The promise of entrepreneurship as a field of research," *Academy of Management Review*, **25** (1), 217–26.

Shaver, K. (2014), "Experimental methods in entrepreneurship research," in A. Carsrud and M. Brännback (eds), *Handbook of Research Methods and Applications in Entrepreneurship and Small Business*, Cheltenham: Edward Elgar, pp. 88–111.

Simmons, S., D. Hsu, A. Wieland, and M. Begelfer (2016), "Experimental methodologies: applications and agendas for entrepreneurship research," paper presented at the USASBE Annual Conference, San Diego, CA, 8–14 January.

Souitaris, V., S. Zerbinati, and A. Al-Laham (2007), "Do entrepreneurship programmes raise entrepreneurial intention of science and engineering students? The effect of learning, inspiration and resources," *Journal of Business Venturing*, **22** (4), 566–91.

Taylor, B.J. (2006), "Factorial surveys: using vignettes to study professional judgement," *British Journal of Social Work*, **36** (7), 1187–207.

Trochim, W. (2001), *Research Methods Knowledge Base*, 2nd edn, Mason, OH: Atomic Dog/ Thomson.

Venkatraman, V., S. Huettel, L. Chuah, J. Payne, and M. Chee (2011), "Sleep deprivation biases the neural mechanisms underlying economic preferences," *The Journal of Neuroscience*, **31** (10), 3712–18.

Venkatraman, V., A. Rosati, A. Taren, and S. Huettel (2009), "Resolving response, decision, and strategic control: evidence for a functional topography in dorsomedial prefrontal cortex," *The Journal of Neuroscience*, **29** (42), 13158–64.

Walker, L. (2014), "Developing your experiment," in M. Webster and J. Sell (eds), *Laboratory Experiments in the Social Sciences*, 2nd edn, Burlington, MA: Academic Press, pp. 127–44.

Webster, M., and J. Sell (2014), "Why do experiments?" in M. Webster and J. Sell (eds), *Laboratory Experiments in the Social Sciences*, Burlington, MA: Academic Press, pp. 5–23.

Weijer, C., T. Bruni, T. Gofton, G. Young, L. Norton, A. Peterson, and A. Owen (2015), "Ethical considerations in functional magnetic resonance imaging research in acutely comatose patients," *Brain*, 139 (1), 292–9.

Wilson, T., E. Aronson, and K. Carlsmith (2010), "The art of laboratory experimentation," in S.T. Fiske, D.T. Gilbert, and G. Lindzey (eds), *Handbook of Social Psychology*, 5th edn, vol. 1, Hoboken, NJ: John Wiley & Sons, pp. 51–88.

Yarkoni, T., and T. Braver (2010), "Cognitive neuroscience approaches to individual differences in working memory and executive control: conceptual and methodological issues," in A. Gruszka, G. Matthews, and B. Szymura (eds), *Handbook of Individual*

Differences in Cognition: Attention, Memory and Executive Control, New York, NY: Springer, pp. 87–108.

Zaro, M., L. da Cruz Fagundes, F. Rocha, and W. Nunes (2016), "Cognitive brain mapping used in the study of entrepreneurial behavior – pilot test with the use of electroencephalogram – EEG during the process of identification of business opportunities," *American Journal of Educational Research*, **4** (6), 472–8.

PART II

NEUROSCIENCE APPLICATIONS – ENTREPRENEURIAL JUDGMENT, DECISION MAKING, AND COGNITION

7. Entrepreneurial return on investment through a neuroentrepreneurship lens
Mellani Day and Mary C. Boardman

INTRODUCTION/LITERATURE REVIEW

For this handbook we present part of an ongoing stream of research and propose some neuroexperimental designs that have potential to enrich and enhance this research. Specifically, this research builds on and helps to refine a model that best describes the internal, possibly even subconscious, cost/benefit decision analysis that an individual undergoes when deciding to engage in entrepreneurship (Shane and Venkataraman, 2000). We then identify data and present the results from our preliminary regression analysis and hypothesis testing. Then we discuss some suggested neuroentrepreneurship research designs that may build upon the decision factors identified in our research thus far, to test our findings and further refine the Day (2014) ROI model.

The entrepreneurship literature discusses both tangible and intangible factors and motivations in determining the entrepreneurial return on investment (ROI) decision. Because of these intangibles, we argue that entrepreneurial ROI goes beyond monetary profit to incorporate these in entrepreneurial decision making (Elkington, 1997; Slaper and Hall, 2011). Such intangibles could both increase and decrease the entrepreneur's perceived and experienced ROI.

An entrepreneur is an individual who perceives an opportunity or problem within a market and then acts upon it with a solution. This individual does not need to personally possess all the resources necessary to bring this solution to market and often convinces others to join in his or her vision (Stevenson and Jarillo-Mossi, 1990). Entrepreneurship carries with it great uncertainty. While many start-ups fail, entrepreneurs expect their own endeavor to be successful. They invest time, energy, and resources, facing a substantial amount of risk and uncertainty. Stanton and Welpe (2010) argue that entrepreneurs do not gamble, rather they take what they perceive to be calculated risks. While from an environmental perspective the "odds" are against these individuals, they invest heavily in the success of their ventures.

This chapter suggests that there is more going on in an entrepreneur's mind than simple financial profit-and-loss calculations. We hypothesize that other factors affect an entrepreneur's perceived and experienced ROI. Just as utility is understood to be subjective, Becker (1993) states, "individuals maximize welfare *as they conceive it*" (emphasis in original). In other words, entrepreneurial ROI can be conceived as a form of subjective utility.

Entrepreneurs also subjectively assess value to and/or create entrepreneurial opportunities in a way that is varied (Alvarez and Busenitz, 2001). The use of heuristics, or simplifying information-processing strategies, that Tversky and Kahneman (1974), Kahneman et al. (1982), Alvarez and Busenitz (2001), and Kahneman (2011) discuss is likely to be a part of entrepreneurial judgment and decision making. However, the focus of our research is not so much on the decision-making processes as it is on the internal priorities and factors behind this subjective utility. In other words, we focus on the "why" instead of the "how." Thus our hypotheses will relate to the "proximate causation of the phenomena" as Harrington (2011) states in her instructional guide, *The Design of Experiments in Neuroscience*.[1]

At this point in our study, we may discover concurrence of a reaction (that is, a chemical and/or electrical response) with a given stimulus. As such, referring back to the discussion in the Introduction to this handbook, we could claim a "nomological" or law-like evidence for causation (Kurthen, 2010). With enough repetition of the particular treatment or stimulus, if we repeatedly get the same category of responses, then we can tie those responses to our stimulus (that is, to be "caused" by our stimulus), and reject other possible explanations for those responses.

DAY (2014) MODEL

As discussed above, entrepreneurial decision making is likely to include other, internal motivating factors in addition to profit (Elkington, 1997). This decision process is likely to contain qualitative and quantitative, internal and external aspects. Day (2014) constructed a model of costs and benefits gleaned from the entrepreneurship literature as a first step toward quantifying the qualitative factors to help lay the foundation for neuroexperimental testing. This line of research is designed to provide a more detailed and explicit understanding of how an entrepreneur might internally evaluate a variety of intangible returns, positive and negative, which by default become motivators at several levels.

Calculating ROI is done with a simple equation: ROI = (Benefits – Cost)/Cost. This is generally widely understood in a financial context. However, not all benefits and costs are financial, external, and relatively easy to measure. The incorporation of benefits and costs that are internal and more intangible adds a great deal of complexity to this calculation, which by nature is highly subjective. Stanton and Welpe (2010) make the argument that calculating ROI objectively is fundamentally different than a subjective calculation.

This applies directly to entrepreneurial decision making, especially since entrepreneurs operate in a highly ambiguous, uncertain environment. While we do not have an objective, measurable way to account for ambiguity or uncertainty, this may not matter. If a true definition of risk means that all the probabilities are known and can be calculated, then it follows that for right or for wrong, entrepreneurs might operate under a perception that they have calculated the risks in a particular undertaking, and have accounted for them. Further, as many have noted (Krueger and Welpe, 2014; Harvey and Evans, 1995, Stanton and Welpe, 2010), entrepreneurship is a dynamic process and risk preferences might be unstable even over the briefest period of time.

Day (2014) builds on the abstract calculation of ROI as: ROI = (benefits – costs)/costs with a subjective analysis that is specific to the entrepreneur and his/her circumstances. The way entrepreneurs subjectively calculate ROI can vary greatly among individuals. Table 7.2 shows the lists of constructs that Day (2014) suggests as possible perceived benefits (Set A) and perceived costs (Set B) for the entrepreneur. It is assumed that each of these benefits and costs could be weighted differently among individual entrepreneurs. However, the perceived benefits and costs, along with the associated weights, have yet to be empirically tested and verified. Day (2014) proposes the following ROI calculation as a function of the sets A and B listed in Table 7.1:

Table 7.1   ROI calculation as a function of the sets A and B

$A \neq B$, and $A \cap B$; and

$$f = [(A_1, \ldots, A_{19}) - (B_1, \ldots, B_{14})] / (B_1, \ldots, B_{14}) \text{ or}$$

$$f = \frac{(A_1, \ldots, A_{19})}{(B_1, \ldots, B_{14})} - 1$$

METHODOLOGY

To empirically test this model, the first step was to assess the current available data that could measure the constructs proposed. In the Appendix we present details of these findings and provide a brief discussion of the implications. Once available data was collected, the second step was to perform basic hypothesis testing on each construct for which data is available.

For each construct, we hypothesized that it is statistically significantly associated with higher or lower degrees of entrepreneurship prevalence. For example, a high level of prevalence or degree of a "benefit," such as a low opportunity cost, could be statistically significantly associated with greater entrepreneurship prevalence. At the same time, the opposite (a high opportunity cost) would be statistically significantly associated with lower entrepreneurship prevalence. Similarly, a high level of prevalence or degree of a "cost," such as fear of failure, would be statistically significantly associated with lower entrepreneurship prevalence. Finally we expected the opposite to be true – a low degree of fear of failure, for example, would be statistically significantly associated with higher entrepreneurship prevalence.

Those constructs that exhibited a statistically significant relationship with entrepreneurship prevalence at the $(p > .1)$ level would remain in the model. Other constructs would be reconsidered in the model. That being said, attempting to calculate ROI in such a way is a complex endeavor involving many variables. Therefore, we expected that many, if not all, of these coefficients would be small. However, even a small, yet statistically significant relationship would be grounds to retain a construct at this point. The available data sets and results of this preliminary regression analysis and hypothesis testing are reported below.

AVAILABLE DATA SETS

To assess the current data availability, we examined two data sets: World Values Survey (WVS) and the Global Entrepreneurship Monitor (GEM). We went through each survey questionnaire and identified items that could measure the proposed constructs. The results are presented in Table 7A.1, showing the data set, item number, question, and relevant construct.

Some constructs were combined and treated as a spectrum, especially when certain question items could measure either cost or benefit. Generally speaking, we found a range from robust data availability for a particular construct to not finding a single item to address others. This may be due to gaps in our current available survey instruments, but it is a topic for another study and outside the scope of this chapter. We present below the data availability for each construct in the Day (2014) model:

Table 7.2   Entrepreneurial benefit and cost-decision variables

Set A – Benefits:
1. Likelihood (risk of) of success (conviction, cognitive biases (Krueger and Dickson, 1994); overlaps with egoistic passion)
2. Passion engaged (driving interest – outward looking)
3. Egoistic passion fed (driving interest – inward looking/narcissistic; feeds from expert scripts: Mitchell et al., 2000)
4. Mission (may overlap with passion; stewardship (Van Duzer et al., 2007; Miller and Timothy, 2010))
5. Contribution
6. Altruism (not necessarily the same as mission, passion, or spiritual fulfillment); other regarding preferences (Fehr et al., 2005)
7. Independence/autonomy (need for freedom from authority)
8. Drive (overlaps with but not the same as passion)
9. Need for achievement (McClelland, 1961), [validation/affirmation, self-serving bias (Baron, 1998), alignment with ideal self (Brockner et al., 2004)]
10. Excitement (variety, change, challenge, seeking)
11. Need for control
12. Social advancement (power, influence, respect, fame)
13. Opportunity cost – nothing to lose (everything to gain)
14. Necessity-based – no other choice (Reynolds et al, 2002; Venkataraman, 1997)
15. Environmental concern (which may be a passion or mission)
16. Spiritual fulfillment (Balog et al, 2014) (which may overlap with passion, mission and/or independence/autonomy)
17. Profit/wealth enhancement
18. Satisfaction (Balog et al, 2014)
19. Legacy

Set B – Costs:
1. Likelihood (risk of) of failure (includes/overlaps with other factors below)
2. Liability of newness (lack of credibility) (Hannan and Freeman, 1984)
3. Liability of smallness (lack of impact in the market) Bruderl et al., 1992
4. Lack of self efficacy/self doubt; regretful thinking (self = venture) (Markman et al., 2002)
5. Lack of security net (alone; alignment with security and safety needs, Brockner et al., 2004)
6. Disappointment
7. Bootstrapping
8. No access to capital
9. Uncertainty (ignorance about the future) (Alvarez and Busenitz, 2001)
10. Stress/pressure
11. Burnout (overextended)
12. Ridicule (social embarrassment)
13. Bankruptcy/financial ruin
14. Family, friends, against it

Robust data availability:

- Drive (overlaps with but not the same as passion) (see for example: Getley, 1979).
- Independence/autonomy (need for freedom from authority)/lack of self-efficacy/self-doubt (regretful thinking; self = venture) (Markman et al., 2002).
- Opportunity cost (nothing to lose, everything to gain)/necessity-based (no other choice) (Reynolds et al., 2002; Venkataraman, 1997).

Moderate data availability:

- Environmental concern (this may be a passion or mission) (York and Venkataraman, 2010).
- Excitement (variety, change, challenge seeking)/stress, pressure (see for example: Kuratko et al., 1997; Nicolaou et al., 2008).
- Likelihood (risk) of success (conviction, cognitive biases (Krueger and Dickson, 1994); overlaps with egoistic passion)/likelihood (risk) of failure (includes/overlaps with other costs).
- Need for control/internal locus of control (Brockhaus, 1982).
- Need for achievement (McClelland, 1961) [validation/affirmation, self-serving bias (Baron, 1998), alignment with ideal self (Brockner et al., 2004)].
- Other-regarding preferences/altruism (not necessarily the same as mission, passion, or spiritual fulfillment) (Fehr et al., 2005).
- Profit (wealth enhancement)/bankruptcy (financial ruin) (Knight, 1921, 1942).
- Social advancement (power, influence, respect, fame)/ridicule (social embarrassment) (see for example: Kets de Vries, 1985).
- Spiritual fulfillment (Balog et al., 2014) (this may overlap with passion, mission, and/or independence/autonomy).

Minimal data availability:

- Access to capital (Coleman, 2000).
- Lack of security net (alone; alignment with security and safety needs, Brockner et al., 2004).
- Legacy/unsupportive social network (family, friends against it) (see for example: Van Auken and Werbel, 2006).
- Mission (may overlap with passion; stewardship) (Van Duzer et al., 2007; Miller and Timothy, 2010).

- Passion engaged (driving interest – outward looking) (see for example: Grilo and Thurik, 2008).
- Satisfaction (Balog et al., 2014)/disappointment.

No data availability:

- Bootstrapping (Winborg and Landstroem, 1997; and others).
- Burnout (overextended) (see for example: Shepherd et al., 2010).
- Contribution (Reynolds, 1987).
- Egoistic passion fed [driving interest – inward looking/narcissistic; feeds from expert scripts (Mitchell et al., 2000)].
- Liability of newness (lack of credibility) (Hannan and Freeman, 1984).
- Liability of smallness (lack of impact in the market) (Bruderl et al., 1992).
- Uncertainty (ignorance about the future) (Alvarez and Busenitz, 2001).

PRELIMINARY DATA ANALYSIS

Our next step was to conduct preliminary regression analysis and hypothesis, using a subset of the data identified in the previous section. The subset of data we chose for this preliminary analysis was the Global Entrepreneurship Development Index (GEDI) score and the World Values Survey (WVS) data for 2014. Specifically, the dependent variable (DV) was the GEDI score for each country. This is appropriate and useful since it is the best quantitative measure of overall entrepreneurial activity at the country level. As the GEDI index is primarily based on GEM data, we chose to explore possible relationships between this and the WVS data for 2014.

The WVS data was the most appropriate data set to use for our independent variables because it is a survey of the general values prevalent across country populations (WVS). As we are concerned with the decision to become an entrepreneur, but cannot know who in a given society is having those thoughts at any given time, a general values survey by country can serve as a proxy. In our data set, there were 48 countries that had both GEDI index scores and WVS data. Since we only used data for 2014, our sample size was limited to this number.

As this research is still at the exploratory, theory-building stage, we used stepwise ordinary least squares (OLS) regression with forward-selection search to identify the model that best predicts country-level GEDI scores.

Table 7.3   Two factors explain ~55 percent of variation in GEDI scores

GEDIscore = -44.89 + 25.61wvsv49 + 15.38wvsv191

```
. regress gediscore wvsv49 wvsv191
```

Source	SS	df	MS		
				Number of obs	= 48
				F(7, 40)	=29.10
Model	6194.36191	2	3097.18095	Prob > F	=0.0000
Residual	4790.02263	45	106.444947	R-squared	=0.5639
				Adj R-squared	=0.5445
Total	10984.3845	47	233.710309	Root MSE	=10.317

gediscore	Coef.	Std. Err.	t	P>|t|	[95% Conf. Interval]	
wvsv49	25.60512	5.043722	5.08	0.000	15.44655	35.7637
wvsv191	15.37582	3.244614	4.74	0.000	8.84083	21.9108
_cons	-44.88666	11.85904	-3.79	0.000	-68.77199	-21.00132

We used both Stata and SPSS software to conduct our analysis. Our expectations were modest for the predictive value of the model since the sample size was only 48 countries, and we were relying solely on aggregate data. However, these models have much greater predictive value than expected.

We identified models that had the highest level of explanatory power at the $p < .1$, $p < .05$, and the $p < .01$ levels. Below are all three models, along with descriptions of the variables.

The first model, represented in Table 7.3, is statistically significant at the $p < .01$ level, with an adjusted r-squared of .5445. The variable wvsv49 corresponds to the question asking if a main goal in life is to make one's parents proud (legacy factor) and the variable wvsv191 corresponds to the question asking if one or one's family went without income at some point in the previous year (opportunity cost/necessity factor). In other words, the variation in the country averages of these two variables, or these two factors, explain nearly 55 percent of the variation in the GEDI scores. Especially given the relatively small sample size, this model has an incredibly high level of explanatory power.

Since part of exploratory research is determining which variables explain the greatest variation in entrepreneurial activity, we next present two models that are significant at the $p < .05$ and $p < .1$ levels, respectively. They include more variables that are likely to be qualitatively meaningful to better understanding entrepreneurial ROI. The model shown in Table 7.4 is statistically significant at the $p < .05$ level, with an adjusted r-squared of .5958. In addition to the above variables measuring the legacy and opportunity cost/necessity factors, this model also includes wvsv236,

Table 7.4   Three factors explain ~60 percent of variation in GEDI scores

GEDIscore = -41.2 + 26.04wvsv49 + 14.18wvsv191 – 3.41wvsv236

```
. regress gediscore wvsv49 wvsv191 wvsv236
```

Source	SS	df	MS		Number of obs	= 48
					F(7, 40)	=24.10
Model	6828.34244	3	2276.11415		Prob > F	=0.0000
Residual	4156.0421	44	94.4555022		R-squared	=0.6216
					Adj R-squared	=0.5958
Total	10984.3845	47	233.710309		Root MSE	=9.7188

gediscore	Coef.	Std. Err.	t	P>|t|	[95% Conf. Interval]	
wvsv49	26.03505	4.754085	5.48	0.000	16.45382	35.61628
wvsv191	14.17583	3.091324	4.59	0.000	7.945676	20.40599
wvsv236	-3.409262	1.31594	-2.59	0.013	-6.061364	-.7571593
_cons	-41.20236	11.26137	-3.66	0.001	-63.89817	-18.50655

corresponding to the question covering the employment status of the primary wage earner of the household (also measuring the opportunity cost/necessity factor). In other words, the variation in the country averages of these three variables, or these two factors, explain nearly 60 percent of the variation in the GEDI scores.

The third and final model, shown in Table 7.5, covers the greatest number of variables, and is statistically significant at the p <.1 level, with an adjusted r-squared of .6958. In addition to the above variables measuring the legacy and opportunity cost/necessity factors, this model also includes wvsv137, wvsv21, wvsv16, and wvsv11. The variable wvsv137 corresponds to the question asking the degree to which income equality is seen as important for democracy (independence/autonomy factor), wvsv21 corresponds to the question asking if children should learn obedience at home (independence/autonomy factor), wvsv16 corresponds to the question asking if children should learn tolerance and respect (other-regarding preferences factor), and wvsv11 corresponds to the question asking about health (satisfaction/disappointment factor). In other words, the variation in the country averages of these seven variables, explain nearly 70 percent of the variation in the GEDI scores.

As next steps, we will expand the sample size greatly by incorporating data from more survey years into our analysis, as well as incorporating data from the Pew survey. We will then conduct a preliminary ranking of costs and benefits that can be performed quantitatively, according to coefficient size and level of statistical significance. These rankings will provide a basis and set of testable hypotheses to eventually conduct neurobased studies. We suggest several experimental approaches below.

Table 7.5   Seven factors explain ~70 percent of variation in GEDI scores

GEDIscore = 26.2 + 21.43wvsv49 + 6.08wvsv191 – 2.87wvsv236 – 1.37wvsv137 + 25.01wvsv21 – 32.43wvsv16 – 11.85wvsv11

```
. regress gediscore wvsv49 wvsv191 wvsv236 wvsv137 wvsv21 wvsv16 wvsv11
```

Source	SS	df	MS		
				Number of obs	= 48
				F(7, 40)	=16.36
Model	8141.00716	7	1163.00102	Prob > F	=0.0000
Residual	2843.37738	40	71.0844344	R-squared	=0.7411
				Adj R-squared	=0.6958
Total	10984.3845	47	233.710309	Root MSE	=8.4312

gediscore	Coef.	Std. Err.	t	P>|t|	[95% Conf. Interval]	
wvsv49	21.42515	4.621298	4.64	0.000	12.08516	30.76514
wvsv191	6.079093	3.329306	1.83	0.075	-.6496845	12.80787
wvsv236	-2.872886	1.248753	-2.30	0.027	-5.396709	-.3490625
wvsv137	-1.371759	1.385455	-0.99	0.328	-4.171869	1.428351
wvsv21	25.06322	7.978561	3.14	0.003	8.937951	41.1885
wvsv16	-32.42504	12.02357	-2.70	0.010	-56.72558	-8.124499
wvsv11	-11.85188	5.959857	-1.99	0.054	-23.89721	.1934375
_cons	26.19623	5.959857	1.04	0.305	-24.77859	77.17105

BUILDING NEUROEXPERIMENTAL MODELS

While there is much to be done to extend the work that has been presented in this research stream thus far, enough groundwork has been established to identify potential neuroexperimental projects. For many of the entrepreneurial constructs that Day (2014) identified in the literature, no matching equivalents were found in the WVS or the GEDI index/GEM data sets. This suggests possible gaps in this survey data, as it pertains to entrepreneurial ROI. However, just using the combined factors in the third model presented above in this initial analysis,[2] and revising our basic ROI model, ROI = (benefits – costs)/costs, we find on the benefits side the following factors (the revised Set A):

- Independence/autonomy (need for freedom from authority).
- Opportunity cost (nothing to lose, everything to gain)/necessity-based (no other choice) (Reynolds et al., 2002; Venkataraman, 1997).
- Other-regarding preferences/altruism (not necessarily the same as mission, passion, or spiritual fulfillment) (Fehr et al., 2005).

On the costs side we found the following factors (the revised Set B):

- Legacy (family, friends against it).
- Disappointment.

The revised ROI calculation:

$$A \neq B, \text{ and } A \cap B; \text{ and}$$
$$f = [(A_1, \ldots, A_3) - (B_{1+}B_2)] / (B_1 + B_2)$$

Or, for our purposes:

ROI Decision = [(autonomy + opportunity cost + other-regarding preferences) – (legacy family friends against it + disappointment)] / (legacy family friends against it + disappointment)

With this foundation we present below a set of experimental design ideas that could be developed and performed in different settings with functional magnetic resonance imaging (fMRI), electroencephalogram (EEG), magnetoencephalography (MEG), and so on. We keep in mind the complicated nature of the logistics and requirements involved for each type of approach, along with potential financial constraints. In the example below we will be developing the background for a series of fMRI experiments. That said, it may be more cost-effective and efficient to go with EEG, and where resources are abundant we would do both.

We initially propose choosing three groups of the same culture or race, each consisting of 16, self-identified as: entrepreneurs,[3] non-entrepreneurs, and potential entrepreneurs (pre-nascent), for a total of 48 participants. Eight males and eight females will be in each group as a control for gender differences. Different designs might call for using the same participants in multiple experiments as well as different groups over time (or combinations).

For each of these initial designs, we propose testing the hypothesis that there is no difference between the groups, along with testing the hypothesis that there are no within-group differences. We further hypothesize that the primary brain activity for this experiment will be in the region of the medial prefrontal cortex (MPFC), since this has been found to be the area that evaluates "experienced risk level of the possible decision options and the valenced magnitude (positive or negative) of the outcome" (Wargo et al., 2010; Xue et.al., 2008).

Next we want to define what we mean by our dependent variable, the ROI decision equation. In general terms we mean that if total perceived and experienced ROI is high (past some threshold in the entrepreneur's mind per the ROI calculation from our third model above), a decision for entrepreneurship might be taken. If perceived and experienced ROI is low, a decision against entrepreneurship might be taken. Since this is exploratory research, how we determine what constitutes a "high" or "low" threshold, given that such thresholds exist, would be revealed after the fact. However, it would presumably entail an evaluation of the "experienced risk" that must accompany each individual variable in the model, as well as that of the whole equation. For example, the generation of blood-oxygen-level-dependent (BOLD)[4] or brain activity when agreeing or disagreeing that each of the third model factors would be, say, of positive impact in their decision process to start a venture.

In the fMRI experiment design itself, first come a series of agree or disagree questions regarding preferences per the ROI model, for example: "I would start my own company because I want to be my own boss" or "I would not start a company if my family was against it" or "I plan to start my own company when I recognize a problem that I can solve," and related questions from the Pew survey, the GEM, and the WVS. Then would come an ordering of priority of importance of a list of the cost/benefit variables from our previous research (Day, 2014), and finally a Likert-type scale from one to six, which provides a limited range, but means to weight how much more important is each variable than the previous variable in the ordered list.

Brain activity correlating to these responses would be compared between and within groups. Technical questions in the experimental design relate to the type of equipment,[5] scanning time, minimizing "dead time," controlling for the distraction of the fMRI (noise, claustrophobic) process itself, length of each treatment (how long it should take to answer a question or to rank order a series of variables), slices per volume, slice thickness and orientation, and so on. Because working out these specifics would require more neuroscience expertise than what is typical of entrepreneurship scholars, we suggest collaboration with colleagues versed in neuroscience to determine these.

Other research designs that build on this work include:

- Asking variations of the five questions from the model to each of the participants.
- Asking questions representing the other factors (keeping in mind fatigue). Introducing "palette cleansing" or neutralizing exercises between treatments as well as positive/negative influencing events that would measure strength of resolve and how "mood" might affect answers; viewing a pleasant scene or cute-cat video versus viewing a dark, dirty alley or news about the falling stock market.

It is important to consider that there may be cultural differences to consider in designing these treatments.

- Introducing scenarios – "if/then." For example: your parents hate the idea of you starting a particular business and would support you until you found a job, but you have tried for a long time and have not found a job. However, you have found the opportunity to start a business that a neighbor has successfully done.[6]
- Collecting longitudinal data for each of the above – six months; annual for five years.
- We are assuming meaningful cultural differences. Therefore, we could perform this series in other countries and/or other contexts.

LIMITATIONS

Having 16 participants in a group represents a low n; however, in neuroexperiments, having a low n is common practice, due to the logistics and financial constraints surrounding this type of research.[7] This is not without controversy, however, and is recognized as a limitation in these types of studies (see for example Button et. al., 2013). Friston et al. (1999) present a case as to why and under what conditions a relatively small set of participants in an fMRI experiment can produce an effect that has some predictive validity.

Schafer et.al (2003) found that more than 15 subjects are needed to provide a representative sample in an "event-related paradigm involving a button press" fMRI experiment. There are many factors involved that would impact the sample size needed, including the type of task (motor versus cognitive skill) and the "signal to noise ratio." While small sample issues will limit the generalizability of our study, we have set our per group size at 16 participants as an initial research program that can be extended over time.

CONCLUSIONS/DIRECTIONS FOR FUTURE RESEARCH

With sufficient subjects in a neuroentrepreneurship study such as this, statistically meaningful results have the potential to create entrepreneur versus non-entrepreneur neurotypes, along with neurotypes among the entrepreneurs. Would such neurotypes, if identified, finally provide some predictive value to the very unpredictable nature of entrepreneurs and entrepreneurship? What would the implications be of identifying such neurotypes?

Once the available data has been through statistical testing, the model will be revised as appropriate. The next step will be additional data collection to fill in the gaps (such as data from the Pew Global Attitudes Project), made apparent in this current stage in our research. We will then conduct another round of statistical testing to formulate a model that is as empirically valid as possible with aggregate data. Once this is completed with ranking, we intend to then work on assessing weights to each construct.

As discussed earlier, we do not assume preferences and subjective ROI calculation to be stable over time. Future research will be useful in gathering data via a survey methodology to assess the weighting of various costs and benefits throughout the various stages of venture creation and growth. Ideally, we would conduct a longitudinal study using a set of the same entrepreneurs throughout their process. There may also be differences in rankings and weights, not only during the entrepreneurial process, but across cultures, nations, and even generations. It would be useful to see if there are such differences moving forward.

With an empirically valid framework for subjective assessments of entrepreneurial ROI, researchers could assess differences among individual entrepreneurs or types of entrepreneurs. Are the ways some entrepreneurs weigh and rank these internal costs and benefits in their ROI calculations more successful than others? Is there truly an "entrepreneurial mindset" that we can identify among individuals within a community, setting them apart from non-entrepreneurs? This empirical research sets a foundation to conduct neuroentrepreneurship experiments that compare how entrepreneurs and non-entrepreneurs subjectively calculate ROI.

Most interesting, this research could provide an empirical basis to conduct further neuroentrepreneurship research. For example, a MEG or fMRI trial could test the subjective ROI model in the most rigorous way possible. At the very least, it could either confirm or inform model revision and/or reconsideration and would be useful regardless of results. For example, if confirmed, the results would tell us that the preconscious reaction to the incentive stimuli reflects stated preferences and choices. If the neuro studies refute or challenge the model, the results would provide valuable guidance to refine our research. If stated preferences and choices differ from the preconscious reactions to incentive stimuli, this would provide the basis for incredibly interesting research. With repeated trials a high-enough n could be established for such research to produce statistically meaningful results.

This novel world of neuroentrepreneurship opens up many new potential research avenues. Could we eventually have at our disposal virtual, perhaps 3-D databases, of neuroimages of entrepreneurs' brains under varying stages of decision making over time and under a variety of conditions and influences – our simulated man, the virtual entrepreneur?

NOTES

1. Harrington, a neuroscience educator, is Tippit Professor in Life Sciences at Smith College in Northampton, MA.
2. p <.1 level, adjusted r-squared of .6958.
3. As our research question involves the decision to engage in entrepreneurship, the entrepreneurs in our study do not necessarily need to have founded successful enterprises. A decision to stay or exit would involve a different, if related, research question.
4. BOLD is the acronym for blood-oxygen-level-dependent contrast imaging used in fMRI brain studies.
5. For example, at the University of Colorado Medical School, they use a G-3 Tesla whole body MRI scanner, equipped with high-performance gradient coils, and so on.
6. There are a lot of confounding factors here, but something like this and other possible scenarios that combine our model factors (for example substitute "wife" or "husband" for parents; add "unhappy at work" or many other variations).
7. Logistical constraints include (but are not limited to) reserving a lab in your area, presumably a hospital or clinic, that allows outside researchers to rent time and talent (those that can run, for example, the fMRI or MEG process and that can help with interpretation of the results). Also, research participants must come to the lab and spend several hours on location. This presents a greater logistical challenge compared to research designs where the researcher travels to the participants (which has its own logistic considerations), or conducting online surveys.

REFERENCES

Alvarez, S. and L. Busenitz (2001), "The entrepreneurship of resource-based theory," *Journal of Management*, **27**, 755–75.

Balog, A., L. Baker, and A. Walker (2014), "Religiosity and spirituality in entrepreneurship: a review and research agenda," *Journal of Management, Spirituality & Religion*, 2014; http://dx.doi.org/10.1080.14766086.2013.836127.

Baron, R. (1998), "Cognitive mechanisms in entrepreneurship: why and when entrepreneurs think differently than other people," *Journal of Business Venturing*, **13**, 275–94.

Becker, G. (1993), "Nobel lecture: the economic way of looking at behavior," *The Journal of Political Economy*, **101** (3), 385–409.

Brockhaus, R. (1982), "The psychology of the entrepreneur," in Calvin A. Kent, Donald L. Sexton, and Karl H. Vesper (eds), *Encyclopedia of Entrepreneurship*, Englewood Cliffs, NJ: Prentice-Hall, pp. 39–57.

Brockner, J., E. Higgins, and M. Low (2004), "Regulatory focus theory and the entrepreneurial process," *Journal of Business Venturing*, **19** (2), 203–20.

Bruderl, J. P. Preisendoerfer, and R. Ziegler (1992), "Survival chances of newly founded business organizations," *American Sociological Review*, *57*, 227–42.

Button, K., J. Ioannidis, C. Mokrysz, B. Nosek, J. Flint, E. Robinson, and M. Munafo (2013), "Power failure: why small sample size undermines the reliability of neuroscience," *Nature Reviews Neuroscience*, **14**, 365–76.

Coleman, S. (2000), "Access to capital and terms of credit: a comparison of men- and women-owned businesses," *Journal of Small Business Management*, **38** (3), 37–52.

Day, M. (2014), "Work problems: intangible returns on investment in the mind of the entrepreneur," presented at the 2014 Academy of Management Conference, Philadelphia, PA.

Elkington, J. (1997), *Cannibals with Forks: The Triple Bottom Line of 21st Century Business*, Oxford: Capstone Publishing.

Fehr, E, M. Kosfeld, and U. Fischbacher (2005), "Neuroeconomic foundations of trust and social preferences," IZA discussion paper No. 1641, IEW working paper No. 221.

Friston, K., A. Holmes, and K. Worsley (1999), "Comments and controversies: how many subjects constitute a study?" *NeuroImage*, **10**, 1–5.

Getley, R. (1979), "Entrepreneurial drive," *Industrial and Commercial Training*, **11** (1), 19–23.

Grilo, I. and R. Thurik (2008), "Determinants of entrepreneurial engagement levels in Europe and the US," *Industrial and Corporate Change*, **17** (6), pp 1113–45.

Hannan, M. and J. Freeman (1984), "Structural inertial and organizational change," *American Sociological Review*, **49**, 149–64.

Harrington, M. (2011), *The Design of Experiments in Neuroscience*, 2nd edn, Los Angeles: Sage Publishing.

Harvey, M. and R. Evans (1995), "Strategic windows in the entrepreneurial process," *Journal of Business Venturing*, **10**, 331–47.

Kahneman, D. (2011) *Thinking, Fast and Slow*, New York, NY: Farrar, Straus, and Giroux.

Kahneman, D., P. Slovic, and A. Tversky (eds) (1982), *Judgment Under Uncertainty: Heuristics and Biases*, Cambridge: Cambridge University Press.

Kets de Vries, M. (1985), "The dark side of entrepreneurship," *Harvard Business Review*, **63** (6), 160–67.

Knight, F. (1921), *Risk, Uncertainty, and Profit*, Boston, MA: Hart, Schaffner & Marx, Houghton Mifflin Company, The Riverside Press.

Knight, F. (1942), "Profit and entrepreneurial functions," *The Journal of Economic History*, **2** (S1), 126–32.

Krueger, N. and P.R. Dickson (1994), "How believing in ourselves increases risk taking: perceived self-efficacy and opportunity recognition," *Decision Sciences*, **25** (3), 385–400.

Krueger, N. and I. Welpe (2014), "Neuroentrepreneurship: what can entrepreneurship learn from neuroscience?," in Michael H. Morris (ed), *Annals of Entrepreneurship Education and Pedagogy – 2014*, Cheltenham: Edward Elgar; doi:http://dx.doi.org/10.4337/97817834714 54.00011.

Kuratko, D., J. Hornsby, and P. Naffziger (1997), "An examination of owner's goals in sustaining entrepreneurship," *Journal of Small Business Management*, **35** (1), 24–33.

Kurthen, M. (2010), "Pushing brains: can cognitive neuroscience provide experimental evidence for brain-mind causation?," *Psyche* **16** (2), 5–22.

Markman, G.D., D.B. Balkin, and R.A. Baron (2002), "Inventors and new venture formation: the effects of general self-efficacy and regretful thinking," *Entrepreneurship Theory & Practice*, Winter, 149–65.

McClelland, D. (1961), *The Achieving Society*, Princeton, NJ: Van Nostrand Co.

Miller, D. and E. Timothy (2010), "Rethinking the impact of religion on business values: understanding its reemergence and measuring its manifestations," *Journal of International Business Ethics*, **3** (2), 49–83.

Mitchell, R.K., B. Smith, K.W. Seawright, and E.A. Morse (2000), "Cross-cultural cognitions and the venture creation decision," *Academy of Management Journal*, **43** (5), 974–93.

Nicolaou, N. S. Shane, L. Cherkas, and T. Spector (2008), "The influence of sensation seeking in the heritability of entrepreneurship," *Strategic Entrepreneurship Journal*, **2** (1), 7–21.

Reynolds, P. (1987), "New firms: societal contribution versus survival potential," *Journal of Business Venturing*, **2** (3), 231–46.

Reynolds, P., W. Bygrave, E. Autio, L. Cox, and M. Hay (2002) "Global entrepreneurship monitor 2002 executive report," Babson College, Ewing Marion Kauffman Foundation and London Business School.

Schafer, J., S. Mostofsky, M. Kraut, A. Boyce, B. Caffo, A. Flower, M. Goldbert, K. Fadonovich, and J. Pekar (2003), "How many subjects are enough; subsampling and consensus in fMRI," *Proceedings of the International Society of Magnetic Resonance in Medicine*, **11**, 383.

Shane, S., and S. Venkataraman (2000), "The promise of entrepreneurship as a field of research," *Academy of Management Review*, **25** (1), 217–26.

Shepherd, C., G. Marchisio, S. Morrish, J. Deacon, and M. Miles (2010), "Entrepreneurial burnout: exploring antecedents, dimensions and outcomes," *Journal of Research in Marketing and Entrepreneurship*, **12** (1), 71–9.

Simons, K. and Astebro, T. (2010), "Entrepreneurs seeking gains: profit motives and risk aversion in inventors' commercialization decisions," presented at the 2006 International Industrial Organization Conference, accessed at http://homepages.rpi.edu/~simonk/pdf/rationalInventors.pdf.

Slaper, T.F. and T.J. Hall (2011), "The triple bottom line: what is it and how does it work?," *Indiana Business Review*, **86** (1), Spring.

Stanton, A. and I. Welpe (2010), "Risk and ambiguity: entrepreneurial research from the perspective of economics," in A. Stanton, M. Day, and I. Welpe (eds), *Neuroeconomics and the Firm*, Cheltenham: Edward Elgar.

Stevenson, H. and J. Jarillo-Mossi (1990), "A paradigm of entrepreneurship: entrepreneurial management," *Strategic Management Journal*, **11** (2), 17–27.

Tversky, A. and D. Kahneman (1974), "Judgment under uncertainty: heuristics and biases," *Science*, **185**, 1124–31.

Tversky, A. and D. Kahneman (1981), "The framing of decisions and the psychology of choice," *Science*, **211**, 453–8.

Wargo, D., N. Baglini, and K. Nelson (2010), "Dopamine, expected utility and decision-making in the firm," in A. Stanton, M. Day, and I. Welpe, I. (eds) *Neuroeconomics and the Firm*, Cheltenham: Edward Elgar.

Winborg, J. and H. Landstroem (1997), "Financial bootstrapping in small businesses – a resource-based view on small business finance," in, P. Reynolds, W. Bygrave N. Carter, P. Davidsson, W. Gartner, C. Mason, and P. McDougall (eds), *Frontiers of Entrepreneurship Research 1997: Proceedings of the Seventeenth Annual Entrepreneurship Research Conference*, Babson College, pp. 471–85.

Van Auken, H. and J. Werbel (2006), "Family dynamic and family business financial performance: spousal commitment," *Family Business Review*, **19** (1), 49–63.

Van Duzer, J. R. Franz, G. Karns, K. Wong, and D. Daniels (2007), "It's not your business: a Christian reflection on stewardship and business," Professional Development Workshop presentation at the Academy of Management Conference, Philadelphia, PA.

Venkataraman, S. (1997), "The distinctive domain of entrepreneurship research: an editor's perspective," *Advances in Entrepreneurship, Firm Emergence, and Growth*, **3**, 119–38.

Xue, G., Z. Lu, I. Levin, J. Weller, X. Li, and A. Bechara (2008), "Functional dissociations of risk and reward processing in the medial prefrontal cortex," *Cerebral Cortex Advance Access*, accessed 13 April 2017 at https://www.ncbi.nlm.nih.gov/pubmed/18842669.

York, J. and S.Venkataraman (2010), "The entrepreneur-environment nexus: uncertainty, innovation, and allocation," *Journal of Business Venturing*, **25** (5), 449–63.

APPENDIX

Table 7A.1　Current available data on the proposed ROI constructs from World Values (WVS), Pew, and Global Entrepreneurship Monitor (GEM) surveys

Item Number	Question	Construct	Data Source
V10	Taking all things together, would you say you are (read out and code one answer): 1 Very happy, 2 Rather happy, 3 Not very happy, 4 Not at all happy	Satisfaction/ Disappointment	WVS
V100	How would you place your views on this scale (from 1–10)?: In the long run, hard work usually brings a better life; Hard work doesn't generally bring success – it's more a matter of luck and connections	Locus of control	WVS
V11	All in all, how would you describe your state of health these days? Would you say it is (read out): 1 Very good, 2 Good, 3 Fair, 4 Poor	Satisfaction/ Disappointment	WVS
V12	Should children be encouraged to learn (independence) at home?	Independence/ Autonomy	WVS
V13	Should children be encouraged to learn (hard work) at home?	Drive	WVS
V131	Please tell me for (Governments tax the rich and subsidize the poor) how essential you think it is as a characteristic of democracy.	Independence/ Autonomy	WVS
V134	Please tell me for (People receive state aid for unemployment) how essential you think it is as a characteristic of democracy.	Independence/ Autonomy	WVS
V136	Please tell me for each of the following things how essential you think it is as a characteristic of democracy. Use this scale where 1 means "not at all an essential characteristic of democracy" and 10 means it definitely is "an essential characteristic of democracy" (Civil rights protect people from state oppression.)	Independence/ Autonomy	WVS

Table 7A.1 continued

Item Number	Question	Construct	Data Source
V137	Please tell me for (The state makes people's incomes equal) how essential you think it is as a characteristic of democracy.	Independence/ Autonomy	WVS
V138	Please tell me for each of the following things how essential you think it is as a characteristic of democracy. Use this scale where 1 means "not at all an essential characteristic of democracy" and 10 means it definitely is "an essential characteristic of democracy" (People obey their rulers.)	Independence/ Autonomy	WVS
V14	Should children be encouraged to learn (feeling of responsibility) at home?	Drive	WVS
V144	Do you belong to a religion or religious denomination? If yes, which one?	Spiritual Fulfillment	WVS
V145	Apart from weddings and funerals, about how often do you attend religious services these days?	Spiritual Fulfillment	WVS
V146	Apart from weddings and funerals, about how often do you pray?	Spiritual Fulfillment	WVS
V147	Independently of whether you attend religious services or not, would you say you are: 1 A religious person, 2 Not a religious person, 3 An atheist	Spiritual Fulfillment	WVS
V148	Do you believe in God?	Spiritual Fulfillment	WVS
V15	Should children be encouraged to learn (Imagination) at home?	Independence/ Autonomy	WVS
V150	With which one of the following statements do you agree most? The basic meaning of religion is: 1 To follow religious norms and ceremonies, 2 To do good to other people	Spiritual Fulfillment	WVS
V152	How important is God in your life?	Spiritual Fulfillment	WVS
V16	Should children be encouraged to learn (tolerance and respect for other people) at home?	Other-regarding preferences	WVS
V160c	I see myself as someone who . . . tends to be lazy: 1 Disagree strongly, 2 Disagree a little, 3 Neither agree nor disagree, 4 Agree a little, 5 Agree strongly, 9 Don't know	Drive	WVS

Table 7A.1   continued

Item Number	Question	Construct	Data Source
V160d	I see myself as someone who . . . is relaxed, handles stress well: 1 Disagree strongly, 2 Disagree a little, 3 Neither agree nor disagree, 4 Agree a little, 5 Agree strongly, 9 Don't know	Excitement/Stress	WVS
V160i	I see myself as someone who . . . gets nervous easily: 1 Disagree strongly, 2 Disagree a little, 3 Neither agree nor disagree, 4 Agree a little, 5 Agree strongly, 9 Don't know	Excitement/Stress	WVS
V160j	I see myself as someone who . . . has an active imagination: 1 Disagree strongly, 2 Disagree a little, 3 Neither agree nor disagree, 4 Agree a little, 5 Agree strongly, 9 Don't know	Passion Engaged	WVS
V17	Should children be encouraged to learn (thrift, saving money and things) at home?	Drive	WVS
V18	Should children be encouraged to learn (determination, perserverance) at home?	Drive	WVS
V181	To what degree are you worried about the following situations? (Losing my job or not finding a job) 1 Very much, 2 A good deal, 3 Not much, 4 Not at all, –1 DK/NA	Opportunity Cost/Necessity	WVS
V182	To what degree are you worried about the following situations? (Not being able to give my children a good education) 1 Very much, 2 A good deal, 3 Not much, 4 Not at all, –1 DK/NA	Opportunity Cost/Necessity	WVS
V188	In the last 12 months, how often have you or your family: (Gone without enough food to eat) 1 Often, 2 Sometimes, 3 Rarely, 4 Never, –1 DK/NA	Opportunity Cost/Necessity	WVS
V19	Should children be encouraged to learn (religious faith) at home?	Spiritual Fulfillment	WVS
V190	In the last 12 months, how often have you or your family: (Gone without medicine or medical treatment that you needed) 1 Often, 2 Sometimes, 3 Rarely, 4 Never, –1 DK/NA	Opportunity Cost/Necessity	WVS

Table 7A.1　continued

Item Number	Question	Construct	Data Source
V191	In the last 12 months, how often have you or your family: (Gone without a cash income) 1 Often, 2 Sometimes, 3 Rarely, 4 Never, –1 DK/NA	Opportunity Cost/ Necessity	WVS
V192	How much you agree or disagree with: Science and technology are making our lives healthier, easier, and more comfortable.	Mission	WVS
V193	How much you agree or disagree with: Because of science and technology, there will be more opportunities for the next generation.	Mission	WVS
V196	How much do you agree or disagree with: It is not important for me to know about science in my daily life.	Mission	WVS
V20	Should children be encouraged to learn (unselfishness/generosity) at home?	Other-regarding preferences	WVS
V21	Should children be encouraged to learn (obedience) at home?	Independence/ Autonomy	WVS
V22	Should children be encouraged to learn (self-expression) at home?	Independence/ Autonomy	WVS
V229	Are you employed now or not? If yes, about how many hours a week?	Opportunity Cost/ Necessity	WVS
V23	All things considered, how satisfied are you with your life as a whole these days? Using this card on which 1 means you are "completely dissatisfied" and 10 means you are "completely satisfied" where would you put your satisfaction with your life as a whole?	Satisfaction/ Disappointment	WVS
V233	How much independence do you have in performing your tasks at work? If you do not work currently, characterize your major work in the past. Use this scale to indicate your degree of independence where 1 means "no independence at all" and 10 means "complete independence".	Independence/ Autonomy	WVS
V235	Are you the chief wage earner in your household?	Opportunity Cost/ Necessity	WVS
V236	Is the chief wage earner of your household employed now or not?	Opportunity Cost/ Necessity	WVS

Table 7A.1   continued

Item Number	Question	Construct	Data Source
V237	During the past year, did your family: 1 Save money, 2 Just get by, 3 Spent some savings, 4 Spent savings and borrowed money	Opportunity Cost/ Necessity	WVS
V238	People sometimes describe themselves as belonging to the working class, the middle class, or the upper or lower class. Would you describe yourself as belonging to the: 1 Upper class, 2 Upper middle class, 3 Lower middle class, 4 Working	Opportunity Cost/ Necessity	WVS
V239	We would like to know in what income group your household is. Please specify the appropriate number, counting all wages, salaries, pensions, and other incomes that come in.	Opportunity Cost/ Necessity	WVS
V25	Could you tell me whether you are an active member, an inactive member or not a member of (a church or religious organization)?	Spiritual Fulfillment	WVS
V30	Could you tell me whether you are an active member, an inactive member or not a member of (an environmental organization)?	Environmental Concern	WVS
V32	Could you tell me whether you are an active member, an inactive member or not a member of (a humanitarian or charitable organization)?	Other-regarding preferences	WVS
V34	Could you tell me whether you are an active member, an inactive member or not a member of (a self-help group, mutual aid group)?	Other-regarding preferences	WVS
V49	For each of the following statements I read out, can you tell me how strongly you agree or disagree with each. Do you strongly agree, agree, disagree, or strongly disagree? (One of my main goals in life has been to make my parents proud.)	Legacy/Unsupportive Social Network	WVS
V55	Some people feel they have completely free choice and control over their lives, while other people feel that what they do has no real effect on what happens to them. Please use this scale where 1 means "no choice at all" and 10 means "a great deal of choice" to indicate how much freedom of choice and control you feel you have over the way your life turns out.	Locus of control	WVS

Table 7A.1   continued

Item Number	Question	Construct	Data Source
V58	Have you had any children?: 0 No children, 1 One child, 2 Two children, 3 Three children, 4 Four children, 5 Five children, 6 Six children, 7 Seven children, 8 Eight or more children	Legacy/Unsupportive Social Network	WVS
V59	How satisfied are you with the financial situation of your household?	Opportunity Cost/ Necessity	WVS
V6	Indicate how important (leisure time) is in your life.	Drive	WVS
V67	Please tell me for (Less importance placed on work in our lives), if it were to happen, whether you think it would be a good thing, a bad thing, or don't you mind?	Drive	WVS
V68	Please tell me for (More emphasis on the development of technology), if it were to happen, whether you think it would be a good thing, a bad thing, or don't you mind?	Mission	WVS
V69	Please tell me for (Greater respect for authority), if it were to happen, whether you think it would be a good thing, a bad thing, or don't you mind?	Independence/ Autonomy	WVS
V70	Would you please indicate for each description whether that person is very much like you, like you, somewhat like you, not like you, or not at all like you: It is important to this person to think up new ideas and be creative; to do things one's own way.	Independence/ Autonomy	WVS
V71	Would you please indicate for each description whether that person is very much like you, like you, somewhat like you, not like you, or not at all like you: It is important to this person to be rich; to have a lot of money and expensive things.	Profit/Bankruptcy	WVS
V73	Would you please indicate for each description whether that person is very much like you, like you, somewhat like you, not like you, or not at all like you: It is important to this person to have a good time; to "spoil" oneself.	Drive	WVS

Table 7A.1   continued

Item Number	Question	Construct	Data Source
V74	Would you please indicate for each description whether that person is very much like you, like you, somewhat like you, not like you, or not at all like you: It is important to this person to do something for the good of society.	Other-regarding preferences	WVS
V74B	Would you please indicate for each description whether that person is very much like you, like you, somewhat like you, not like you, or not at all like you: It is important for this person to help the people nearby; to care for their well-being.	Other-regarding preferences	WVS
V75	Would you please indicate for each description whether that person is very much like you, like you, somewhat like you, not like you, or not at all like you: Being very successful is important to this person; to have people recognize one's achievements.	Need for Achievement	WVS
V76	Would you please indicate for each description whether that person is very much like you, like you, somewhat like you, not like you, or not at all like you: Adventure and taking risks are important to this person; to have an exciting life.	Excitement/ Stress	WVS
V77	Would you please indicate for each description whether that person is very much like you, like you, somewhat like you, not like you, or not at all like you: It is important to this person to always behave properly; to avoid doing anything people would say is wrong.	Social Advancement/ Ridicule	WVS
V78	Would you please indicate for each description whether that person is very much like you, like you, somewhat like you, not like you, or not at all like you: Looking after the environment is important to this person; to care for nature and save life resources.	Environmental Concern	WVS
V79	Would you please indicate for each description whether that person is very much like you, like you, somewhat like you, not like you, or not at all like you: Tradition is important to this person; to follow the customs handed down by one's religion or family.	Independence/ Autonomy	WVS

Table 7A.1   continued

Item Number	Question	Construct	Data Source
V79	Would you please indicate for each description whether that person is very much like you, like you, somewhat like you, not like you, or not at all like you: Tradition is important to this person; to follow the customs handed down by one's religion or family.	Social Advancement/ Ridicule	WVS
V8	Indicate how important (work) is in your life.	Drive	WVS
V82	During the past two years have you given money to an ecological organization?	Environmental Concern	WVS
V83	During the past two years have you participated in a demonstration for some environmental cause?	Environmental Concern	WVS
V96	How would you place your views on this scale (from 1–10)?: issue: Incomes should be made more equal; We need larger income differences as incentives for individual effort	Drive	WVS
V97	How would you place your views on this scale (from 1–10)?: Private ownership of business and industry should be increased; Government ownership of business and industry should be increased	Independence/ Autonomy	WVS
V98	How would you place your views on this scale (from 1–10)?: Government should take more responsibility to ensure that everyone is provided for; People should take more responsibility to provide for themselves	Drive	WVS
V99	How would you place your views on this scale (from 1–10)?: Competition is good. It stimulates people to work hard and develop new ideas; Competition is harmful. It brings out the worst in people	Drive	WVS
Q74	And do you ever use social networking sites like Facebook, Twitter (INSERT COUNTRY-SPECIFIC EXAMPLES) to share your views about (INSERT) or not?	Access to Capital	Pew

Table 7A.1   continued

Item Number	Question	Construct	Data Source
Q5	And over the next 12 months do you expect the economic situation in our country to improve a lot, improve a little, remain the same, worsen a little, or worsen a lot?	Likelihood of Success/Risk of Failure	Pew
Q7	And over the next 12 months do you expect your personal economic situation to improve a lot, improve a little, remain the same, worsen a little, or worsen a lot?	Opportunity Cost/ Necessity	Pew
Q72	Do you ever use online social networking sites like (Facebook, Twitter, INSERT COUNTRY-SPECIFIC EXAMPLES)?	Access to Capital	Pew
Q73	Do you ever use social networking sites like Facebook, Twitter (INSERT COUNTRY-SPECIFIC EXAMPLES) to stay in touch with family and friends or not?	Access to Capital	Pew
Q21b	Do you think (a lack of employment opportunities) is a very big problem, a moderately big problem, a small problem, or not a problem at all in our country?	Opportunity Cost/ Necessity	Pew
Q21d	Do you think (public debt) is a very big problem, a moderately big problem, a small problem, or not a problem at all in our country?	Access to Capital	Pew
Q21a	Do you think (rising prices) is a very big problem, a moderately big problem, a small problem, or not a problem at all in our country?	Likelihood of Success/Risk of Failure	Pew
Q21c	Do you think (the gap between the rich and the poor) is a very big problem, a moderately big problem, a small problem, or not a problem at all in our country?	Social Advancement/ Ridicule	Pew
Q24	Do you think the gap between the rich and the poor in (survey country) has increased, decreased, or stayed the same in the last five years?	Social Advancement/ Ridicule	Pew
Q182c	Have there been times during the last year when you did not have enough money: to buy clothing your family needed?	Opportunity Cost/ Necessity	Pew

Table 7A.1   continued

Item Number	Question	Construct	Data Source
Q182a	Have there been times during the last year when you did not have enough money: to buy food your family needed?	Opportunity Cost/ Necessity	Pew
Q182b	Have there been times during the last year when you did not have enough money: to pay for medical and health care your family needed?	Opportunity Cost/ Necessity	Pew
Q4	Now thinking about our economic situation, how would you describe the current economic situation in (survey country) – is it very good, somewhat good, somewhat bad, or very bad?	Likelihood of Success/Risk of Failure	Pew
Q129	Thinking about yourself, how confident are you that you will have an adequate standard of living in your old age – very confident, somewhat confident, not too confident, not confident at all?	Safety Net	Pew
Q8	When children today in (survey country) grow up, do you think they will be better off or worse off financially than their parents?	Legacy/ Unsupportive Social Network	Pew
		Bootstrapping Burnout Contribution Egoistic Passion Fed	
i5	In your country, most people would prefer that everyone had a similar standard of living {EQUALINC} 1 Yes, 2 No, -1 Don't know, -2 Refused	Independence/ Autonomy	GEM
1K2	Which one of the following, do you feel, is the most important motive for pursuing this opportunity? {SUOPTYPE} 1 Greater independence, 2 Increase personal income, 3 Just to maintain income, 4 None of these (SPECIFY) {SUOPTYPE_OTH}, –1 Don't know, –2 Refused	Independence/ Autonomy	GEM
2K2	Which one of the following, do you feel, is the most important motive for pursuing this opportunity? {SUOPTYPE} 1 Greater independence, 2 Increase personal income, 3 Just to maintain income, 4 None of these (SPECIFY) {SUOPTYPE_OTH}, –1 Don't know, –2 Refused	Independence/ Autonomy	GEM

Table 7A.1   continued

Item Number	Question	Construct	Data Source
E	How many members make up your permanent household, including you? {HHSIZE} Enter the actual number of the household's size _____, –1 Don't know, –2 Refused	Legacy/ Unsupportive Social Network	GEM
		Liability of Newness	GEM
		Liability of Smallness	GEM
i2	In the next six months, will there be good opportunities for starting a business in the area where you live? {OPPORT} 1 Yes, 2 No, –1 Don't know, –2 Refused	Likelihood of Success/Risk of Failure	GEM
i3	Do you have the knowledge, skill, and experience required to start a new business? {SUSKILL} 1 Yes, 2 No, –1 Don't know, –2 Refused	Likelihood of Success/Risk of Failure	GEM
i4	Would fear of failure prevent you from starting a business? {FEARFAIL} 1 Yes, 2 No, –1 Don't know, –2 Refused	Likelihood of Success/Risk of Failure	GEM
5E2	Employed by others in part-time work {OCCUPART} 1 Yes, 2 No, –1 Don't know, –2 Refused	Opportunity Cost/ Necessity	GEM
5E3	Self-employed {OCCUSELF} 1 Yes, 2 No, –1 Don't know, –2 Refused	Opportunity Cost/ Necessity	GEM
5E4	Seeking employment {OCCUSEEK} 1 Yes, 2 No, –1 Don't know, –2 Refused	Opportunity Cost/ Necessity	GEM
1K2	Which one of the following, do you feel, is the most important motive for pursuing this opportunity? {SUOPTYPE} 1 Greater independence, 2 Increase personal income, 3 Just to maintain income, 4 None of these (SPECIFY) {SUOPTYPE_OTH}, –1 Don't know, –2 Refused	Opportunity Cost/ Necessity	GEM
2K2	Which one of the following, do you feel, is the most important motive for pursuing this opportunity? {SUOPTYPE} 1 Greater independence, 2 Increase personal income, 3 Just to maintain income, 4 None of these (SPECIFY) {SUOPTYPE_OTH}, –1 Don't know, –2 Refused	Opportunity Cost/ Necessity	GEM

Table 7A.1   continued

Item Number	Question	Construct	Data Source
2K1	Did you become involved in this firm to take advantage of a business opportunity or because you had no better choices for work? {OMREASON} 1 Take advantage of business opportunity, 2 No better choices for work, 3 Combination of both of the above, 4 Have a job but seek better opportunities, 5 Other (SPECIFY) {OMREASON_OTH}, –1 Don't know, –2 Refused	Opportunity Cost/ Necessity	GEM
1K2	Which one of the following, do you feel, is the most important motive for pursuing this opportunity? {SUOPTYPE} 1 Greater independence, 2 Increase personal income, 3 Just to maintain income, 4 None of these (SPECIFY) {SUOPTYPE_OTH}, –1 Don't know, –2 Refused	Profit/Bankruptcy	GEM
2K2	Which one of the following, do you feel, is the most important motive for pursuing this opportunity? {SUOPTYPE} 1 Greater independence, 2 Increase personal income, 3 Just to maintain income, 4 None of these (SPECIFY) {SUOPTYPE_OTH}, –1 Don't know, –2 Refused	Profit/Bankruptcy	GEM
2K1	Did you become involved in this firm to take advantage of a business opportunity or because you had no better choices for work? {OMREASON} 1 Take advantage of business opportunity, 2 No better choices for work, 3 Combination of both of the above, 4 Have a job but seek better opportunities, 5 Other (SPECIFY) {OMREASON_OTH}, –1 Don't know, -2 Refused	Profit/Bankruptcy	GEM
i6	In your country, most people consider starting a new business a desirable career choice {NBGOODC} 1 Yes, 2 No, –1 Don't know, –2 Refused	Social Advancement/ Ridicule	GEM

Table 7A.1   continued

Item Number	Question	Construct	Data Source
i7	In your country, those successful at starting a new business have a high level of status and respect {NBSTATUS} 1 Yes, 2 No, –1 Don't know, –2 Refused	Social Advancement/ Ridicule	GEM
i8	In your country, you will often see stories in the public media about successful new businesses {NBMEDIA} 1 Yes, 2 No, –1 Don't know, –2 Refused	Social Advancement/ Ridicule	GEM
		Uncertainty Overconfidence Bias Representative Bias	

8. The cognitive neuroscience of entrepreneurial risk: conceptual and methodological challenges

Kelly G. Shaver, Leon Schjoedt, Angela Passarelli, and Crystal Reeck

INTRODUCTION

Do entrepreneurial ventures involve risk? The quick answer to this question is, "Well, of course they do!" And there is no shortage of supportive data. For example, the US Panel Studies of Entrepreneurial Dynamics (PSED; Gartner et al., 2004; Reynolds and Curtin, 2009; Reynolds and Curtin, 2011) shows that as many as 72 months after a business-organizing venture begins, only some 30 percent of efforts have produced new firms. As another example, the industry analytics provider CB Insights (https://www.cbinsights.com/industry-analytics) pointed out that from 2010 to 2015 a total of 83 ventures, each of which had raised at least US \$50 million in venture capital, have exited for less than they had raised. Spending six years trying to organize a company "risks" at least the time and opportunity cost; selling a company for less than the venture capital raised "risks" the wealth of the investors. But there are at least two important differences. First, investors can take a portfolio approach to try to balance risks and rewards. Individuals, however, typically start only one enterprise at a time, so they stand to lose "all," not just "some." Second, investment decisions made by angels or venture capitalists are typically collective decisions, involving the best guesses of multiple brains. By contrast, business-organizing decisions are typically made by a single brain. At the present stage of theory and research, the single-brain decisions have been most heavily studied by the methods of neuroscience. Consequently, this chapter restricts its focus to the judgments of risk made by individual entrepreneurs.

When the goal is to examine the brain correlates of variations in risk judgments, restricting the investigation to an individual person is merely the beginning. At least four other design elements need to be considered for the final answers to be clear:

1. There must be a conceptual analysis that distinguishes one sort of risk from others.
2. The research designs chosen must maximize the opportunity to obtain meaningful results.
3. The concepts selected for testing must be operationalized unambiguously.
4. Potential methodological confounding must be avoided.

This chapter is organized to address each of these concerns in turn to identify practices that might better enable researchers to understand the cognitive neuroscience of entrepreneurial risk.

CONCEPTUAL ANALYSIS OF RISK

Uncertainty and Risk

Nearly 100 years ago Knight (1921) drew a distinction between uncertainty (a situation in which many of the potential outcomes of action are unknown) and risk (a situation in which the potential outcomes of action are known, but their probabilities must be estimated). Thus, risk is measurable, whereas uncertainty is not. This fundamental distinction remains in current conceptions of risk such as the ISO 31000 and its Guide 73:2009, conceptions that typically consider (1) the valence – positive or negative – of events; and (2) the likelihood that each of these outcomes might occur. As March and Shapira (1987) note, "In classical decision theory, risk is most commonly conceived as reflecting variation in the distribution of possible outcomes, their likelihoods, and their subjective values" (p. 1404). Thus for our purposes, overall risk (R) involves three separate elements: the number of individual negative consequences that can be enumerated (C), the severity (S) of each of those consequences, and the probability that each consequence will occur (prC):

$$R = \sum_{i=1}^{k}((C_i \times S_i) \times Pr\,C_i)$$

It is important to note that each of the components of risk is subjective: individuals will differ in the number and kind of consequences that they could anticipate, what Sitkin and Pablo (1992) call "outcome uncertainty." They will differ in the severity attached to each anticipated consequence, and what Sitkin and Pablo call "outcome potential" ("How bad could it get?"). Finally, they will differ in the estimated probabilities they attach to the occurrence of each consequence.

Varieties of Risk

A broad conception of the ways in which risk might arise was outlined by Jackson et al. (1972). These investigators examined the literature and found four major categories of situations in which risk might vary. Not surprisingly, the first of these was *monetary* risk, a willingness to take chances for financial gain, to sacrifice job security for a better payoff, or in other ways to bet on one's own future. The second is *physical* risk, the enjoyment of adventurous activities that could lead to personal injury. The third is *social* risk, a willingness to express oneself fully, regardless of the consequences (for example, answering, "How do I look?" with complete candor may not always be safe). The fourth is *ethical* risk, a willingness to contravene normative standards or to use deceit to gain one's objectives. Jackson et al. (1972) investigated these four sorts of risk using a combination of direct self-assessments, vocational choices, vignettes describing a choice facing another person, and true–false statements that were part of a larger personality inventory. Data from the study were subjected to principal components analysis that showed the four expected separate factors, but also a second-order factor encompassing all four. This means that although there is "generalized risk taking" (p. 497), it is also permissible to use one or another facet individually. Just such a domain-specific scale of risk taking, the DOSPERT is available in several languages in a 30-item form (Blais and Weber, 2006).

Given Jackson's participation in this classification of risk, it is not surprising that the Jackson Personality Inventory (JPI; Jackson, 1976) has been a popular measure used to assess entrepreneurial risk. The JPI consists of 22 separate scales designed to instantiate all the elements of Murray's (1938) need-based view of personality structure. The JPI contains two scales, Harm Avoidance (HA) and Risk Propensity (RP) that assess, respectively, an individual's desires for self-protection from physical harm, and his or her willingness to engage in behavior that most people would consider risky (primarily monetary risk but not confined specifically to entrepreneurial risk). Because of their frequency of occurrence in the literature, both of these scales should be considered in studies of entrepreneurial risk.

As noted by Palich and Bagby (1995) the notion of risk was a central element in the first formal theory of entrepreneurship, posed by Cantillon, a French economist, in 1755. The notion that "entrepreneurs are risk-takers" remains part of the popular conception of entrepreneurship, though the scientific literature in the field now paints a more nuanced picture (Jain, 2011; Niess and Biemann, 2014; Stewart and Roth, 2001, 2004; Zhao and Seibert, 2006). First, regardless of whether the people involved are entrepreneurs or not, there can be problems in the way risk is measured. In an early study attempting to find convergent validity among various measures of a general risk propensity, Slovic (1962) had male subjects complete three response set measures of risky behavior, two questionnaire measures (including a job preference inventory), three experimental gambling measures, and one self-rating of risk. The highest pairwise intercorrelation was between the self-rating of risk and a life experience inventory ($r = .34$), but among the 36 possible correlations only nine were significant (one-tailed tests), and three of those were significantly negative. Reasoning that the substantial differences among tasks might have obscured an underlying regularity in risk preferences, Slovic (1972) constructed gamble pairs that could be answered either by choosing one element of each pair or by setting a "selling price" for each element. Female and male undergraduates evaluated 36 pairs of such bets and the results showed that although there was substantial *within*-task consistency, the *cross*-task consistency was disappointingly low.

The importance of such framing effects is an essential ingredient in prospect theory (Kahneman and Tversky, 1979), developed as a critique of expected utility theory as a normative model of rational choice. Prospect theory holds that there are two phases of evaluating a potential monetary gamble (a "prospect"). In the "editing" phase individuals establish a "frame" for their judgments, then in the "evaluation" phase they make choices based on the combination of the frame and the probabilities inherent in the gamble. One of the frames is the "certainty effect" in which people overweight positive outcomes that are certain relative to those that are merely probable, even though the expected values are identical. In short, they are risk averse. Another frame is the "reflection effect" that occurs when the potential outcomes are negative. In this circumstance people are risk seeking, preferring a probable loss to a certain loss, even when the expected value of the probable loss is more extreme (that is, worse) than the certain loss. As Kahneman and Tversky note, "an essential feature of the present theory is that the carriers of value are changes in wealth or welfare, rather than final states" (1979, p. 278). For judgments of entrepreneurial risk, this means that the person's current circumstances will have a substantial influence on any estimates of just how "risky" a particular course of business action might be. In addition to the person's current circumstances, other work building on prospect theory indicates that the individual's recent gains or losses will affect the choices made (Thaler and Johnson, 1990). If one is, as Thaler and Johnson describe it, "playing with house money," one tends to be risk seeking, rather than risk averse. This suggests, for example, that an experienced entrepreneur financing a new start-up from part of the proceeds from the sale of a first company might be more risk seeking than would a first-timer with no financial cushion.

Not only are estimates of risk complicated by the perceiver's immediate past results and current circumstances, they are also likely to be influenced by what sort of risk is being considered. Following Stoner (1961), Kogan and Wallach (1964) introduced a risk measurement task called the Choice Dilemmas Questionnaire (CDQ). This consists of 12 vignettes, each of which poses a choice between two alternative courses of action, and asks what probability of success would be necessary for the less certain alternative to be chosen. In addition to the CDQ, Kogan and Wallach administered other measures of risk propensity. But they experienced little more cross-measure success than had been achieved in earlier research. Although the Kogan/Wallach CDQ has been used in subsequent studies on entrepreneurial risk taking (for example, Brockhaus, 1980), it may not be the best choice. Of the 12 vignettes, only three deal directly with business in the sense that we would use the word today. Three others are career choices, two involve the potential for physical risk, and three others involve potential social risk.

Other measures of risk have been constructed in the management literature, notably by MacCrimmon and Wehrung (1986, 1990) and March and Shapira (1987). The extensive work by MacCrimmon and Wehrung involved 13 separate measures of risk broadly categorized into those derived from standardized hypothetical situations (gambles), those arising from behavior in risky situations, and those based on self-reported attitudes toward risk. Items in the first set were based on (1) the risk in-basket, which asks respondents to assume the role of an executive deciding between a risky action and an action with certain consequences, and (2) investment decisions grounded in utility theory. The second set included a variety of personal investment risks, such as the percentage of gross assets in risky asset classes, the percentage of personal gross assets held as debt, and the amount spent in the previous year on recreational gambling. The third set consisted of attitude choices, many of which were derived from Zuckerman's (Zuckerman et al., 1964) sensation-seeking scale. A factor analysis of the 13 items revealed eight factors accounting for 68 percent of the variance. It may be worth noting that to obtain eight factors from 13 items is not the level of simplification one normally hopes will result from a factor analysis.

Although classical decision theory is often the starting point for discussions of risk, March and Shapira (1987) have suggested that some traditional elements need modification when it comes to the risky decisions of managers (and, we would argue, entrepreneurs). For example, though overall variability in the probability distributions for consequences should be related to perceptions of risk, managers (and entrepreneurs) are relatively unconcerned about the degree of variability of *positive* consequences, preferring to concentrate on the absolute value of the ends to be achieved. As another example, managers (and also entrepreneurs, see Keyes, 1965) often do not take stated risk as a given, but rather seek either to revise the risk estimates or to search for ways to manage and control the risk (thus, obviously, changing its psychological implications).

Other factors that might affect the psychological perception of risk have been identified by Vlek and Stallen (1980), and Baird and Thomas (1985). Mostly, these are characteristics of the setting for the decision, or of the conditions under which the decision is to be made. One of the first is the controllability of the consequences – if an outcome can be contained or reversed, the perceived risk will be smaller. If there is greater knowledge of the positive consequences than of the negative consequences, the activity is more likely to be undertaken. Potential risk can also be discounted in time (intended benefits precede potential failures) or in space (benefits are accrued by the actor, potential negative consequences fall to others). Do these discounting principles operate in the same way, and involve identical neurological mechanisms, if entrepreneurs (novice or habitual) are compared to other people?

Returning to entrepreneurial risk, Brockhaus (1980) used the Kogan-Wallach CDQ to compare risk-taking preferences between entrepreneurs and managers. There were three groups of respondents. The entrepreneurial group had left their employers to own or manage new businesses within the preceding three months; the second group had changed organizations within the past three months; the third group had changed their roles within the same organization during the same time period. The results of this comparison showed no differences in CDQ scores across the three groups, leading to the conclusion that "general risk-taking propensity does not distinguish entrepreneurs from nonentrepreneurs" (p. 519). However, as noted above, only one-quarter of the items deal with what would today be considered business risk (and only one that even mentions a start-up); thus, the failure to find "risk propensity" differences between entrepreneurs and nonentrepreneurs might not be very informative.

The CDQ was put to a slightly different use by Schwer and Yucelt (1984). These authors used a convenience sample of "small business entrepreneurs" in Vermont to examine differences in responses to the CDQ when particular segments were divided into business risk, personal risk, career-related risk, and "trivial decisions." Unfortunately for our purposes, their selection of items for particular subscales was done a priori, not as the result of any factor-analytic or clustering procedure. So Item A – the decision to leave a corporate position to join a start-up – was not included in "business risk" though it is the only item that actually mentions a start-up company. Rather, their third "business risk" item was L, the choice by a research scientist of whether to work on a risky long-term problem or more certain short-term problems. Obviously, our division of the items above is also done a priori, but the fact that two different sets of investigators could create different, though reasonable-sounding, divisions of items is another indication of why the CDQ is not a satisfactory measure of entrepreneurial risk. Schwer and Yucelt appear to have conducted a series of one-way analyses of variance on individual CDQ items (not averages within risk types) with a succession of demographic and business characteristics used as the independent variables. Among the 108 comparisons reported, there were only 12 significant differences.

Meta-analyses of Risk

Even with the space limitations of this chapter, it is useful to spend this much time on procedural details of past research on "entrepreneurial risk," because current views of the problem rely primarily on meta-analyses. The technique of meta-analysis permits mathematical combination of the effect sizes of differences between groups (Hunter and Schmidt, 1990). The typical measure is d, a fraction whose numerator is the mean difference between groups and whose denominator is the pooled standard deviation of the two groups (and therefore is independent of the sample sizes). Though meta-analysis can correct for measurement reliability and overcome many concerns about statistical power, it does *not* correct for flaws in experimental design or inappropriate operationalization of conceptual variables. And several studies that suffer from these difficulties nonetheless find their way into more than one meta-analysis.

For example, in a first meta-analysis of entrepreneurial risk, Stewart and Roth (2001) conducted a thorough search of articles that compared managers to entrepreneurs, retaining those whose statistical reports were sufficiently detailed to allow computation of d. These included four published articles that had used the CDQ (Brockhaus, 1980; Masters and Meier, 1988; Seth and Sen, 1995; and Sexton and Bowman, 1983) and seven that had used HA, RPS, or some larger version of the JPI (Ahmed, 1985; Begley and Boyd, 1987; Carland and Carland, 1991; Carland et al., 1995; Palich and Bagby, 1995; Sexton and Bowman, 1983; and Stewart et al., 1999). Results of this meta-analysis revealed a somewhat higher risk propensity among entrepreneurs than among managers (corrected d

= 0.36). This positive difference was much higher (corrected d = 0.84) if only the three studies where the entrepreneurs had growth intentions were considered. Finally, on the basis of their analysis, Stewart and Roth (2001) recommend using the RPS as a measure of entrepreneurial risk propensity.

Very soon Stewart and Roth's (2001) meta-analysis was followed by another (Miner and Raju, 2004) that arrived at different conclusions. This meta-analysis also followed the Hunter and Schmidt (1990) procedures for computing d that were used by Stewart and Roth (2001). The difference is that the Miner and Raju paper concentrated almost exclusively on studies using the Miner Sentence Completion Scale Form T (MSCS-T) (Miner, 1986). The MSCS-T is a semi-projective test based on McClelland's achievement motivation theory (McClelland, 1961) rather than on Murray's (1938) need structure. The test is semi-projective because each element consists of a stem with an ending blank that is to be filled in by the respondent. The basic argument is that projective and semi-projective tests encourage the expression of "motives below the level of consciousness" (2004, p. 4). Because the MSCS-T is proprietary, and because the scoring of the end-of-sentence fragments requires training and comparisons to normative data, its use is not as pervasive as that of tests that involve less overhead.

The Miner and Raju (2004) article reported 14 "studies," two of which also included a version of the Shure and Meeker (1967) Risk Avoidance Scale of 17 items dealing with "material and physical risk taking" (Miner and Raju, 2004, p. 5). Note that the Risk Avoidance Scale is *not* described as containing items relevant to entrepreneurial risk. Across the 14 reports, there is one common author for six of the reports and another individual common author for seven of the others, some of which were published in a single article. Moreover, as pointed out in a reply by Stewart and Roth (2004), there are problems of independence in some of the reports and inconsistent operationalizations of what constitutes an "entrepreneur" (indeed, there were instances in which the "experimental" group included no firm founders, and instances in which the "control" group may have included firm owners).

PSYCHOLOGICAL CHARACTERISTICS AND RISK PROPENSITY

Although psychologically based studies of entrepreneurs are still decidedly in the minority (Shaver, 2014b, found only 15 percent of the articles published between 2007 and 2010 in the *Journal of Business Venturing* and in *Entrepreneurship Theory and Practice* – the only two entrepreneurship journals in the 45-entry *Financial Times* list – involved individual-level psychological attributes), there have still been a number of narrative and meta-analytic reports of psychological characteristics related to entrepreneurial performance. Many of these have dealt with what is known as the Big Five personality dimensions: conscientiousness, agreeableness, neuroticism, openness to experience, and extraversion (Costa and McCrae, 1985). These five dimensions are based on lexical analysis of personality trait words, frequently taken from the public domain International Personality Item Pool (IPIP) of 2,413 separate descriptors. Factor analyses of the lexical domain in English typically produce the Big Five dimensions, and Johnson (2014) has shown how 30 facets of the Big Five dimensions can be measured with an inventory of only 120 items. Other work with international samples now adds a sixth dimension – honesty/humility (Ashton and Lee, 2007). The six-dimensional structure is referred to as HEXACO (emotionality rather than neuroticism; eXtraversion rather than extraversion).

In an early one of the studies testing the Big Five with entrepreneurs, Ciavarella et al. (2004) found conscientiousness positively related to venture survival. Interestingly, extraversion, emotional stability (the positive end of neuroticism), and agreeableness were unrelated to venture survival. A meta-analytical review of the relationship between the Big Five and entrepreneurial status was conducted by Zhao and Seibert (2006). They found that compared to managers, entrepreneurs were, on balance, (1) higher in conscientiousness, (2) higher in openness to experience, (3) lower in agreeableness, and (4) lower in neuroticism. Whether these entrepreneurial characteristics are intimately related to risk remains an open question, as Ashton et al. (1998) found that RPS and harm avoidance (HA) do not map directly onto any of the Big Five personality dimensions.

For our purposes, it is important to note that Zhao and Seibert were more restrictive than some have been in constructing their definition of what constitutes an "entrepreneur." Specifically, they required that an entrepreneur be "the founder, owner, and manager of a small business and whose principal purpose is growth" (p. 263). Many past studies of "entrepreneurs" have included owner/managers, whether or not they were also founders. Still others have included founder/owner/managers without ascertaining whether *growth* was one of their primary motivations. Indeed, one of the most widely used and cited data sets on entrepreneurship, the Panel Studies of Entrepreneurial Dynamics (PSED; Gartner et al., 2004; Reynolds and Curtin, 2009) did not require growth aspirations as a criterion for participation. On the other hand, when the research objective is to identify neurological concomitants of risk judgments among entrepreneurs, it may be important to restrict the sample to founder/owners who do have growth as a primary motivation. The additional restriction more precisely defines the "known group" whose brain activity will be examined.

One consistent contributor to the literature on the psychological characteristics of entrepreneurs is Chell (1985, 2008). Her 2008 book discusses not the Big Five, but what she calls the "Big Three": achievement motivation, locus of control, and risk propensity. The argument is that in McClelland's (1961) treatment of achievement motivation the incentive value of success was inversely related to the probability of success and the incentive value of failure was inversely related to the probability of failure (with that probability considered "risk"). In her narrative (in other words, not meta-analytic) review Chell concludes that:

> The findings from studies on risk-taking indicate a need to consider fundamentally how risk is constructed. The methodological issues of general concern are: (a) how the measure is constructed, using an inadequate measure; (b) the research design, e.g. use of control groups, composition of the sample (e.g. nascent entrepreneurs, single-occasion measures, lack of before/after or longitudinal studies, absence of controls for other variables such as sex, prior founding experience, the effect of learning); (c) the relationship with performance issues. (pp. 109–10)

Two studies that address some of these concerns are based on the German Socio-Economic Panel (SOEP), a representative panel survey of some 22,000 individuals living in 12,000 households in Germany. In the first of these, Caliendo et al. (2009) examined the relationship between risk attitudes and a transition to self-employment. Note that this definition – self-employment – does not rise to the restrictive standard used by Zhao and Seibert. In the USA, for example, one can be classified as "self-employed" simply by filing Schedule C in the Internal Revenue Service's Form 1040. No company needs to be formed, no articles of organization need to be written, no separate company tax identification number is needed, and there is no need for a separate bank account or a Dun & Bradstreet registration. The attitude questions dealt with the self-described willingness to "take risks" in general, in financial matters, and in your occupation. The risk questions had been tested by Dohmen et al. (2005), who found that they predicted how much real money people were willing to bet. There was also a lottery-like question asking how much of lottery winnings the person would be willing to invest with a chance to double the money (or a like chance to lose half of it) within two years. This lottery-like question is, of course, equivalent to what Thaler and Johnson (1990) would consider "playing with the house's money," so it is unfortunate that "Our primary analysis is based on the lottery question" (2009, p. 156). In any event, the results of this study showed that risk preferences predicted the transition to self-employment only for individuals who were transitioning from previous employment. There was no attitudinal difference for people who were previously unemployed. Additionally, the attitude questions showed that women were significantly more risk averse than men.

The second SOEP study, by Niess and Biemann (2014), also uses the transition to "self-employment" as the primary dependent variable. Because the risk propensity items had been added to the SOEP only in 2004 (the SOEP actually began in 1984), Niess and Biemann followed 2,772 men and 2,201 women until 2010. Interestingly, the mean age of this sample was over 42 years in 2004. As before, although there were multiple specific contexts in which risk preferences were assessed, "we decided to operationalize risk propensity as a single-item measure based on this general question" (p. 1002) but also added questions about investment risk and occupational risk to create a three-item scale "used for robustness analyses as an alternative operationalization of risk propensity" (p. 1002). Over the five years of the study, three sorts of self-employment were coded: transitions from employment ($n = 141$), continued self-employment ($n = 524$), and failures of self-employment (transition to paid work, $n = 160$). Event history analysis of the data showed: (1) that risk propensity was positively related to self-employment entry, but that (b) already self-employed individuals of moderate risk propensity were more likely to survive in that role than were those either high or low in risk propensity.

In a third German study (but not using the SOEP), Block et al. (2015) compared what are known as "opportunity entrepreneurs" to what are known as "necessity entrepreneurs." The opportunity–necessity distinction arises from studies in the Global Entrepreneurship Monitor (GEM) that in 2015 covered 90 percent of the world's gross domestic product (GDP) in 73 countries (Singer et al., 2015). The point is that in some less developed countries, entrepreneurship is the only choice other than unemployment, whereas in highly developed countries much of entrepreneurial activity is designed to pursue attractive opportunities. The risk propensity measures were: (1) a general question about willingness to take risks in "your entrepreneurial decisions," and (2) a hypothetical lottery investment. Control variables included some measures of the Big Five. Major results showed lower risk tolerance among necessity entrepreneurs (compared to a mixed-motive set) and higher risk tolerance among opportunity entrepreneurs (again compared to the mixed-motive benchmark group). Women showed less risk tolerance than men. For our present purposes, one of the study's overall conclusions is especially important: "further research, such as focusing on differences in risk perception within the group of entrepreneurs . . . seems promising"

(p. 200). Additionally, Block et al. (2015) argued for comparisons between novice entrepreneurs and habitual entrepreneurs, and for comparison of risk attitudes across different entrepreneurial decision-making situations, such as entrepreneurial exit.

Where to Go From Here

Even this brief review shows that the topic of entrepreneurial risk has been of interest ever since the early work of Cantillon (1755). Yet, the findings pertaining to entrepreneurial risk are at conflict. For example, it is not clear whether entrepreneurs are uniformly risk seeking, uniformly risk averse, or some combination of the two depending on situational factors. This may be due to the methods employed by researchers, such as the selection of study participants, measures, data collection methods, and analyses (see for example, Chell, 2008). Consequently, what we suggest in the remainder of the chapter is a set of research guidelines that: (1) relies heavily on experimentation, (2) includes individual difference measures to use as controls, and (3) employs methods of neuroscience to provide dependent variables that are substantially more than the self-reports often seen. Experimentation holds potential to overcome threats of limited measurement validity, internal validity, and statistical conclusion validity that affect most research on entrepreneurial risk. Thus the use of experimental designs to study entrepreneurial risk holds potential to settle the conflicting findings inherent in the literature.

RESEARCH DESIGN

For business scholars raised on regression methods, it is probably useful to say some things about experimentation in psychological research (see also Shaver, 2014a). Though the literature in entrepreneurship is beginning to show occasional experimental studies (see, for example, Fairlie and Holleran, 2012; Fiet and Patel, 2008; Gatewood et al., 2002; Grichnik, 2008), they are still unusual enough that some general background is in order. If you were to begin reading a text on experimental methods, the first chapter would likely point out the uses to which they should – and should not – be put. This might be followed by a discussion of validity of various forms. Next there would be simple experimental designs and eventually there would be discussion of complex designs and the ways in which they should be analyzed. The purpose of this section is to give an abbreviated treatment of all of these topics, ending with the sort of experimental designs that are commonly used in cognitive neuroscience research, particularly research on entrepreneurial risk.

Research in social psychology is sometimes accused of being "the study of the college sophomore." True, a great deal of published research in the field involves experimentation using participants from introductory psychology classes that typically carry a requirement that students participate in a certain number of research projects. But it is critical to note that such studies are specifically *not* designed to tell us more than anyone would want to know about what goes on in a college student's head. Rather, experiments in social psychology are designed to *test theory* that has been developed in other circumstances. This can be done only if: (1) the conceptual issues are stated very clearly (more about this in the 'Operationalization' section below), and (2) there are sufficient controls present in the setting that extraneous influences on the results can be ruled out convincingly.

Random Assignment

One of the primary such controls is the random assignment of participants to experimental conditions. Random assignment is considered to "rule out" the individual differences that participants bring with them into the experiment. The basic idea is that the things that make us unique people will contribute to the *error* in each condition, but will not contribute to any systematic differences between conditions. As important as random assignment is, it is not always well understood. The fundamental principle is that each succeeding person has a probability of being assigned to one condition or another, independent of the condition assignments that have been made before. Suppose that there is a list of 100 research participants to assign to one of two experimental conditions. If one simply flips a coin 100 times, two things will be true. First, every one of the 100 participants has exactly a 50–50 chance of being assigned to one condition or the other. Second, because the assignment is truly random, the number of cases in each condition may (or may not) be 50. With multiple repetitions of the assignment process, the asymptote will be 50, but that need not be true for any particular assignment process. This has implications for the data analysis. Experimental data are typically analyzed with some form of analysis of variance (ANOVA). The calculations in ANOVA are simpler if all of the treatment conditions (called "cells" in the design) have the same number of participants. Fortunately, apart from students learning the techniques (and perhaps not even them), no one does ANOVA calculations by hand these days, and as long as the distributions of participants are relatively close (and there is a total number of participants that exceeds a minimum value), the fact that the cell ns are unequal is not a concern.

The reason to emphasize what random assignment accomplishes is that it is not always applied properly. Every now and then one sees a piece of research in which participants are placed in a list, the first participant is selected by a true random device, but then every kth person after that first one is placed in the same condition as the first one. So if our 100 participants were separated into four groups, and person #3 was chosen randomly for Condition A, person #7, person #11, person #15, and so forth would be placed in the same Condition A. The problem is that once the first person is chosen for each condition, every succeeding person has either a zero percent chance or a 100 percent chance (not a 25 percent chance) of being placed in the same condition, simply by his or her location in the list.

Instructions

An additional approach to establishing control over the setting in an experiment is based on the "instructions" that are provided to research participants. This has two central elements. First, what is said to each participant should be exactly what is said to every other participant. Note that this is quite different from the normal procedure that occurs in a great deal of qualitative research, where the elements of the "semi-structured" interview might be specifiable in advance, but where the conversation will grow, expand, and proceed in a different direction depending on a respondent's responses to the initial interview question. As an aside, this is why experimentalists are so adamant about seeing the complete "codebook" for any interview study. In an experiment, there is no "conversation." There is what the experimenter says to describe the research and that is pretty much all there is. If a "response" is actually expected from a participant, the "conversation" will have been pre-tested so much that the experimenter knows essentially all of the probable responses and, consequently, knows which part of the script to follow from that point forward. Research assistants in social psychology are normally not allowed to see the first participant until their part of the interaction has been rehearsed to a point that it can be delivered "naturally," but without variation, from one participant to the next.

The second critical aspect of delivering experimental instructions is the control that must be exercised over the *experimenter's* expectations. There is a long history of methodological advice in experimental social psychology that: (1) recognizes that an interaction between an experimenter and a participant is a human interaction, in all the complexity that entails, and (2) attempts to minimize any systematic effects arising from that interaction

(Aronson et al., 1985; Rosenberg, 1965; Rosenthal, 1966; Smith, 2014). For starters, it is standard practice for the people who developed the hypotheses for the research *not* to be the same people who "run the subjects." Investigators do not assign graduate students to conduct the experiments out of laziness, they do it for better methodological control. Better, if there are two different theoretical constructs being tested in one experimental design, it is accepted practice for one experimenter to deliver the first set of instructions and for a second experimenter (unaware of what the first one has done) to deliver the second set of instructions. This way, if a predicted interaction between the two conceptual variables emerges, it is impossible for that to have been produced by experimenter expectancies.

Validity

In a classic treatment of the subject, Cook and Campbell (1979) discussed several forms of validity in research designs. These are statistical conclusion validity, internal validity, construct validity, and external validity. We have discussed these in detail elsewhere (Shaver, 2014a) and will only summarize that discussion here. To begin with the one most familiar to entrepreneurship scholars, there is *external* validity: what is the likelihood that the results of our research tell us something valuable about the way things are in the "real world" (as opposed, often, to the world of the college sophomore). The greatest external validity is achieved when the people being studied are like (if not "the") the people to whom it is hoped the research will apply. Even better when those people are doing, in their everyday lives, what the people to whom we hope to generalize are doing. This is why an interview study of a few established entrepreneurs might be seen as preferable to an experimental study conducted with, say, entrepreneurship undergraduate or MBA students. Frankly, if the objective is to determine how "experienced entrepreneurs think about various forms of term sheets," an experiment of any sort is the wrong technique. Experiments are only rarely good for external validity.

Another form of validity discussed by Cook and Campbell is "statistical conclusion validity." As the number of people whose responses contribute to a mean score increases, the stability of the estimate of the true mean will also increase. As a rule of thumb (and that is all it is), social psychologists need to have a grand total of 30 participants (or, if it is a complex experimental design, at least 10 participants per treatment cell) to be comfortable. This is why American Psychological Association (APA) style insists that effect sizes, as well as mean scores, be presented in articles intended for publication in psychological journals. On the other hand, one of the authors has fond personal memories of presenting the results of a student's research at an APA conference. The author's presentation followed that of a researcher who studied the performance of army recruits, so his work included literally thousands of participants. There were two conditions. The two graphs differed by only the width of a pencil lead. But of course with thousands of participants, the difference was highly statistically significant. The author and student had done an experiment with four conditions and fewer than 40 participants. But the design had been so well controlled that we *also* had statistical significance (indeed, though this was before effect sizes became required, the likelihood is that our effect sizes were larger).

The final sort of validity to be mentioned here is internal validity. Basically, this is freedom from confounding variables, a claim that the differences shown in the research are real, not artifactual. If a research project involves "in-depth interviews" with multiple entrepreneurs, the external validity will likely be high. But the number of confounding variables can be legion. What is there about the particular entrepreneurs selected for interviews? Were they selected on the basis of convenience, or a known list (for example, graduates of an MBA program), or on a "snowball" fashion where they were referred to the project by other participants? And did the referring entrepreneur call to make the appointment or otherwise communicate the nature of the research prior to the time that the investigator showed up at the person's office? Does the person conducting the research know the hypotheses? Has the protocol been practiced to the point of being standardized, or is the researcher "winging it?" All of these factors (and more) can compromise the internal validity of a research project. By contrast, an experiment in which (1) respondents are randomly assigned to conditions, (2) the experimental setting is highly controlled, and (3) the instructions are as thoroughly practiced as the work of a professional auctioneer, is likely to minimize the effect of potential confounding variables.

Experimental Design

The very simplest experimental design has two conditions. One of these is a "treatment" condition; the other is a "control" condition. Respondents assigned to the treatment condition receive whatever instructions are specific to the treatment; respondents in the control condition are typically given a general description of the research, but none of the specific instructions. Though this is a very simple design, it has at least one substantial drawback: because the control condition contains none of the stage-setting (and extraneous variable limiting) instructions, it is basically an "individual differences" condition. Statistically speaking, a control condition of this form may very well have a larger within-cell variance than the treatment condition does, thereby compromising one of the assumptions of the analysis of variance.

For this reason, even in a two-cell design, most researchers prefer for both cells to have instructions, with one cell receiving instructions designed to produce a high level of whatever variable is being examined and the other cell receiving instructions designed to produce a very low level of the same variable (sometimes a "control" condition is added "between" these two). But here is the rub: for even this simple two-cell design to work, there must be some relatively strong *theory* that distinguishes what will create a high value on the dimension of interest from what will create a low value on that dimension. It is worth noting that even with instructions in both conditions, the simple two-cell design is highly likely to be unsatisfactory in at least one sense. So far, we have been speaking of "respondents" as if they were an undifferentiated category of people who come to the research with no individual differences that cannot be overcome with random assignment. Unfortunately, to paraphrase the French, "Vive la différence!" Men and women are so different from each other in so many different ways that it is a serious error not to take the sex of the participant into account (see, for example, Bleidorn et al., 2016; Sullivan and Meek, 2012). What this means is that a "two-cell" design really needs to be *four* cells: women who do (and do not) receive the treatment and men who do (and do not) receive the treatment. This can be clarified by noting the form of the basic equation in the analysis of variance (the generally preferred method for analyzing experimental data. That equation (the form of the *F* test) is:

$$\frac{\text{Treatment effect} + \text{error}}{\text{Error}}$$

The null hypothesis is, of course, that there is no treatment effect (so the fraction becomes 1.0).

If respondent sex is not taken into account, all variation based on sex appears in the denominator. However, if sex is considered a factor in the design (notwithstanding the fact that it is an organismic – not manipulated – variable), then the F equation becomes:

$$\frac{\text{Treatment effect} + \text{sex effect} + \text{error}}{\text{Error}}$$

Table 8.1   The Solomon four-group design

Group 1	Pre-test	Treatment	Post-test
Group 2	Pre-test		Post-test
Group 3		Treatment	Post-test
Group 4			Post-test

In addition to the biological differences, there are differences in experience that should not be overlooked. For example, almost no one would argue that an entrepreneur who is starting his or her fifth business is psychologically the same as a novice entrepreneur attempting to organize his or her first venture. But obviously, entrepreneurial experience cannot be randomly assigned (any more than respondent sex can be randomly assigned). A design that incorporates a pre-existing variable is technically a quasi-experimental design (West et al., 2014). How can such a source of variability be controlled? The answer is that each group of respondents can be *pre-tested* before being subjected (or not) to the experimental treatment, and then all respondents can be post-tested. Then the score that gets analyzed is not the absolute score on the post-test, but rather the *difference* between the pre-test and the post-test for each respondent group.

But suppose the investigator is concerned that the pre-test itself might sensitize participants to the nature of the research, thus changing their responses. In that case one can employ a version of the Solomon four-group design shown in Table 8.1. Pre-test sensitization alone can be determined by comparing groups 2 and 4; effects of the treatment alone can be determined by comparing groups 3 and 4; effects of the individual difference variable can be identified by comparing groups 1 and 2. What you will quickly notice here is the reason that the design is not used very often (despite DeTienne and Chandler, 2004). Not only are there several different sorts of "control" groups (which increases the overhead associated with doing the research), some of the groups are involved in more than a single comparison, which makes the statistical analysis very challenging, even in the age of computerized statistical analysis.

In part to achieve greater experimental efficiency, and in part to try to better approximate the complexity of the "real world," most social psychologists prefer full factorial designs such as the one shown in Table 8.2. In this design there are two factors of interest, each of which has two "levels." In such a design either factor could be "organismic" (for example, respondent sex) or "manipulated" (produced in the setting by variations in the experimental instructions). In such a design every respondent is exposed to both (all) of the factors being examined. This

Table 8.2   A full two-factor design

Factor A	Factor B	
	Low	High
Low		
High		

is a 2 x 2 design. Then the ANOVA can identify three different effects: a main effect for Factor A (the row totals collapsed across columns), a main effect for Factor B (the column totals collapsed across rows), and an interaction effect that considers all four cells. Obviously, more factors can be added, and each added factor might have a different number of levels. The challenge for a researcher is that with every (2-level) factor added, the number of participants required doubles. This is why, when there are several factors of interest, researchers do what is called "conjoint analysis" (Shepherd and Zacharakis, 1999), which is actually an *incomplete* factorial design. In other words, a conjoint design allows for the testing of all or most main effects but few if any interaction effects.

So far we have been assuming that each cell in a design is populated by a particular set of respondents: no participant appears in more than one cell of the design. When the objective is to conduct neuroscientific investigations of the psychological processes of entrepreneurs, such completely "between subjects" designs are out of reach of all but the most highly funded investigators. With a single functional magnetic resonance imaging (fMRI) session costing as much as US $500 or substantially more, as much information as possible needs to be obtained from every single participant. If there are to be multiple "treatments," each participant needs to receive them all. Moreover, if the participants differ on some important element of life experience (such as being either novice or experienced entrepreneurs), there needs to be a way to eliminate "but they are just different people" as an explanation for any results achieved in the research.

The way to accomplish both of these objectives is to use a "repeated measures" factorial design. Suppose, for example, we are interested in determining whether the entrepreneurial risk associated with starting a company is perceived differently by novice and experienced entrepreneurs. The first problem is that the entrepreneurial risk cannot be assessed in an absolute sense. Rather, it must be *compared* (see Shaver, 2007) to some other sort of risk, preferably one for which it has already been determined that there are no differences between entrepreneurs and non-entrepreneurs, or between novice and experienced entrepreneurs. For example, let's assume that both novice and experienced entrepreneurs would consider it quite risky to lend a personal automobile to a teenager with a less-than-perfect driving record. If this assumption is granted, then "lending my car to an unreliable teenager" can be a baseline against which various sorts of *entrepreneurial* risk can be compared. Now a comparison between the novices and the experienced is not being made on an absolute scale, but rather on a *difference* between entrepreneurial risk and "ordinary" risk. The question is not how much risk is perceived by the two groups, but how much *more* risk is perceived than the baseline. Exactly the same method would be used to compare entrepreneurs of any sort to non-entrepreneurs. Obviously, what this means is that there must be pre-testing to determine what non-entrepreneurial risks would produce comparable levels between, for example, novices and experienced entrepreneurs, or men and women, or people who differ on some other variable that cannot be eliminated by instructions.

In any repeated-measures design, there will be an order effect of the treatments presented to participants. The number of different orders will depend on the number of different measures being taken. Suppose, for example, that in an fMRI study of entrepreneurial risk, an investigator desires to compare (1) entrepreneurial risk to (2) social risk to (3) ethical risk. Then participant #1 might get a–b–c, participant #2 might get b–a–c, and so forth. This can be accomplished most efficiently with some version of a Latin square, an example of which is shown in Table 8.3. If the number of participants is a multiple of the number of boxes in the design, the experimental conditions can be examined independently of the order in which they were presented. Because of the need to obtain dependent variable measures that are as stable as they can be, in a neuroscience context each of these rows might be repeated two or three times per respondent. As a final nuance, if there is some individual difference variable that cannot be controlled adequately by the design, that variable can be assessed in advance of the research and used as a *covariate* in the ANOVA, making it an ANCOVA. Repeated-measures designs, either with or without a covariate, are likely to be the most effective for research into the neuropsychological correlates of entrepreneurial risk.

Table 8.3   A sample Latin square

A	B	C	D
B	C	D	A
C	D	A	B
D	A	B	C

METHODOLOGICAL CHALLENGES

Many of the design issues raised in the section on research design will apply to experimental studies of entrepreneurial risk regardless of the particular measurement method used in the research. However, a number of additional design considerations exist for neuroscience studies. Additionally, there are "statistical, technological, and human factors" that are unique to neuroimaging research (Berkman et al., 2014, p. 125). For more technical details than are provided below, Berkman et al. recommend works by Harmon-Jones and Beer, 2009 and Huettel et al., 2009. Our purpose here is to raise – not solve – some of these additional design considerations.

Method Selection

Method selection is, necessarily, an early consideration in research design. A host of methods is used in cognitive neuroscience, including lesion studies; functional imaging – for example, fMRI, and positron emission tomography, (PET); and electrophysiological recording – for example, event-related potential (ERP), electroencephalography (EEG), and magnetoencephalography (MEG). All of these methods have strengths and weaknesses, some of which overlap and others that do not. For example, all of these methods share issues of interpretation that arise from assigning a single cognitive process to a particular neural region when, in fact, that region may be involved in multiple cognitive processes (Fellows et al., 2005; Horwitz et al., 2000). Imaging and electrophysiological approaches provide an advantage in dealing with this issue as they allow for studying activity of the whole brain and, thus, offer the potential of identifying the interrelationships among brain regions. However, the inferences drawn from imaging studies are constrained by their correlational nature (Fellows et al., 2005).

Selecting between imaging and electrophysiological methods (for example, fMRI and EEG, respectively) has further decision points. fMRI provides more precise localization of neural activity, including subcortical areas of the brain, than EEG. On the other hand, EEG offers better temporal resolution (Lieberman, 2010; for a more detailed account of these techniques, see Lee and Chamberlain, 2007). A complete program of research would include multimethod triangulation. As a starting point, however, we have selected to focus on functional imaging, and fMRI in particular. fMRI provides better data on subcortical structures likely involved in risk perception and decision making than does EEG, and allows for examination of network relationships across the brain. Finally, imaging studies have had a significant scholarly impact in the cognitive neuroscience literature (Chatterjee, 2005; Fellows et al., 2005) and fMRI is the most prominent among imaging techniques (Horwitz et al., 2000).

Study Design

Statistically, there are sufficient individual differences in neural responses that conceptually important issues must be treated as within-subjects variables, as described above. Moreover, the human organism's neural adaptability is such that responses must be assumed to be autocorrelated. What the fMRI actually measures is a blood-oxygenation-level-dependent (BOLD) signal. The onset of this BOLD response follows, but is not coterminous with, the stimulus provided by the experimenter; the duration of the BOLD response may last for several seconds following a stimulus as short as 100 ms. To deal with such issues, Berkman et al. (2014) suggest two different designs for presentation of stimuli. First, any given experimental treatment could be presented in *blocks* lasting 30–50 seconds, with a fixation-point resting space between blocks. To return to the Latin square design described above, several successive trials of (A) would be followed by a rest, followed by several successive trials of (B), then a rest, then several successive trials of (C) before the order was changed. Second, multiple event types can be interleaved (along with rest) in a sequence that allows detection of contrasts between conditions. If the interleaved sequence is randomly presented (rather than following the design of a Latin square), it is considered an event-related design (see D'Esposito et al., 1999). Event-related designs allow for greater certainty that findings are the result of differences in neural response to the task demands, rather than confounding factors such as change in arousal (Gazzaniga et al., 2014).

Technological and Human Factors

Practical considerations of conducting neurobiological research involve both technological and human factors. On the technological side, fMRI scanning is expensive and loud (Berkman et al., 2014). When conducted in an academic medical center by researchers who are not on the medical center's faculty, the charge for scanner time can easily run to US $500 per hour or substantially more in machine time (not including the time charges for professional staff to supervise the sessions). Research participants hear instructions through earbuds covered by noise-reducing headphones, but task-relevant instructions must be presented in frequencies that do not fall into the range of the scanner itself. Responses are typically collected using joy sticks or limited-alternative choice boxes, not exactly the way that entrepreneurs are accustomed to connecting to their worlds. For people whose daily success likely depends on facility with the spoken language, pressing buttons with a couple of fingers is a relatively impoverished way of responding.

Not surprisingly, there are also problems associated with the fact that many humans – especially those with attention deficit hyperactivity disorder (ADHD) – are very uncomfortable lying motionless in a supine position with their heads stabilized while spending an hour or more placed in a loud, dark, narrow tube (Berkman et al., 2014). This could be a particular problem in studying entrepreneurial experience in that Wiklund's (2016) research suggests that people with ADHD might be overrepresented among habitual entrepreneurs. Participants must be screened for claustrophobia, for presence of psychotropic medications, ferrous metal in or adorning the body, for handedness (typically only right-handed individuals are used), and, of course, every one of these necessary controls reduces the pool of potential participants and generalizability of any conclusions reached.

Human factors may also be the source of biological and psychological confounds. Biological confounds can arise from such things as neurological and degenerative disorders, the presence of psychotropic medications, and handedness. Gender is another issue that can present confounds because of systematic differences in brain functioning. This issue is often addressed by either including equal numbers of males and females in the study or conducting the study on only one gender, the latter of which has obvious drawbacks to generalizability. Other individual differences, such as mathematical ability, may explain differences in neural response to risk perception, rather than entrepreneurial experience. These potential confounds must be identified and measured at the onset of the study so that they can be accounted for by statistical analysis. A final consideration unique to neuroscience studies is how to handle the reporting of neurological abnormalities that are detected during the course of the study. Although established procedures for the responsible conduct of research specify how such problems should be handled, we should note that, at a bare minimum, the consent forms that participants sign must indicate the possibility that brain anomalies might be discovered. Researchers planning to conduct imaging studies should expect that their institutional review boards will likely require full committee review of the submitted research protocols.

Operationalization

If an entrepreneurship scholar uses a secondary database to study the issues of interest, that scholar is necessarily limited by what the original creators of the database considered important. Even a nationally representative and longitudinally gathered database as extensive as the PSED has its limitations, because there are conceptual issues of current interest that were not among the variables originally included. This is not the case in most experimentation. The experimenter can consider the particular respondents to be included, the conceptual variables to be examined, the controls that must be included in the design, and then create dependent variables that serve exactly the purpose desired. Unfortunately, in neuroimaging studies of entrepreneurial risk, there are limits on the experimenter's freedom to create dependent variables that precisely operationalize the conceptual variables of interest. Indeed, there is a sizable array of operational choices, thus complicating the experimenter's task. As operational decisions are made, they must further be linked to regions of interest (ROI) in the brain hypothesized to be involved in the variables of interest.

Initial neuroimaging research on risky decision making focused on examining which brain regions were activated when people selected options involving risk compared to which regions were activated when they selected risk-free options. For example, one of the first experiments to study the neural precursors to choosing a risky or safe option focused on the domain of financial decision making (Kuhnen and Knutson, 2005). In this experiment participants were presented on each trial with a choice among three options: a safe bond (that always paid $1), a good stock (expected value of $2.50), and a bad stock (expected value of –$2.50). On each trial, each stock would offer a return drawn from a probabilistic distribution, whereas the bond always returned a consistent payment. As with the real stock market, at the end of each trial participants learned the return of all three assets, but only experienced the outcome of the asset they had selected. Neuroimaging analyses revealed that prior to making a safe choice (that is, choosing the bond) participants exhibited greater activation in the anterior insula than when they chose a risky option (either the good stock or the bad stock). Conversely, activation in the ventral striatum increased prior to making a risky choice compared to a safe choice.

Another measure of risk is the Columbia Card Task (Figner and Weber, 2011). This task comes in two versions, a "hot" version (hCCT) with multiple choices per round and immediate feedback on success or failure, and a "cold" version with only one choice per round and feedback delayed until all choices have been made. In the hCCT respondents begin with a score of zero and then are presented with 32 cards that can be turned over one at a time. Some cards present a gain, others present a loss. The magnitude of the gain/loss and the gain/loss probability can be varied. A round ends either when the participant decides to stop turning over cards and collect his/her winnings, or when a loss card is encountered. Brain regions activated during this task include the ventromedial prefrontal cortex (VMPC), the prefrontal cortex (PFC), as well as the anterior insula, and dorsal medial PFC (van Duijvenvoorde et al., 2015).

Another measure of risk tolerance is the Balloon Analogue Risk Task (BART; Lejuez et al., 2002). This task presents participants with "balloons" that can be pumped to increase in size. At any time, the participant can decide to stop pumping and collect the money accrued or can decide to add another pump. Adding another pump increases the balloon value, but also risks the balloon popping which results in the loss of the money accrued thus far. The amount of money that can be earned per pump varies from a low value to a high value, and on each trial the computerized screen shows the current value of the balloon, a balloon pump, and a reset button that is labeled "Collect $$$." Each balloon is programmed to pop between 1 and 128 pumps, with an average break point of 64 pumps. At any point the participant can end the trial by collecting the earnings up to that point. The measure of risk propensity is simply the adjusted average pumps (the number of pumps on which the balloon did not pop). Generally, the BART shows activation in the PFC, with losses activating the dorsal lateral PFC (Cazzell et al., 2012).

Although risk and reward often co-occur, they are not identical, so disentangling their distinct neural representations has presented a challenge. In order to distinguish between the two, Preuschoff and colleagues (Preuschoff et al., 2006; Preuschoff et al., 2008) developed a task that featured independent aspects of risk and reward. In this card-drawing task, on each trial participants draw two cards from a set of ten and bet whether the second card will be higher or lower than the first. The first card is then revealed, and after a short delay the second card is also revealed, indicating whether the bet has been won or lost. This design allows the value of the outcome and the probability of its occurrence to vary independently. In this case, value and expected reward increase linearly with the probability of winning, whereas estimates of risk vary quadratically with the probability of winning (for example, both a 10 percent chance of winning and a 90 percent chance of winning have a similar variance in the outcomes). Neuroimaging analyses separately modeled the value of each trial and its associated risk, allowing delineation of separate neural signals tracking risk and reward. Activation in the ventral striatum correlated with the value of outcomes, whereas activation in the anterior insula correlated with risk and prediction errors related to risk.

Many of the tasks discussed thus far involve situations in which, although an outcome is unknown, the probability of different outcomes occurring is known. For example, when betting on whether a coin will land heads or tails, the outcome is uncertain but the probability of both outcomes is 50 percent. However, decisions involving uncertainty do not always feature known probabilities; one may be aware of the possible outcomes but unable to estimate the likely probabilities of these outcomes. Such contexts, which feature an unknown probabilistic distribution of outcomes, are said to involve ambiguity rather than risk (Ellsberg, 1961). Ambiguity may be particularly relevant in entrepreneurship because an entrepreneur may not have sufficient evidence or history in order to predict the probability of an outcome. Previous research has established that people are often much more likely to embrace risk than ambiguity (Camerer and Weber, 1992; Ellsberg, 1961). Neural investigations identify several regions that discriminate between ambiguity and risk. Both the amygdala and the lateral orbitofrontal cortex exhibit greater activation when decisions feature ambiguous rather than risky options, whereas the ventral striatum and precuneus exhibit greater activation when decisions feature risk compared to ambiguity (Hsu et al., 2005). These findings highlight the dissociation between ambiguity and risk at both the neural and behavioral levels, and suggest that distinct psychological and neural mechanisms underlie decisions involving these different types of uncertainty.

When considering entrepreneurial decision making, the symmetry of the distribution of potential outcomes is also relevant. Entrepreneurs may encounter decisions with positively skewed outcomes (in which there is a very small likelihood of high-value outcomes and high probability of low-value outcomes, such as the chance that one's new start-up will become the next tech star) or negatively skewed outcomes (in which there is a very small likelihood of a very negative outcome and high probability of low-value outcomes, such as the chance that one's business will fail catastrophically and consume all of one's personal wealth). Such heavily skewed outcomes may be processed slightly differently from normal risky decisions, as decision makers may overweigh the low-probability outcome in their decision making (Tversky and Kahneman, 1992). In general, positively skewed decisions evoke positive arousal for people, while negatively skewed decisions evoke negative arousal for people (Wu et al., 2011). However, only negatively skewed decisions also evoke greater judgments of perceived risk (Wu et al., 2011). Negatively and positively skewed decisions also evoke activation in distinct neural regions, with activation in the anterior insula tracking the former and activation in ventral striatum tracking the latter (Wu et al., 2011).

Overall, these findings point to a core network of regions implicated in processing risk and uncertainty during decision making. The anterior insula appears to support the processing of risk independent of the expected value of options and may be especially engaged in response to negatively skewed outcomes (Kuhnen and Knutson, 2005; Mohr, Biele, and Heekeren, 2010; Mohr, Biele, Krugel, et al., 2010; Preuschoff et al., 2008; Singer et al., 2009; Wu et al., 2011). The ventral striatum, on the other hand, appears to support reward processing and also tracks positively skewed decisions (Kuhnen and Knutson, 2005; Preuschoff et al., 2006; Wu et al., 2011; Wu et al., 2012). Both of these regions are heavily implicated in emotional processing as well, consistent with the notion that risk is related to affective processing (Loewenstein et al., 2001; Quartz, 2009; Singer et al., 2009; Wu et al., 2012). Despite the core network, there are substantial individual differences in responses to risk, with some people seeking risk and others preferring to eschew it. Particularly in the context of entrepreneurship, where some entrepreneurs may have a relatively high tolerance for uncertainty, understanding heterogeneity in responses to risk may help discriminate entrepreneurs from the general population, as well as identifying subgroups of entrepreneurs with a higher tolerance for uncertainty.

There are three main findings with respect to individual differences in neural responses to uncertainty. First, in some cases regions generally identified as responding to uncertainty also exhibit differential responding among those who are more or less risk averse. For example, in the context of financial risk those who are more likely to choose a safe option after having previously selected a risky option also exhibit greater activation in the anterior insula (Kuhnen and Knutson, 2005). Moreover, those who were more likely to make risk-averse mistakes (selecting the safe option when embracing risk would result in a higher expected value) also exhibited heightened anterior insula activation (Kuhnen and Knutson, 2005). These findings suggest that those who are most sensitive to risk – and also the most risk averse – also exhibit the strongest neural responses to risk in the anterior insula. Second, neural responses in regions that track subjective value are also modulated by individual risk preference. For instance, an area of the lateral PFC exhibits greater activation in response to larger expected utility of options (Tobler et al., 2009). This same region also exhibits slightly different responses depending on the risk tolerance of the individual, such that activation increases in response to uncertainty for those who are risk seeking, but decreases in response to uncertainty for those who are risk averse (Tobler et al., 2009). These findings suggest that risk attitudes modify neural representations of subjective value. Finally, individual differences in responses to risk also evoke differential responding in neural regions that do not typically process risk or reward. For example, one investigation found that the lateral orbitofrontal cortex independently tracked individual differences in risk attitudes while participants were choosing between risky and safe options (Mohr, Biele, Krugel et al., 2010). Consistent with other experiments demonstrating that distinct neural regions track ambiguity and risk, studies of individual differences reveal that activation in the posterior parietal cortex correlates with risk preference while activation in the lateral PFC correlates with preference for ambiguity (Huettel et al., 2006). This set of findings suggests that a broader set of regions may modify signals related to risk and reward during decision making. For example, the posterior parietal cortex may track quantitative representations of uncertainty (Feigenson et al., 2004), consistent with its role in magnitude representation, supporting decisions about risk.

The distinct advantage of using any of these tasks (or some of the others described by Defoe et al., 2015; or Platt and Huettel, 2008) is that their properties are well known and the brain regions of interest involved are also well documented. But that does not automatically make them completely suitable for the study of entrepreneurial risk. There are several reasons why this is true. First, several incorporate an element of randomness that is fully outside the participant's control (for example, when the stock loses, when the "loss card" appears in the Columbia Card Task, when the balloon pops in the Balloon Analogue Risk Task). By contrast, in the entrepreneurial world, the loss may never happen or the participant's actions could alter the result. Second, these tasks typically involve monetary outcomes, so none is capable of operationalizing *other* sorts of risk: physical, ethical, social, etc. This makes it very challenging to compare, for example, entrepreneurial risk to some other form on which novices and experienced entrepreneurs might actually be the same. These elements necessarily reduce the external validity of any findings that might be obtained and suggest areas for future research.

Data Preparation

Before any data can be analyzed, substantial preprocessing is required (Berkman et al., 2014). The scanner produces a series of slices through the brain, with each slice typically taken at a resolution of 64 x 64, or 4,096 volume elements (*voxels*). A typical whole-brain volume then comprises 30–35 slices, gathered in approximately two seconds (Berkman et al., 2014). The slices may be collected sequentially (1, then 2, then 3, then 4, and so on), or they may be collected in "interleaved" order (1, 3, 5, then 2, 4, 6, and so on). Preprocessing of the images requires: (1) corrections for distortions in the magnetic field map at boundaries between tissue and air-filled cavities (for example, nasal passages); (2) correction for the acquisition timing of each slice across the brain; (3) co-registration of the slices with reference to fixed structural scans; (4) realignment to correct for movement that may have occurred between the time of the structural scans and the time of the functional scans; (5) normalization to adjust for the fact that the physical brain of one participant is not an identical shape to the physical brain of another participant. This latter step is frequently conducted with reference to the Montreal Neurological Institute (MNI) atlas, a composite of 152 brains. The preprocessed data are then analyzed first on a subject-by-subject basis (first-level models) and then combined into a second-level model of whole-brain comparisons, or comparisons of particular regions of interest (ROIs).

CONCLUDING THOUGHTS

Research on entrepreneurial risk is important to entrepreneurs and stakeholders of entrepreneurship because it holds the potential to explain how and why people make entrepreneurial risk judgments. Despite the importance of research on entrepreneurial risk, the literature provides findings that are frequently at odds, thus reducing the value to entrepreneurs and their stakeholders in making risk judgments that might improve entrepreneurial outcomes.

Scholars have pointed out that one reason for the conflicting findings inherent in the literature on entrepreneurial risk is the methods employed by researchers. Many studies are based on post-hoc methodologies that have potential to generate biased findings. Results may be affected by post-hoc rationalization, sample bias, and measurement validity, among other threats to the findings. One way to overcome these challenges and to generate valid findings is the use of experimentation as the research design. This provides real-time data on entrepreneurial risk judgments. A risk judgment is a latent construct. Even though announcing a risk judgment is a recordable behavior (Bird and Schjoedt, 2009), it could be biased by a social researcher and participant expectations and self-presentation. Employing neuroscience data-collection techniques while participants make entrepreneurial risk judgments can remove many of these self-presentational effects, potentially enhancing the validity of the information obtained. Yet the methods of neuroscience are themselves not without methodological challenges. They provide an important new avenue for research, but one that must be followed with appropriate care.

REFERENCES

Ahmed, S.U. (1985), "nAch, risk-taking propensity, locus of control and entrepreneurship," *Personality and Individual Differences*, **6** (6), 781–2.

Aronson, E., M.B. Brewer, and J.M. Carlsmith (1985), "Experimentation in social psychology," in G. Lindzey and E. Aronson (eds), *Handbook of Social Psychology* (3rd edn), vol. 1, New York, NY: Random House, pp. 441–86.

Ashton, M.C., D.N. Jackson, E. Helmes, and S.V. Paunonen (1998), "Joint factor analysis of the Personality Research Form and the Jackson Personality Inventory: comparisons with the Big Five," *Journal of Research in Personality*, **32**, 243–50.

Ashton, M.C. and K. Lee (2007), "Empirical, theoretical, and practical advantages of the HEXACO model of personality structure," *Personality and Social Psychology Review*, **11**, 150–66.

Baird, I.S. and H. Thomas (1985), "Toward a contingency model of strategic risk taking," *Academy of Management Review*, **10** (2), 230–243.

Begley, T.M. and D.P. Boyd (1987), "A comparison of entrepreneurs and managers of small business firms," *Journal of Management*, **13** (1), 99–108.

Berkman, E.T., W.A. Cunningham, and M.D. Lieberman (2014), "Research methods in social and affective neuroscience," in H.T. Reis and C.M. Judd (eds), *Handbook of Research Methods in Social and Personality Psychology*, 2nd edn, New York, NY: Oxford University Press, pp. 121–58.

Bird, B. and L. Schjoedt (2009), "Entrepreneurial behavior: its nature, scope, recent research and future research," in A.L. Carsrud and M. Brännback (eds), *Understanding the Entrepreneurial Mind: Opening the Black Box*, Dordrecht, Germany: Springer, pp. 327–58.

Blais, A.-R. and E.U. Weber (2006), "A domain-specific risk-taking (DOSPERT) scale for adult populations," *Judgment and Decision Making*, **1**, 33–47.

Bleidorn, W., R.C. Arslan, J.J.A. Denissen, P.J. Rentfrow, J.A. Jaap, P. Renfrow, J.E. Gebauer, J. Potter, and S.D. Gosling (2016), "Age and gender differences in self-esteem – a cross cultural window," *Journal of Personality and Social Psychology*, **111** (3), 396–410; dx.doi.org/10.1037/pspp0000078.

Block, J., P. Sandner, and F. Spiegel (2015), "How do risk attitudes differ within the group of entrepreneurs? The role of motivation and procedural utility," *Journal of Small Business Management*, **53** (1), 183–206; doi:10.1111/jsbm.12060.

Brockhaus Sr., R.H. (1980), "Risk taking propensity of entrepreneurs," *Academy of Management Journal*, **23** (3), 509–20.

Caliendo, M., F. Fossen, and A. Kritikos (2009), "Risk attitudes of nascent entrepreneurs— new evidence from an experimentally validated survey," *Small Business Economics*, **32**, 153–67.

Camerer, C.F. and M. Weber (1992), "Recent developments in modeling preferences: uncertainty and ambiguity," *Journal of Risk and Uncertainty*, **5**, 325–70.

Cantillon, R. (1755), *Essai sur la Nature du Commerce en General [Essay on the nature of trade in general]*, London: Macmillan.

Carland, J.C. and J.W. Carland (1991), "An empirical investigation into the distinctions between male and female entrepreneurs and managers," *International Small Business Journal*, **9**, 62–72.

Carland III, J.W., J.W. Carland, J.C. Carland, and J.W. Pearce (1995), "Risk taking propensity among entrepreneurs, small business owners, and managers," *Journal of Business and Entrepreneurship*, **7**, 15–23.

Cazzell, M., L. Li, Z.-J. Lin, S.J. Patel, and H. Liu (2012), "Comparison of neural correlates of risk decision making between genders: an exploratory FNIRS study of the Balloon Analogue Risk Task (BART)," *NeuroImage*, **62** (3), 1896–911; doi:10.1016/j.neuroimage.2012.05.030.

Chatterjee, A. (2005), "A madness to the methods in cognitive neuroscience?" *Journal of Cognitive Neuroscience*, **17** (6), 847–9; doi:10.1162/0898929054021085.

Chell, E. (1985), "The entrepreneurial personality: a few ghosts laid to rest?" *International Small Business Journal*, **3**, 43–54.

Chell, E. (2008), *The Entrepreneurial Personality: A Social Construction*, 2nd edn, London: Routledge.

Ciavarella, M.A., A.K. Buchholtz, C.M. Riordan, R.D. Gatewood, and G.S. Stokes (2004), "The Big Five and venture survival: is there a linkage?" *Journal of Business Venturing*, **19**, 465–83.

Cook, T.D. and D.T. Campbell (1979), *Quasi-experimentation: Design and Analysis Issues for Field Settings*, Chicago, IL: Rand McNally.

Costa, P.T. and R.R. McCrae (1985), *The NEO Personality Inventory Manual*, Odessa, FL: Psychological Assessment Resources.

Defoe, I.N., J.S. Dubas, B. Figner, and M.A.G. van Aken (2015), "A meta-analysis on age differences in risky decision making: adolescents versus children and adults," *Psychological Bulletin*, **141** (1), 48–84; doi:10.1037/a0038088.

D'Esposito, M., E. Zarahn, and G.K. Aguirre (1999), "Event-related functional MRI: implications for cognitive psychology," *Psychological Bulletin*, **125** (1), 155–64; doi:10.1037/0033-2909.125.1.155.

DeTienne, D.R. and G.N. Chandler (2004), "Opportunity identification and its role in the entrepreneurial classroom: a pedagogical approach and empirical test," *Academy of Management Learning & Education*, **3** (3), 242–57; doi:10.5465/AMLE.2004.14242103.

Dohmen, T., A. Falk, D. Huffman, U. Sunde, J. Schupp, and G. Wagner (2005), *Individual Risk Attitudes: New Evidence from a Large, Representative, Experimentally-validated Survey*, DIW. Berlin, Germany.

Ellsberg, D. (1961), "Risk, ambiguity, and the savage axioms," *Quarterly Journal of Economics*, **75** (4) 643–69.

Fairlie, R.W. and W. Holleran (2012), "Entrepreneurship training, risk aversion and other personality traits: evidence from a random experiment," *Journal of Economic Psychology*, **33** (2), 366–78; doi:10.1016/j.joep.2011.02.001.

Feigenson, L., S. Dehaene, and E. Spelke (2004), "Core systems of number," *Trends in Cognitive Sciences*, **8** (7), 307–14.

Fellows, L.K., A.S. Heberlein, D.A. Morales, G. Shivde, S. Waller, and D.H. Wu (2005), "Method matters: an empirical study of impact in cognitive neuroscience," *Journal of Cognitive Neuroscience*, **17** (6), 850–858; doi:10.1162/0898929054021139.

Fiet, J.O. and P.C. Patel (2008), "Entrepreneurial discovery as constrained, sytematic search," *Small Business Economics*, **30** (3), 215–29; doi:10.1007/s11187-006-9010-5.

Figner, B. and E.U. Weber (2011), "Who takes risks when and why? Determinants of risk taking," *Current Directions in Psychological Science*, **20** (4), 211–16; doi:10.1177/0963721411415790.

Gartner, W.B., K.G. Shaver, N.M. Carter, and P.D. Reynolds (2004), *Handbook of Entrepreneurial Dynamics: The Process of Business Creation*; Thousand Oaks, CA: Sage Publications.

Gatewood, E.J., K.G. Shaver, J.B. Powers, and W.B. Gartner (2002), "Entrepreneurial expectancy, task effort, and performance," *Entrepreneurship: Theory & Practice*, **27** (2), 187–206.

Gazzaniga, M.S., R.B. Ivry, and G.R. Mangun (2014), *Cognitive Neuroscience: The Biology of the Mind*, 4th edn, New York, NY: W.W. Norton.

Grichnik, D. (2008), "Risky choices in new venture decisions – experimental evidence from Germany and the United States," *Journal of International Entrepreneurship*, **6** (1), 22–47; doi:10.1007/s10843-008-0019-5.

Harmon-Jones, E. and J.S. Beer (2009), *Methods in Social Neuroscience*, New York, NY: Guilford Press.

Horwitz, B., K.J. Friston, and J.G. Taylor (2000), "Neural modeling and functional brain imaging: an overview," *Neural Networks*, **13** (8), 829–46.

Hsu, M., M. Bhatt, R. Adolphs, D. Tranel, and C.F. Camerer (2005), "Neural systems responding to degrees of uncertainty in human decision-making," *Science*, **310** (5754), 1680–83; doi:10.1126/science.1115327.

Huettel, S.A., A.W. Song, and G. McCarthy (2009), *Functional Magnetic Resonance Imaging*, 2nd edn, Sunderland, MA: Sinauer Associates.

Huettel, S.A., C.J. Stowe, E.M. Gordon, B.T. Warner, and M.L. Platt (2006), "Neural signatures of economic preferences for risk and ambiguity," *Neuron*, **49** (5), 765–75.

Hunter, J.E. and F.L. Schmidt (1990), *Methods of Meta-analysis: Correcting Error and Bias in Research Findings*, Newbury Park, CA: Sage.

Jackson, D.N. (1976), *Jackson Personality Inventory Manual*, Port Huron, MI: Research Psychologists Press.

Jackson, D.N., L. Hourany, and N.J. Vidmar (1972), "A four-dimensional interpretation of risk-taking," *Journal of Personality*, **40** (3), 483–501.

Jain, R.K. (2011), "Entrepreneurial competencies: a meta-analysis and comprehensive conceptualization for future research," *Vision*, **15** (2), 127–52; doi:10.1177/097226291101500205.

Johnson, J.A. (2014), "Measuring thirty facets of the Five Factor Model with a 120-item public domain inventory: development of the IPIP-NEO-120," *Journal of Research in Personality*, **51**, 78–89.

Kahneman, D. and A. Tversky (1979), "Prospect theory: an analysis of decision under risk," *Econometrica*, **47** (2), 263–91.

Keyes, R. (1965), *Chancing It*, Boston, MA: Little, Brown.

Knight, F.H. (1921), *Risk, Uncertainty and Profit*, Chicago, IL: Houghton-Mifflin.

Kogan, N. and M.A. Wallach (1964), *Risk Taking: A Study in Cognition and Personality*, New York, NY: Holt, Rinehart, & Winston.

Kuhnen, C.M. and B. Knutson (2005), "The neural basis of financial risk taking," *Neuron*, **47** (5), 763–70.

Lee, N. and L. Chamberlain (2007), "Neuroimaging and psychophysiological measurement in organizational research: an agenda for research in organizational cognitive neuroscience," *Annals of the New York Academy of Sciences*, **1118**, 18–42.

Lejuez, C.W., J.P. Read, C.W. Kahler, J.B. Richards, S.E. Ramsey, G.L. Stuart, and R.A. Brown (2002), "Evaluation of a behavioral measure of risk taking: the Balloon Analogue Risk Task (BART)," *Journal of Experimental Psychology: Applied*, **8** (2), 75–84; doi:10.1037/1076-898X.8.2.75.

Lieberman, D.A. (2010), "Social cognitive neuroscience," in S.T. Fiske, D.T. Gilbert, and G. Lindzey (eds), *Handbook of Social Psychology*, 5th edn, New York, NY: McGraw-Hill, pp. 143–93.

Loewenstein, G.F., E.U. Weber, C.K. Hsee, and N. Welch (2001), "Risk as feelings," *Psychological Bulletin*, **127** (2), 267–86; doi:10.1037/0033-2909.127.2.267.

MacCrimmon, K.R. and D.A. Wehrung (1986), *Taking Risks: The Management of Uncertainty*, New York, NY: Free Press.

MacCrimmon, K.R. and D.A. Wehrung (1990), "Characteristics of risk taking executives," *Management Science*, **36** (4), 422–35.

March, J.G. and Z. Shapira (1987), "Managerial perspectives on risk and risk taking," *Management Science*, **33** (11), 1404–18.

Masters, R. and R. Meier (1988), "Sex differences and risk-taking propensity of entrepreneurs," *Journal of Small Business Management*, **26** (1), 31–5.

McClelland, D.C. (1961), *The Achieving Society*, New York, NY: D Van Nostrand Company.

Miner, J.B. (1986), *Scoring Guide for the Miner Sentence Completion Scale: Form T*, Atlanta, GA: Organizational Measurement Systems Press.

Miner, J.B. and N.S. Raju (2004), "Risk propensity difference between managers and entrepreneurs and between low- and high-growth entrepreneurs: a reply in a more conservative vein," *Journal of Applied Psychology*, **89** (1), 3–13.

Mohr, P.N.C., G. Biele, and H.R. Heekeren (2010), "Neural processing of risk," *The Journal of Neuroscience*, **30** (19), 6613–19; doi:10.1523/JNEUROSCI.0003-10.2010.

Mohr, P.N.C., G. Biele, L.K. Krugel, S.-C. Li, and H.R. Heekeren (2010), "Neural foundations of risk–return trade-off in investment decisions," *NeuroImage*, **49** (3), 2556–63; doi:10.1016/j.neuroimage.2009.10.060.

Murray, H.A. (1938), *Explorations in Personality*, Oxford: Oxford University Press.

Niess, C. and T. Biemann (2014), "The role of risk propensity in predicting self-employment," *Journal of Applied Psychology*, **99** (5), 1000–1009.

Palich, L.E. and D.R. Bagby (1995), "Using cognitive theory to explain entrepreneurial risk-taking: challenging conventional wisdom," *Journal of Business Venturing*, **10** (6), 425–38.

Platt, M.L. and S.A. Huettel (2008), "Risky business: the neuroeconomics of decision making under uncertainty," *Nature Neuroscience*, **11** (4), 398–403; doi:10.1038/nn2062.

Preuschoff, K., P. Bossaerts, and S.R. Quartz (2006), "Neural differentiation of expected reward and risk in human subcortical structures," *Neuron*, **51** (3), 381–90.

Preuschoff, K., S.R. Quartz, and P. Bossaerts (2008), "Human insula activation reflects risk prediction errors as well as risk," *The Journal of Neuroscience*, **28** (11), 2745–52; doi:10.1523/JNEUROSCI.4286-07.2008.

Quartz, S.R. (2009), "Reason, emotion and decision-making: risk and reward computation with feeling," *Trends in Cognitive Sciences*, **13** (5), 209–15; doi:10.1016/j.tics.2009.02.003.

Reynolds, P.D. and R.T. Curtin (eds) (2009), *New Firm Creation in the United States: Initial Explorations with the PSED II Data Set*, New York, NY: Springer.

Reynolds, P.D. and R.T. Curtin (2011), *PSED I, II Harmonized Transitions, Outcomes Data Set*, accessed 3 April 2017 at http://www.psed.isr.umich.edu/psed/data.

Rosenberg, M.J. (1965), "When dissonance fails: on eliminating evaluation apprehension from attitude measurement," *Journal of Personality and Social Psychology*, **1**, 28–42.

Rosenthal, R. (1966), *Experimenter Effects in Behavioral Research*, New York, NY: Appleton-Century-Crofts.

Schwer, R.K. and U. Yucelt (1984), "A study of risk-taking propensities among small business entrepreneurs and managers: an empirical evaluation," *American Journal of Small Business*, **8** (3), 31–40.

Seth, S. and A. Sen (1995), "Behavioural characteristics of women entrepreneurs and executives vis-a-vis their male counterparts: an empirical study," *Social Science International*, **11** (1–2), 18–33.

Sexton, D. and N. Bowman (1983), "Determining entrepreneurial potential of students," *Academy of Management Proceedings*, Academy of Management Conference, Dallas, TX, pp. 408–12; doi: 10.5465/AMBPP.1983.4976385.

Shaver, K.G. (2007), "C2D2: psychological methods in entrepreneurship research," in J.R. Baum, M. Frese, and R.A. Baron (eds), *The Psychology of Entrepreneurship*, Mahwah, NJ: Lawrence Erlbaum Associates, pp. 335–46.

Shaver, K.G. (2014a), "Experimentation in entrepreneurship research," in A.L. Carsrud and M. Brännback (eds), *Handbook of Research Methods and Applications in Entrepreneurship and Small Business*, Cheltenham: Edward Elgar, pp. 88–111.

Shaver, K.G. (2014b), "Psychology of entrepreneurial behavior," in A. Fayolle (ed.), *Handbook of Research on Entrepreneurship: What We Know and What We Need to Know*, Cheltenham: Edward Elgar, pp. 262–80.

Shepherd, D.A. and A.L. Zacharakis (1999), "Conjoint analysis: a new methodological approach for researching the decision policies of venture capitalists," *Venture Capital*, **1** (3), 197–217.

Shure, G.H. and R.J. Meeker (1967), "A personality/attitude schedule for use in experimental bargaining studies," *The Journal of Psychology: Interdisciplinary and Applied*, **65** (2), 233–52.

Singer, S., J.E. Amorós, and D.M. Arreola (2015), *Global Entrepreneurship Monitor 2014 Global Report*, accessed 17 April 2017 at http://www.gemconsortium.org/report.

Singer, T., H.D. Critchley, and K. Preuschoff (2009), "A common role of insula in feelings, empathy and uncertainty," *Trends in Cognitive Sciences*, **13** (8), 334–40; doi:10.1016/j.tics.2009.05.001.

Sitkin, S.B. and A.L. Pablo (1992), "Reconceptualizing the determinants of risk behavior," *Academy of Management Review*, **17** (1), 9–38; doi:10.5465/AMR.1992.4279564.

Slovic, P. (1962), "Convergent validation of risk taking measures," *The Journal of Abnormal and Social Psychology*, **65** (1), 68–71.

Slovic, P. (1972), "Information processing, situation specificity, and the generality of risk-taking behavior," *Journal of Personality and Social Psychology*, **22** (1), 128–34.

Smith, E. (2014), "Research design," in H.T. Reis and C.M. Judd (eds), *Handbook of Research Methods in Social and Personality Psychology*, 2nd edn, New York, NY: Oxford University Press, pp. 27–48.

Stewart Jr, W.H. and P.L. Roth (2001), "Risk propensity differences between entrepreneurs and managers: a meta-anaalytic review," *Journal of Applied Psychology*, **86**, 145–53.

Stewart Jr, W.H. and P.L. Roth (2004), "Data quality affects meta-analytic conclusions: a response to Miner and Raju (2004) concerning entrepreneurial risk propensity," *Journal of Applied Psychology*, **89** (1), 14–21; doi:10.1037/0021-9010.89.1.14.

Stewart Jr., W.H., W.E. Watson, J.C. Carland, and J.W. Carland (1999), "A proclivity for entrepreneurship: a comparison of entrepreneurs, small business owners, and corporate managers," *Journal of Business Venturing*, **14**, 189–214.

Stoner, J.A.F. (1961), "A comparison of individual and group decisions including risk," master's degree, Boston, MA: Massachusetts Institute of Technology.

Sullivan, D.M. and W.R. Meek (2012), "Gender and entrepreneurship: a review and process model," *Journal of Managerial Psychology*, **27**, 428–58.

Thaler, R.H. and E.J. Johnson (1990), "Gambling with the house money and trying to break even: the effects of prior outcomes on risky choice," *Management Science*, **36** (6), 643–60.

Tobler, P.N., G.I. Christopoulos, J.P. O'Doherty, R.J. Dolan, and W. Schultz (2009), "Risk-dependent reward value signal in human prefrontal cortex," *Proceedings of the National Academy of Sciences of the United States of America*, **106** (17), 7185–90.

Tversky, A. and D. Kahneman (1992), "Advances in prospect theory: cumulative representation of uncertainty," *Journal of Risk and Uncertainty*, **5**, 297–323.

van Duijvenvoorde, A.C.K., H.M. Huizenga, L.H. Somerville, M.R. Delgado, A. Powers, W.D. Weeda, . . . and B. Figner (2015), "Neural correlates of expected risks and returns in risky choice across development," *The Journal of Neuroscience*, **35** (4), 1549–60; doi:10.1523/JNEUROSCI.1924-14.2015.

Vlek, C. and P.J. Stallen (1980), "Rational and personal aspects of risk," *Acta Psychologica*, **45**, 273–300.

West, S.G., H. Cham, and Y. Liu (2014), "Causal inference and generalization in field settings: experimental and quasi-experimental designs," in H.T. Reis and C.M. Judd (eds), *Handbook of Research Methods in Social and Personality Psychology*, 2nd edn, New York, NY: Oxford University Press, pp. 49–80.

Wiklund, J. (2016), "Making a difference as an entrepreneurship scholar," paper presented at the United States Association for Small Business and Entrepreneurship, San Diego, CA.

Wu, C.C., P. Bossaerts, and B. Knutson (2011), "The affective impact of financial skewness on neural activity and choice," *Plos One*, **6** (2); doi:e16838; doi: 10.1371/journal.pone.0016838.

Wu, C.C., M.D. Sacchet, and B. Knutson (2012), "Toward an affective neuroscience account of financial risk taking," *Frontiers In Neuroscience*, **6**; doi:doi:10.3389/fnins.2012.00159.

Zhao, H. and S.E. Seibert (2006), "The Big Five personality dimensions and entrepreneurial status: a meta-analytical review," *Journal of Applied Psychology*, **91**, 259–71.

Zuckerman, M., E.A. Kolin, L. Price, and I. Zoob (1964), "Development of a sensation-seeking scale," *Journal of Consulting Psychology*, **28** (6), 477–82.

9. A few words about entrepreneurial learning, training, and brain plasticity
Aparna Sud

A PLUG FOR STANDARDIZATION IN ENTREPRENEURSHIP EDUCATION

As demand and supply for entrepreneurship based education flourishes and active based learning in the classroom is increasingly adopted, there is a need to develop a level of standardization in the field that has never before existed. A standard for entrepreneurial education acknowledged by both practioners and academics can help drive continuous improvement in how we teach entrepreneurship as well as evaluate entrepreneurial programs, and hold those that have been created by market opportunity to a higher standard. If we review prior art in the field of entrepreneurship research, a trend of retrospective studies can be observed. Compared to observational studies which lack the ability to prove causality, retrospective studies are the preferred method for study design. Prospective studies, although stronger studies for demonstrating causation between exposure and outcome, are also limited due to difficulty in recruiting and conducting experiments that require following entrepreneurs over time. Yet, retrospective studies are still prone to a recall bias which can be prevented if we adopt best practices from alternate disciplines.

Take the biomedical field for example: interventional studies are designed to evaluate impacts of a new treatment or preventive measure. They consist of three well-defined elements: an exposure or treatment that defines the principal experimental cohort, a measurable outcome as a result of the treatment, and a statistical comparison among the groups to assess the relationship between treatment and health outcome.

The strongest type of interventional study is a randomized controlled trial (RCT). In such studies, a homogenous population is divided into two separate groups and the intervention is selectively administered to one cohort. Clinical trials are powerful tools for assessing the benefits of one treatment over another by controlling for confounding variables. Pre-post studies, similar to RCTs, are proven to be a good experimental design method. But unlike RCTs, these studies are conducted as single-arm studies in which outcome variables are measured before and after the intervention without any comparison among groups.

Such studies can be leveraged in the entrepreneurship field to understand the impact of entrepreneurial education in a measurable way. As the market saturation of startup accelerator programs grows and demand on a global scale for entrepreneurship based education spikes, it will be increasingly vital for practioners and academics to work together in creating a baseline standard for entrepreneurship education. To do so, such programs and educational modules must first be evaluated on their impact relative to students and entrepreneurs. Applying research methods from other fields can be a means to reach this end goal quicker. A set standard can help refine design of entrepreneurial programs and support continued funding for entrepreneurial education due to proven impact.

Furthermore, as we work towards a better understanding of the effects of entrepreneurial education and uptake various study design from non-adjacent industries, we can look to existing resources such as the CONSORT statement. In order to standardize experimental studies, the healthcare industry has adopted a certain evidence-based set of recommendations that provide a guideline for reporting randomized trials. The CONSORT statement outlines a checklist of factors relating to design, analysis, and interpretation of a study and can be useful as we work toward implementing a similar guildeline in the field of entrepreneurship.

BACKGROUND ON BRAIN PLASTICITY

Until the 1960s brain development was believed to be only possible during early childhood and infancy. However, the new mode of thought backed by recent research in neural circuitry is that even the adult brain has the ability to rewire, reconstruct, grow neurons, and form new synapses. The hippocampus in particular is one region of the brain that continues to generate new neurons well into adulthood. This region is responsible for our long-term memories, learning, and emotions.

Our brains are incredibly dynamic, constantly adapting to fresh stimulus, changing environments, solidifying and creating new neural pathways. When we learn new motor skills, plastic changes occur in the structure of brain cells. Connections are strengthened or eliminated over time to increase efficiencies, a process known as synaptic pruning. Experiences such as stress can also induce hard-wired changes in the brain acting as a powerful modulators of brain plasticity.

In a similar fashion, our daily habits make a sizable impact on neural pathways, leaving permanent imprints to our brain wiring. Our brain cells have a fascinating way of communicating with one another. According to the well-known Hebbian principle, neurons that fire together wire together. During the process of long-term potentiation, an electric current sends neurotransmitters across the gap between neurons, the synapse, where adjacent neurons are stimulated. The firing response is then cascaded between cells until an entire neural pathway is stimulated and continually strengthened by recurring activation.

Many of us hone the same brain patterns on a daily basis with routine activities. On one hand we have adapted to our changing environments and become more efficient at using our brain power. However, on the other hand, we have become less adept at adapting to changes in our environment. One remedy to prevent against solidification of brain wiring is to continually introduce new stimulus into our environments in efforts to maintain diverse connectivity among neurons. Similar to physical exercise, we can stretch and work our brain pathways in different ways training our brain to re-fire in the directions of new neural pathways through our activities.

Exercise for instance produces brain neurogenesis; however, exercise alone is not enough to maintain mental flexibility. Our brains need to attempt to coordinate complex limb movements with a particular activity, engaging in motor learning. Moreover, activities such as musical training that involve multimodal sensory coordination (auditory, visual, motor) can be particularly beneficial in maintaining and generating synaptic connections. Research indicates that motor learning is key to growing new synapses, and synaptogenesis is vital to adapting to new contexts.

Thus, if we strive to stimulate synaptic connections through novel activity, strengthening our pathways just enough to ensure we do not lose them, we can retain a sense of fluidity that can allow us to adapt to any environment and changes within that environment. Whether we choose to take an unfamiliar route to work or attempting a new skill, one that relies on linking movement with brain activity such as dancing, we can reap long-term benefits with minor, simple adjustments to our daily habits. One may consider this neural flexibility to be a classic "entrepreneurial" trait. As such, due to brain plasticity one may consider if this entrepreneurial trait can be learned over time.

AN INTERVENTION-BASED APPROACH TO ENTREPRENEURIAL RESEARCH

If we take what we know about brain plasticity and adopt the frame of mind that entrepreneurship can be learned, we can start to seed insights into the effectiveness of entrepreneurial education. Instead of conducting research based principally on past data sets, we could gather, analyze, and interpret data in real time. Not only would this give us an enhanced understanding of the neural correlates to traits common to entrepreneurs, helping us to better define the ever-nebulous "entrepreneurial" mindset, but it would also provide important clues into the effectiveness of entrepreneurial education.

If we use what we know about the human brain being plastic, and apply a clinical-trial-design research approach to the entrepreneurial domain, we can not only start to uncover novel facets of entrepreneurial wiring, but also test hypotheses regarding certain interventions that can be applied over time in order to encourage learned behaviors exhibited by entrepreneurs.

As an example, we can take a closer look into the interconnectivity of entrepreneurs versus non-entrepreneurs. Is an entrepreneur who frequently faces challenging and changing environments by the nature of his or her day-to-day job able to form more connections when novel stimulus is exposed to him/her with a greater processing speed than a non-entrepreneur? Such questions can now be answered by utilizing experimental designs within cognitive science.

To offer an alternate case, meditation practices are highly effective modes of intervention that can mitigate stress. As such, they can be studied for their effectiveness on entrepreneurs many of whom don't have the luxury of emotional stability due to working in rapidly dynamic, high pressure, and fast-paced environments. Stress may impair our ability to form new synapses in regions associated with higher-order thinking (for example, the prefrontal cortex). Significant stress activates the amygdala and chronic psychological stress can even have detrimental effects on telomerase activity.

Although there are differing methods to meditation, recent literature has drawn an interesting link between open monitoring or mindfulness meditation and divergent thinking, associated with creativity. Mindfulness training has even proven to be capable of improving working memory capacity and reducing distractibility – in a mere two weeks. Practicing mindfulness meditation may result in greater curiosity and openness to new experiences. It has also been suggested that meditation may reduce the likelihood of hippocampal atrophy.

By implementing an intervention-based study of mindfulness we can seek to better understand the neural correlates of specific meditative practices in the context of an entrepreneurial frame of mind. If mindfulness is correlated to an increase in creativity, then we can observe the effects of a mindfulness based educational module on entrepreneurs evaluating creative capabilities over time as the outcome measure. For example, we can introduce mindfulness-based cognitive therapy (MBCT) to entrepreneurs, focused on shifting frame of reference, and analyze how that changes how they perceive opportunities. To take a step further, interventions can span from yoga to visualization techniques, to practical entrepreneurial courses aimed at creating new ventures in a real-world setting and can vary. However, the vital point is that as a result of this new frame of reference that builds on prior art in neuroplasticity and overlays research methodologies borrowed from the biomedical world, we can start to fathom the nature of entrepreneurs on a more granular, defined, and quantifiable level. In doing so, we have the ability to perhaps discover exciting new findings that will positively impact and shape the future of entrepreneurial education and research.

SUGGESTED FURTHER READING

Black, J.E., K.R. Isaacs, B.J. Anderson, A.A. Alcantara, and W.T. Greenough (1990), "Learning causes synaptogenesis, whereas motor activity causes angiogenesis, in cerebellar cortex of adult rats," *Proceedings of the National Academy of Sciences of the United States of America*, **87** (14), 5568–72.

Colzato, L.S., A. Ozturk, and B. Hommel (2012), "Meditate to create: the impact of focused-attention and open-monitoring training on convergent and divergent thinking," *Frontiers in Psychology*, **3**, 116.

Han, J.-Y. and S.-H. Han (2014), "Primary prevention of Alzheimer's disease: is it an attainable goal?," *Journal of Korean Medical Science*, **29** (7), 886–92.

Luders, E., N. Cherbuin, and F. Kurth (2014), "Forever young(er): potential age-defying effects of long-term meditation on gray matter atrophy," *Frontiers in Psychology*, **5**, 1551.

Marciniak, R., K. Sheardova, P. Čermáková, D. Hudeček, R. Šumec, and J. Hort (2014), "Effect of meditation on cognitive functions in context of aging and neurodegenerative disease,." *Frontiers in Behavioral Neuroscience*, **8**, 17.

Mohan, A., R. Sharma, and R.L. Bijlani (2011), "Effect of meditation on stress-induced changes in cognitive Functions." *The Journal of Alternative and Complementary Medicine*, **17** (3), 207–12; doi:10.1089/acm.2010.0142.

Newberg, A.B., M. Serruya, N. Wintering, A.S. Moss, D. Reibel, and D.A. Monti (2014), "Meditation and neurodegenerative diseases," *Annals of the New York Academy of Sciences*, **1307**, 112–23; doi: 10.1111/nyas.12187.

Thiese, M.S. (2014) "Observational and interventional study design types; an overview," *Biochemia Medica*, **24** (2): 199–210.

10. A few words about neuroexperimental designs for the study of emotions and cognitions in entrepreneurship
Theresa Treffers

INTRODUCTION

Recent technological developments have provided for the application of neuroscientific methods in the behavioral sciences. Psychologists have picked up these methods fast and academic fields such as affective and cognitive neuroscience have emerged. Economists apply neuroscientific methods and call it neuroeconomics. Eventually, neuroscience made an entry into the field of management and streams like neuromarketing or neurostrategy have emerged. The academic field of entrepreneurship, an area that interests scholars from several fields, is now attempting to form a research stream on neuroentrepreneurship. But what is this new research stream going to avail? How can neuroscientific methods be valuable to further our understanding of entrepreneurship?

Emotion and cognition research is still a hot topic in entrepreneurship. Initial advances have been made to empirically investigate the impact that emotions and cognitions have throughout the start-up process (see Cardon et al., 2009; Foo, 2009; Shepherd, 2003; Welpe et al., 2012). For example, emotions can influence how entrepreneurs perceive entrepreneurial opportunities, how they evaluate them, and how persistent they are in exploiting an opportunity. While behavioral evidence about the impact of emotions and cognitions on the entrepreneurial process is important and valuable, neuroscientific methods can help solve contradicting evidence or confirm existing evidence from a different perspective. In short, neuroscience can provide new tools to answer old questions and ask new ones to gain a comprehensive picture of how emotions and cognitions influence the entrepreneurial process.

This chapter seeks to give insights into how the study of emotions and cognitions in entrepreneurship can benefit from the application of neuroscientific methods, in particular functional magnetic resonance imaging (fMRI). Because there is already abundant knowledge about emotions and cognitions from the fields of affective and cognitive neuroscience, this knowledge may help us better understand their influence in entrepreneurship and design studies and answer contradicting or new questions.

For this purpose, this chapter seeks to give insights into the fields of affective and cognitive neuroscience and how these fields may be valuably linked to entrepreneurship. This review will open up new research gaps and new research ideas that cannot be addressed with behavioral studies, but only with neuroscientific methods. In addition, by providing concrete methods for possible neuroimaging studies, I hope to stimulate more neuroentrepreneurial research in the future. At the same time, by discussing potential limitations and practical pitfalls, I also want to raise awareness for the challenges that neuroscientific studies entail. I am confident that this chapter can also increase scholars' trust for the application of neuroscientific methods in entrepreneurship research. Although the field of neuroscience applies several distinct methods, this chapter focuses on fMRI.

AFFECTIVE NEUROSCIENCE

Affective neuroscience studies the neural mechanisms of emotion. Two hypotheses from the neurological study of emotion have emerged over time. First, the right hemisphere hypothesis proposes that the expression and perception of emotion is processed in the right hemisphere (Borod, 1992; Borod et al., 1983; Yokoyama et al., 1987). Second, the valence hypothesis recognizes the importance of the right hemisphere for the processing of emotion, but suggests that the right hemisphere processes negative emotions, while the left hemisphere processes positive emotions (Davidson et al., 1990; Fox, 1991; Silberman and Weingartner, 1986).

Recent meta-analyses also rely predominantly on two theoretical approaches (Barrett, 2006; Kober et al., 2008; Lindquist et al., 2012; Murphy et al., 2003; Phan et al., 2002; Vytal and Hamann, 2010). First, the psychological construction approach assumes that a network of brain regions underlies emotions such as happiness, fear, sadness, or anger (Barrett and Wager, 2006; Lindquist et al., 2012). In particular, scholars supporting this approach suggest that there is one network of brain regions underlying the valence (pleasantness versus unpleasantness) and arousal (activation level) dimension of emotion. Second, the locationist approach assumes that specific emotions are biologically basic and that all emotional states relate to a distinct brain region or network of brain regions (Ekman and Cordaro, 2011; Izard, 2011; Panksepp and Watt, 2011).

In general, emotional processing has been related to the anterior cingulate cortex and the medial prefrontal cortex; emotional information has been related to the dorsal frontomedial cortex (Damasio, 1996; Ferstl et al., 2005; Phan et al., 2002). Recently, brain areas could also be identified for the processing of specific emotions. For example, fear has been related to the amygdala (LeDoux, 2003; Murphy et al., 2003; Phan et al., 2002); anxiety – the pathological counterpart to fear – to the amygdala, inferior frontal gyrus (Brodman Area 45), and the ventromedial prefrontal cortex (Bishop, 2007; Mujica-Parodi et al., 2007); sadness to the subcallosal cingulate cortex (Murphy et al., 2003; Phan et al., 2002); anger to the lateral orbitofrontal cortex (Murphy et al., 2003); disgust to the insular cortex (Britton et al., 2006; Lane et al., 1997; Murphy et al., 2003; Phan et al., 2002); displeasure to the amygdala, hippocampus, insular cortex, and the superior temporal gyrus (Britton et al., 2006; Casacchia et al., 2009); pleasure – as positive state – to the anterior cingulate cortex, putamen, medial prefrontal cortex, and the nucleus accumbens (Sabatinelli et al., 2007; McLean et al., 2009); and happiness – as positive trait – to basal ganglia (Murphy et al., 2003; Phan et al., 2002).

All these results show that affective neuroscience has provided ample evidence for the study of emotion in the brain. These results are important and helpful in designing neuroentrepreneurial studies because we can build on a large body of existing studies and apply them to research questions that are relevant to the field of entrepreneurship. However, as entrepreneurship is an applied field, the study of emotions may not be sufficient to understand entrepreneurship as a phenomenon. Instead, we need to add cognitive evidence from the field of neuroscience to be able to neurologically study entrepreneurial outcomes.

COGNITIVE NEUROSCIENCE

Cognition refers to all mental processes that precede most human behavior. Cognitive neuroscience studies the neural circuits in the brain that underlie cognitive activities. Because we want to link emotion and cognition to the field of neuroentrepreneurship, we rely on evidence from the cognitive neuroscience of emotion, that is, cognitive neuroscience research, including the study of emotion.

Several constructs that contain emotional and cognitive elements, and which are of interest to the study of neuroentrepreneurship, have been related to specific brain areas. For instance, flow has been related to the dorsomedial prefrontal cortex and the medial parietal cortex (Iacobini et al., 2004); optimism to the rostral anterior cingulate cortex and the amygdala (Sharot et al., 2007); frustration to the right anterior insula and the right ventral prefrontal cortex (Abler et al., 2005); trust to the anterior paracingulate cortex, caudate nucleus, and putamen (King-Casas et al., 2005; Dimoka 2010); distrust to the amygdala and insular cortex (Winston et al., 2002; Dimoka 2010); and envy to the anterior cingulate cortex (Takahashi et al., 2009). Finally, self-regulation of emotion, or emotion regulation as it is often called, in psychological research has been linked to the amygdala, dorsolateral prefrontal cortex, and hypothalamus (Beauregard et al., 2001).

Constructs that are mainly cognitive but likely evolve emotional responses (and are thus relevant to neuroentrepreneurship) have also been studied in cognitive neuroscience. For example, risk is related to the nucleus accumbens (Knutson et al., 2001); uncertainty to the orbitofrontal and parietal cortex (Krain et al., 2006; Huettel et al., 2005); ambiguity to the insular cortex and the parietal cortex (Krain et al., 2006); reward and utility to the anterior cingulate cortex, caudate nucleus, nucleus accumbens, and putamen (Bush et al., 2002; McClure et al., 2004; Delgado et al., 2005); loss to the insular cortex (Paulus and Frank, 2003); competition to the inferior parietal cortex and the medial prefrontal cortex (Decety and Jackson, 2004); cooperation to the amygdala, orbitofrontal cortex, and dorsolateral prefrontal cortex (Rilling et al., 2002; Rilling et al., 2007); intentions to the ventrolateral prefrontal cortex and Brodman Area 47 (Dove et al., 2008; Okuda et al., 1998); and task intentions to the anterior cingulate cortex, and the medial and lateral prefrontal cortex (Haynes et al., 2007; Winterer et al., 2002).

Again, all these studies help us better understand emotional and cognitive constructs from a neurological perspective and apply them to the field of neuroentrepreneurship. The cognitive neuroscience of emotion in particular helps us understand entrepreneurial outcomes because it studies cognition and emotion at the same time. Given extant evidence from this field, neuroentrepreneurial scholars can formulate hypotheses based on certain brain areas that are implicated in certain processes of functions, and better interpret findings from fMRI in conjunction with these extant studies.

NEUROEXPERIMENTAL DESIGNS FOR THE STUDY OF EMOTIONS AND COGNITIONS IN ENTREPRENEURSHIP

Technicalities

Although there are several neuroscientific methods, which all have their benefits and limitations, our suggestions for experimental designs mainly focus on fMRI because it is the most commonly used neuroscientific method in affective and cognitive neuroscience. An fMRI experiment should be planned to complement existing behavioral evidence. It is one of the most fine-grained and expensive methods and therefore is much too precious to apply randomly and without proper preparation. fMRI is suitable to measure constructs such as sensitive issues, hidden emotions, automated processes, complex processes, and moral issues, which cannot be easily measured with existing methods. Besides masked stimuli, which are not consciously observed but are likely to trigger brain activity (see Vuilleumier et al., 2001) – such as experiencing work stress, constructs that are open to subjectivity bias such as the self-report of emotions (see LeDoux 2003), or constructs that fall prey to social desirability such as the recruitment propensity of entrepreneurs – all may be better captured with fMRI than with behavioral data. With fMRI, study participants cannot manipulate their brain responses, because fMRI measures the objective physiological responses.

Experiments can typically be designed as between-subjects or within-subjects manipulations. In between-subjects designs, different groups of participants receive different stimuli, for example, one group receives a treatment and the other group does not. The group difference may be some intrinsic qualifier, such as male versus female or entrepreneur versus non-entrepreneur, or it may be randomly assigned by the experimenters. In fMRI studies, between-subjects designs are most common in the examination of the effects of a drug or disease state. Because there is a large inter-subject variability in fMRI studies, most fMRI studies use within-subjects designs. In within-subjects designs, each participant receives all experimental conditions, as in control and treatment conditions (Huettel et al., 2004).

As behavioral experimental designs, neuroentrepreneurial designs need one or more suitable control groups to which the effect that is most relevant to the research question is compared. Oftentimes, the design of the control condition(s) is more difficult than the design of the treatment condition(s). Researchers have to think carefully to which standard they want to compare the treatment condition(s). Control condition(s) should therefore be as similar to the treatment condition as possible, but differ only in the effect of interest.

fMRI experiments can be designed as blocked designs or as event-related designs (Huettel et al., 2004). In blocked designs, experimental conditions are separated into distinct blocks, so that each condition is presented for an extended period of time. The main advantage of blocked designs is high statistical power due to the repetitive stimuli that creates an additive effect on the resulting brain activations. In event-related designs, discrete, short-duration events are presented whose timing and order may be randomized. By allowing randomization across conditions, event-related designs minimize anticipation and habituation effects. However, as a result, event-related designs have lower statistical power than blocked designs (Dimoka, 2012). In general, event-related designs are more complex than blocked designs and blocked designs should be applied when seeking to capture the cognitive strategies used by a participant to perform a given task.

Suggestions for Neuroentrepreneurial Research Designs

Neuroexperimental designs aim at manipulating emotional or cognitive processes while the corresponding brain activations are recorded within an fMRI scanner. Relative to behavioral laboratory experiments, experimental tasks in fMRI studies must be simpler and shorter to enable a straightforward link between the experimental tasks and the observed brain activations. To have relevance to the field of entrepreneurship, participants in fMRI studies should be entrepreneurs. However, one could also invite entrepreneurs and non-entrepreneurs, or economic and social entrepreneurs, or nascent and experienced entrepreneurs and compare their neural activities during experimental tasks. If only entrepreneurs are invited, neuroimaging studies could complement behavioral evidence in, for example, shedding light on underlying mechanisms or on competing hypotheses. If different groups are invited, neuroimaging findings can give new insights in how (certain kinds of) entrepreneurs are different from others.

Suggestion 1: emotional or rational entrepreneurial decision making
A very basic, but useful, application of an fMRI study is to find out if a decision is made emotionally or rationally. Although we know that no decision is possible without emotion and reason (Damasio, 1996), an fMRI study can give insight into which (brain) part outweighs the other. In an entrepreneurial context, it would be interesting to know if the decision to start a new venture is more emotional or rational, or if an entrepreneurial opportunity is evaluated emotionally or rationally. Also, it would be interesting to know if strategic or tactic decisions are mainly made emotionally or rationally. Finally, it would be interesting to know if financial decisions, which are argued to be mainly based on reason, contain a smaller or lager part of emotion.

In a neuroentrepreneurial study, entrepreneurs can be faced with quick-decision scenarios, for example, how they would evaluate different opportunities. When presenting the different opportunities the corresponding brain responses are recorded. The activated brain areas give insight into the level of emotion and reason in an evaluation decision and additionally shed light on which emotions and which rational processes are involved.

Such a study can, for instance, complement, possibly contradict, existing behavioral evidence stating that entrepreneurs' decisions are more influenced by emotions than by reason (Baron, 1998, 2008). The reasoning behind this argument is that entrepreneurs base their decisions more on emotions because their emotions are the only reliable cue in an uncertain environment. From the cognitive neuroscience of emotion, we know which brain areas should be involved when faced with risk, uncertainty, and ambiguity, and if any of the emotional brain circuits will be activated if conducting a neuroentrepreneurial study.

Suggestion 2: emotional Stroop for entrepreneurs
The emotional Stroop task measures attentional bias toward emotional stimuli (Stroop, 1935). Participants are asked to name the color of the presented word instead of the word itself (Pratto and John, 1991). In general, it is more difficult for participants to name the ink color of emotionally valenced words (for example, death, failure) than of emotionally neutral words (for example, iron, face) (Wentura et al., 2000; Williams and Broadbent 1986). The response time is used to measure the magnitude between the differently valenced words.

For a neuroentrepreneurial study, entrepreneurs and non-entrepreneurs could be presented with the same set of words such as failure, grief, layoff, or millionaire as treatment conditions, and words such as face, desk, telephone, or carpet as control conditions. The related brain activations when presenting a word can be recorded and compared between the groups. The response time can be used as a behavioral robustness measure. The brain activations will show us – besides the activated brain regions – for instance, if non-entrepreneurs really show a higher fear of failure than entrepreneurs, or if entrepreneurs are really more aroused when they imagine themselves as millionaires.

Suggestion 3: entrepreneurial emotions as reaction to stimuli
Entrepreneurial emotions can also be studied as reaction to a stimuli. Situational stimuli that are relevant to the study of entrepreneurship are, for instance, entrepreneurial opportunities, negotiations, or failure. For a neuroentrepreneurial study, participants could be presented with different negotiation scenarios, including different behavioral aspects of the counterpart such as direct, transparent, emotional, or cool. The according brain activations can tell us which emotions are

experienced and how strongly entrepreneurs experience emotions when negotiating.

Knowing which emotions and how strongly entrepreneurs experience emotions when negotiating can not only help entrepreneurs themselves to improve their negotiation behavior, but also help coaches to train entrepreneurs in how to appropriately deal with their emotions during negotiations. In self-report data, it may not be as clear which emotions entrepreneurs really experience, and honestly indicating emotions such as helplessness or fear during negotiations requires a lot of self-confidence and reflection. Through fMRI, entrepreneurs' emotions during a negotiation situation can be transparently displayed and the findings can be used for practical purposes.

Suggestion 4: testing potential biases against entrepreneurs on the labor market

Recent evidence indicates that entrepreneurs face difficulties on the labor market when applying for corporate jobs (Koellinger et al., 2015; Treffers et al., 2016). Because recruiters are the first to screen a job applicant's résumé, they are the ones likely rejecting entrepreneurs for job interviews. While some of them may have rational reasons not to select entrepreneurs as potential job candidates, others could have formed biases against entrepreneurs. Hence, an fMRI study can be suitable to examine potential (hidden) biases of recruiters against entrepreneurs.

In a neuroentrepreneurial study, recruiters could be invited as participants. A conjoint experiment could be designed where recruiters have to react to different word combinations such as entrepreneur and extroverted, manager and dominant, entrepreneur and creative, or manager and persistent. Brain activation will show us to which words recruiters associate negative or positive emotions. Activations can also give insights into which brain areas are involved for potentially biased decisions against entrepreneurs. Previous studies about the brain areas can help explain why these brain areas may be active in recruiters' brains when deciding against entrepreneurs as potential job candidates.

Suggestion 5: neuromarketing

Eventually, fMRI could deliver promising insights into neuroentrepreneurial marketing. By scanning potential customers of new ventures, entrepreneurs – and possibly interested venture capitalists – could test the value of their brand, logo, or slogan. Customers could be presented with different slogans and their according brain responses can be recorded. By comparing the brain areas and their level of activation, findings give insights into which slogans are related to which emotions (but possibly also to other neural correlates) and how strongly. Such results can help entrepreneurs to formulate their marketing strategy because they know what their potential customers truly think about their marketing instruments.

Other Design Issues to Consider

In medical and some psychological fields, it is common standard to determine the sample size *ex ante*. The benefit of this procedure is that the exact sample size can be determined with the desired statistical power. The challenge, however, is that researchers need to be clear about the expected effect size. This can be difficult to determine if only a few studies on the estimated effect size of the relationship exist. Researchers are advised to follow a conservative approach and assume a smaller effect size rather than a liberal approach assuming large effect sizes.

If an *ex ante* determination of the sample size is not possible for some reason, the statistical power of the study should at least be calculated *post hoc*. Early neuroscience experiments in psychology had an average power of only 50 percent (Maxwell, 2004). However, statistical power of > 80 percent is desirable. An easy and free tool for conducting power analyses is G*Power (Faul et al., 2007, 2009).

Besides statistical power calculations, there is a much larger statistical burden to face when analyzing data from a neuroimaging experiment. There are several steps to take before the data is even ready for analysis. The preprocessing of the data includes slice timing, realignment, co-registration, segmentation, normalization, and smoothing (for an extensive description of these steps see Dimoka, 2012; and Huettel et al., 2004). After the preprocessing, the data can be analyzed with region of interest analysis or individual and group comparisons. Hence, the statistical analysis of a neuroimaging study is a serious effort and is expensive in computer storage and time. Thus before starting to design an experimental study, scholars should think about how the data can be analyzed.

Finally, it is strongly recommended to join forces with experienced scholars from the field of affective and/or cognitive neuroscience before conducting a neuroentrepreneurial study. Scholars in entrepreneurship bring expertise from practice and applied research questions, but they usually have less experience with neuroscientific methods. Although it is not impossible to learn how to conduct a neuroentrepreneurial study by the book, entrepreneurship scholars should not underestimate the time and energy that goes into such a project. In addition, many practices are not easily learned by the book, but can only be learned in practice.

CONCLUSION

While behavioral evidence about the impact of emotions and cognitions on the entrepreneurial process is important and valuable, neuroscientific methods can help solve contradicting evidence or confirm existing evidence from a different perspective. Neuroscience can provide new tools to answer old questions and ask new ones to gain a comprehensive picture of how emotions and cognitions influence the entrepreneurial process. This chapter reviewed literature from affective and cognitive neuroscience and described several brain areas that are related to emotions, cognitive processing, and decision making in the entrepreneurial process. Furthermore, I presented suggestions for neuroexperimental designs that can be applied to the study of emotions and cognitions in entrepreneurship. With this chapter, I hope to have stimulated more thoughts for the neurological study of emotions and cognitions in entrepreneurship and inspired some ideas for neuroentrepreneurial study designs.

REFERENCES

Abler, B., H. Walter, and S. Erk (2005), "Neural correlates of frustration," *Neuroreport*, **16** (7), 669–72.

Baron, R. (1998), "Cognitive mechanisms in entrepreneurship: why and when entrepreneurs think differently than other people," *Journal of Business Venturing*, **13**, 275–94.

Baron, R.A. (2008), "The role of affect in the entrepreneurial process," *Academy of Management Review*, **33** (2), 328–40.

Barrett, L.F. (2006), "Are emotions natural kinds?" *Perspectives on Psychological Science*, **1**, 28–58.

Barrett, L.F. and T. Wager (2006), "The structure of emotion: evidence from the neuroimaging of emotion," *Current Directions in Psychological Science*, **15** (2), 79–85.

Beauregard, M., J. Lévesque, and P. Bourgouin (2001), "Neural correlates of conscious self-regulation of emotion," *The Journal of Neuroscience*, **21**, 1–6.

Bishop, S.J. (2007), "Neurocognitive mechanisms of anxiety: an integrative account," *Trends in Cognitive Sciences*, **11** (7), 307–16.

Borod, J.C. (1992), "Intel-hemispheric and intrahemispheric control of emotion: a focus on unilateral brain damage," *Journal of Consulting and Clinical Psychology*, **60** (3), 339–48.

Borod, J.C., E. Koff, and H.S. Caron (1983), "Right hemispheric specialization for the expression and appreciation of emotion: a focus on the face," in E. Perecman (ed.), *Cognitive Functions in the Right Hemisphere*, New York: Academic Press, pp. 83–110.

Britton, J.C., K.L. Phan, S.F. Taylor, R.C. Welsh, K.C. Berridge, and I. Liberzon (2006), "Neural correlates of social and nonsocial emotions: an fMRI study," *NeuroImage*, **31**, 397–409.

Bush, G., B.A. Vogt, J. Holmes, A.M. Dale, D. Greve, M.A. Jenike, and B.R. Rosen (2002), "Dorsal anterior cingulate cortex: a role in reward-based decision making," *Proceedings of the National Academy of Sciences*, **99** (1), 523–28.

Cardon, M.S., J. Wincent, J. Singh, and M. Drnovsek (2009), "The nature and experience of entrepreneurial passion," *Academy of Management Review*, **34**, 511–32.

Casacchia, M., M. Mazza, A. Catalucci, R. Pollice, M. Gallucci, and R. Roncone (2009),

"Abnormal emotional responses to pleasant and unpleasant visual stimuli in first episode schizophrenia: f-MRI investigation," *European Psychiatry*, **24** (1), S700.

Damasio, A.R. (1996), "The somatic marker hypothesis and the possible functions of the prefrontal cortex," *Philos Trans R Soc Lond B Biol*, **351** (1346), 1413–20.

Davidson, R., P. Ekman, C.D. Saron, J.A. Senulis, and W.V. Friesen (1990), "Approach-withdrawal and cerebral asymmetry: emotional expression and brain physiology I," *Journal of Personality and Social Psychology*, **58** (2), 330–41.

Decety, J. and P. Jackson (2004) "The functional architecture of human empathy," *Behavioral and Cognitive Neuroscience Reviews*, **3**, 71–100.

Delgado, M.R., M.M. Miller, S. Inati, and E.A. Phelps (2005), "An fMRI study of reward-related probability learning," *NeuroImage*, **24**, 862–73.

Dimoka, A. (2010), "What does the brain tell us about trust and distrust? Evidence from a functional neuroimaging study," *MIS Quarterly*, **34** (2), 373–96.

Dimoka, A. (2012), "How to conduct a functional magnetic resonance (fMRI) study in social science research," *MIS Quarterly*, **36** (3), 811–A11.

Dove, A., T. Manly, R. Epstein, and A.M. Owen (2008), "The engagement of mid-ventrolateral prefrontal cortex and posterior brain regions in intentional cognitive activity," *Human Brain Mapping*, **29**, 107–19.

Ekman, P. and D. Cordaro (2011), "What is meant by calling emotions basic," *Emotion Review*, **3**, 364–70.

Faul, F., E. Erdfelder, A. Buchner, and A.-G. Lang (2009), "Statistical power analyses using G*Power 3.1: tests for correlation and regression analyses," *Behavior Research Methods*, **41**, 1149–60.

Faul, F., E. Erdfelder, A.-G. Lang, and A. Buchner (2007), "G*Power 3: a flexible statistical power analysis program for the social, behavioral, and biomedical sciences," *Behavior Research Methods*, **39**, 175–91.

Ferstl, C., M. Rinck, and D.Y. von Cramon (2005), "Emotional and temporal aspects of situation model processing during text comprehension: an event-related fMRI study," *Cognitive Neuroscience*, **17** (5), 724–39.

Foo, M.-D. (2009), "Emotions and entrepreneurial opportunity evaluation," *Entrepreneurship Theory and Practice*, **35** (2), 375–93.

Fox, N.A. (1991), "If it's not left, it's right," *American Psychologist*, **46** (8), 863–72.

Haynes, J.-D., K. Sakai, G. Rees, S. Gilbert, C. Frith, and R.E. Passingham (2007), "Reading hidden intentions in the human brain," *Current Biology*, **17**, 323–8.

Huettel, S.A., A.W. Song, and G. McCarthy (2004), *Functional Magnetic Resonance Imaging*, Sunderland, MA: Sinauer Associates.

Huettel, S.A., A.W. Song, and G. McCarthy (2005), "Decisions under uncertainty: probabilistic context influences activation of prefrontal and parietal cortices," *Journal of Neuroscience*, **25** (13), 3304–11.

Iacoboni, M., M.D. Lieberman, B.J. Knowlton, I. Molnar-Szakacs, M. Moritz, J.C. Throop, and A.P. Fiske (2004), "Watching social interactions produces dorsomedial prefrontal and medial parietal BOLD fMRI signal increases compared to a resting baseline," *NeuroImage*, **21**, 1167–73.

Izard, C.E. (2011), "Forms and functions in emotions: matters of emotion-cognition interactions, *Emotion Review*, **3**, 371–8.

King-Casas, B., D. Tomlin, C. Anen, C.F. Camerer, S.R. Quartz, and P.R. Montague (2005), "Getting to know you: reputation and trust in a two-person economic exchange," *Science*, **308** (5718), 78–83.

Knutson, B., G.W. Fong, C.M. Adams, J.L. Varner, and D. Hommer (2001), "Dissociation of reward anticipation and outcome with event-related fMRI," *Neuroreport*, **12**, 3683–7.

Kober, H., L.F. Barrett, J. Joseph, E. Bliss-Moreau, K. Lindquist, and T.D. Wager (2008), "Functional grouping and cortical-subcortical interactions in emotion: a meta-analysis of neuroimaging studies," *NeuroImage*, **42** (2), 998–1031.

Koellinger, P.D., J.N. Mell, I. Pohl, C. Roessler, and T. Treffers (2015), "Self-employed but looking: a labour market experiment," *Economica*, **82** (325), 137–61.

Krain, A., A.M. Wilson, R. Arbuckle, F.X. Castellanos, and M.P. Milham (2006), "Distinct neural mechanisms of risk and ambiguity: a meta-analysis of decision-making," *NeuroImage*, **32** (1), 477–84.

Lane, R.D., E.M. Reiman, G.L. Ahern, G.E. Schwartz, and R.J. Davidson (1997), "Neuroanatomical correlates of happiness, sadness, and disgust," *American Journal of Psychiatry*, **154**, 926–33.

LeDoux, J. (2003). "The emotional brain, fear, and amygdala," *Cellular & Molecular NeuroBiology*, **23**, 727–38.

Lindquist, K., T. Wager, H. Kober, E. Bliss-Moreau, and L.F. Barrett (2012), "The brain basis of emotion: a meta-analytic review," *Behavioral and Brain Sciences*, **35** (3), 121–43.

Maxwell, S.E. (2004), "The persistence of underpowered studies in psychological research: causes, consequences, and remedies," *Psychological Methods*, **9**, 147–63.

McClure, S.M., D.I. Laibson, G. Loewenstein, and J.D. Cohen (2004), "Separate neural systems value immediate and delayed monetary rewards," *Science*, **306** (5695), 503–507.

McLean, J., D. Brennan, D. Wyper, B. Condon, D. Hadley, and D. Cavanagh (2009), "Localisation of regions of intense pleasure response evoked by soccer goals," *Psychiatry Research: Neuroimaging*, **171**, 33–43.

Mujica-Parodi, L.R., M. Korgaonkar, B. Ravindranath, B. Greenberg, D. Tomasi, M. Wagshul, B. Ardekani, D. Guilfoyle, S. Khan, Y. Zhong, K. Chon, and D. Malaspina (2007), "Limbic dysregulation is associated with lowered heart rate variability and increased trait anxiety in healthy adults," *Human Brain Mapping*, **30** (1), 47–58.

Murphy, F.C., I. Nimmo-Smith, and A.D. Lawrence (2003), "Functional neuroanatomy of emotions: a meta-analysis," *Cognitive, Affective, and Behavioral Neuroscience*, **3** (3), 207–33.

Okuda, J., F. Toshikatsu, A. Yamadori, R. Kawashima, T. Tsukiura, R. Fukatsu, K. Suzuki, M. Ito, and H. Fukuda (1998), "Participation of the prefrontal cortices in prospective memory: evidence from a PET study in humans," *Neuroscience Letters*, **253**, 127–30.

Panksepp, J. and D. Watt (2011), "What is basic about basic emotions? Lasting lessons from affective neuroscience," *Emotion Review*, **3**, 387–96.

Paulus, M.P. and L.R. Frank (2003), "Ventromedial prefrontal cortex activation is critical for preference judgments," *Neuroreport*, **14** (10), 1311–15.

Phan, K.L., T. Wager, S.F. Taylor, and I. Liberzon (2002), "Functional neuroanatomy of emotion: a meta-analysis of emotion activation studies in PET and fMRI," *NeuroImage*, **16**, 331–48.

Pratto, F. and O.P. John (1991), "Automatic vigilance: the attention grabbing power of negative social information," *Journal of Personality and Social Psychology*, **61** (3), 380–91.

Rilling, J.K., A.L. Glenn, M.R. Jairam, G. Pagnoni, D.R. Goldsmith, H.A. Elfenbein, and S.O. Lilienfeld (2007), "Neural correlates of social cooperation and non-cooperation as a function of psychopathy," *Biological Psychiatry*, **61** (11), 1260–71.

Rilling, J.K., D.A. Gutman, T.R. Zeh, G. Pagnoni, G.S. Berns, and C.D. Kilts (2002), "A neural basis for social cooperation," *Neuron*, **35** (2), 395–405.

Sabatinelli, D., M.M. Bradley, P.J. Lang, V.D. Costa, and F. Versace (2007), "Pleasure rather than salience activates human nucleus accumbens and medial prefrontal cortex," *Journal of Neurophysiology*, **98**, 1374–9.

Sharot, T., A. Riccardi, C. Raio, and E. Phelps (2007), "Neural mechanisms mediating optimism bias," *Nature*, **450** (7166), 102–106.

Shepherd, D.A. (2003), "Learning from business failure: propositions of grief-recovery for the self-employed," *Academy of Management Review*, **28** (2), 318–418.

Silberman, E.K. and H. Weingartner (1986), "Hemispheric lateralization of functions related to emotion," *Brain and Cognition*, **5** (3), 322–53.

Stroop, J.R. (1935), "Studies of interference in serial verbal reactions," *Journal of Experimental Psychology*, **18** (6), 643–62.

Takahashi, H., M. Kato, M. Matsuura, D. Mobbs, T. Suhara, and Y. Okubo (2009), "When your gain is my pain and your pain is my gain: neural correlates of envy and schadenfreude," *Science*, **323** (5916), 937.

Treffers, T., P. Sandner, and E. Stam (2016), "Recruiters' perceptions of entrepreneurs' human capital," working paper.

Vuilleumier, P., J.L. Armony, J. Driver, and R.J. Dolan (2001), "Effects of attention and emotion on face processing in the human brain," *Neuron*, **30** (3), 829–41.

Vytal, K. and S. Hamann (2010), "Neuroimaging support for discrete neural correlates of basic emotions: a voxel-based meta-analysis," *Journal of Cognitive Neuroscience*, **22** (12), 2864–85.

Welpe, I.M., M. Spörrle, D. Grichnik, T. Michl, and D.B. Audretsch (2012), "Emotions and opportunities: the interplay of opportunity evaluation, fear, joy, and anger as antecedent of entrepreneurial exploitation," *Entrepreneurship Theory and Practice*, **36** (1), 69–96.

Wentura, D., K. Rothermund, and P. Bak (2000), "Automatic vigilance: the attention-grabbing power of approach and avoidance-related social information," *Journal of Personality and Social Psychology*, **78** (6), 1024–37.

Williams, J.M. and K. Broadbent (1986), "Distraction by emotional stimuli: use of a Stroop task with suicide attempters, *British Journal of Clinical Psychology*, **25** (2), 101–10.

Winston, J.S., B.A. Strange, J. O'Doherty, and R.J. Dolan (2002), "Automatic and intentional brain responses during evaluation of trustworthiness of faces," *Nature Neuroscience*, **5**, 277–83.

Winterer, G., C.M. Adams, D.W. Jones, and B. Knutson (2002), "Volition to action – an event-related fMRI study," *NeuroImage*, **17**, 851–8.

Yokoyama, K., R. Jennings, P. Ackles, B.S. Hood, and F. Boiler (1987), "Lack of heart rate changes during an attention-demanding task after right hemisphere lesions," *Neurology*, **37** (4), 624–30.

11. Which tool should I use? Neuroscience technologies for brain-driven entrepreneurship researchers
Víctor Pérez-Centeno

Venturing into an entrepreneurship study from a brain-driven perspective requires two major components: an experimental design and the use of a proper neuroscience technology. A variety of neuroscience techniques are available for use in humans (Bunge and Kahn, 2009). These methods on one hand aim to determine which neural structures are active during certain mental operations (Carter and Shieh, 2015) and, on the other hand, explore the brain mechanisms behind this activity (Bunge and Kahn, 2009). These technologies address different aspects of neural function, hence the interpretation of a given result strongly depends on what is being measured: neuronal firing, brain metabolism, neuro transmitter levels, and so on (Ruff and Huettel, 2014). From the plethora of existing neuroscience techniques, this chapter deals only with the techniques that fulfil three requirements: gathering data directly from the brain, being non-invasive, and holding potential to advance entrepreneurship research.

Many new techniques and improvements to existing techniques that could be applicable to entrepreneurship research continue to emerge and can be categorized into four classes. The first type consists of methods for directly measuring electrical activity associated with neuronal firing, such as electroencephalography (EEG) and magnetoencephalography (MEG) (Bunge and Kahn, 2009). Both EEG and MEG are known as electromagnetic recording methods (Banich and Compton, 2011).

The second class pertains to methods for indirectly measuring neuronal activity. These methods operate under the principle that neural activity is supported by increased local blood flow and metabolic activity (Bunge and Kahn, 2009). Methods under this category are known as functional brain-imaging methods and include functional magnetic resonance imaging (fMRI). Positron emission tomography (PET) is also a functional brain-imaging tool, but it is not considered here because it is invasive, therefore unlikely to be used on entrepreneurs.

A third class concerns techniques for influencing or modulating the activity of the human brain (Banich and Compton, 2011; Lewis et al.,

2016). These techniques are regarded also as "brain stimulation" or "neuromodulation," including transcranial magnetic stimulation (TMS), transcranial direct current stimulation (tDCS), and neurofeedback, among others. Neuromodulation techniques manipulate neuronal activity in humans without penetrating the skull. It has been said that these methods hold the potential for "neuro-enhancement," improving human attention, memory, and cognitive abilities in those with existing normal function (Carter and Shieh, 2015).

A fourth class refers to optical imaging techniques. These methods produce images of neural activity by measuring changes in blood flow and metabolism from the surface of the brain (Carter and Shieh, 2015). Rather than detecting changes in the magnetic or electrical properties of neurons, as in fMRI, EEG, or MEG, optical imaging detects changes in light reflectance from the surface of the brain due to changes in the amount of blood flowing to neural tissue (Carter and Shieh, 2015). Optical imaging requires the brain surface to be exposed to allow light to penetrate and reflect back to a camera, but near-infrared spectroscopy (NIRS) is a non-invasive optical imaging alternative that enables the recording of light reflectance through the scalp (Carter and Shieh, 2015). I particularly focus on functional near-infrared spectroscopy (fNIRS), which consists in the use of NIRS for the purpose of functional brain imaging. fNIRS is also considered a functional brain-imaging technique because it measures neuronal activity indirectly (Bunge and Kahn, 2009).

Functional brain-imaging methods[1] are also known as "measurement techniques" because they measure changes in brain function while a research participant engages in some cognitive activity (Ruff and Huettel, 2014), whereas neuromodulation tools are regarded as "manipulation techniques" (Ruff and Huettel, 2014) or stimulation techniques (Charron et al., 2008) because they examine how perturbations of the brain function change cognitive functions or behavior, either by transiently changing neuronal firing rates or neurotransmitter levels (Ruff and Huettel, 2014).

The application of these techniques could forward entrepreneurship research, however their use requires much learning and knowledge of the field (Krueger and Day, 2010). To provide a broader idea of the level of technical competence demanded, the next section introduces each tool, highlights its strengths and weaknesses, and advocates some entrepreneurship research topics for which these tools could be applied. Additionally, three principles are presented to orient the selection of a fitting technology. See Carter and Shieh (2015) for a detailed account of the whole range of technologies available in neuroscience.

ELECTROENCEPHALOGRAPHY (EEG)

To the best of my knowledge, Ortiz-Terán et al. (2013) and Zaro et al. (2016) are the only scholars who have used EEG in entrepreneurship research, the former exploring entrepreneurial decision-making speed and the latter studying entrepreneurial behavior during business opportunity discoveries. Both studies compared entrepreneurs and non-entrepreneurs.

EEG recordings were the first method developed for direct and non-invasive measurement of brain activity for human subjects (Woodman, 2010). It is a harmless technique (Bear et al., 2007) that records the brain's electrical signals through a series of electrodes placed on different points of the scalp (Bear et al., 2007; Eysenck and Keane, 2000). EEG measures the gross electrical activity of the surface of the brain (Carter and Shieh, 2015). Though it is not truly a brain-imaging technique, since no meaningful images of the brain can be produced using this technique alone, it can be used to ascertain certain states of consciousness with an excellent temporal resolution (Carter and Shieh, 2015). EEG equipment is low priced and widely available as compared to MEG or fMRI (Bear et al., 2007). One of its disadvantages, however, is that it possesses a poor spatial resolution (Bear et al., 2007). It is hard to determine where in the brain the electrical activity is coming from. EEG recordings, as such, reveal little about cognitive processes because the recordings reflect the brain's global electrical activity, but coupled with a technique named "event-related potential" (ERP), it allows the exploration of how brain activity is modulated in response to a particular task (Gazzaniga et al., 2014).

The ERP logic is as follows: EEG traces, recorded from a series of trials, are averaged together by aligning them relative to an external event, such as the onset of a stimulus or response (Gazzaniga et al., 2014). This alignment eliminates variations in the brain's electrical activity that are unrelated to the events of interest. The evoked response, or event-related potential (ERP), is a tiny signal embedded in the ongoing EEG that was triggered by the stimulus (Gazzaniga et al., 2014). By averaging the traces, investigators can extract this signal, which reflects neural activity related to the sensory, motor, or cognitive event that evoked it, henceforth the name "event-related potential" (Gazzaniga et al., 2014).

EEG/ERP is ideal for exploring brain mechanisms (Bunge and Kahn, 2009) because it allows a detailed investigation of the processes underlying cognitive functions. Furthermore, EEG/ERP yields a measure between stimulus and response, allowing a much better understanding of the effects of experimental manipulations than behavioral responses (Bear et al., 2007); providing a continuous measure of processing between stimulus and response, making it possible to determine which stage or stages of processing are affected by a specific experimental manipulation (Luck, 2014); and affording online measures of the processing of stimuli, even when there is no behavioral response (Luck, 2014).

The most notorious ERP disadvantage is that the functional significance of an ERP component is virtually never as clear as the functional significance of a behavioral response (Luck, 2014). Moreover, ERP are so small that it often requires a large number of trials to measure them accurately. In most behavioral experiments, a reaction time difference can be observed with only 20–30 trials per subject in each condition, whereas ERP effects often require 50, 100 or even 1,000 trials per subject in each condition (Luck, 2014). This places a limitation on the types of questions that ERP recordings can realistically answer (Luck, 2014).

As per Brandeis and Lehmann (1986), EEG/ERPs have been widely used to examine a number of cognitive processes such as selective attention, decision processes, and language. Aside from the importance of decision making and language to entrepreneurship scholars (Clarke and Cornelissen, 2014; Maine et al., 2015), I also think that the issue of attention should be assessed using EEG/ERPs; the reason is obvious: before any stimulus, attention is one of the earliest cognitive processes that takes place between the entrepreneur and the outer world where "opportunities" lie. For instance, using EEG/ERP to study how attentional processes operate in the identification of a business opportunity between entrepreneurs and non-entrepreneurs may shed new light on the stages of discovery (idea development) and exploitation (behaviors that make it happen), as these could presumably be induced in the laboratory (Davidsson, 2007).

MAGNETOENCEPHALOGRAPHY (MEG)

To this point there is no entrepreneurship study that has benefited from the advantages of MEG. This technique measures the magnetic fields produced by electrical activity in the brain (Bear et al., 2007; Eysenck and Keane, 2000). MEG uses a superconducting quantum interference device (SQUID) to measure the magnetic fields produced by electrical brain activity (Eysenck, 2006). This measurement can only be performed in a magnetically shielded room; there must be no external magnetic properties that would potentially interfere with the MEG signal (Charron et al., 2008). This technique is complex because the size of the magnetic field created by the brain is extremely small relative to the earth's magnetic field (Eysenck, 2006).

Similar to EEG, MEG has a good temporal resolution, which makes it a great tool to assess brain mechanisms (Bunge and Kahn, 2009). Unlike EEG, MEG provides better spatial resolution (2–3 mm) (Bear et al., 2007). The major MEG disadvantage is that it is expensive and less widely available than EEG (Bear et al., 2007).

As argued by Ruff and Huettel (2014), MEG offers five advantages. It is non-invasive and well-tolerated by humans, can be used with a wide range of experimental paradigms, records data from the entire brain simultaneously, and can yield insight into the combined location and timing of cortical activity with accuracy unmatched by any other technique. If that is so, why has it not been used in entrepreneurship research? A major MEG limitation lies in its inaccessibility. Purchasing a new scanner and setting it up can require 2–3 million USD. These costs are similar to those of fMRI (Ruff and Huettel, 2014). There is nonetheless a central difference between these two techniques. fMRI can be conducted using a standard MRI scanner, a very common diagnostic device for various clinical conditions. In contrast, there are only a few hundred research MEG systems in the world (Ruff and Huettel, 2014).

MEG has better source localization than EEG, in part because magnetic fields more readily pass through the skull and scalp. The inverse problem still holds, and researchers cannot fully identify the generating neural sources from a MEG recording (Ruff and Huettel, 2014). This method has been extensively applied to the study of a variety of cognitive neuroscience functions (Bauer et al., 2003). It has been applied to explore the lateralization-localization of language functions (Roberts et al., 2000), the localization of memory processes (Castillo et al., 2001), emotions (Parkes et al., 2016), and attention (Assadollahi and Pulvermüller, 2001). The study of these topics is related to the arena of entrepreneurial cognition. In this line MEG could be applied, for example, to unravel the cognitive processes behind the interaction of a variety of emotions and efficient decision making among expert and novice entrepreneurs and non-entrepreneurs. What is more, the simultaneous use of MEG and fMRI may allow a deeper understanding of the corresponding brain mechanisms in terms of its intrinsic brain networks. Such an aim is technically viable and beyond the identification of the brain regions involved.

FUNCTIONAL MAGNETIC RESONANCE IMAGING (fMRI)

Laureiro-Martínez et al. (2014) have produced the only article using fMRI to observe efficient decision making among entrepreneurs and managers. This technique utilizes a magnetic resonance imaging (MRI) machine

(Eysenck and Keane, 2000) to track blood-flow changes in the brain, which are thought to be correlated with local changes in neuronal activity (Gazzaniga et al., 2014). fMRI applies a strong magnetic field to the subject and records the variations of the magnetic field induced by a local increase in blood flow in the brain. This indirect measure of brain activity is known as a blood-oxygenation-level-dependent "BOLD" signal. The main goal of fMRI is to detect the local variation of the BOLD signal in the brain and its potential correlation in a given task or action (Charron et al., 2008).

The physiological changes captured by this technique fluctuate between a typical timescale of several hundreds of milliseconds at best, making it excellent at mapping the regions involved in task performance (Fox and Raichle, 2007) but incapable of resolving the flow of rapid brain activity that unfolds with time (Baillet, 2011). In simple words, fMRI is a very expensive technology, highly fitting to examine the "where" but inefficient to explore the "when" due to its poor temporal resolution.

Mather et al. (2013) state that fMRI results can inform our understanding of cognition in four ways. First, fMRI can answer questions about which functions can be localized to specific brain regions. Second, fMRI data can be utilized as markers of particular mental processes, allowing insight into what processes are being engaged during different tasks. Third, fMRI can answer questions about exactly what information is represented in each part of the brain. Fourth, fMRI can answer questions about whether two tasks engage common or distinct processing mechanisms.

As with any other method, fMRI has some weaknesses. Mather et al. (2013) underline three major fMRI shortfalls. First, fMRI cannot address the causal role of a particular brain region in a particular task, though showing correlations between fMRI signals and behavior help somewhat. Second, fMRI does not have the necessary temporal resolution to unveil the workings of thought, the component stages of which generally proceed on the scales of tens or hundreds of milliseconds. Third, even with high-resolution fMRI, the signal that can be seen is a subsampled version of the actual language in which neurons talk to each other. Mather et al. (2013) indicate that fMRI cannot tell whether the same neurons are involved even when activity looks the same across multiple conditions. Like other techniques, a question mark remains on the origin of a specific neural representation: local or resulting from an earlier stage of processing.

Like EEG and MEG, fMRI has been used to investigate an array of cognitive functions (Cabeza and Nyberg, 2000). fMRI studies carried out on short-term working memory could be significant to entrepreneurship scholars (D'Esposito et al., 2000) for the study of encoding and retrieval into long-term memory (Mcintosh, 1998); language generation and comprehension (de Zubicaray et al., 1998); attention (LaBar et al., 1999); emotions (Norris et al., 2007); and emotional processing (Rämä et al., 2001). Cognizant of the ties between emotions and entrepreneurship (Morris et al., 2012), including entrepreneurial decision making (Michl et al., 2009), entrepreneurship researchers may take advantage of existing well-defined fMRI paradigms for the study of emotions. Norris et al. (2007) highlight some of these studies. A safe strategy to this end would be to identify a meaningful entrepreneurship research question that fits within the boundaries of an established fMRI paradigm; there is no need to reinvent the wheel.

FUNCTIONAL NEAR-INFRARED SPECTROSCOPY (fNIRS)

As with MEG, there is not a single entrepreneurship study that has employed this technique to date. NIRS is an optical imaging technology that offers the advantage of making measurements in vivo of changes in cerebral hemodynamics and oxygenation (Soul and du Plessis, 1999). fNIRS indicates the use of NIRS for the purpose of functional brain imaging. Because fNIRS is non-invasive and portable, it can provide real-time measurements of these changes at bedside (Soul and du Plessis, 1999).

fNIRS produces images of neural activity by measuring changes in blood flow and metabolism from the surface of the brain (Carter and Shieh, 2015). This technique operates according to the same principle as optical brain-imaging technologies. It capitalizes on the fact that changes in hemoglobin concentration in cortical tissue affect the absorption of infrared light in the tissue (Bunge and Kahn, 2009). Try this: shine a flashlight over the palm of your hand and see the light coming out the other side. This is how fNIRS operates, except the light is shown on the head to understand what is happening inside the brain.

Crosson et al. (2010) outlines that fNIRS has spatial resolution of slightly less than 1 cm, temporal resolution of milliseconds to tens of milliseconds, and light penetration of only about 1 cm into the superficial portions of the brain. Thus, for superficial brain regions, it is a useful complement to fMRI. Its portability, relatively low cost (Carter and Shieh, 2015), and ability to be used in a normal and unconfined environment make it a powerful tool (Crosson et al., 2010). Where fMRI is limited due to the constraints induced by the scanning environment, fNIRS measurements may be recorded in a more comfortable and natural environment (Dieler et al., 2012). fNIRS produces a high signal-to-noise ratio (Koch et al., 2010). Unlike fMRI, fNIRS does not produce instrumental noise, allowing the execution of tasks that require subtle acoustic features – such as words or conversations – to be distinguished (Cutini et al., 2012; Obrig et al., 2010).

Notably, fNIRS can be used in hyper-scanning with no particular disadvantages (for example, simultaneous brain activity recording of more than one participant), while hyper-scanning with fMRI is expensive and technically challenging (Cutini et al., 2012). For instance, a recent study adopted fNIRS hyper-scanning to measure brain activity coherence between two participants during a social game (with two main conditions: cooperation and competition) (Cui et al., 2012). Such a feature may enormously facilitate the study of entrepreneurs' social interactions, entrepreneurial teams, and so on.

Although fNIRS is a versatile instrument to investigate the neural correlates of human cognition (Cutini et al., 2012), its signal is much weaker than invasive optical imaging, as light must pass through the superficial layers of the head to the brain, and then from the brain to optical electrodes, placed on the surface of the scalp (Carter and Shieh, 2015). Furthermore, it is blind to subcortical activity, and anatomical information must be obtained with other techniques or inferred with specific methods such as fMRI (Cutini et al., 2012).

fNIRS can be applied to the examination of almost all cognitive function. In some cases, it can provide converging evidence in regard to a specific cognitive theory by confirming previous results obtained with different brain-imaging techniques (Cutini et al., 2012). I suggest that entrepreneurship scholars take a look into the strengths of fNIRS to investigate emotions (Glotzbach et al., 2011), memory (Rugg et al., 2008), attention (Toichi et al., 2004), and language processing (Noguchi et al., 2002) to see how fNIRS cognitive paradigms might be adapted to further our understanding on the phenomena of entrepreneurship.

Like tDCS, TMS and neurofeedback, NIRS can also be used as a therapy. For instance, Pablo Cassano, a psychiatrist at Massachusetts General Hospital in Boston, is successfully applying NIR to restore normal function within the brain of people suffering from depression. His hypothesis is that in depression, deeper brain areas are overly firing, especially the emotion-driving amygdala, which overwhelm more superficial areas in the front of the brain that usually help control or prevent that excessive activity. What if similar mechanisms could be operating behind a lack of entrepreneurial action, lack of self-confidence, fear of failure, and so on? For instance, NIRS could be used to target accessible brain regions linked to emotions, memory, attention, perception, and others, to elucidate its potential to nurture or boost entrepreneurial self-regulation.

TRANSCRANIAL MAGNETIC STIMULATION (TMS)

Regardless of the technological advantages it yields, TMS has not yet been adopted into the realms of entrepreneurship research. TMS is a valuable and established research tool in cognitive neuroscience (Walsh and Cowey, 1998) because of its ability to induce "virtual lesions" (Pascual-Leone et al., 1999). By stimulating the brain, the experimenter can disrupt normal activity in a selected region of the cortex. The behavioral consequences of the stimulation are used to shed light on the normal function of the disrupted tissue. This method is appealing because it allows the comparison of performance between stimulated and non-stimulated conditions in the same individual (Gazzaniga et al., 2014).

In a TMS measurement, a coil (often in the shape of a figure "eight") is placed close to the participant's head (Eysenck, 2006). Then, a very brief (less than 1 ms) but large magnetic pulse of current is run through it (Eysenck, 2006). This produces a short-lived magnetic field that generally inhibits processing in the brain area affected (Eysenck and Keane, 2000).

Ruff and Huettel (2014) point out three advantages of TMS. First, TMS allows the non-invasive manipulation of neural processing with high spatial resolution (around 1 cm) and exceptional temporal resolution (milliseconds). Second, TMS can be employed quite flexibly in regard to temporal profiles and patterns of stimulation that can have markedly different effects on neural processing and behavior. Third, TMS can be applied in almost any healthy subject (Rossi et al., 2009). Moreover, this approach allows causal links to be drawn between neural states and behavior, whereas techniques such as fMRI, ERPs, and MEG can only report co-variations between brain activity and behavior and cannot tell whether a given neural substrate is necessary or not for a specific behavior (Walsh and Cowey, 2000).

A TMS disadvantage is that, due to the drop-off of the magnetic field with increasing distance from the coil, it is only feasible to target brain areas on the cortical surface (Ruff and Huettel, 2014). A second shortfall is that the noise and tactile sensations generated by TMS can be experienced as distracting or painful by some participants. Although this can be partially mitigated, these side effects may complicate comparison of behavioral effects for different stimulation sites. Also, TMS can make it difficult to conduct blind studies in which participants and/or experimenters are unaware of specific stimulation conditions (Ruff and Huettel, 2014).

Since its inception TMS has been used in studies of cognitive functions, although much less extensively than fMRI (Walsh and Cowey, 2000). TMS paradigms applied to the studies of perception (Amassian et al., 1993), attention (Ashbridge et al., 1997), plasticity (Stefan et al., 2000), decision making (Van't Wout et al., 2005), and learning (Pascual-Leone et al., 1994) could be useful to advance the understanding of the entrepreneurial phenomena. For instance, TMS paradigms could be adapted to assess and compare the give-and-take of the various regions of the prefrontal cortex with attentional (dorsolateral area), decision making (ventrolateral area), and emotional responses (orbitofrontal area) faced by entrepreneurs and non-entrepreneurs at various stages of the entrepreneurial process. Since TMS magnetic fields have the capacity to stimulate nerve cells in the brain, the evidence obtained in the assessment of these regions may serve as a basis for implementing a TMS therapy to attempt enhancing entrepreneurial performance. Entrepreneurship scholars avid for intellectual challenges should scrutinize this possibility.

TRANSCRANIAL DIRECT CURRENT STIMULATION (tDCS)

Akin to TMS, the capabilities of tDCS have not been taken advantage of in entrepreneurship research, despite being an attractive tool for use in humans that permits painless modulation of cortical activity and excitability through the intact skull (Nitsche et al., 2015).

tDCS is a technique that induces and modulates neuroplasticity in the human cerebral cortex in order to elicit prolonged and yet reversible shifts of cortical excitability (Nitsche et al., 2015; Ouellet et al., 2015) and behavior (Stagg and Nitsche, 2011). From a technical point of view, tDCS is simple. It involves attaching two electrodes to the scalp and applying a constant electric potential difference, thus running a weak but constant electrical current between them (Ruff and Huettel, 2014).

tDCS holds four major advantages. First, it does not have any distracting side effects such as noise or persisting tactile distractions. Second, tDCS offers a very good control condition. Third, it is inexpensive and easy to use. Fourth, its capacity to either up- or down-regulate neural excitability allows for the conduction of tests of the functional roles of both enhancements and reductions of neural function (Ruff and Huettel, 2014).

In the same fashion, tDCS is not free of limitations, especially in regards to TMS (Ruff and Huettel, 2014). Its spatial resolution is much lower, so it is hard to assume that neural processing only changes in a very focal cortical region. tDCS is not temporarily precise, as its effects are continuously expressed through the stimulation period and continue in its aftermath (Ruff and Huettel, 2014). Another factor that could be considered a disadvantage is that the behavioral effects of single sessions of tDCS are relatively short-lived, lasting for a maximum of a few tens of minutes (Stagg and Nitsche, 2011).

tDCS is most often used to modulate ongoing task-related neural activity in a way that is undetectable to participants, whereas TMS is most often used to disrupt normally occurring patterns of neural activity in a spatially and temporally precise manner (Ruff and Huettel, 2014). In summary, tDCS is a valuable tool in neuroscience research, as its focality can be used to explore several brain aspects (Brunoni et al., 2012) germane to entrepreneurship research, such as cognition (Kincses et al., 2004), decision making (Pripfl et al., 2013), risk taking (Minati et al., 2012), and exploration (Beharelle et al., 2015). For example, tDCS studies on healthy subjects have shown positive changes in attention and memory (Bolognini et al., 2010). It has also been alleged that tDCS is well suited for assessing subtle decision processes (Ruff and Huettel, 2014), including inducing changes in decision-making behavior (Boggio et al., 2010).

The results achieved by tDCS in experimental psychology and neuroscience studies pull out an inevitable question that ought to be inspected by entrepreneurship scholars: can tDCS be useful to augment entrepreneurial performance (for example, across the stages of evaluation, discovery, and exploitation)?

NEUROFEEDBACK

It is not surprising that only one study has utilized neurofeedback, specifically EEG Biofeedback to gauge the improvement of cognitive processes in entrepreneurial skills (Rahmati et al., 2014). Although this method has a long history (Chapin and Russell-Chapin, 2013) and is claimed to enhance human potential (Moss, 1998), its use remains overlooked in entrepreneurship research.

Neurofeedback is a form of brain-wave training that makes use of the principle of learning, defined as the general process by which an organism alters its behavior according to certain goals. By measuring and proving feedback related to brain-wave activity, the process of neurofeedback provides an additional channel of information that increases awareness of brain behavior by creating subjective experiences that are derived from electroencephalography (Smith et al., 2014). This technique involves a brain computer interphase (BCI) that maps certain aspects of subjects' neurophysiology (for example, brain-wave amplitudes for various frequency bands) to some form of feedback, usually audio or video, that allows the brain to monitor and manipulate the underlying EEG activity

(Chapin and Russell-Chapin, 2013). The process of neurofeedback consists of recording a brain-related signal, usually the EEG, using electronics and computers to create a representation of that signal to teach the brain to change. In doing so, neurofeedback provides another channel of information for the brain to understand its own process (Smith et al., 2014). Like EEG, neurofeedback can also be implemented using MEG, fMRI, and fNIRS (Thibault et al., 2016).

Neurofeedback has its own pros and cons. Though it is a safe and non-invasive procedure that has showed improvement in the treatment of anxiety, depression, insomnia, memory, learning disabilities, and dyslexia, its validity has been questioned in terms of conclusive scientific evidence of its effectiveness (Marzbani et al., 2016). It is also an expensive, time-consuming procedure, and its benefits are not long-lasting (Marzbani et al., 2016); it might take months to see the desired improvements (Mauro and Cermak, 2006).

Marzbani et al. (2016) posit that neurofeedback has some methodological limitations. It is not fully certain how many sessions are needed before participants can learn to exert an alert control over their own waves, or how many sessions are needed before such training procedures produce the expected effect on the optimal performance, and how long the desired effects last without feedback (long-term effects). Thus, standard protocols are vital to perform neurofeedback. Some of the applications of neurofeedback could be useful to entrepreneurship scholars. For instance, neurofeedback is used to enhance human performance (Moss, 2012; Othmer and Othmer, 2012), particularly improving an athlete's self-confidence (Blumenstein et al., 2002). Studies have shown that professional athletes have distinct patterns of brain activity compared to those of beginners (Vernon, 2005). Recognition of the status of the professional's EEG before and during performance provides a rationale for the use of neurofeedback training to create or imitate these patterns and to improve the performance of unprofessional individuals (Vernon, 2005).

Other studies suggest that neurofeedback could improve self-confidence (Werthner and Dupee, 2010), increase perceived motivation (Vernon, 2005), increase energy, heighten composure and tolerance (Hammond, 2007), increase focus, reduce stress, improve emotional control, and increase workload tolerance and self-efficacy (Rahmati et al., 2014). The study undertaken by Rahmati et al. (2014) contends that neurofeedback affects the development of entrepreneurial personality traits, such as creativity and the internal locus of control. Neurofeedback has also proved to be effective in memory improvement (Escolano et al., 2011). This is good news because memory is claimed to be one of the two major components of entrepreneurial excellence (Baron, 2013).

The advantages of neurofeedback sound promising for plunging into some of the challenges in entrepreneurship research. If this tool has shown effectiveness in upgrading athletes' self-confidence, why could it not help to revamp entrepreneurs' self-confidence? Should entrepreneurs' brain patterns be decoded with the aid of this tool? Should specific neurofeedback protocols be built to test the readiness of this method in order to raise entrepreneurial behavior? I think so; this research method definitely deserves to be given a try.

WHAT NEUROSCIENCE TECHNIQUE IS THE BEST?

There is no single answer to the question as to which neuroscience technique is the best. In principle there is not an ideal method that may provide answers to all questions of interest (Banich and Compton, 2011) within the spectrum of entrepreneurship research. Even supposing the seven tools introduced in this chapter could be used in entrepreneurship research, each has its limitations. Therefore, it is the job of the investigator to match the technique with the research question (Eysenck and Keane, 2000).

At a basic level, the techniques vary in the precision with which they identify the brain areas when a task is performed (spatial resolution) and the time course of such activation (temporal resolution). The techniques also differ in their capacity to provide precise information regarding where and when the brain activity takes place (Eysenck and Keane, 2000). In addition to the factors of temporal and spatial resolution, portability and usage costs should also be taken into account to select a suitable neuroscience tool.

For example, Ramón y Cajal (1999, p. 65) recommends achieving mastery of the most difficult tool:

> The latest research techniques can be given preference, but first priority must go to the most difficult because they are the least exploited. Time wasted on experiments that do not work does not matter. If the method has very high resolution, the desired results will have real importance, and will repay our eagerness and zeal quite handsomely. Moreover, difficult techniques provide us the inestimable advantage of proceeding almost alone, finding very few imitators and competitors along the way.

A more middle-of-the-road approach would suggest considering the use of a tool that is both accessible and powerful enough to provide substantial data of a particular brain process. EEG falls within this range because it is available in the majority of departments of psychology, and its excellent temporal resolution allows an in-depth study of almost any cognitive phenomena. Other powerful tools that could be used are tDCS and fNIRS; they are less available than EEG but relatively inexpensive (Bunge and Kahn, 2009) compared to techniques such as MEG or fMRI. The use of EEG is recommended for "how/when" research questions, whilst fMRI is the ideal tool to dive into "where/type" enquiries.

As pertinent as identifying the adequate technique to address a particular research enquiry is the verification of its availability and operational costs during the design of an experiment. This is fundamental because the unavailability of a selected technology or the lack of funding to back its operational expenses may jeopardize the execution of a study. For instance, usually 10–20 subjects are necessary (twice that for a between-subjects study) for a typical experiment to reach an appropriate, statistically significant conclusion (Carter and Shieh, 2015). Usually data acquisition takes two hours per participant. The costs of using fMRI and MEG are comparatively higher, with prices that vary across laboratories (Martinez et al., 2015). It is not unusual for scanner time to be an average cost of 500 USD per hour (Thibault et al., 2016). TMS and neurofeedback are less expensive technologies than fMRI, with costs of 100–300 USD, whereas the usage costs of EEG, fNIRS, and tDCS usually require no extra fees (Thibault et al., 2016). Most of these technologies should be located in the departments of psychology or medicine, thus an extra networking effort is required to verify their availability and access.

Before unveiling the four principles to guide the selection of an appropriate technique, let me punctuate that the technique shall be chosen in terms of how it best addresses the hypothesis of the study and not the other way around.

Target Spatial Resolution if Assessing Neuronal Activations

The accuracy with which the imaging techniques are able to provide definite images of the anatomy of the centres of the central nervous system and/or the activation of these centres, in order to be able to localize them accurately, is defined as spatial resolution (Zani et al., 2003). For instance, indirect measures of neural activity have better spatial resolution than EEG (10 mm) or MEG (5 mm) but poor temporal resolution (Bunge and Kahn, 2009).

Particularly, there are two tools that allow accurate spatial localization throughout the brain: fMRI and PET. For the purposes of entrepreneurship research, the application of PET is discarded because it is invasive. fMRI is the most widely used brain-imaging technique, for a number of reasons: high availability, relatively low cost per scan, lack of recognized risks for properly screened subjects, and excellent spatial resolution (1 mm) (Bunge and Kahn, 2009). It should be noted that fMRI has low temporal resolution (1 s) and relies on correlative links between neurometabolism and neural activity (Ruff and Huettel, 2014).

Thus, there is a tradeoff between high temporal precision and high spatial precision. One solution to this problem is to use fMRI data to limit the possible sources of neural activity in EEG and MEG data. Another even more challenging solution is multimodal imaging, for example, the concurrent acquisition of fMRI and EEG data (Bunge and Kahn, 2009).

fMRI might be the right choice for entrepreneurship scholars looking to address "where"-type questions such as those pointed out by McMullen et al. (2014) in relation to opportunity beliefs: identification of the brain regions that are activated for people who attentively and accurately monitor the physical and social environments, mapping brain activity of novices and experts to examine the role of expertise in the formation and execution of opportunity beliefs, and so on. Seeing that fMRI has the potential to identify which brain areas are consistently associated with particular types of emotional states (Wager et al., 2008) this opens up the doors to explore and compare the incidence of diverse emotions on expert and novice entrepreneurs.

MEG is the second best tool in terms of spatial resolution (5 mm) after fMRI. Because MEG provides a reasonably good temporal resolution (0.05 s), it could be used to address "where"-type questions pointed out by McMullen et al. (2014) and the brain processes involved. Were MEG more accessible and less expensive than fMRI, it would be the ideal tool to use for entrepreneurship research. Brain processes mainly consist of three aspects: encoding – "what is extracted from available input"; retrieval – "what is recalled and integrated in to judgment"; and weighting – "what is assigned greater and what lesser importance" (Balcetis and Granot, 2015).

Target Temporal Resolution if Examining Brain Processes

The speed with which the techniques can keep on scanning the central nervous system (CNS) anatomy and physiology, taking into account all intrinsic limitations (as in the minimum time that must necessarily pass between the collection of a measure of one CNS activation and the successive one) is described as temporal resolution (Zani et al., 2003).

Inasmuch as the final goal of research on the mind and brain should be to construct a model of functional relation between the pathways and centres of the brain, it is essential to have a temporal resolution of milliseconds for the processes involved. The only techniques that hold such good temporal resolution are the techniques used systematically on single cells that measure the electromagnetic activity of the brain directly (Zani et al., 2003). But it is not possible to use these techniques in entrepreneurship research due to their invasiveness; it would demand neurosurgery to implant the microelectrodes.

Contrary to single unit recordings, there are two other tools that provide good temporal resolution that can be used for entrepreneurship research: EEG/ERPs (0.05 s) and MEG (0.05 s). The use of EEG/ERPs has the advantage of temporal resolution, but its poor spatial resolution makes it difficult to identify the precise origin of the signal, hence it is not the best tool for localization purposes (Bunge and Kahn, 2009).

Like EEG, MEG has the same exquisite temporal resolution (Bunge and Kahn, 2009; Zani et al., 2003); it is sensitive to changes in neural activity (Bunge and Kahn, 2009). Inasmuch as MEG is minimally influenced by the no uniform conductivity of the brain, skull, and scalp, it is a second-best option to assess brain processes within the realm of entrepreneurship research. MEG is the only technique that has high levels of both spatial and temporal resolution. The spatial resolution of this technique ranges from 1.5 mm to 4 mm for the cortical areas of the brain, but this resolution decreases substantially by some centimetres for subcortical regions. MEG could therefore be the technique of choice for localizing activity in the superficial areas of the brain (for example, the cerebral cortex, which is responsible for mental processes in general). Regrettably, this technique is very expensive to become as widely used as the ERPs (Zani et al., 2003).

The golden rule for entrepreneurship scholars is to consider the use of EEG when the research question deals with the scrutiny of cognitive brain processes.

Target Multimodal Methods if Examining both Neuronal Activations and Brain Mechanisms

The joint use of several of the described methods to advance entrepreneurship research is powerful but very challenging. It is recommended after a prior reasonable technical competence has been acquired at least in a single technique.

In short, the use of a unique technology is not enough (Banich and Compton, 2011) to probe an entrepreneurship research question, because the limitation of each method curtails the explanatory power of data obtained with only one technique (Ruff and Huettel, 2014). Even if it is accurate to ascertain that the different methods are very useful individually, only integration of the techniques with different spatial and temporal resolutions can provide valuable information on the neurofunctional mechanisms of mental processes and on the temporal course of their activation.

Because of this fact, researchers have started to use a multimodal approach, applying multiple methods in tandem (Banich and Compton, 2011). For instance, combining fMRI with either EEG/ERP (Zani et al., 2003) or MEG (Charron et al., 2008) could avail the spatial resolution of fMRI and reliable information about source location with the temporal resolution of the electrophysiological techniques that provide the time course of neural activation (Charron et al., 2008).

Combination methods can be based on a direct or an indirect approach. The former uses hemodynamic images to obtain a real structural basis of the estimates of functional activation acquired separately, whereas the latter involves parallel recording of these parameters in a single experiment (Zani et al., 2003). There exists equipment that allows for the simultaneous recording of fMRI and EEG, whereas MEG and fMRI have to be recorded separately (Charron et al., 2008).

Another possible combination is the simultaneous recording of EEG and MEG (Bunge and Kahn, 2009; Grabowski and Damasio, 1996), fNIRS–fMRI (Cui et al., 2011), and fNIRS–EEG (Ehlis et al., 2009). For instance, studies may first spatially localize specific neuronal computations with fMRI, and then test the specific role of activated brain areas with brain stimulation techniques such as TMS or tDCS (Beharelle et al., 2015). Moreover, a combination of fMRI–EEG has currently been successfully used for the study of decision-making processes (Fouragnan et al., 2015).

Also possible is the simultaneous recording of two interacting subjects called dual-EEG (Oullier et al., 2008; Tognoli et al., 2007) and hyper-scan fMRI (King-Casas et al., 2005), which allows for studying the brain activity of different individuals while they are interacting with each other (Charron et al., 2008).

As much as multimethod approaches are often used in combination because converging evidence from various techniques is the most powerful tool for uncovering fundamental aspects of brain-behavior relationships (Banich, 2004), they often require using twice as much equipment, collecting and analysing twice as much data, carrying out additional analyses to link them together, and usually the cooperation of researcher subjects to do multiple sessions of similar tasks in each modality. Therefore, the benefits of a multimodal approach, in terms of the extra knowledge that can be obtained, must justify the effort required (Banich and Compton, 2011).

None of these methods are perfect, but different techniques can be combined either sequentially or in parallel to provide converging evidence for a specific neural model of behavior (Ruff and Huettel, 2014). Such integration of research methods may help for achieving what I consider the two most far-reaching goals within the field of entrepreneurship: to attain a higher and deeper understanding of how entrepreneurs evaluate, discover, and exploit opportunities across the entrepreneurial process from a brain viewpoint; and to apply these insights to the enhancement of entrepreneurial performance. Lastly, before deciding on the use of a combined approach, entrepreneurship scholars must justify their decision for the selection of each tool and be absolutely clear about the individual need and contribution of each tool to ponder a particular research question.

Target Neuromodulation Techniques if Aiming to Stimulate the Brain

The development of techniques for influencing the activity of the brain is taking place rapidly (Lewis et al., 2016). Entrepreneurship, a field increasingly concerned with developing a deeper understanding about how entrepreneurs think and make decisions (Mitchell et al., 2004), a process that entirely takes place in the brain, entitles entrepreneurship scholars to use neuroscience technologies not only to collect data from entrepreneurs' brains, but also to examine numerous brain processes or gauge the location of independent or networked neural activations. Non-invasive neuromodulation technologies such as tDCS, fNIRS, and TMS can also be used to stimulate the activity of the entrepreneurial brain and, in doing so, dive deeper into the scrutiny of the entrepreneurial journey.

The fact that neuromodulation is mainly used to address disorders associated with the nervous system (Henry et al., 2016) should not prevent entrepreneurship scholars from using these tools to stimulate (tDCS and fNIRS) or even temporally interrupt (TMS) the functioning of specific brain regions to probe a variety of cognitive processes in sheer interest of the field, such as in decision making (prefrontal cortex), memory (hippocampus), emotions (amygdala), attention (prefrontal and parietal cortex), and learning (hippocampus and prefrontal cortex).

Of the above techniques, electrical neural stimulation is the most widely used today (Luan et al., 2014). I would particularly suggest using tDCS because it is the most accessible and economic tool compared to fNIRS and TMS. On the other hand, tools such as EEG, MEG, fMRI, and fNIR can be part of a neurofeedback study or training method to induce entrepreneurial learning because it plainly puts entrepreneurs in the driver's seat of their own mind by teaching them to train their brain waves. For instance, recently a decoded neurofeedback experiment based on fMRI signals has demonstrated the possibility to conquer fear. As Schiller (2016) claims, the next steps should assess the efficacy of this technique for real-life memories, especially those that are old, strong, and complex, as well as the stability of the change. One of those real-life memories of interest to entrepreneurship scholars and novice entrepreneurs has to do with the "fear of failure."

From these technologies, I recommend starting with neurofeedback based on EEG recordings (EEG biofeedback), as it is the most economic and available technology. It is also the major tool applied for neurofeedback purposes. If neurofeedback has proved useful for a wide variety of psychological and medical conditions, if it has the capacity to optimize the central nervous system and condition brain electrical activity (Smith et al., 2014), then why not use neurofeedback's benefits to forward the development of entrepreneurial theory and practice? It is an unchartered territory, but it is also fair to claim that these tools possess the capacity to nourish and leverage entrepreneurial behavior in ways unforeseen a decade ago.

CONCLUDING REMARKS

Neuroscience technologies provide unprecedented access to brain function (Ruff and Huettel, 2014) from which entrepreneurship scholars could gain great leverage. For instance, decoded neurofeedback (DecNef), one of the many neuroscience techniques available, is being used by researchers of the Centre for Information and Neural Networks (CINET) to erase subjects' fear memories (Koizumi et al., 2016). In the same spirit, a team of neuroscientists at the RIKEN Brain Science Institute in Japan have found in zebra fish a deep-brain structure called "habenula" that determines winning or losing behavior (Chou et al., 2016). They believe a similar circuit exists in humans.

The promise of these technologies for entrepreneurship research is, then, substantial. For instance, the "fear of failure," one of the major obstacles to entrepreneurial success, could be mitigated with the aid of DecNef. Moreover, Adolphs (2015) contends that issues regarding how we make decisions and how learning and memory work should be solved by neuroscience within the next 50 years.

This chapter discloses seven major neuroscience technologies that could be applied in the execution of any entrepreneurship study envisioned under the umbrella of a brain-driven approach. Gaining knowledge on the existing technological options and their capabilities to advance entrepreneurship research is important, taking into account that to date only fMRI and EEG have barely been used in available studies.

I also argue that future brain-driven entrepreneurship scholars need to have a clear understanding of the tools available, and their pros and cons, but also should become competent in at least one neuroscience technique, preferably EEG because it is the most accessible, powerful, and economic technology. Seeing, for instance, that learning how to design a good experiment and collecting and processing data using EEG may easily consume two years of study, the deploying of this approach should be evaluated in terms of its added value to entrepreneurship research.

Becoming familiar with the use of a single neuroscience technique is a challenge, but in all honesty it is not enough. Learning one technique is a good start but not a place to stop. For instance, the poor spatial resolution of EEG might and should be compensated by a method that makes up for this deficiency, usually MEG or fMRI.

The complementarity of neuroscience technologies requires considering a multimodal use. For example, currently becoming more and more popular is the joint use of EEG–MEG (Baillet, 2011; Grabowski and Damasio, 1996), EEG–fMRI (Charron et al., 2008), and MEG–fMRI (Charron et al., 2008). After the mastering of a single method, the next natural step is the implementation of a multimodal approach, because it combines the spatial resolution and reliable information about the source location of a tool such as fMRI with the temporal resolution of an electrophysiological technique such as EEG that is capable to provide the time course of neural activation (Charron et al., 2008). Likewise, entrepreneurship scholars should earnestly consider the use of neuromodulation techniques such as transcranial magnetic stimulation (TMS), transcranial direct current stimulation (tDCS), and neurofeedback methods, because they hold the potential to alter entrepreneurial behavior.

These neuroscience technologies, however, should never be the guiding force behind doing experiments in entrepreneurship research, hence a technique should not be used for its own sake but because it is the best technique to address a particular research question (Carter and Shieh, 2015).

I believe that I have not given the idea that carrying out brain-driven entrepreneurship research is near to impossible; it is not, especially for those who are equipped with the theoretical and methodological toolboxes of an established discipline, such as psychology (Davidsson, 2007). As Davidsson (2007) points out, all one has to accomplish is to do a little better than one's predecessors, and with the help of the tools and another's experiences, it should be possible to reach that goal in this young field.

NOTE

1.   Used to gain knowledge on which structures are activated during a cognitive task and the interactions between the structures that are activated (Zani et al., 2003).

REFERENCES

Adolphs, R. (2015), "The unsolved problems of neuroscience," *Trends in Cognitive Sciences*, **19** (4), 173–5.

Amassian, V., P. Maccabee, R. Cracco, J. Cracco, A. Rudell, and L. Eberle (1993), "Measurement of information processing delays in human visual cortex with repetitive magnetic coil stimulation," *Brain Research*, **605** (2), 317–21.

Ashbridge, E., V. Walsh, and A. Cowey (1997), "Temporal aspects of visual search studied by transcranial magnetic stimulation," *Neuropsychologia*, **35** (8), 1121–31.

Assadollahi, R. and F. Pulvermüller (2001), "Neuromagnetic evidence for early access to cognitive representations," *Neuroreport*, **12** (2), 207–13.

Baillet, S. (2011), "Electromagnetic brain mapping using MEG and EEG," in J. Decety and J.T. Cacioppo (eds), *The Oxford Handbook of Social Neuroscience*, Oxford: Oxford University Press, pp. 97–133.

Balcetis, E. and Y. Granot (2015), "Under the influence and unaware: unconscious processing during encoding, retrieval, and weighting in judgment," in G. Keren and G. Wu (eds), *The Wiley Blackwell Handbook of Judgment and Decision Making*, vol. 2, Chichester: John Wiley and Sons, pp. 333–55.

Banich, M.T. (2004), *Cognitive Neuroscience and Neuropsychology*, 2nd edn, Boston, MA: Houghton Mifflin.

Banich, M.T. and Compton, R. (2011), *Cognitive Neuroscience*, 3rd edn, Belmont, CA: Wadsworth Publishing.

Baron, A. (2013), *Enhancing Entrepreneurial Excellence: Tools for Making the Possible Real*, Cheltenham: Edward Elgar.

Bauer, R., E. Leritz, and D. Bowers (2003) "Neuropsychology," in I. Weiner, J. Schinka, and W. Velicer (eds), *Research Methods in Psychology: Vol. 2. Handbook of Psychology*, Hoboken, NJ: John Wiley and Sons, pp. 289–322.

Bear, M., B. Connors, and M. Paradiso (2007), *Neuroscience: Exploring the Brain*, 3rd edn, Baltimore, MD: Lippincott Williams & Wilkins.

Beharelle, A., R. Polanía, T. Hare, and C. Ruff (2015), "Transcranial stimulation over frontopolar cortex elucidates the choice attributes and neural mechanisms used to resolve exploration–exploitation trade-offs," *The Journal of Neuroscience*, **35** (43), 14544–56.

Blumenstein, B., M. Bar-Eli, and D. Collins (2002), "Biofeedback training in sport," in B. Blumenstein, M. Bar-Eli and G. Tenenbaum (eds), *Brain and Body in Sport and Exercise: Biofeedback Applications in Performance Enhancement*, Chichester: Jonh Wiley & Sons, pp. 55–76.

Boggio, P., C. Campanhã, C. Valasek, S. Fecteau, A. Pascual-Leone, and F. Fregni (2010), "Modulation of decision-making in a gambling task in older adults with transcranial direct current stimulation," *European Journal of Neuroscience*, **31** (3), 593–7.

Bolognini, N., F. Fregni, C. Casati, E. Olgiati, and G. Vallar (2010), "Brain polarization of parietal cortex augments training-induced improvement of visual exploratory and attentional skills," *Brain Research*, **1349**, 76–89.

Brandeis, D. and D. Lehmann (1986), "Event-related potentials of the brain and cognitive processes: approaches and applications," *Neuropsychologia*, **24** (1), 151–68.

Brunoni, A., M. Nitsche, N. Bolognini, M. Bikson, T. Wagner, L. Merabet, and A. Pascual-Leone (2012), "Clinical research with transcranial direct current stimulation (tDCS): challenges and future directions," *Brain Stimulation*, **5** (3), 175–95.

Bunge, S. and I. Kahn (2009), "Cognition: an overview of neuroimaging techniques," in L.H. Squire (ed.), *Encyclopedia of Neuroscience*, vol. 2, Oxford: Academic Press, pp. 1063–7.

Cabeza, R. and L. Nyberg (2000), "Imaging cognition II: an empirical review of 275 PET and fMRI studies," *Journal of Cognitive Neuroscience*, **12** (1), 1–47.

Carter, M. and J. Shieh (2015), *Guide to Research Techniques in Neuroscience*, 2nd edn, Burlington, MA: Academic Press.

Castillo, E., P. Simos, R. Davis, J. Breier, M. Fitzgerald, and A. Papanicolaou (2001),

"Levels of word processing and incidental memory: dissociable mechanisms in the temporal lobe," *Neuroreport*, **12** (16), 3561–6.

Chapin, T. and L. Russell-Chapin (2013), *Neurotherapy and Neurofeedback: Brain-Based Treatment for Psychological and Behavioral Problems*, New York, NY: Routledge.

Charron, S., A. Fuchs, and O. Oullier (2008), "Exploring brain activity in neuroeconomics," *Revue d'Economie Politique*, **118** (1), 97–124.

Chou, M., R. Amo, M. Kinoshita, B. Cherng, H. Shimazaki, M. Agetsuma, and M. Yamazaki (2016), "Social conflict resolution regulated by two dorsal habenular subregions in zebrafish," *Science*, **352** (6281), 87–90.

Clarke, J. and J. Cornelissen (2014), "How language shapes thought: new vistas for entrepreneurship research," in J.R. Mitchell, R.K. Mitchell, and B. Randolph-Seng (eds), *Handbook of Entrepreneurial Cognition*, Cheltenham: Edward Elgar, pp. 383–97.

Crosson, B., A. Ford, K. McGregor, M. Meinzer, S. Cheshkov, X. Li, and R. Briggs (2010), "Functional imaging and related techniques: an introduction for rehabilitation researchers," *Journal of Rehabilitation Research and Development*, **47** (2), 7–33.

Cui, X., S. Bray, D. Bryant, G. Glover, and A. Reiss (2011), "A quantitative comparison of NIRS and fMRI across multiple cognitive tasks," *Neuroimage*, **54** (4), 2808–21.

Cui, X., D. Bryant, and A. Reiss (2012), "NIRS-based hyperscanning reveals increased interpersonal coherence in superior frontal cortex during cooperation," *Neuroimage*, **59** (3), 2430–2437.

Cutini, S., S. Moroa, and S. Biscontib (2012), "Functional near infrared optical imaging in cognitive neuroscience: an introductory," *Journal of Near Infrared Spectroscopy*, **20** (1), 75–92.

Davidsson, P. (2007), "Method challenges and opportunities in the psychological study of entrepreneurship," in B.J. Robert, M. Frese, and R. Baron (eds), *The Psychology of Entrepreneurship*, Mahwah, NJ: Lawrence Erlbaum Associates, pp. 287–323.

D'Esposito, M., B. Postle, and B. Rypma (2000), "Prefrontal cortical contributions to working memory: evidence from event-related fMRI studies," *Experimental Brain Research*, **133** (1), 3–11.

de Zubicaray, G., S. Williams, S. Wilson, S. Rose, M. Brammer, E. Bullmore, and A. Brown (1998), "Prefrontal cortex involvement in selective letter generation: a functional magnetic resonance imaging study," *Cortex*, **34** (3), 389–401.

Dieler, A., S. Tupak, and A. Fallgatter (2012), "Functional near-infrared spectroscopy for the assessment of speech related tasks," *Brain and Language*, **121** (2), 90–109.

Ehlis, A., T. Ringel, M. Plichta, M. Richter, M. Herrmann, and A. Fallgatter (2009), "Cortical correlates of auditory sensory gating: a simultaneous near-infrared spectroscopy event-related potential study," *Neuroscience*, **159** (3), 1032–43.

Escolano, C., M. Aguilar, and J. Minguez (2011), "EEG-based upper alpha neurofeedback training improves working memory performance," paper presented at the 33rd Annual International Conference of the IEEE Engineering in Medicine and Biology Society, Boston, 30 Aug–3 Sep.

Eysenck, M. (2006), *Fundamentals of Cognition*, Hove: Psychology Press.

Eysenck, M. and M. Keane (2000), *Cognitive Psychology: A Student's Handbook*, 4th edn, Hove: Psychology Press.

Fouragnan, E., C. Retzler, K. Mullinger, and M. Philiastides (2015), "Two spatiotemporally distinct value systems shape reward-based learning in the human brain," *Nature Communications*, **6** (8107), 8 September; doi: 10.1038/ncomms9107.

Fox, M. and M. Raichle (2007), "Spontaneous fluctuations in brain activity observed with functional magnetic resonance imaging," *Nature Reviews Neuroscience*, **8** (9), 700–711.

Gazzaniga, M., R. Ivry, and G. Mangun (2014), *Cognitive Neuroscience: The Biology of the Mind*, 4th edn, New York, NY: Norton and Company, Inc.

Glotzbach, E., A. Mühlberger, K. Gschwendtner, A. Fallgatter, P. Pauli, and M. Herrmann (2011), "Prefrontal brain activation during emotional processing: a functional near infrared spectroscopy study (fNIRS)," *The Open Neuroimaging Journal*, **5** (1), 33–9.

Grabowski, T. and A. Damasio (1996), "Improving functional imaging techniques: the dream of a single image for a single mental event," *Proceedings of the National Academy of Sciences*, **93** (25), 14302–3.

Hammond, D. (2007), "What is neurofeedback?" *Journal of Neurotherapy*, **10** (4), 25–36.

Henry, R., M. Deckert, V. Guruviah, and B. Schmidt (2016), "Review of neuromodulation techniques and technological limitations," *IETE Technical Review*, **33** (4), 368–77.

Kincses, T., A. Antal, M. Nitsche, O. Bártfai, and W. Paulus (2004), "Facilitation of probabilistic classification learning by transcranial direct current stimulation of the prefrontal cortex in the human," *Neuropsychologia*, **42** (1), 113–17.

King-Casas, B., D. Tomlin, C. Anen, C. Camerer, S. Quartz, and P. Montague (2005), "Getting to know you: reputation and trust in a two-person economic exchange," *Science*, **308** (5718), 78–83.

Koch, S., C. Habermehl, J. Mehnert, C. Schmitz, S. Holtze, A. Villringer, and H. Obrig (2010), "High-resolution optical functional mapping of the human somatosensory cortex," *Frontiers in Neuroenergetics*, **2** (12).

Koizumi, A., K. Amano, A. Cortese, K. Shibata, W. Yoshida, B. Seymour, and H. Lau (2016), "Fear reduction without fear through reinforcement of neural activity that bypasses conscious exposure," *Nature Human Behaviour*, **1**, 0006.

Krueger, N. and M. Day (2010), "Looking forward, looking backward: from entrepreneurial cognition to neuroentrepreneurship," in Z.J. Acs and D.B. Audretsch (eds), *Handbook of Entrepreneurship Research*, New York: Springer, pp. 321–57.

LaBar, K., D. Gitelman, T. Parrish, and M. Mesulam (1999), "Neuroanatomic overlap of working memory and spatial attention networks: a functional MRI comparison within subjects," *Neuroimage*, **10** (6), 695–704.

Laureiro-Martínez, D., N. Canessa, S. Brusoni, M. Zollo, T. Hare, F. Alemanno, and S. Cappa (2014), "Frontopolar cortex and decision-making efficiency: comparing brain activity of experts with different professional background during an exploration-exploitation task," *Frontiers in Human Neuroscience*, **7** (927), 1–10.

Lewis, P., R. Thomson, J. Rosenfeld, and P. Fitzgerald (2016), "Brain neuromodulation techniques: a review," *Neuroscientist*, **22** (4), 406–21.

Luan, S., I. Williams, K. Nikolic, and T. Constandinou (2014) "Neuromodulation: present and emerging methods," *Frontiers in Neuroengineering*, 15 July; https://doi.org/10.3389/fneng.2014.00027.

Luck, S. (2014), *An Introduction to the Event-Related Potential Technique*, 2nd edn, Cambridge, MA: MIT Press.

Maine, E., P. Soh, and N. Dos Santos (2015), "The role of entrepreneurial decision-making in opportunity creation and recognition," *Technovation*, **39–40** (May–June), 53–72.

Marzbani, H., H. Marateb, and M. Mansourian (2016), "Neurofeedback: a comprehensive review on system design, methodology and clinical applications," *Basic and Clinical Neuroscience*, **7** (2), 143–58.

Mather, M., J. Cacioppo, and N. Kanwisher (2013), "How fMRI can inform cognitive theories," *Perspectives on Psychological Science*, **8** (1), 108–13.

Mauro, T. and S. Cermak (2006), *The Everything Parent's Guide to Sensory Integration Disorder: Get the Right Diagnosis, Understand Treatments, and Advocate for Your Child*, Avon, MA: Adams Media.

Mcintosh, A. (1998), "Understanding neural interactions in learning and memory using functional neuroimaging," *Annals of the New York Academy of Sciences*, **855** (1), 556–71.

McMullen, J., M. Wood, and L. Palich (2014), "Entrepreneurial cognition and social cognitive neuroscience," in J.R. Mitchell, R.K. Mitchell, and B. Randolph-Seng (eds), *Handbook of Entrepreneurial Cognition*, Cheltenham: Edward Elgar, pp. 316–63.

Michl, T., I. Welpe, M. Spörrle, and A. Picot (2009), "The role of emotions and cognitions in entrepreneurial decision-making," in L.A. Carsrud and M. Brännback (eds), *Understanding the Entrepreneurial Mind*, New York, NY: Springer, pp. 167–90.

Minati, L., C. Campanha, H. Critchley, and P. Boggio (2012), "Effects of transcranial direct-current stimulation (tDCS) of the dorsolateral prefrontal cortex (DLPFC) during a mixed-gambling risky decision-making task," *Cognitive Neuroscience*, **3** (2), 80–88.

Mitchell, R., L. Busenitz, T. Lant, P. McDougall, E. Morse, and J. Smith (2004), "The distinctive and inclusive domain of entrepreneurial cognition research," *Entrepreneurship Theory and Practice*, **28** (6), 505–18.

Morris, H., G. Pryor, and M. Schindehutte (2012), *Entrepreneurship as Experience: How Events Create Ventures and Ventures Create Entrepreneurs*, Cheltenham: Edward Elgar.

Moss, D. (1998), "Biofeedback, mind-body medicine, and the higher limits of human nature," in D. Moss (ed.), *Humanistic and Transpersonal Psychology: A Historical and Biographical Sourcebook*, Westport, CT: Greenwood Press, 145–61.

Moss, D. (2012), "The use of general biofeedback in the pursuit of optimal performance," in W.A. Edmonds and G. Tenenbaum (eds), *Case Studies in Applied Psychophysiology: Neurofeedback and Biofeedback Treatments for Advances in Human Performance*, Chichester: John Wiley & Sons, pp. 1–16.

Nitsche, M.., M. Kuo, W. Paulus, and A. Antal (2015), "Transcranial direct current stimulation: protocols and physiological mechanisms of action," in H. Knotkova and D. Rasche (eds), *Textbook of Neuromodulation: Principles, Methods and Clinical Applications*, New York, NY: Springer, pp. 101–11.

Noguchi, Y., T. Takeuchi, and K. Sakai (2002), "Lateralized activation in the inferior frontal cortex during syntactic processing: event-related optical topography study," *Human Brain Mapping*, **17** (2), 89–99.

Norris, C., J. Coan, and T. Johnstone (2007), "Functional magnetic resonance imaging and the study of emotion," in J.A. Coan and J.J.B. Allen (eds), *Handbook of Emotion Elicitation and Assessment*, Oxford: Oxford University Press, pp. 440–59.

Obrig, H., S. Rossi, S. Telkemeyer, and I. Wartenburger (2010), "From acoustic segmentation to language processing: evidence from optical imaging," *Frontiers in Neuroenergetics*, **2** (13).

Ortiz-Terán, E., A. Turrero, J. Santos, P. Bryant, T. Ortiz, E. Ortiz-Terán, and T. Ortiz (2013), "Brain cortical organization in entrepreneurs during a visual Stroop decision task," *Neuroscience and Neuroeconomics*, **2**, 33–49.

Othmer, S. and S. Othmer (2012), "Performance enhancement applications of neurofeedback," in W.A. Edmonds and G. Tenenbaum (eds), *Case Studies in Applied Psychophysiology: Neurofeedback and Biofeedback Treatments for Advances in Human Performance*, Chichester: John Wiley & Sons, pp. 17–30.

Ouellet, J., A. McGirr, F. Van den Eynde, F. Jollant, M. Lepage, and M. Berlim (2015), "Enhancing decision-making and cognitive impulse control with transcranial direct current stimulation (tDCS) applied over the orbitofrontal cortex (OFC): a randomized and sham-controlled exploratory study," *Journal of Psychiatric Research*, **69** (October), 27–34.

Oullier, O., J. Kelso, and A. Kirman (2008), "Social neuroeconomics: a dynamical systems perspective," *Revue d'Economie Politique*, **118** (1), 51–62.

Parkes, L., C. Perry, and P. Goodin (2016), "Examining the N400m in affectively negative sentences: a magnetoencephalography study," *Psychophysiology*, **53** (5), 689–704.

Pascual-Leone, A., D. Bartres-Faz, and J. Keenan (1999) "Transcranial magnetic stimulation: studying the brain-behaviour relationship by induction of 'virtual lesions'," *Philosophical Transactions of the Royal Society of London*, Series B, 354, pp. 1229–38.

Pascual-Leone, A., J. Grafman, and M. Hallett (1994), "Modulation of cortical motor output maps during development of implicit and explicit knowledge," *Science*, **263** (5151), 1287–9.

Pripfl, J., R. Neumann, U. Köhler, and C. Lamm (2013), "Effects of transcranial direct current stimulation on risky decision making are mediated by 'hot' and 'cold' decisions, personality, and hemisphere," *European Journal of Neuroscience*, **38** (12), 3778–85.

Rahmati, N., R. Rostami, M. Zali, S. Nowicki, and J. Zarei (2014), "The effectiveness of neurofeedback on enhancing cognitive process involved in entrepreneurship abilities among primary school students in district No. 3 Tehran," *Basic and Clinical Neuroscience*, **5** (4), 277–84.

Rämä, P., S. Martinkauppi, I. Linnankoski, J. Koivisto, H. Aronen, and S. Carlson (2001),

"Working memory of identification of emotional vocal expressions: an fMRI study," *Neuroimage*, **13** (6), 1090–1101.

Ramón y Cajal, S. (1999), *Advice for a Young Investigator (N. Swanson & LW Swanson, Trans.)*, Cambridge, MA: MIT Press.

Roberts, T., P. Ferrari, D. Perry, H. Rowley, and M. Berger (2000), "Presurgical mapping with magnetic source imaging: comparisons with intraoperative findings," *Brain Tumor Pathology*, **17** (2), 57–64.

Rossi, S., M. Hallett, P. Rossini, A. Pascual-Leone, and S. o. T. C. Group (2009), "Safety, ethical considerations, and application guidelines for the use of transcranial magnetic stimulation in clinical practice and research," *Clinical Neurophysiology*, **120** (12), 2008–39.

Ruff, C. and S. Huettel (2014), "Experimental methods in cognitive neuroscience," in P.W. Glimcher and E. Fehr (eds), *Neuroeconomics: Decision Making and the Brain*, 2nd edn, San Diego, CA: Academic Press, pp. 77–108.

Rugg, M., J. Johnson, H. Park, and M. Uncapher (2008) "Encoding-retrieval overlap in human episodic memory: a functional neuroimaging perspective," *Progress in Brain Research: Vol. 169. Essence of Memory*, Amsterdam, the Netherlands: Elsevier, pp. 339–53.

Schiller, D. (2016), "Neuroscience: hacking the brain to overcome fear," *Nature Human Behaviour*, **1**, 0010.

Smith, M., T. Collura, and J. Tarrant (2014), "Neurofeedback," in K. Nidal and A.S. Malik (eds), *EEG/ERP Analysis: Methods and Applications*, Boca Raton, FL: CRC Press.

Soul, J. and A. du Plessis (1999), "Near-infrared spectroscopy," *Seminars in Pediatric Neurology*, **6** (2), 101–10.

Stagg, C. and M. Nitsche (2011), "Physiological basis of transcranial direct current stimulation," *The Neuroscientist*, **17** (1), 37–53.

Stefan, K., E. Kunesch, L. Cohen, R. Benecke, and J. Classen (2000), "Induction of plasticity in the human motor cortex by paired associative stimulation," *Brain*, **123** (3), 572–84.

Thibault, R., M. Lifshitz, and A. Raz (2016), "The self-regulating brain and neurofeedback: experimental science and clinical promise," *Cortex*, **74** (January), 247–61.

Tognoli, E., J. Lagarde, G. DeGuzman, and J. Kelso (2007), "The phi complex as a neuromarker of human social coordination," *Proceedings of the National Academy of Sciences*, **104** (19), 8190–95.

Toichi, M., R. Findling, Y. Kubota, J. Calabrese, M. Wiznitzer, N. McNamara, and K. Yamamoto (2004), "Hemodynamic differences in the activation of the prefrontal cortex: attention vs. higher cognitive processing," *Neuropsychologia*, **42** (5), 698–706.

Van't Wout, M., R. Kahn, A. Sanfey, and A. Aleman (2005), "Repetitive transcranial magnetic stimulation over the right dorsolateral prefrontal cortex affects strategic decision-making," *Neuroreport*, **16** (16), 1849–52.

Vernon, D. (2005), "Can neurofeedback training enhance performance? An evaluation of the evidence with implications for future research," *Applied Psychophysiology and Biofeedback*, **30** (4), 347–64.

Wager, T., L. Barrett, E. Bliss-Moreau, K. Lindquist, S. Duncan, H. Kober, and J. Mize (2008), "The neuroimaging of emotion," in M. Lewis, J.M. Haviland-Jones, and L.F. Barrett (eds), *The Handbook of Emotions*, 3rd edn, New York, NY: Guilford Press, pp. 249–71.

Walsh, V. and A. Cowey (1998), "Magnetic stimulation studies of visual cognition," *Trends in Cognitive Sciences*, **2** (3), 103–10.

Walsh, V. and A. Cowey (2000), "Transcranial magnetic stimulation and cognitive neuroscience," *Nature Reviews Neuroscience*, **1** (1), 73–80.

Werthner, P. and M. Dupee (2010), "Bio/neurofeedback: an effective tool for athlete psychological preparation leading up to and during the 2010 Winter Olympic Games," *Journal of Exercise, Movement, and Sport*, **42** (1), accessed 15 April 2016 at https://www.ncbi.nlm.nih.gov/pmc/articles/PMC5105966/.

Woodman, G. (2010), "A brief introduction to the use of event-related potentials in studies of perception and attention," *Attention, Perception, & Psychophysics*, **72** (8), 2031–46.

Zani, A., G. Biella, and A. Proverbio (2003), "Appendix F – brain imaging techniques: invasiveness and spatial and temporal resolution," in A. Zani and A.M. Proverbio (eds), *The Cognitive Electrophysiology of Mind and Brain*, San Diego, CA: Academic Press, pp. 417–22.

Zaro, M., L. da Cruz Fagundes, F. Rocha, and W. Nunes (2016), "Cognitive brain mapping used in the study of entrepreneurial behavior – pilot test with the use of electroencephalogram – EEG during the process of identification of business opportunities," *American Journal of Educational Research*, **4** (6), 472–8.

12. A few words about what neuroentrepreneurship can and cannot help us with

Sean Guillory, Mary C. Boardman, and Mellani Day

Now is a great time to pursue neuroentrepreneurship. In this chapter, we provide a quick overview of the topics discussed in previous chapters, and then place this in context. Specifically, we discuss the benefits and limitations of neuroentrepreneurship research.

The first two content chapters in this handbook were designed to introduce entrepreneurship scholars to neuroscience research. Specifically, they provide an overview of past studies (Chapter 2), the present fields that make up cognitive neuroscience (Chapter 2), and the litany of noninvasive methods one can use for studying cognitive neuroscientific phenomena (Chapter 3). The next few chapters (Chapters 4–6) go more into how these neuroscience methods have been used in previous studies. Then, chapters 7–10 provide examples of how neuroscience methods can inform entrepreneurship research: a framework for examining entrepreneurial return on investment (ROI) (Chapter 7), risk calculation (Chapter 8), brain plasticity (Chapter 9), and emotion/cognitions (Chapter 10). After all of this, Chapter 11 provides several technologies and principles as to which tools would best be used for which types of questions. A researcher could synthesize the information from these previous chapters and from this know how to get started in conducting neuroentrepreneurship studies. This chapter lays out what researchers should assess when deciding to devote the time and resources to pursuing this field of study.

This is a bigger decision for one to make than may be expected at face value. At the time of publication of this handbook, the field of neuroentrepreneurship is nascent. There are currently experts in the separate neuroscience fields but few neuroentrepreneurship experts. There are also few, if any, established funding sources specifically for neuroentrepreneurship studies. As with any nascent field, we are tasked with convincing both scholars, and those who can fund research, of the importance of neuroentrepreneurship, and that the timing is now.

Essentially, these are the same issues entrepreneurs themselves face when assessing whether they should move forward with any new venture.

It is both interesting and exciting to make the case that entrepreneurship scholars should make a business decision (either way) to further a field that has potential to help entrepreneurs. This is an opportunity for scholars to both contribute to their field of research and gain their own valuable experience as entrepreneurs. This is a venture that presents both risks and opportunities; below we discuss both. Risks may include the following:

1.   *There is a noted bias from entrepreneurship scholars to publish experimental research.* A theme that was repeated several times at the 2016 Academy of Management Conference in Anaheim, CA was that while journal editors and entrepreneurship scholars acknowledge the importance of experimental research, there is only a very small percentage of experimental research that makes its way into the top entrepreneurship journals (Williams et al., 2016). It seems that both entrepreneurship researchers and journal editors are hesitant to create and publish experimental research. Neuroentrepreneurship research is by default experimental. This can either be negative, in that neuroentrepreneurship articles may never see publication, or positive, in that as more and more experimental research of this sort is carried out, there will be more need for forums for this research to be shared. Perhaps (and hopefully) there will eventually be a journal created that is solely devoted to neuroentrepreneurship.

2.   *The topic of entrepreneurship is currently little discussed by human neuroscience scholars.* While there are a handful of neuroscientists interested in the phenomena of entrepreneurship, the neuroscience domain has focused more on the study of diseased or injured brains. However, in early 2017 in the Netherlands, one neuroscience conference series presented a session entitled: Neuro-entrepreneurship: Vascular Dementia. The session explored such topics as simulation semantics, cognitive science, computational theory of mind, next generation of entrepreneurs in neuroscience, neuroscience and brain game, neuromanagement, and neuro-industrial-engineering. Neuroentrepreneurship within the domain of vascular dementia may raise eyebrows for entrepreneurship researchers, but the fact that there is converging interest on the part of both fields is encouraging. Another example is the 40th Annual Meeting of the Japan Neuroscience Society, also in 2017, in which several presentations in the area of brain-driven entrepreneurship research are proposed. However, currently these are the exceptions, not the rule.

3.   *There is no "gold standard" neuroscience method that doesn't have*

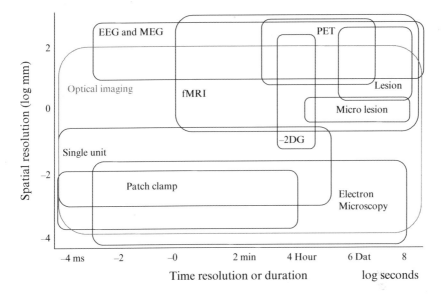

Source: Sejnowski et al. (2014).

Figure 12.1   Comparison of spatio-temporal resolutions

tradeoffs in interpretations. Figure 12.1 depicts many different neuroscience methods and the spatio-temporal resolutions that each one covers (not all techniques are available for study on in-vivo humans).

For human-based methods, Chapter 8 in this handbook provides valuable insight into the tradeoffs of different noninvasive human methods. An example of this tradeoff is between functional magnetic resonance imaging (fMRI) and electroencephalogram (EEG) studies. For fMRI studies, the spatial resolution is around 3 mm^3 per voxel to get the entire brain. The speed of this is a sample being taken every two to three seconds. While this sounds fast and high-resolution, neurons can fire up to 3,000 times within a three-second window and are usually measured in the micron (micrometer) scale. In layman's terms, this produces a slow, grainy picture relative to actual brain activity. This is on top of the fact that fMRI is not directly measuring electrical signals.[1]

For EEG, the activity being measured is electrical activity and the coverage depends on the number of electrodes used. The limitations depend on the exact location these signals may be coming from. This includes both issues with the inverse problem,[2] and the fact that

EEG electrodes are very sensitive to movement (even uncontrolled movements such as eye blinks). We mention these two examples not to denigrate them compared to other methods, but to point out that there is still currently no single method/device that can record and/or stimulate the whole brain at the level of individual neurons. This is why these many different methods are being used to better understand neuroscience phenomena and why a variety of different methods will be needed to truly understand neuroentrepreneurship phenomena.

4. *Internal/external validity concerns.* This is an issue with any experimental discipline that uses both lab and field tests within their experiments. However, this is worth a special mention when it comes to neuroscience methods. Many methods (including EEG and fMRI) can have their signals disturbed by things like body movements, head movements, and even blinking. While a sneeze in most lab studies would ruin perhaps a trial at most, a sneeze (or similar movement) could cause a total recalibration of the signal, and one could have to start the entire experiment over. Also, with such methods that use MRI, there are constraints in studying people with implanted medical devices or who are claustrophobic.

5. *Some methods are very expensive.* MRI costs about $600 an hour to run a session – just for materials alone. Good EEG equipment costs thousands of dollars, and good MRI systems cost millions of dollars. A budding neuroentrepreneurship scholar is going to need money and/or access (which will likely take a good explanation for why you need either one).

6. *2016 replication crisis.* This one may touch a nerve but it bears mentioning as insight into the current state of the cognitive neuroscience and psychology fields. There was a high-profile (Open Science Collaboration, 2015) attempt to replicate 100 famous psychology studies. Only 36 percent of these replicated to a significant finding (the effects sizes were typically half as strong as reported in the original studies). This groundbreaking study is also on the heels of two previous cognitive neuroscience studies that found deficiencies in standard analyses that fMRI researchers commonly used (Vul et al., 2009; Bennett et al., 2011). These challenges to the field have triggered a reflection period in trying to discover the best ways to move forward.

7. *Most research in cognitive neuroscience and psychology is conducted without a specific application purpose in mind.* In these academic fields, the focus and incentives are on contributing to theory more than its application. Even neuroeconomics studies are simply an extension of previous behavioral economics and game-theory studies designed to further support the theory and not necessarily to help

economists to make better decisions. Without a specific application to help people in some way, it is really just research for research's sake. Such basic research is perfectly appropriate in some disciplines. However, in entrepreneurship research, knowledge is created to better understand, predict, encourage, and even promote entrepreneurial behavior. Researchers should keep this in mind as a strength and carry it forward in neuroentrepreneurship research.

The intention behind outlining the risks in initiating neuroentrepreneurship research is to provide a realistic picture, not to discourage research in this field. With this in mind, below are opportunities available to neuroentrepreneurship scholars:

1. *Buying low.* Currently in neuroscience, conditions are similar to a financial bubble bursting but with the added vulnerability of being supported almost entirely by federal grants and not generated revenue. The neuroscience field itself is going through a time of reflection to discover the changes that need to be made moving forward (including methods and incentives). This "crisis" and subsequent finger-pointing may scare off some researchers, possibly even reducing competition in neuroscience. Now is an excellent time to act on this opportunity and build a new field on rigorous foundations. We have been fortunate to witness the many "wrong" ways to conduct neuroscience research. Thus the field of neuroentrepreneurship has the advantage of leapfrogging those pioneers to build a scalable, reliable product, taking into account the mistakes of those who have gone before.

2. *Neuroentrepreneurship has the potential to be cognitive neuroscience's "killer app."* The issues that lead to the current crises for the cognitive neuroscientist are systemic in nature. Incentives exist to produce many publications a year, but do not strongly exist to apply research in a product-focused way. While a business perspective may not be appropriate for all applications, having this applied perspective may mitigate some of the current issues. Findings, like products, that are built from tenuous work, could rightfully earn a researcher (just as a company) a bad reputation, a lawsuit, and/or lost revenue. If neuroentrepreneurship focuses on research that can directly be translated to helping entrepreneurs (and potential entrepreneurs) make better decisions, this application-focused neuroscience could be the field that established researchers, funding agencies, and investors are going to want to follow.

Below are just a few possible applications:

3. *Profiling/taxonomy/typing entrepreneurial personality.* Anecdotally there are many different "types" of entrepreneurs. But entrepreneurship research thus far has turned up no discernable personality traits. Have we been asking the right questions? Neuroscience methods give us another way to explore this nebulous phenomenon. If there were a set of methods based upon neuroentrepreneurship discoveries that could reliably predict the personality and thinking processes for specific entrepreneurs, there would be potential to have tailored help toward identifying their strengths and weaknesses and how best to educate them.

4. *Surveys/questionnaires that correspond to neuroentrepreneurial profiling.* Assuming entrepreneurs have a distinct neuroprofile or set of profiles, we could use this to develop surveys that have the potential to reliably predict a certain brain state of an individual. Specifically, we could validate a survey/questionnaire designed to predict the brain state that they currently have. With a tool like this, researchers could check in on the entrepreneur routinely without having to do a brain scan each time.

5. *Studying causes (not just correlations).* Entrepreneurship is embedded in a complex social environment where there are many different drivers for actions. It is currently very challenging to pinpoint what caused certain entrepreneurial events to happen the way that they did. There are some methods such as transcranial magnetic stimulation (TMS) that can noninvasively send a magnetic pulse to a targeted part of a subject's brain. This allows us to see which parts of a brain are directly responsible for a certain action in a causal sense. Pinpointing causes to this level of specificity would be a first for the entrepreneurship literature and could be applied to help entrepreneurs in very interesting ways.

6. *Nootropics/cognitive enhancements.* Perhaps far into the future, when the neuroscience that can help to predict accurately entrepreneurial decision making is much better understood, there can be targeted drugs/supplements that can help enable entrepreneurs toward amplifying/enhancing their behavior in wanted ways, spawning a whole new type of industry.

Our hope is that these above ideas effectively demonstrate neuroentrepreneurship's potential as a field in theory and in practice. This is not just research for research's sake. It is not just using the tools of neuroscience so the processes that entrepreneurial researchers already know can be pinpointed in the brain. While this information may be helpful and potentially validating to neuroscience and entrepreneurship theorists alike, the information created has great potential for applied methods and products as well. Hopefully we have demonstrated that while not necessarily easy, it is absolutely possible and potentially very rewarding. The time is ripe to move forward in this new field of neuroentrepreneurship.

NOTES

1. See Logothetis (2008) for more on the parameters and limitations of fMRI methods: http://www.nature.com/nature/journal/v453/n7197/abs/nature06976.html.
2. Per Neidermeyer and da Silva (2004), the quick way to describe the inverse problem is that this is a complication inherent to many signal processing methods (not just scalp EEG). The forward problem would be going from source to signal/data. This is to say that the signal from a single electrode is picking up signal from multiple sources similar to leaving a microphone on in a crowded room. The audio signal presented on the screen is the totality of all the different noises in the room that it is picking up. The inverse problem is when you try to infer those sources from the signal (going from signal/data to sources). In this problem, there are infinitely many source configurations that could lead to the signal that is shown. In terms of EEG, it is not certain where in the brain the EEG is picking up signal from, how many sources there are, how large these sources are, and which sources have the most weighting on the signal, which is not necessarily the cortex directly underneath the electrode).

REFERENCES

Bennett, S., I. Agyepong, K. Sheikh, K. Hanson, F. Ssengooba, and L. Gilson (2011), "Building the field of health policy and systems research," *PLoS Medicine*, **8** (8); Doi:10.1371/journal.pmed.1001081.

Logothetis, N. (2008), "What we can do and what we cannot do with fMRI," *Nature*, **453** (12), 869–78; doi:10.1038/nature06976.

Niedermeyer E. and F.L. da Silva (2004), *Electroencephalography: Basic Principles, Clinical Applications, and Related Fields*, New York: Lippincot Williams & Wilkins.

Open Science Collaboration (2015), "Estimating the reproducibility of psychological science," *Science* **349** (6251); dx.doi.org/10.1126/science.aac4716.

Sejnowski, T., P. Churchland, and A. Movshon (2014), "Putting big data to good use in neuroscience," *Nature Neuroscience*, **17**, 1440–41; doi:10.1038/nn.3839.

Vul, E., C. Harris, P. Winkielman, and H. Pashler (2009), "Puzzlingly high correlations in fMRI studies of emotion, personality, and social cognition," *Perspectives on Psychological Science*, **4** (3), 274–90; doi:10.1111/j.1745-6924.2009.01125.x.

Williams, D., M. Wood, D. Gregoire, D. Urbig, J. McMullen, A. Rauch, and L. Busenitz (2016), "Publishing entrepreneurship research using experimental methods: best practices and advice," Professional Development Workshop, Academy of Management, Anaheim, CA.

Index